W9-DGV-584

STRUCTURES IN THE SUBJECTIVE LEXICON

STRUCTURES IN THE SUBJECTIVE LEXICON

SAMUEL FILLENBAUM
AMNON RAPOPORT
University of North Carolina,
Chapel Hill

1971

 *ACADEMIC PRESS*   *New York and London*

ACADEMIC PRESS, INC.
111 Fifth Avenue, New York, New York 10003

United Kingdom Edition published by
ACADEMIC PRESS, INC. (LONDON) LTD.
Berkeley Square House, London W1X 6BA

LIBRARY OF CONGRESS CATALOG CARD NUMBER: 74-154407

PRINTED IN THE UNITED STATES OF AMERICA

CONTENTS

	Preface	vii
Chapter 1	**Introduction**	**1**
	Relations to Other Approaches	3
	Selection of Semantic Domains	4
	Selection of Methods	8
Chapter 2	**Methodology**	**13**
	Linear Graphs	14
	Multidimensional Scaling	20
	Cluster Analysis	28
	Other Data Analysis Procedures	35
Chapter 3	**Color Names**	**41**
	Method	42
	Results	44
	Discussion	55
Chapter 4	**Kinship Terms**	**58**
	Method	61
	Results	62
	Discussion	79
Chapter 5	**Pronouns**	**85**
	Method	87
	Results	88
	Discussion	96

Chapter 6	**Emotion Names**	**100**
	Method	111
	Results	111
	Discussion	122
Chapter 7	**Prepositions**	**125**
	Method	129
	Results	131
	Discussion	141
Chapter 8	**Conjunctions**	**148**
	Method	151
	Results	153
	Discussion	163
Chapter 9	**HAVE Verbs**	**168**
	Method	172
	Results	172
	Discussion	183
Chapter 10	**Verbs of Judging**	**190**
	Method	193
	Results	194
	Discussion	201
Chapter 11	**Good–Bad Terms**	**209**
	Method	211
	Results	213
	Discussion	230
Chapter 12	**Assessment**	**235**
	Methodological Issues	235
	Substantive Issues	243
	References	**252**
	Author Index	259
	Subject Index	262

PREFACE

This work represents an approach to the study of structures in the subjective lexicon. On the assumption that the meaning of a lexical item is a function of the meaning relations obtaining between that item and other items in the same domain, we sought to determine how people "reckon" in assessing similarity relations among terms in a given domain. This research constitutes an empirical investigation of structures characterizing nine selected semantic domains which run the gamut from delimited well-specified domains for which articulated models are available, such as pronouns and kinship terms, to broad, open, and ill-specified ones about which little is known, such as verbs of judging and evaluative adjectives. Similarity data, obtained in a number of different ways, are subjected concurrently to a number of recently developed procedures for the structural analysis of ordinal data such as nonmetric multidimensional scaling, graph theoretic analysis, and hierarchical clustering analysis. These procedures are employed in an attempt to discover underlying meaning properties and to characterize the nature of their organization, i.e., in order to provide appropriate representations for the structural properties of these domains.

After an introductory chapter and a chapter which deals with methodological issues, nine substantive chapters follow, each directed to research on a particular domain; finally there is a chapter by way of assessment of the whole enterprise. The substantive chapters concern (a) Color Names, (b) Kinship Terms, (c) Pronouns, (d) Emotion Names, (e) Prepositions, (f) Conjunctions, (g) Verbs of Possession, (h) Verbs of Judging, and (i) Evaluative Terms. Although the ordering of these chapters is principled in that it reflects differences in regard to the specification of the various domains and differences in the availability of independent well-developed theoretical accounts, each one is relatively self contained, as the study of a particular domain, and may thus be read independently.

Our interest is both methodological and substantive. It is methodological with regard to problems encountered in any attempt to uncover underlying structures, to problems in assessing the extent to which procedures for gathering and analyzing data may have Procrustean properties which impose structure, and to problems that arise in evaluating the fit between data and theory. Our interest is substantive with regard to the actual yield of the various studies and what this may reveal as to the way in which each of the domains is, in fact, organized. The methodology and the findings should be of general interest to cognitive psychologists, and to behavioral scientists concerned with problems arising in the structural representation of similarity data. This work should be specifically pertinent for psychologists, anthropologists, and linguists interested in the empirical examination of semantic structures.

The research reported in this book was supported by PHS Research Grant No. MH-10006 from the National Institute of Mental Health to the L. L. Thurstone Psychometric Laboratory. Part of the work in Chapters 2, 3, 4, and 9 has been presented in two Psychometric Laboratory Reports ("Undirected Graphs and the Structural Analysis of Proximity Matrices," Report No. 53, July 1967, and "A Structural Analysis of the Semantic Space of Color Names," Report No. 60, May 1968), in a paper given at the MSSB Advanced Research Seminar on Measurement and Scaling, June 1969 ("An Experimental Study of Semantic Structures"), and in a paper given at the December 1969 meetings of the Linguistic Society of America ("An Experimental Study of Semantic Structure: English Kin Terms").

The Psychometric Laboratory has provided us with a setting that makes research possible and enjoyable. We are indebted to all the staff and students, but particularly to the director of the laboratory, Lyle V. Jones, for his encouragement. We are grateful to Herbert Clark, James E. Deese, Forrest W. Young, and Lyle V. Jones for reading and commenting on the manuscript. We wish to thank Charles E. Clifton, then at the University of Iowa, for carrying out some early multidimensional scaling of a part of our data, and Atar Ornan and Sandra G. Funk, for help with data analysis. We are greatly indebted to our typists Betsy Schopler, Susan Seifer, and Patty Snell. Finally, we thank our wives, Gerda and Aviva, for their encouragement and understanding.

For permission to present quoted materials we are grateful to Academic Press, Inc.; American Anthropological Association; Blackwell & Mott, Ltd.; Cambridge University Press; International Journal of American Linguistics; Linguistic Research, Inc.; M. I. T. Press; Psychometrika; and John Wiley & Sons, Inc.

This book and the research on which it is based constitute a joint effort of the two authors; the order of authorship reflects only the alphabetical ordering of our names. Neither of us alone would have had the patience to carry the work to completion.

Samuel Fillenbaum

Amnon Rapoport

STRUCTURES IN THE SUBJECTIVE LEXICON

Chapter 1   *INTRODUCTION*

Natural languages are patterned on a number of different levels, and it is the recognition of various interrelated levels of structure which characterizes current approaches to the study of phonology, grammar, and semantics. To quote from a recent introduction to theoretical linguistics,

> The most characteristic feature of modern linguistics—one which it shares with a number of other sciences—is "structuralism" (to use the label which is commonly applied, often pejoratively). Briefly, this means that each language is regarded as a *system of relations* (more precisely, a set of interrelated systems), the elements of which—sounds, words, etc.—have no validity independently of the relations of equivalence and contrast which hold between them [Lyons, 1968, p. 50].

Relational systems in linguistics are characterized by their elements and the types of relations holding among them. The syntactic system generates strings of minimal syntactically functioning elements and specifies the structural interrelationships among them. The phonological system converts a string of elements of specified syntactic structure into a phonetic representation. And the semantic system assigns a semantic interpretation or "meaning" to an abstract structure generated by the syntactic system.

Although semantic theories of natural languages are a part of linguistic descriptions of those languages, linguists have paid relatively little attention to them (see, however, recent investigations of the semantic component of a transformational grammar by Katz and Fodor, 1963; Katz and Postal, 1964; see also other attempts to devise ways for the study of semantic problems by Weinreich, 1963, 1966). In part this is so because many linguists still doubt whether the meaning of words and sentences can be studied as rigorously and objectively as phonology and grammar. Whereas these studies quite clearly fall within the domain of linguistics, semantics might seem to be of equal, if not greater, concern to philosophy, psychology, and, perhaps, also to other social science disciplines such as sociology and anthropology. Basically this stems from the fact that while work on syntax and phonology may be almost exclusively formal, studies of semantics go necessarily beyond the limits of formal linguistics because in dealing with problems of semantics we seek to coordinate the structures of language to the external world, as perceived and understood by human observers.

Even though the high level of formalism and sophistication characterizing recent theories of grammar and phonology cannot be presently achieved by semantic theories, problems of meaning are clearly much too important to be ignored. Indeed, despite the scant attention devoted to semantics by linguists, the empirical analysis of structured semantic domains has been one of the main concerns of a number of social science disciplines. Anthropologists have developed methods of componential analysis and applied various formal techniques to the study of restricted semantic domains such as pronouns and kinship terms (Hammel, 1965; Romney and D'Andrade, 1964; Wallace and Atkins, 1960). Psychologists have also directed their research to this issue. The bulk of the work by Osgood and his associates has involved the use of antonymously anchored rating scales to obtain similarity data, and has employed factor analytic techniques for specifying connotative or affective aspects of meaning. Recently, Osgood (1968a, b) has begun work on what he calls a semantic feature analysis, where an attempt is made to discover underlying features by examining conditions of semantic interaction which yield anomalous, apposite, or simply possible word combinations.

More directly to this point is recent work by Deese (1965) and his students, and by Miller (1967). Deese and his group have used a variety of techniques (including learning, association, and multidimensional scaling methods) to investigate such domains as English prepositions (Clark, 1968), a semantic field of animal terms (Henley, 1969), and a subset of kin terms (Henley, Noyes, and Deese, 1968). Miller, arguing that classification methods may reveal some aspects of the subjective lexicon better than the association techniques used by Deese, or rating methods of the sort used by Osgood, has, among other things, reanalyzed some of Deese's association data and some of Osgood's semantic differential data by use of cluster analytic procedures. Miller's results attest to the promise of cluster analytic techniques both in the classification of widely different concepts and for "investigating the finer details of closely related meanings."

RELATIONS TO OTHER APPROACHES

The present work constitutes an approach to the study of the subjective lexicon; it is concerned with the empirical investigation of the structures characterizing selected semantic domains. These structures are assumed to be "real" only in the sense that they represent the way that a particular individual under certain circumstances organizes the meaning relations among a set of lexical items. The work, then, is based on the assumption, implicit in the above-mentioned studies, that the meaning of a lexical item is a function of the set of meaning relations which hold between that item and other items in the same domain. We shall explore a variety of techniques for the discovery of semantic structures, and present the outcomes of analyses of a number of different domains. Applying some recently developed procedures for data analysis such as multidimensional scaling, and graph theoretic and clustering techniques, to be described in detail below, our work presents a methodology and the results of studies of selected semantic domains, ranging from domains which are delimited and well specified to domains which are broad and ill-defined.

Like previous empirical studies of language statistics our approach to the study of meaning relations has been influenced by De Saussure's conceptual distinction between *la langue* and *la parole*.

> If *la langue* represents an underlying "universe" and *la parole* samples taken from that universe, one can by studying the statistics of the sample infer something about the underlying universe [Rapoport, Rapoport, Livant, and Boyd, 1966, p. 338].

In the present work we have used as basic data college students' judgments of similarity (or dissimilarity) in meaning among lexical items constituting various domains. A careful analysis of the statistics obtained from different samples of individuals judging similarity in meaning among lexical items constituting the same semantic domain, or of the statistics obtained from the same sample of individuals judging similarity in meaning among items constituting different semantic domains, may uncover some properties of the semantic domains in question.

As the terms "semantic structure" and "semantic domain" suggest, our work retains one of the main ideas of the Semantic Differential method of Osgood, Suci, and Tannenbaum (1957). Their method first requires a subject to associate pairs of bipolar adjectives (scales) with selected nouns (concepts); a matrix of intercorrelations among the scales is then computed and factor analyzed to yield a "semantic space" with a relatively small number of dimensions. Each of the concepts can then be assigned a set of coordinates which uniquely determines its position in the space. Following Rapoport *et al.* (1966), the present approach generalizes the idea of "semantic space" in several important ways. First, we have not used bipolar scales to determine the location of concepts in a space, and the space we are concerned with is a denotative rather than a connotative, affective space. Second, the dimensionality of the space has been investigated by means of recently developed nonmetric multidimensional scaling methods which make considerably weaker assumptions about the data. Third, and most important, we have not confined ourselves to the study of dimensionality of semantic spaces; rather, employing graph and clustering techniques which make minimal assumptions about the data, we have attempted to extract additional structural properties.

We consider a generalized "semantic space" and relax or dispense with various conditions or constraints for a reason absolutely basic to our whole enterprise. We do not want to prejudge the sort of organization that may characterize a particular semantic field or domain; insofar as possible we want to avoid forcing or imposing a particular structure on the data. In general it would seem foolhardy in the extreme to insist, in advance, that a particular kind of structure, whether metric or nonmetric, cross-classificatory or hierarchic, must describe a given domain. This is particularly the case if the dependence of semantic structures on individuals and contexts is explicitly recognized. While any particular technique for data analysis will tend to impose a certain structure on the data, the concurrent application of techniques based on quite different assumptions should yield results which may guide us in selecting that structural representation which appears to be the most, or more, appropriate one. In particular cases, strong assumptions about underlying structural properties may, in fact, suggest the selection of particular analytic techniques, but even in such cases the availability of alternative solutions should provide a useful check on the adequacy of the preferred or theoretically demanded solution. We shall recur to some of these very basic issues when considering the results of particular studies, and also in the general discussion of the last chapter.

Our methodological approach is also close to that of Cliff and Young (1968) and Shepard and Chipman (1970) in that it is explicitly cognitive and assumes that an individual can meaningfully organize a set of terms having psychological referent values according to the subjective significance of their relationships. Adopting Cliff and Young's terminology, it is assumed that an individual has an internal *configuration* of terms which he can use in various ways. We use the term *representation* to denote the description of a set of related terms which results from the individual's judgments of similarity among them.

SELECTION OF SEMANTIC DOMAINS

The following considerations governed the selection of lexical items. First, in each study an attempt was made to choose items in such a fashion as to ensure that they formed a structurally related coherent set. Second, the domains investigated were chosen so as to be quite diverse. Since one of our main purposes is to exemplify and evaluate the uses of various techniques for the analysis of the semantic structure of the general vocabulary of the language, we need to examine not only highly structured or relatively limited, well-defined domains, but also cases where matters are not so clear cut, where the class of terms is open and its boundaries are quite unclear. Third, the domains were chosen so as to represent cases of some intrinsic interest or importance, where previous analyses or results were generally already available, so as to permit comparisons of our results with those of other studies.

We chose to study (1) color names, (2) kinship terms, (3) pronouns, (4) emotion names, (5) prepositions, (6) conjunctions, (7) the HAVE family of verbs, (8) verbs of JUDGING, and (9) the GOOD-BAD families of adjectives.

Color Names

These constitute a relatively well-defined domain. There has been much concern with the description of color space. Several studies have used multidimensional scaling methods to characterize color space or parts of it (Helm and Tucker, 1962; Shepard, 1962b), and there has also been some interest in "Color Names for Color Space" to cite the title of a recent important paper by Chapanis (1965). We wished to examine the structure that characterizes a set of color names, and to compare it with the color space, the underlying dimensionality of which is already known.

Kinship Terms

In anthropological linguistics kinship terminology has provided what is perhaps the paradigm case for the application of componential analysis. With regard to American-English kinship terminology at least two somewhat different componential analyses are available due to Wallace and Atkins, and to Romney (Romney and D'Andrade, 1964). What is more, Romney and D'Andrade have also presented "the results of a series of psychological tests designed to measure different aspects of the individual's cognitive structure concerning kin terms." See also Wexler and Romney (1969). Consequently, there is the opportunity to compare our results obtained by use of a rather different technique with those of Romney and D'Andrade, and Wexler and Romney, and to assess the adequacy of the componential analyses offered to our results.

Pronouns

Like kinship terms, pronouns constitute a restricted structured set of terms with obvious differences in regard to number, person, and case. We were interested in seeing whether such components would emerge from an analysis of similarity judgments, and how the structure emerging from such an analysis would compare with that yielded by an analysis of confusion matrices resulting from errors made during learning of such terms in a paired-associate task.

Emotion Names

There have been a number of attempts to provide a structural analysis of facial expressions as pictured emotions (Schlosberg, 1954; Abelson and Sermat, 1962), and to develop dimensional theories of emotion by an analysis of the relationships obtaining among a set of emotion terms (Block, 1957; Ekman, 1955). In the present study we seek to compare results obtained by use of four different scaling methods with each other, and with results obtained by previous investigations which used various other methods to obtain and analyze their data.

Prepositions

Prepositions, many of which seem to involve some sort of spatial reference, constitute a relatively small set of terms which are often critical for accurate description of action and location. What can be said of the structure of the relations among English prepositions? There are already available some data due to Clark (1968), who used a variety of tasks to examine the similarity among a set of 33 prepositions, arguing that "the total pattern similarity gives a comprehensive picture of the semantic relationships among all the prepositions." In addition, Deese (1965) has factor analyzed the associative overlaps (intersection coefficients) of some English prepositions using free association data obtained by Fillenbaum and Jones (1965). The results obtained in this study may thus be compared with these other findings, as well as being compared with "a semantic analysis of English locative prepositions" due to Cooper (1968).

Conjunctions

Conjunctions constitute one important class of propositional operators. Even a cursory inspection of English conjunctions reveals that these appear to make up at least two gross groups, more or less simple conjunctions as AND, ALSO, AS WELL AS, etc., and conjunctions which, in addition, have some sort of contrastive or counter-to-expectation component, such as BUT, NEVER-THELESS, YET, etc. As Weinreich (1963) has noted, following some suggestions of Strawson (1952) toward the analysis of the "operators" of everyday English, conjunctions may involve a fusion of logical operations and pragmatic components.

HAVE Family

We decided on the HAVE family (including verbs such as FIND, GAIN, GIVE, HOLD, TAKE, etc.) because these terms constitute a semantic field whose boundaries are rather ill-defined and indefinite, because of the intrinsic importance and generality of use of these verbs, and because, for a restricted subset, a structural analysis has recently been offered by Bendix (1966), who carried out a cross-linguistic study in English, Hindi, and Japanese, requiring subjects to respond to a number of semantic tests including matching and interpretation tasks. It might be noted that very recently (1970a, b) Wexler has presented a reanalysis of most of the verbs considered by Bendix, providing both a theoretical model of "embedding structures" or "hierarchical features" and some pertinent experimental data.

Verbs of JUDGING

As is true of the HAVE family, verbs of JUDGING (including terms such as ACCUSE, APPROVE, BLAME, CONDEMN, CRITICIZE, PRAISE, etc.) extend over a broad and ill-defined semantic domain. These interpersonal verbs are of great significance in everyday social intercourse, involving as they do evaluations of others and their actions. In addition we were interested in these verbs since recently Osgood (1966b, 1968a) has sought to provide an analysis of a large set of interpersonal verbs, including a substantial number of verbs of JUDGING, in terms of a cross-classification on the basis of 10 semantic features. And Fillmore (1969a), from a very different perspective, has attempted to provide an account of some 10 or 11 verbs of "praising and blaming" by means of an examination of the "role structure" of these verbs, distinguishing primarily between the implicit presuppositions of each verb and its explicit assertions. We shall be interested to see to what extent our results are consistent with Osgood's analysis, and whether they can capture some of the distinctions suggested by Fillmore, particularly that between the presuppositions of a verb and its assertions.

GOOD-BAD Families

The general logic governing our selection of these sets of terms was the same as that indicated above in the case of the HAVE family, and for verbs of JUDGING. In this instance, however, no independent external analysis was available with which to compare our results, so we attempted to choose our items in such a manner as to permit internal matching analyses. The two sets of adjectives were chosen such that all the terms in one set were "good" terms and all the terms in the other set were "bad" terms (i.e., the two sets of terms used tend to fall at the opposite extremes of any sort of Evaluation factor). We were interested not only in seeing what structure might emerge in each set, but particularly in seeing whether much the same structure would emerge in both sets, since in a sense the two sets were very similar, differing principally in their polarized opposed location on an Evaluation dimension.

By way of recapitulation it may be noted, first, that we have attempted to sample a variety of content domains ranging from logical operators (conjunctions), to spatial terms (prepositions), to descriptive terms (GOOD-BAD family and emotion terms), to properties of action (HAVE family and verbs of JUDGING), to names of relatively elementary properties of sensory experience (color names), to names of socially defined relatives (kin terms and pronouns); second, that these terms come both from well specified, or limited, closed classes (e.g., kin terms and pronouns, and conjunctions or prepositions, respectively), and from open, ill-defined classes (e.g., the GOOD-BAD family, the HAVE family, verbs of JUDGING, and emotion terms); third, that these items have sampled some of the principal grammatical classes, viz. conjunctions, prepositions, adjectives (GOOD-BAD family), verbs (HAVE family, verbs of JUDGING), nouns (kin terms, emotion terms, and color names, although of course the latter terms also have an adjectival role), and pronouns; and, fourth, that in a number of cases some independent analyses or results are already available for comparison, these findings having been obtained by anthropologists, linguists, philosophers, and other psychologists.

SELECTION OF METHODS

The multidimensional scaling (MDS) and clustering procedures, to be described in the next chapter, have been designed for the analysis of two-way arrays of numerical or ordinal data. In an excellent chapter on the spatial representation of behavioral science data, from which we shall borrow freely, Shepard (1969) distinguishes among three basic types of data to which MDS and clustering procedures have so far been applied—proximity, dominance, and profile data. The classification of a particular array of numerical or ordinal data into one of these three types, Shepard notes, does not depend upon properties of the data in that matrix as such. Rather, it depends upon the kind of model suggested for those data. Since it is often the case that the same set of data may be consistent with two or more different models, each of which is based on a different set of assumptions and implies a different method of analysis, applying different methods of analysis to the same set of data, of whichever kind, may uncover different but equally significant aspects of the underlying structure.

The basic data in our work are symmetric arrays of proximity measures between all pairs of lexical items drawn from a specific semantic domain. In terms of the relation between the data and the model, it is assumed that the data are measured on an ordinal scale. To quote from Shepard (1969, p. 9),

> The numbers in a matrix are considered as proximity data when the spatial model that we have in mind is one in which it is the spatial proximities among points in the model that are to represent the given numbers. More precisely, the model is a spatial configuration of points—one point for each row and each column of the matrix; and the relation between the model and the data is to be one of a monotonic transformation from the distance between the points corresponding to any row and any column to the given number in the cell at the intersection of that row and column of the matrix.

Proximity data include almost any measure of similarity, substitutability, cooccurrence, and association between every two stimulus objects or sets of stimulus objects (words, persons, groups, etc.) under study. In psychological experiments, proximity measures have been obtained traditionally by asking subjects which of two pairs of stimulus objects are more similar (or dissimilar), by asking them to rate each pair of stimulus objects according to the strength of similarity between its elements, or by rank-ordering some or all pairs of stimulus objects with respect to similarity, dissimilarity, substitutability, cooccurrence, etc. Proximity measures have also been obtained indirectly by measuring the degree to which two stimulus objects are confused in a learning or memory experiment, or by computing the correlation between their occurrences. For reviews of scaling, association, substitution, and classification methods for collecting proximity data as employed in psychology and biology, see Miller (1967), Torgerson (1958), and Sokal and Sneath (1963).

A basic distinction can be made between direct and derived measures of proximity (Shepard, 1969). A direct measure is one that emerges from each pair of stimulus objects under study "as a primitive datum about that pair." The degree of association between words or the degree of mutual choice between individuals serve as typical examples. A derived measure, on the other hand, does not emerge directly. Rather, it is computed from a larger set of data given certain assumptions concerning the type of data involved and the scale of measurement. The product moment correlation is a typical example. Purely direct or purely derived measures of proximity are extreme though not atypical cases. There are various kinds of proximity measures that fall intermediate between them. As we shall see later, the proximity data for individual subjects considered in this work are either direct or intermediate, depending upon the particular method used for collecting the data. When proximity data are averaged over subjects, as we do for each of our data-collecting methods, the mean proximity measures are closer to the derived measures of proximity mentioned above.

Before describing briefly each of the three data-collecting methods used in our work a few words are in order regarding the type of proximity matrix (a two-way array of proximity measures) that has been used. Whether proximity data are direct, derived, or of some intermediate type, they may appear in different kinds of matrices, square or rectangular, symmetric or asymmetric. Proximity matrices include the (unconditional) *rectangular* proximity matrix of order $N \times M$, in which a set of N stimulus objects is used to represent the rows, and a different set of M stimulus objects is used to represent the columns. Another kind is the *conditional* proximity matrix, which can best be thought of as a "subject" by "stimulus" rectangular matrix in which the M columns represent M "stimulus objects," the N rows represent N "subjects," and the number in cell (n, m), $(n = 1, 2, \ldots, N; m = 1, 2, \ldots, M)$, is the expressed preference or actual frequency of choice of "subject" n for "object" m. MDS programs for analyzing these cases have been recently developed. (See Shepard, 1969, for a discussion of the different kinds of proximity matrices.)

We shall be concerned here with only the simplest kind of proximity matrix, the one first studied by MDS procedures (Shepard, 1962a), which is square and *symmetric* and in which the N rows and N columns are represented by the same set of N points in the model. As we shall see below, symmetry is not achieved in our studies by averaging each entry with its diagonally opposite counterpart, rather it is a by-product of each of our data-collection methods.

Three procedures were employed to obtain the proximity data in our studies: (1) tree construction, (2) construction of complete undirected graphs, and (3) direct grouping or classification; all three procedures will be described in detail in Chapter 2. Briefly, the tree construction method requires subjects to construct ordinary linear graphs by linking words in a given vocabulary set in terms of some specified similarity criterion. Nodes are words, and edges are defined by the relation linking pairs of words. If the resulting graph is a tree, the method determines all $N \times N$ proximity measures among the words. One of the purposes of this study was to extend the use of this method, which had been employed previously in the study of relatively heterogeneous sets of concepts (Rapoport *et al.,* 1966; Rapoport, 1967), to the study of coherent, related sets of terms.

The method of constructing complete, undirected linear graphs requires the complete rank-ordering of all pairs of N words. Like the tree construction method, it also allows for the sequential construction of proximity matrices. Whereas the first method yields only the first $N-1$ ranked pairs of nodes, and certain assumptions must be made to obtain the remaining ranks, the second method yields all $N(N-1)/2$ ranked pairs. This is done at a certain cost, however, for the task is tiring and exhausting, demanding the continuous rescanning of the large subset of remaining pairs.

The method of direct grouping simply requires subjects to sort the words into as many classes as they wish, with any number of words placed in any class. (See Clark, 1968, for use of this procedure in the study of English prepositions; also see Miller, 1967, 1969.) We shall be interested in comparing results obtained by using the three different data-collection methods.

Following Shepard (1969), one may distinguish between two approaches to data analysis: one that is primarily oriented toward the detection and statistical evaluation of structures of an already specified form, and one that is primarily oriented toward the discovery of new structures. Since some of the semantic domains that will be examined are ill-defined, and since, with only few exceptions, there have been no semantic theories prescribing a detailed structure for these domains, we shall be characteristically concerned with the latter approach to data analysis. Even in the two semantic domains of color names and kinship terms, which are well-defined and highly structured, there may be more than just a few patterns whose form is explicitly specified in advance. Linguists have clearly demonstrated (see Lyons, 1968) that the same substance of colors may have a different form imposed upon it by different languages, and one should therefore be wary of any *a priori* assumption that the semantically relevant dimensions of color are necessarily those selected by physics. Various structural models may turn out to be adequate depending upon the assumptions made about the lexical distinctions drawn in a particular language, and the weighting of dimensions such as hue, brightness, and saturation. Similarly, as mentioned in the preceding section, alternative structural analyses of kinship terms may be suggested even for the same language. By attempting to discover underlying structures, one may not only succeed in providing structure for previously poorly structured semantic domains, but one may be able also to decide between alternative models, or perhaps assess individual differences among structures in the same semantic domain.

We shall employ MDS, clustering, and graph theoretic procedures. The latter procedure, applied only when the graph construction methods are used to obtain proximity data, is concerned not with the structural analysis of proximity matrices but mainly with their "evolution." Examining such properties of graphs as connectivity, cycle size, distribution of node degree, etc., we shall first determine whether or not the proximity matrices were randomly constructed, and, if not, what "biases" operated in different stages of their construction. Given that the proximity matrices were not constructed at random, we shall analyze the complete matrices by means of a nonmetric MDS technique due to Young and Torgerson (1967), and by means of a hierarchical clustering technique due to Johnson (1967).

The MDS method is not used, characteristically, for the purpose of testing for the presence of any particular structure or trend in a given proximity matrix, but, rather, for the purpose of discovering what sort of structure, in fact, obtains. The method has two characteristic properties: (1) it transforms a proximity matrix into a spatial model of sufficiently low dimensionality, and (2) it does this "on the basis of assumptions about the general form of the to-be-revealed structure that seem minimally vulnerable and, hopefully, provide for the possibility of an acceptable reconstruction of the original data (Shepard, 1969, p. 6)." The spatial model has been typically Euclidean, but can be easily extended to include non-Euclidean metrics. Since the Euclidean condition is rather specific, there has been some apprehension that it may be too restrictive for certain kinds of psychological data (Attneave, 1950; Shepard, 1964; Torgerson, 1958). For this reason, several of the more recent MDS programs have been extended to accommodate various of these more general metrics such as the Minkowski r-metrics (Kruskal, 1964a; Young, 1969). However, it appears that the assumption of the Euclidean metric is quite robust as long as there is a continuous underlying space of well-defined dimensionality.

When the assumption of a "continuous underlying space of well-defined dimensionality" is questionable, or does not hold, the Euclidean model becomes inappropriate and dimension free methods associated with more abstract metrics—such as Johnson's hierarchical clustering method—should be employed to discover structural properties in the data. The "continuity" assumption can be considered from several viewpoints, each of which has different implications for data analysis, when the structure of semantic domains is under study. The most conservative viewpoint, arguing that, since the lexical items to be scaled are discrete, continuity should not be assumed, implies that the use of a Euclidean model is objectionable. A more liberal viewpoint, arguing that continuity is a property of the semantic space and not of the set of lexical items that are embedded in it, allows for the Euclidean model. Regardless of the point of view taken concerning the "continuity" assumption, it seems advisable to supplement the Euclidean model by analyses of structure based on considerably weaker assumptions such as graph theoretic and clustering methods. These methods can provide a different kind of insight into the proximity data as well as a check upon the adequacy of a dimensional representation. Of course, the basic reason for use of hierarchic clustering techniques is simply that the structure underlying a particular configuration may, in fact, be taxonomic or hierarchic rather than, say, linear or a cross-classification; this applies since, as Miller (1969) has argued, "hierarchical (taxonomic) organization based on relations of class inclusion is a pervasive feature of the (subjective) lexicon". Indeed, a common case may involve a mixture with both dimensional and taxonomic properties.

In the next chapter we shall examine in detail the methods used to obtain and analyze the data. The following chapters will present the results of the nine studies *seriatim*, and in the final chapter we will assess and consider some implications of these results.

Chapter 2   *METHODOLOGY*

Our approach is concerned primarily with discovering appropriate representations for the structural properties of selected semantic domains. The theory of graphs is employed for testing several statistical hypotheses concerned with the proximity data obtained by the two graph construction methods. Of the various possible approaches for the representation of structure, two were selected—typal and dimensional approaches. The former assumes that the stimulus objects are members of inclusive and mutually exclusive nominal or hierarchical clusters, such that membership in a cluster accounts for all the consistent variation in the proximity data. The latter attempts to embed the stimulus objects in some metric space of low dimensionality, and then to interpret the dimensions in terms of psychological attributes. To the extent that it succeeds, proximities may be considered as a function of the psychological components defining these dimensions.

These two approaches to the representation of structure, which have been employed in both the behavioral and biological sciences, have yielded two distinct classes of analytic techniques: cluster analysis or cluster seeking procedures, on one hand, and factor analysis or nonmetric MDS, on the other hand. The present study employs MDS and hierarchical clustering methods, viewing them as quantitative psycholinguistic models rather than as methods for merely organizing, summarizing, and displaying data. The methods differ in the assumptions they make about the structure of the semantic domain in question, in their output, and, as we hope to show, in their appropriateness for different semantic domains.

LINEAR GRAPHS

The principal object of the studies reported here is an ordinary linear graph, in which nodes (vertices) are words and links (edges) are certain similarity relations joining pairs of words. Our methodological approach calls for investigating different statistical properties of linear graphs and providing some psycholinguistic interpretation for observed properties which distinguish linear graphs constructed by our subjects from randomly constructed graphs (Rapoport *et al.*, 1966). Since the terminology currently in use in graph theory is not standardized, we follow the conventions of Busacker and Saaty (1965).

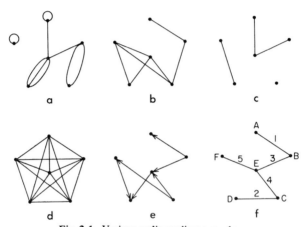

Fig. 2-1. Various ordinary linear graphs.

A linear graph is defined as a nonempty set V, the elements of which are called *nodes* (vertices), a (possibly empty) set E disjoint from V, the elements of which are called *links* (edges), and a mapping ϕ, called the *incidence mapping*, of E into the unordered product of V with itself. If the sets V and E are both finite, the graph is *finite*. When a link e connects two nodes v_i and v_j, these nodes are called the *end points* of e. If $v_i = v_j$, then v_i is the only end point of e, and e is called a *loop*. If at least two links connect v_i and v_j they are called *parallel links*. A graph is said to be *simple* if it has no loops and no parallel links. Figure 2-1 portrays several finite graphs, each with six nodes. Part a shows a graph with two loops and two parallel links, while the other graphs are simple. Graph a has nine links, graph b has seven links, graph c has three links, etc.

A graph is *complete* if every two distinct nodes are joined by a link. Part d exhibits a complete graph. If it is possible to reach every node in a graph from every other node by passing along links over intervening nodes, the graph is called *connected*. Clearly, every complete graph is connected, but not conversely. Connected graphs are portrayed in parts b, d, e, and f.

A finite sequence $e_1, e_2, \ldots, e_f$ of links of a graph is said to constitute a *link progression* of length f if there exists an appropriate sequence of $f + 1$ nodes, $v_0, v_1, \ldots, v_f$, such that e_i joins nodes v_{i-1} and v_i, $i = 1, 2, \ldots, f$. If all the elements of a closed progression represent distinct links, the progression is called a *cycle progression,* and the set of links is said to constitute a *cycle*. The graph presented in part b has two cycles, whereas the one presented in part e has only one cycle.

The connecting links in a graph may be directed, i.e., going from one node to another, or undirected, i.e., connecting two nodes without reference to direction. In the former case we have a *directed graph,* and in the latter an *undirected graph*. A connected undirected graph without cycles is called a *tree*. Part e shows a directed graph; all other graphs in the figure are undirected. The graph exhibited in part f is a tree. The present work discusses only undirected graphs.

The number of links converging at a node in an undirected graph is called the *degree* of this node. Part c has one node with degree two, whereas every node in part d has a degree of five. If each link in a graph is assigned a real-valued number, and the N nodes are numbered from 1 to N, we shall call the graph *labeled* (or weighted). Part f shows a labeled tree.

In gathering proximity data we have attempted to use methods which are efficient, can handle a relatively large N, seem meaningful to the subjects, and make it possible to obtain the proximity data sequentially. The tree construction method satisfies all of these requirements. The instructions for this method, which will be referred to in the following chapters, were as follows:

> You will be given a list of N words arranged in alphabetical order, and a blank sheet of paper. Read the list carefully several times.
>
> From the list of N words, pick the two words which you think are *most similar* to each other. Write the pair you have chosen on the blank paper and connect them with a line. Label the connecting line 1. Now you have two options:
>
> *Option 1:* You may go carefully over the remaining words in the list (which now includes $N-2$ words) and pick the word which you think is most similar to *either* of the *two* words you have already selected. Write this word down on your paper and connect it to the appropriate word already selected. Label the connecting line 2.
>
> *Option 2:* You may look over the remaining words on the list and decide that two of them are more similar to each other than any one of them is to either of the two words already selected and joined together. If so, you may select these words and write them down on the paper, just as you did with the first pair. Connect the two new words with a line and label it 2.
>
> After taking option 1 or 2, proceed in exactly the same way. Search carefully

the remaining words on the list and continue with option 1 or option 2. When you take option 1 you add a word to an already linked group of words (which is called a tree). When you take option 2 you start a new tree.

Option 3: As the experiment proceeds (after your second choice) you have a third option. If you find that you have made several trees, you may want to connect any two of them together. If you find two words, on two separate trees, that are more similar to each other than any other word on the remaining list is to any other word on the trees, you should connect these words (and thus connect the two trees). Label the connecting line according to the sequence already started.

In short, you have the following options:
1. Adding a new word to one of the trees you have already made.
2. Starting a new tree with two new words.
3. Connecting two separate trees.

Please continue in this way until all N words have been exhausted and until you have connected *all* separate trees into one tree. When you have finished, you will have made one tree of N words connected by $N-1$ numbered lines.

Figure 2-1f portrays a labeled tree with six nodes labeled A, B, C, D, E, and F. Inspection of the graph reveals that the most similar nodes are A and B, the second most similar nodes are C and D, the third most similar nodes are B and E, and so on. Proximity measures between any two nodes are obtained by adding the ranks (weights) of the links of the path connecting them. Thus, the "distance" between nodes A and E is 4, the one between D and F is 11, and so on. The tree construction method requires, then, that the subject directly specifies only $N-1$ out of the $\binom{N}{2}$ possible proximities where the selection of the particular subset of proximities is left up to him. The rather strong assumption of additivity of the proximities along the tree's "branches" is invoked in order to generate the remaining $(N^2 - 3N + 2)/2$ proximities. We shall comment on this assumption in later chapters, and, on occasion, relax it.

The tree construction method allows the subject two different ways of constructing a labeled tree. Using just option 1, he can build one tree only, always adding new nodes to an old tree. Options 2 and 3 allow him considerably more flexibility, since at each stage of the construction he can either add new nodes to an old tree, start a new tree, or join two trees together. Whether the subject uses just option 1 or all three options, the end result is one tree. The labeling of the links makes it possible to discover which option was selected at each stage and the number of subtrees that were constructed.

Instructions for constructing a complete graph were considerably more straightforward. Unlike the previous method, the subject was not asked to construct a graph but was given a simpler task which amounted to filling the entries in the corresponding proximity matrix. The subject was given a list of the N words arranged alphabetically, and a list of the M word pairs arranged randomly; he was asked to decide which was the most similar pair of words in the list, which the next most similar pair, etc. Specifically, the subject was told:

> You will be given a randomly arranged list of M pairs of words, where each word is paired with every other word. *Go carefully through the list and thoroughly study all the pairs.* Then write 1 by the pair which is least (most) similar, 2 by the next least (most) similar pair, 3 by the next pair . . . and so until M for the most (least) similar pair. *Work slowly and carefully; this is a difficult task; take your time.*

Statistical Properties of Linear Graphs

Consider an undirected graph, denoted $G_{N,n}$, with N labeled nodes $v_1, v_2, \ldots, v_N$, and n links, $n = 0, 1, \ldots, \binom{N}{2}$. $G_{N,n}$ is called a *random graph* if it is chosen randomly from all the $\binom{M}{n}$ graphs which can possibly be formed from all the N labeled nodes by selecting n links from all the M possible links, $(M = \binom{N}{2})$. Alternatively, if the graph $G_{N,n}$ is constructed sequentially, we say that $G_{N,n}$ is random if the first link is chosen with equal probability from all the M links, if the second link is chosen randomly from the remaining $M-1$ links, and, in general, if $k < n$ links are already chosen, any of the remaining $M-k$ links has an equal probability of being chosen. In most of our studies, the individual proximity matrices are either trees or complete graphs. Since the subjects constructed the graphs sequentially, statistics computed on the observed graphs may be compared with various statistical properties of random graphs to test the hypothesis that the proximity data are random. Several such statistical properties are listed below.

Suppose a random graph is constructed sequentially until it becomes connected, i.e., until it is possible to reach any node v_i from any node v_j, $i \neq j$, by passing along links over intervening nodes. Let v_N denote the number of links of the resulting connected random graph, G_{N,v_N}. Erdös and Rényi (1959, p. 291) have proved that the probability that v_N assumes a given integer value between 1 and M is given by

$$P\left(v_N = \left[\frac{N}{2} \log_e N\right] + m\right) \sim \frac{2}{N} \exp\left(\left(-\frac{2m}{N}\right) - \exp\left(-\frac{2m}{N}\right)\right) \quad (1)$$

for $|m| = 0(N)$, where $[x]$ denotes the integer part of x. One may fix v_N in (1), solve for m, and then compute the probability that the random graph G_{N,v_N} is completely connected. Values yielded by the function (1) may be compared with the frequency of connected graphs actually observed in a sample of graphs constructed by subjects.

The degree of a node in an undirected graph was defined above as the number of links affixed to it. Observing the fraction of all nodes with a given degree in a population of random graphs, the probability distribution of the random variable representing the degree of a node may be derived analytically. Let

$P(d(v_i) = r)$ denote the probability that a node v_i is connected in $G_{N,n}$ with exactly r other nodes, $r = 0, 1, \ldots, N-1$, where $d(v_i)$ denotes the degree of node v_i. Erdös and Rényi (1960, p. 58) showed that

$$P(d(v_i) = r) = \frac{\binom{N-1}{r}\left(\binom{\binom{N-1}{2}}{n-r}\right)}{\binom{M}{n}}. \tag{2}$$

In addition to deriving the probability that a random graph is connected, and the probability distribution of node degree, Erdös and Rényi (1960) derived the expected number of cycles of a given order in a random graph. This number is given as a function of N and n and can also serve as a basis for comparisons with the observed frequency of cycles consisting of k links (of order k, $k = 3, 4, \ldots$) in a sample of graphs constructed by subjects. Let g_k denote the number of cycles of order k, $k \geqslant 3$, in a random graph, and let $M(g_k)$ denote the expected value of g_k. $M(g_k)$ is given (Erdös and Rényi, 1960, p. 35) by

$$M(g_k) = \frac{(k-1)! \binom{N}{k}\binom{M-k}{n-k}}{2\binom{M}{n}}. \tag{3}$$

There is a unique path (link progression) in a tree connecting every pair of nodes. It is easily shown that a tree with N nodes has $n = N-1$ links. We shall denote such a tree by G_N. A random tree G_N is a tree selected randomly with probability $1/N^{N-2}$ from all possible N^{N-2} trees that can be formed, each having N labeled nodes. We now describe several properties of random trees.

Consider first the distribution of node degree in a random tree. It has been shown (Rapoport $et\ al.$, 1966) that this distribution is well approximated for a large N by the Poisson distribution

$$P_N(r) = \frac{e^{-\lambda}\lambda^{r-1}}{(r-1)!}, \qquad r = 1, 2, \ldots, N-1, \qquad \lambda = \frac{N-1}{N}, \tag{4}$$

where $P_N(r)$ is the probability of encountering a node of degree r in a random tree with N nodes. Note that the only constraints on the number of links per node are (1) that a tree will contain at least two nodes with degree 1, (2) that the number of nodes with odd degree will be even, and (3) that there will be no node with degree higher than $N-1$.

Instead of comparing the theoretical and observed distributions of node degree, a simpler test is obtained by comparing the theoretical and observed number of nodes with degree 1 (the number of endpoints of G_N). This number is large relative to N—the expected proportion of nodes with degree 1 in a random tree is at least 1/3. Let w_N denote the number of nodes with degree 1 in a random tree, G_N, and let $M(w_N)$ and $D(w_N)$ denote the expected value and standard deviation, respectively, of w_N. $M(w_N)$ and $D(w_N)$ are given (Rényi, 1959, pp. 80-81) by

$$M(w_N) = N\left(1-\frac{1}{N}\right)^{N-2} \tag{5}$$

$$D(w_N) = \left((N^2-N)\left(1-\frac{2}{N}\right)^{N-2} + N\left(1-\frac{1}{N}\right)^{N-2} - N^2\left(1-\frac{1}{N}\right)^{2N-4}\right)^{\frac{1}{2}}. \tag{6}$$

Note that $\lim M(w_N) = N/e$ as $N \to \infty$, a result corresponding to that obtained from (4) with $r = 1$ and $\lambda = 1$. Note also that $\lim D(w_N) = N(e-2)/e^2$ as $N \to \infty$.

We shall call two nodes *adjacent* if they are connected by only one link. There are M possible pairs and $N-1$ actual pairs of adjacent nodes in G_N. Since each pair may or may not be chosen when a random tree is constructed, the distribution of the number of pairs of adjacent nodes in a sample of random trees is binomial with parameter $b = (N-1)/M$. The parameter b designates the probability that a pair will be selected in a random tree.

Define a new parameter $\lambda = bY$, where Y is the size of a sample of subjects, each of whom is required to construct a tree from the same set of N words. We can interpret λ as the "popularity bias" of a given pair of words relative to a set of N words and a sample of Y subjects. If all trees are constructed randomly, all pairs of adjacent nodes will have the same popularity bias. The assumption that the popularity bias of different pairs is not constant but is distributed in the population may lead to a distribution of the number of pairs chosen by y subjects, $y = 0, 1, \ldots, Y$. In particular, assuming that λ is gamma distributed, it can be shown (Rapoport *et al.*, 1966) that the distribution of the number of pairs chosen y times is given by the negative binomial distribution with parameters p and s:

$$P(s,y) = \binom{s+y-1}{y} p^s q^y, \qquad 0 < p < 1, \qquad q = 1-p, \qquad s > 0. \tag{7}$$

In interpreting the parameters of the negative binomial distribution, s is treated as a free parameter but p is not. The latter parameter is obtained from $p = s/(s + \lambda)$, where $\lambda = Y(N-1)/M$, and is determined uniquely once s is fixed. The value of s is related to the variance of the gamma distribution, in that a small s indicates a highly peaked gamma distribution, and as s increases the negative binomial distribution approaches the Poisson distribution with parameter $\lambda = bY$ and the model approaches the case of no popularity bias. A small s, then, reflects a strong "popularity bias."

Listed above are several statistical properties of random undirected graphs. Since most of these properties are a function of n, one may study the "evolution" of random graphs and compare these properties with statistics computed on observed graphs at different stages of their construction. Significant differences between observed statistics and theoretical properties of random graphs indicate biases operating in different stages of construction of the graphs, and will be considered as evidence against the null hypothesis of random proximity data, justifying further analyses of the data by MDS and cluster techniques.

MULTIDIMENSIONAL SCALING

Proximity measures, suggested as indices of cognitive and perceptual structure (Attneave, 1950; Coombs, 1964; Isaac, 1968), can be processed by means of nonmetric MDS techniques to construct a representation of the internal configuration ("psychological space"). The first nonmetric MDS technique, written as a computer program, was developed by Shepard in two pioneering papers (1962a, b). At least four additional algorithms for analyzing symmetric proximity matrices have been presented (Kruskal, 1964a, b, Lingoes, 1965; McGee, 1966; Young and Torgerson, 1967), and additional algorithms have been constructed, extending the basic concepts of MDS to rectangular and conditional proximity matrices, multidimensional unfolding, nonmetric factor analysis, and polynomial conjoint measurement. (See Guttman, 1968; Young, 1969, and references cited there.)

The five MDS methods differ in terms of their rationale, generality, and flexibility (see Roskam, 1969, for discussions of the relations among the five methods), but all share a common goal, namely, to find the spatial configuration of a set of points in a low dimensionality in which the rank order of the interpoint distances is maximally inversely correlated with the rank order of the corresponding $\binom{N}{2}$ inter-item similarity measures. The procedures start with a representation of points (which may or may not be arbitrary), and iteratively attempt to find some arrangement of the points such that the rank order of the interpoint distances is exactly the opposite of the rank order of the similarity measures. When this happens, the resulting representation fits the data perfectly. The procedures assume that the entries in the proximity matrix have been measured on an ordinal scale. The resulting interpoint distances are measurable, however, on a ratio scale, i.e., are unique up to multiplication by a positive constant.

Goodness of Fit

As the dimensionality of the space is reduced, departures from perfect fit are likely to appear. Approaching nonmetric MDS from a statistical viewpoint, Kruskal (1964a) has furnished a measure of departure from perfect fit, the *stress* of a representation, which indicates how closely the function relating interpoint distances to ranked proximity measures approaches monotonicity. The stress is a normalized sum of squared deviations and can be thought of as an analogue to the standard error of estimate in regression analysis. It is computed for a prespecified number of dimensions, m, by

$$S = \left(\frac{\underset{i<j}{\Sigma} (d_{ij} - \hat{d}_{ij})^2}{\underset{i<j}{\Sigma} d_{ij}^2} \right)^{1/2}, \qquad i, j = 1, 2, \ldots, N$$

where d_{ij} denotes a (Euclidean or non-Euclidean) distance between points v_i and v_j, and $\hat{d}_{ij}$ is a function of a proximity measure s_{ij} such that (1) $s_{ij} < s_{kl}$ implies $\hat{d}_{ij} > \hat{d}_{kl}$; (2) $\hat{d}_{ii} = 0$; and (3) $s_{ij} = s_{kl}$ implies $\hat{d}_{ij} = \hat{d}_{kl}$. The algorithms constructed by Lingoes and by Young and Torgerson also compute the stress for each representation in a given dimensionality.

Since the algorithms are iterative, the stress value for any set of data is to some extent a function of the number of iterations employed. More important in determining the stress value is the number of items, N, the statistical variability inherent in the data, and the dimensionality of the space. Kruskal suggested three criteria by which to discover the proper value of m. He recommended, first, plotting S as a function of m and selecting a value of m making S acceptably small. A second criterion is to choose m such that the interpretability of the m-dimensional representation is not improved if the number of dimensions is increased beyond m. The third criterion concerns the amount of error inherent in the data; the more accurate the data the more dimensions one may extract.

These three criteria are not always applicable. An additional procedure might be to obtain the distribution of values of S that would be obtained by analyzing, in a given dimensionality, all $\binom{N}{2}!$ possible rankings of the $\binom{N}{2}$ interpoint distances and then to test the null hypothesis that an experimentally obtained value of S is a random sample from this distribution (Stenson and Knoll, 1969). This procedure is particularly useful when the prior subjective probability of supporting the null hypothesis is quite high, as in many of our studies, in which proximity measures were experimentally obtained by new methods in circumstances where the severity of restrictions these methods place on the judgmental process and the biases they introduce are poorly understood.

Since the distribution of S for a given pair of N and m is not presently known, Stenson and Knoll (1969) and Klahr (1969) investigated through Monte Carlo simulation the question of how likely one is to reject the null hypothesis that the proximity data to be scaled are randomly generated. Stenson and Knoll report values of S obtained by analyzing random permutations of the first $\binom{N}{2}$ positive integers, letting N vary from 10 to 60 in steps of 10, m vary from 1 to 10 in steps of 1, and using, throughout the Euclidean distance metric and Kruskal's

MDS procedure. Not surprisingly, the average stress value, obtained from analyzing three randomly chosen permutations for each combination of N and m, increased in N and decreased in m. The ranges of S proved to be extremely small for the various combinations of N and m, indicating that the distribution of S is highly peaked. Sampling randomly from a uniform distribution on the open interval from 0 to 1, Klahr scaled 100 sets of proximities generated for each value of $N = 6, 7, 8$ and 10, and 50 sets for each value of $N = 12$ and $N = 16$. Kruskal's nonmetric MDS program was applied throughout in spaces having $m = 1, 2, \ldots, 5$ dimensions. For a small number of points ($N = 6, 7, 8$), Klahr's results show that it is very likely that a good fit will be obtained in two or more dimensions when in fact the data are generated by a random process. For $N = 10, 12$, and 16, his results correspond fairly close to the ones obtained by Stenson and Knoll.

Adopting Stenson and Knoll's suggestion, we decided to use the mean stress value minus twice the width of the range for that value as a critical cut-off point for rejecting the null hypothesis that the proximity data are randomly generated. Eight different values for N were used in our studies: 14, 15, 16, 18, 20, 24, 29, and 30. Using the results reported by Klahr, interpolating when necessary the mean stress values portrayed graphically by Stenson and Knoll (p. 123), and then subtracting at least twice the width of the obtained range for each point, the critical cut-off points, denoted by $S(N,m)$, were obtained for the above values of N and for $m = 1, 2, 3$. The values of $S(N,m)$ are presented in Table 2-1. Further cut-off points were not obtained since we were only interested in $m \leqslant 3$. Considering the results reported by Klahr, and by Stenson and Knoll, the chosen values of $S(N,m)$ constitute a rather conservative test of a fairly weak null hypothesis.

TABLE 2-1   Critical Cut-off Points, $S(N,m)$

				N				
m	14	15	16	18	20	24	29	30
1	0.22	0.25	0.28	0.32	0.45	0.46	0.50	0.51
2	0.18	0.22	0.25	0.26	0.29	0.30	0.32	0.33
3	0.13	0.15	0.17	0.18	0.20	0.21	0.23	0.23

It should be noted that Kruskal's "stress" is not the only measure of goodness of fit that has been suggested. It can be shown, however, that other measures yield about the same results and "that in most standard cases of interest the data so heavily overdetermine the solution that the particular measure of goodness of fit that is optimized generally has only a negligible effect on the result (Shepard, 1969, p. 30)."

Metric Determinacy

As noted above, the MDS techniques permit their user to obtain a set of interpoint distances measured on a ratio scale from a set of proximity measures assumed to have only ordinal characteristics. The degree of success in obtaining a ratio scaled solution is known as the degree of metric determinacy (Young, 1970). If one is successful in obtaining a truly ratio scale, then the degree of metric determinacy is maximal, and conversely, if the scale has no ratio properties the degree of metric determinacy is minimal. Performing systematic Monte Carlo experiments on error-free data known to be two-dimensional, Shepard (1966) found that the degree of metric determinacy increased as N increased. In particular he found that with as few as 10 points, the original and the reconstructed configurations were almost identical: the square root of the average squared correlation between the original distances (taken from the data of Coombs and Kao, 1960) and the derived distances was 0.998.

Shepard's conclusion is limited since the proximity data he examined were two-dimensional and error-free. Noting that in typical applications of MDS neither of these two assumptions would hold, Young (1970) investigated the metric determinacy afforded by nonmetric MDS as a function of (1) the amount of error contained in the proximity data, (2) N, and (3) m. Young developed an index of metric determinacy, reflecting the relationship between the reconstructed distances and the true distances, and employed it as his dependent variable in a 3 x 5 x 5 factorial design with five replications, where the three independent variables were the number of dimensions in the true configuration ($m = 1, 2, 3$), the number of stimulus elements ($N = 6, 8, 10, 15, 30$), and five different levels of random normal error added to the true distances. The results of the Monte Carlo runs were orderly and sensible: the index of metric determinacy increased directly as N increased. For the experiments reported in this monograph, where $14 \leqslant N \leqslant 30$, $m = 2$, and the stress values are typically smaller than 0.25, the results reported by Young (1970, Table 3) strongly suggest that there is a sufficiently high degree of metric determinacy in the proximity data to justify the application of nonmetric MDS.

The Minkowski Exponent

As mentioned briefly in Chapter 1, several of the more recent MDS programs have considered a more general class of distance functions, e.g., the Minkowski r-metric, where d_{ij}, the distance between stimulus objects v_i and v_j, is defined by

$$d_{ij} = \left(\sum_{k=1}^{m} |x_{ik} - x_{jk}|^r \right)^{1/r}.$$

In the above equation, x_{ik} represents the value of the ith stimulus object on the kth dimension, m represents the dimensionality of the space, and r is known as the Minkowski exponent or constant. The Euclidean distance is obtained by setting $r = 2$ in the above equation, whereas $r = 1$ yields the "City Block" distance. Torgerson (1958), Attneave (1962), and Shepard (1964) have suggested that the type of spatial model which best fits the proximity data is related to the nature of the stimulus objects. When the dimensions of the stimuli are perceptually distinct the City Block model may provide a better fit, and when the dimensions are less distinct the Euclidean scaling function may yield a better spatial model. Some experimental confirmation of the perceptual separability hypothesis has been provided by Hyman and Well (1967), who have also suggested that the appropriate value of r might reflect individual differences with respect to the ability of subjects to extract information from the m component dimensions.

The implication of the perceptual separability hypothesis for our studies is not clear; it may not hold when one generalizes from perceptual to semantic separability of dimensions, and in any case results may depend on the particular set of stimulus objects under examination. In the study of color names, for example, where the dimensions of hue, saturation, and brightness may be reasonably expected to determine similarity judgments, the Euclidean model may be expected to provide a better fit to the data than the City Block model. Different results might perhaps be expected in the study of kinship terms, where the dimensions of sex, generation, and lineality are much more distinct. In order not to prejudge the issue, the proximity data for each stimulus set will be scaled for both $r = 1$ and $r = 2$.

Our concern with the particular value of r may seem to be quite unnecessary in light of Shepard's work (1969), indicating that the Euclidean metric is quite robust, and implying that there is very little to be gained by developing methods to deal with Minkowski r-metrics. Shepard notes that as long as there is a continuous underlying space of well-defined dimensionality, "the data so overdetermine the representation that the erroneous assumption of a Euclidean metric will still permit a satisfactory recovery of the true underlying structure and, indeed, even a determination of the nature of the unknown metric (Shepard, 1969, p. 34)." However, Sherman's thesis (1970), which investigated by Monte Carlo techniques the metric determinacy of nonmetric MDS as a function of N, m, r, and the amount of error in the proximity data to be scaled, only partially supports Shepard's conclusion. In providing a list of guidelines to help the experimenter to use and evaluate results from nonmetric MDS, Sherman (1970, p. 56) suggests that, "It is probably a good idea to scale data according to several different values of the Minkowski constant (say 1.0, 2.0, and 15.0)." Moreover, he implies that the assumption of a "continuous underlying space of well-defined dimensionality" is not sufficient to guarantee robustness, and asserts that when accurate estimation of the true dimensionality of the model is to be achieved, a proper estimation of the Minkowski exponent may be of importance.

Individual Differences

In applying MDS procedures, individual differences in the proximity data are of a particular concern. To the extent that differences between individuals are consistent and systematic, they become interesting and worthy of careful investigation. Isaac (1968) formulated two hypotheses to account for individual differences:

1. The response bias hypothesis—differences in response habits, preferences, and strategies account for differences between people in their responses.

2. The perceptual structure hypothesis—people differ from one another in their responses as a result of differences in the perceived structure of a stimulus set.

Clearly these two hypotheses are not exhaustive, nor are they mutually exclusive. Differences between individuals in their proximity data may be attributed to differences in motivation and preference as well as differences in cognitive structure. It is an open question as to whether, and to what extent the two types of differences may interact.

There have been several experimental studies showing that similarity judgments are not made from the same point of reference. Helm and Tucker (1962), studying color perception, have shown that differences between normal and color-deficient subjects are due to the relative suppression of a dimension by the color-deficient group, and that there remains a dimension common to both groups. Shepard (1964) used two-dimensional stimuli that consisted of a circle and a radial line, and instructed his subjects to take account of differences both in size of the diameter and inclination of the line in judging the similarity of each stimulus to a given standard stimulus. His results show that subjects may fluctuate in attention, and in so doing may ignore one of the two dimensions or otherwise distort the space.

The first systematic attempt to incorporate individual difference considerations into MDS procedures is due to Tucker and Messick (1963), who introduced the "point of view" analysis. In this method, a matrix of observations with rows representing stimulus pairs and columns representing subjects is factorized by the Eckart-Young procedure.

> The factor space gives the number of "viewpoints" which may be considered as ideal observers representing groups relatively homogeneous with respect to judgment of inter-pair-differences. It is understood that these groups may overlap; a "viewpoint" is a factor in a factor-space of individuals, and the "group" consists of those individuals with high loadings on this factor (Horan, 1969, p. 140).

The similarity judgments of these "idealized subjects" are then subjected individually to nonmetric MDS.

Studies by Cliff and Young (1968) and Green and Morris (1969) indicate that the "point of view" method may not be particularly sensitive to individual differences. Cliff and Young scaled similarity judgments of facial expressions, trait-descriptive adjectives, and simulated air raids. The "point of view" method revealed no major individual differences in any of the three experiments. Green and Morris asked two groups of subjects, business students and music majors, to judge the similarity between names of 11 well-known musical artists. Although they found differences between the two groups, with the music students being somewhat more heterogeneous in their perceptual judgments of the artists, they concluded, after applying the "point of view" method, "that in each group a dominant (single) point of view existed, coupled with unsystematic individual variation (p. 71)."

Moreover, the "point of view" method may impart a structure to the set of stimulus objects which is not to be found in the proximity data of any of the individual subjects (Ross, 1966). Cliff (1968) has argued that a reinterpretation of the "point of view" analysis may successfully answer the objections raised by Ross. But Carroll (1969) has argued against Cliff that if finding "idealized" subjects is the object of the "point of view" analysis, a clustering rather than a factor analysis of the subjects should be the first step. Carroll and Chang (1970) have further criticized the "point of view" method noting that it is "little more powerful than doing separate scalings on the individual subjects—and it makes no explicit assumptions about possible or probable communality of the dimensional structures for different real or idealized individuals. It would be very surprising if the various configurations had no structure in common. Rather, one might suspect that, for example, one or two dimensions are the same in two different configurations while a third is different, or that the same dimensions are present, but they have different relative *saliences,* or importances, for different people (p. 284)." Finally, there is an additional difficulty with the method that makes it inapplicable to our studies. The results yielded by the "point of view" method are not invariant up to monotonic transformations of the proximity data. The justification for using the procedure before applying MDS seems questionable when the proximity data are assumed to be measured on an ordinal scale.

Other more promising ways of dealing with individual differences have recently been incorporated by Kruskal (1968) and McGee (1968) into their MDS procedures. Kruskal has two approaches: the first assumes that each subject has a different monotone function relating proximity measures to distances, but constrains all subjects to have the same configurations; the second, on the other hand, assumes that all subjects have the same monotone function, but allows each subject his own idiosyncratic configuration. As for McGee's approach,

McGee allows for either the case in which each subject has his own monotone function, or all are constrained to have the same. He then introduces a parameter that monitors the degree to which the configurations for different subjects are constrained to be similar. At one extreme, these configurations must be identical; at the other there is no constraint at all on how similar they must be. At intermediate values of this parameter, they must be "intermediately" similar (Carroll and Chang, 1970, p. 300).

Kruskal's and McGee's methods, although considerably more promising than the "point of view" method, are also somewhat limited. Kruskal's two approaches represent only two extremes of a continuum in which there are many intermediate cases, and McGee's approach says nothing explicit about how the configurations may depart from identity (Carroll and Chang, 1970).

Adopting a different philosophy from the three approaches discussed above, and in line with Carroll and Chang's criticism of the "point of view" analysis, Horan (1969) has addressed himself to the problem of individual differences in MDS, making very explicit an assumption about the communality among dimensions. His model assumes that different individuals perceive the stimulus objects in terms of a common set of independent dimensions, called the *normal attribute space,* but that these dimensions are differentially salient in the perception of different individuals. His proposed method is based on the observation, supported by analyses of artificially generated data, that taking means of individual distance estimates leads to a distortion, possibly quite small, of the configuration and, hence, that the mean data matrix cannot serve as a basis for the recovery of the normal attribute space, or any simple transform of it, except under very special conditions. A way out of this difficulty is offered by using the square root of the mean squared individual distance estimates as a group estimate. Under this procedure, the obtained configuration is a linear transformation of the original configuration. Horan thus shows that if the proximity data are sufficiently strong to estimate distances on a ratio scale, averaging the data via root mean squares will, apart from the question of error, produce distances between points in a space which includes all the requisite dimensions. The individual spaces, or *perceptual spaces* as Horan calls them, will then be related to the normal attribute space by, at most, a linear transformation.

Horan's method has also received its share of criticism:

The problem with this, from our point of view, is that there is nothing in Horan's averaging procedure to guarantee that the "common space" as derived from it will be described in terms of the correct orientation of axes. Since his procedure reduces all the distances to a common set of Euclidean distances, and then applies a scaling procedure to produce a space from these distances, the rotationally invariant property of Euclidean distances means that no unique orientation of axes will be defined. While one *can* uniquely define the orientation of axes by fiat (say, by rotating to principal axes), there is nothing at all to guarantee that such an orientation will correspond to the "correct" orientation (Carroll and Chang, 1970, p. 302).

The most satisfying solution thus far to the individual differences problem has been proposed by Carroll (1969) and Carroll and Chang (1970). The model is similar to the one proposed by Horan, but is more sophisticated in that it makes a difference in the model as to which set of dimensions is differentially weighted by subjects (i.e., even though the metric in each individual perceptual space is assumed to be Euclidean, rotations are not permissible). Thus, unlike Horan's method, the solution obtained by Carroll and Chang is unique up to a permutation of coordinate axes. Furthermore, their procedure solves at the same time for the subjects by dimensions matrix of weights. "A principal disadvantage of the method is that it is limited to the case in which individual subject spaces are related by *linear* transformations of a common space (Carroll and Chang, 1970, p. 316)." The method may require too many dimensions in cases where the individual perceptual spaces represent nonlinear distortions of a common space. Another limitation of the model, also recognized by the authors, is that the method of analysis is based on a relatively strong metric assumption; it requires distances measured on at least an interval scale rather than on a merely ordinal scale. This limitation whose severity and whose distortive effects on the solutions obtained is presently unknown may be partially alleviated. To quote Carroll (1969, p. 6), ". . . the method can be made at least 'quasi-metric' by procedures essentially the same as those used by Torgerson (see, for example, Young and Torgerson, 1967)."

In view of these criticisms and since, when analyzing the present data, none of the more recent procedures for systematically factoring subjects in terms of their proximity measures was available, the MDS method was applied to both average and individual proximity matrices. Since many subjects participated in each of our studies, the proximity matrices, randomly chosen, of only about one-fourth of them were analyzed.

CLUSTER ANALYSIS

As noted earlier, the goal of nonmetric MDS is to obtain a geometric representation of low dimensionality whose interpoint distances best reproduce the order of the entries in the proximity matrix. It ought to be emphasized, however, that "the possibility of embedding ordinal similarity data in specific types of metric space is by no means assured. Such representations carry strong implications that should not be overlooked (Beals, Krantz, and Tversky, 1968, p. 128)." The evaluation of the adequacy of metric models is a delicate problem. The difficulty lies in the fact that some of their assumptions cannot be easily tested when the proximity data are ordinal. Beals *et al.* (1968) specified certain qualitative properties that ought to be satisfied by ordinal proximity data in order to justify the construction of metric and/or dimensional representations. However, very special experiments using restricted sets of carefully chosen items have to be conducted in order to test these qualitative properties. When the structure of semantic domains is under investigation, such experiments cannot be conducted, and, as we noted in the previous chapter, if the Euclidean model seems too restrictive it ought to be supplemented by dimension free analyses such as Constantinescu's (1966, 1967) clustering program or Johnson's (1967) hierarchical clustering technique.

Sokal and Sneath (1963) have used the term "cluster analysis" to denote a large class of numerical procedures for defining groups of related taxonomic units on the basis of proximity measures. Several types of clustering procedures have been developed, mostly by psychologists and biologists, with particular attention given to hierarchical clustering procedures that establish discrete clusters, each subdivided into subclasses (McQuitty, 1960, 1964; Ward, 1963; Ward and Hook, 1963). Since the advantages of hierarchies are great, especially in biological taxonomy, they have been generally employed in the structural analysis of proximity data even if this meant that the data had to be distorted to some extent.

Since the major purpose of biological numerical taxonomy is to classify organisms into a hierarchic system, it is almost inevitable that the use of hierarchical clustering procedures be widespread. Classification in psychology, it has been argued, need not always be hierarchically structured, e.g., one may have a linear or paradigmatic organization (cross classification) of the stimulus objects (Miller, 1969). In our studies of semantic structures the choice of a particular clustering technique was dictated by the methods used to gather the data and by our wish to compare results from MDS, cluster, and graph analyses of the data. Since the data were gathered either by a direct grouping technique, requiring a subject to put N lexical items into an unspecified number of clusters, or by graph construction methods, allowing the investigation of the "evolution" of graphs, and since, as we show later, the tree construction method yields directly a hierarchical system of clustering representations, it was decided to apply a hierarchical clustering procedure to our data. Another reason for applying Johnson's clustering program to our data was its availability and its previous use in studies of semantic domains (Miller, 1967, 1969). Miller (1967) has maintained that this procedure "seems to offer more promise for semantic theory than any of the other techniques psychologists have used to probe the structure of the subjective lexicon (p. 70)."

Johnson's program is a recursive algorithm that, when applied to a symmetric proximity matrix, constructs a hierarchical system of clustering representations, ranging from a *weak* clustering in which each of the N stimulus objects is represented as a separate cluster to a *strong* cluster in which all N objects are grouped together as a single cluster. The algorithm assumes that there are N stimulus objects $v_1, v_2, \ldots, v_N$, and a sequence of $w+1$ clusterings, $C_0, C_1, \ldots, C_w$, where each clustering C_h ($h = 1, 2, \ldots, w$) has associated with it a number α_h, its *value*. C_0 is the weak clustering, with $\alpha_0 = 0$, and C_m is the strong clustering. The clusterings are assumed to "increase," i.e., $C_{h-1} < C_h$, meaning that every clustering C_h is the *union* of clusters in C_{h-1}. This arrangement of clusterings is called a *hierarchical clustering scheme* (HCS). The values of α_h either increase or decrease (i.e., $\alpha_{h-1} \leqslant \alpha_h$ or $\alpha_h \leqslant \alpha_{h-1}$) depending on whether dissimilarities or similarities, respectively, are considered.

The input to the algorithm consists of a symmetric matrix of ordinal proximity measures s_{ij} ($i, j = 1, 2, \ldots, N$), where $s_{ii} = 0$ and $s_{ij} > 0$ ($i \neq j$). In our studies, ordinal proximity measures result from constructing a labeled tree and taking the proximity measure s_{ij} between nodes v_i and v_j to be the sum of ranks (weights) of the links in the path (link progression) connecting v_i and v_j. Ordinal proximity measures also result when a labeled complete graph is constructed in such a way that each link has a unique integer value between 1 and M. When the direct grouping method is used, requiring subjects to sort N lexical items into as many clusters as they wish, the data are summarized by an $N \times N$ data matrix, where the entry y_{ij} gives the number of subjects who put items v_i and v_j together in the same cluster ($y_{ij} = 0, 1, \ldots, Y$). Since it is quite simple to prove that y is a metric (Miller, 1969), the data matrix can be regarded as a proximity matrix, where y_{ij} is a measure of the semantic proximity of items v_i and v_j. The proximity matrices obtained by the direct grouping or graph construction methods can serve then as input to Johnson's program.

The program consists of two clustering methods—the Connectedness method and the Diameter method. The former constructs an HCS as follows:

Step 1. C_0 is the weak clustering with $\alpha_0 = 0$.

Step 2. Assume a given clustering C_{h-1} with the proximity function s defined for all stimulus objects or clusters in C_{h-1} and let α_h be a minimal nonzero entry in the proximity matrix. Merge the pair of stimulus objects and/or clusters with distance α_h to create C_h of value α_h.

Step 3. A new proximity function is created for C_h in the following way. If c_i and c_j are stimulus objects and/or clusters in C_h and not in C_{h-1} (i.e., $s_{ij} = \alpha_h$), then the distance from the cluster (c_i, c_j) to any third stimulus object or cluster, c_k, is defined by

$$s_{(i,j)k} = \min (s_{ik}, s_{jk}).$$

If c_i and c_j are stimulus objects and/or clusters in C_{h-1}, not clustered in C_h, s_{ij} is not changed.

Step 4. Repeat Steps 2 and 3 until the strong clustering is obtained.

The diameter method is the same as the Connectedness method, except in Step 3, where we define

$$s_{(i,j)k} = \max (s_{ik}, s_{jk}).$$

To demonstrate how the two clustering methods work consider the proximity matrix presented in Table 2-2, which was obtained from the graph G_6 portrayed in Fig. 2-1f. Applying the Connectedness method to Table 2-2

TABLE 2-2   A Proximity Matrix for G_6 in Fig. 2-1f

	Node					
	A	B	C	D	E	F
A	0	1	8	10	4	9
B	1	0	7	9	3	8
C	8	7	0	2	4	9
D	10	9	2	0	6	11
E	4	3	4	6	0	5
F	9	8	9	11	5	0

resulted in the HCS presented in Fig. 2-2. Figure 2-3 shows the HCS built by the Diameter method. Consider Fig. 2-2 first. The first clustering (top row) is the weak clustering with N clusters, the value of which is $\alpha_0 = 0$. C_1 has five clusters—(A, B), (C), (D), (E), and (F), with $\alpha_1 = 1$. C_2 has four clusters, (A, B), (C, D), (E), and (F), with $\alpha_2 = 2$. And, finally, at level 5 we have the strong clustering, C_5, with all words in the same cluster. Figure 3-3 shows a different HCS, indicating that the two clustering methods may yield different results.

As was noted above, the clustering techniques are particularly useful for analyzing proximity data obtained by the direct grouping technique. When this technique is used, judges are asked to sort a set of lexical items into clusters, as

```
                        Node

    Level    F    D    C    E    B    A    α

      0      .    .    .    .    .    .    0

      1      .    .    .    .    X    X    X    1

      2      .    X    X    X    .    X    X    X    2

      3      .    X    X    X    X    X    X    X    X    3

      4      .    X    X    X    X    X    X    X    X    X    4

      5      X    X    X    X    X    X    X    X    X    X    X    5
```

Fig. 2-2. HCS for the graph 2-1f (Connectedness method).

Node

Level	D	C	F	E	B	A	α
0	.	.	.	.	.	.	0
1	.	.	.	.	X	X X	1
2	X X X			.	.	X X X	2
3	X X X			.	X X X X X		4
4	X X X			X X X X X X X			9
5	X X X X X X X X X X X						11

Fig. 2-3. HCS for the graph 2-1f (Diameter method).

many as they wish, and data from all subjects are pooled. This technique was used in several of our studies. Subjects were told that they would be required "to sort words in *terms of similarity in meaning.*" For each deck they were instructed as follows:

> Lay out the cards and look carefully over all the words. Then arrange the words into piles on the basis of similarity or closeness in meaning. *You can use as many piles as you wish and you can have as many or as few words as you like in any pile*–all the way from a large number down to just one. When you have done this look over your piles, make any adjustments or changes you may feel appropriate, and then put a rubber band around each pile and around each single card that you may have, and another rubber band around the whole deck. Then put the deck in the envelope, pull out the deck with the 2 on it, and proceed in the same fashion until you have gone through all decks. Remember, be sure to look carefully over all the words in each deck before starting and then, in terms of similarity or closeness in meaning, sort the words into as many different piles as you feel appropriate.

Both clustering methods share one property, namely, "the clusterings are unaffected by monotone transformations of the similarity matrix (Johnson, 1967, p. 249)." Moreover, the values assigned to the clusterings have simple meanings in the two methods. Let the *size* of a path (link progression) connecting any two nodes, v_i and v_j, be the largest link rank on this path. Given a clustering, we say that the *path distance s'* from v_i to v_j is the minimal path size of all paths connecting v_i and v_j. The value of a Connectedness method clustering is max s'_{ij}, where v_i and v_j are in the same cluster. Clearly, when the tree construction method is used to obtain the proximity measures, the value of a Connectedness method clustering is equal to its level. When either of the two graph construction methods is used to obtain the proximity measures, the Diameter method minimizes at each stage the *diameter* of the clusters (the largest intracluster proximity measure).

Statistics for Cluster Analysis

Rejection of the null hypothesis that the proximity data are random is recommended before attempts are made at psychological interpretation of structural statistics. Tests on statistics of random undirected graphs were described earlier in the present chapter. A useful statistic for cluster analysis has been examined by Johnson (unpublished manuscript, a), who addressed himself to the problem of testing the hypothesis that some subset of k stimulus objects make a cluster. More specifically, given an $N \times N$ symmetric matrix with ordinal proximity measures, he attempted to test the null hypothesis that these k stimulus objects are significantly closer together than one would expect by chance alone.

Suppose that all M proximity measures are converted to ranks. A useful cluster statistic is defined by

$$\lambda_{k,N} = \bar{R}_m(k,N) - \bar{R}_i(k,N)$$

where k is the number of stimulus objects in the cluster, $\bar{R}_m(k,N)$ is the mean of all $\binom{k}{2}$ distances (ranks) within this cluster, and $\bar{R}_i(k, N)$ is the mean of all $k(N-k)$ distances (ranks) from the k stimulus objects in the cluster to the remaining $N-k$ stimulus objects outside this cluster. To test the null hypothesis that an observed value of $\lambda_{k,N}$ is not significantly different from a value expected by chance, the sampling distribution of $\lambda_{k,N}$ is required. Although this distribution is unknown, Johnson has derived the mean $\bar{\lambda}_{k,N}$ and standard deviation $\sigma_{k,N}$ of $\lambda_{k,N}$, allowing him to compute the following "z score":

$$z_{k,N} = \frac{\lambda_{k,N} - \bar{\lambda}_{k,N}}{\sigma_{k,N}}.$$

Since the sampling distribution of $\lambda_{k,N}$ is unknown, Chebyshev's inequality may be used to obtain an upper bound, $1/z_{k,N}^2$, on the probability of obtaining a cluster of size k which is "better" than a given cluster. Stated differently, the probability of obtaining another cluster of the same size with a larger value of $\lambda_{k,N}$ is less than or equal to $1/z_{k,N}^2$. Fixing the desired level of significance at 0.05, the critical z value, $z_{0.05}$, is $\sqrt{20} = 4.47$. Since Chebyshev's inequality is very conservative, the criterion was slightly relaxed and we settled at $z_{0.06} = 4$ for testing the hypothesis that an observed cluster differs significantly from one expected by chance alone.

There are several ways to interpret an HCS, depending on the purpose of the investigator. If he wishes to locate the largest number of significant clusters, regardless of the proportion of stimulus objects that they include, he should scan the HCS from top to bottom. If he is interested in finding the largest number of stimulus objects which form significant clusters, the HCS should be scanned from bottom to top. Another alternative, which we adopted, is to consider the largest number of significant clusters, each of which includes a maximum number of stimulus objects. That is, we first find the largest number of significant clusters and then let each of them "grow" to its maximum size (provided it still remains significant). A clustering constructed by this procedure will be referred to as a MAXC clustering.

Another notion that we shall make use of is the distance between two clusterings, discussed by Johnson (unpublished manuscript, b). Define an *incidence matrix* corresponding to a given clustering C_h as an $N \times N$ matrix of 0's and 1's, where entry (i,j) in the matrix contains 1 if and only if stimulus objects v_i and v_j are in the same cluster in C_h. A *distance between two clusterings*, C_h and C_h', each of which is of size N, is defined by $d(C_h, C_h')$ = the number of entries in the incidence matrices of C_h and C_h' that are different, normalized by division by $N(N-1)$. $d(C_h, C_h')$ is positive and symmetric; it satisfies the triangle inequality, and $0 \leqslant d(C_h, C_h') \leqslant 1$. No restrictions are placed on C_h and C_h' except that they should be partitions of the same set of N stimulus objects. One may measure the distance $d(\text{MAXC}_h, \text{MAXC}_h')$ between two clusterings, or if C_h is a clustering of a particular subject and C_h' is a group clustering (obtained from a mean proximity matrix), $d(C_h, C_h')$ shows how closely the subject respects the group clustering. The distance between C_3 in Fig. 2-2 and C_3 in Fig. 2-3 is $d(C_3, C_3) = 0$, while $d(C_4, C_4) = 0.600$.

In applying cluster analysis we shall mainly be concerned with discovering and interpreting MAXC clusterings, departing from this procedure and discussing nonsignificant clusterings when no significant clusters are obtained or when their number is very small. Our experience has repeatedly been that the number of significant clusters in MAXC clusterings of individual subjects and the number of stimulus objects that these consist of are almost always smaller than the number of significant clusters and the number of stimulus objects these include in group MAXC clusterings. When the number of clusters in C_h is smaller than that in C_h', and both clusterings are partitions of the same set of stimulus objects, the distance $d(C_h, C_h')$ may be quite large even if the clusters of C_h' are subclusters of the clusters of C_h. Since it frequently happened in our studies that distinct significant clusters of a group MAXC clustering were merged together in MAXC clusterings of individual subjects, we computed distances only (1) between two group MAXC clusterings yielded by different clustering methods (the Connectedness and the Diameter methods), (2) between clusterings of two subjects participating under the same experimental condition, and (3) between group and individual clusterings, provided the number of clusters in each (with two stimulus objects or more) was the same.

There is a close relationship between a labeled tree, when the weights of its links are assumed to be measured on an ordinal scale, and an HCS built by the Connectedness method (HCSC). A labeled tree whose links are rank-ordered from 1 to $N-1$ leads directly to an HCSC without going through the intermediate stage of adding ranks to compute the entire $N \times N$ proximity matrix. To see this, consider Figs 2-1f and 2-2. The first two nodes connected in Fig. 2-1f are A and B, the same nodes which make the first cluster in Fig. 2-2. The next two nodes connected in Fig. 2-1f are C and D, resulting in the second cluster in Fig. 2-2. Next, B and E are connected in Fig. 2-1f, corresponding to the merging of the clusters (A, B) and (E) in Fig. 2-2, and so on. Thus, the tree construction method is simply a direct method for building an HCSC. Any labeled tree constructed by our subjects is directly convertible to an HCSC. The converse is not true, however, since both clustering methods merge clusters (and not elements), while under the tree construction method nodes (and not trees) are connected to each other.

Since any labeled complete graph whose links are labeled from 1 to M can be expressed as a symmetric proximity matrix, the statistic $\lambda_{k,N}$ may be reinterpreted within the context of graph theory. Testing the significance of $\lambda_{k,N}$ provides an answer to the question whether the k nodes of a labeled complete graph, $G_{k,\binom{k}{2}}$, which is in itself a subgraph of a labeled complete graph, $G_{N,M}$, are significantly closer together than one would expect by chance alone. (Actually $G_{N,M}$ does not have to be complete. It is only required to have $M-\binom{N-k}{2}$ labeled links.) Similarly, if distances between nonadjacent nodes in a tree are defined as the sum of ranks of the links in the path connecting these two nodes, $\lambda_{k,N}$ may be used to test the hypothesis that the k nodes of a subtree G_k of a tree G_N are closer together than one would expect by chance alone.

OTHER DATA ANALYSIS PROCEDURES

Competing successfully with various metric procedures for analyzing multidimensional proximity data, such as factor analysis and multiple discriminant analysis, nonmetric procedures for analyzing the same type of data have been recently developed under a wide range of assumptions, and presently constitute a fast growing branch of psychometrics. We have discussed above some of the recently developed multidimensional scaling methods which attempt to cope with the problem of individual differences, e.g., Carroll and Chang (1970), Horan (1969), Kruskal (1968), McGee (1968), and Tucker and Messick (1963). In this section we shall describe briefly two procedures which purport to account for typal variation, namely, an "iterative clique detection" procedure developed by Peay (1970), and a "class-quantitative" procedure due to Degerman (1968); the latter procedure considers a class of structures containing both typal and dimensional variation.

Using the terminology of graph theory presented in the first section of the present chapter, Peay (1970) defines a *clique* of a graph G as "a maximal complete subgraph of G (p. 1)." According to this definition, a clique is a subset of nodes in a graph G, every two of which are adjacent, such that there is no other node of G which is adjacent to every node in the subset. Thus, each node of graph G lies in at least one clique; an isolated node, or a pair of adjacent nodes (not contained in a larger complete subgraph) constitute a clique, and if G is complete there is one clique exactly containing all the nodes. The set of all cliques of a graph G is called the *clique set* for G, and it is easy to show that such a set is unique.

Peay's procedure starts with a symmetric (numerical) proximity matrix of order N (or, equivalently, with the corresponding labeled graph with N nodes). Arbitrarily setting a *criterion distance* d_0, the procedure first determines a unique graph by specifying that a link joins a pair of nodes in the graph if and only if the corresponding value in the proximity matrix is less than or equal to d_0, and then determines the unique clique set for the resulting graph. "Thus, a graph is determined for each setting of the criterion distance, and it is easy to see that as the criterion distance is increased, the effect is to add lines successively to the graph (pp. 2-3)." If one determines a clique set for a given graph G at each criterion level, a *hierarchical clique structure* results, corresponding to Johnson's (1967) HCS. For an illustrative example consider the labeled tree in Fig. 2-1f and the corresponding proximity matrix, obtained by summing the values of the links joining each pair of nodes, presented in Table 2-2. The hierarchical clique structure presented in Table 2-3 gives the clique set for each level of the criterion distance d_0.

TABLE 2-3   The Clique Set for G_6 in Fig. 2-1f

d_0	The clique set
0	[A], [B], [C], [D], [E], [F]
1	[A, B], [C], [D], [E], [F]
2	[A, B], [C, D], [E], [F]
3	[A, B], [B, E], [C, D], [F]
4	[A, B, E], [C, D], [C, E], [F]
5	[A, B, E], [C, D], [C, E], [E, F]
6	[A, B, E], [C, D, E], [E, F]
7	[A, B, E], [B, C, E], [C, D, E], [F]
8	[A, B, C, E], [C, D, E], [B, E, F]
9	[A, B, C, E, F], [B, C, D, E]
10	[A, B, C, E, F], [A, B, C, D, E]
11	[A, B, C, D, E, F]

The two clustering methods due to Johnson (1967) and Peay (1970) are very similar in that both allow for hierarchical clustering and both make very weak assumptions regarding the nature of the proximity data, namely, that they are ordinal. The two procedures differ from each other in that the former requires mutually exclusive clusters whereas the latter, like Constantinescu's (1966, 1967) procedure, relaxes this assumption, allowing the clusters to overlap. We shall only make the very obvious remark that hypotheses or expectations concerning the structural properties of the stimulus domain under consideration must determine to a large extent the choice of an appropriate clustering procedure. Among the more obvious circumstances that might give rise to overlapping clusters one may note (1) perhaps most common, the case where there are fringe terms that could fall equally well into two or more clusters, (2) the case where some terms are polysemous and understood differently by different subjects, and (3) the case where a cross-classificatory or paradigmatic structure really obtains and, consequently, terms may be clustered differently by different subjects as a function of the order in which the cross-classifying features are considered. If the stimulus objects constitute geometric objects, kinship terms, or animal names, clustering methods such as Johnson's would seem more appropriate; if the stimulus domain is more open and ill-defined, there would seem to be no sufficiently convincing reasons, *a priori*, for preferring one method over the other. Interpretability of the clustering results cannot, of itself, determine preference since we suspect that, with more experience gained in analyzing multidimensional ordinal data, overlapping clusters may often be as easy to label and interpret as mutually exclusive clusters. When possible, we would recommend, in the spirit of the present work, application of both kinds of clustering procedures, if only to permit examination of the amount of agreement between them.

Considered as quantitative psycholinguistic models, the various MDS and hierarchical clustering procedures discussed above represent alternative structural models as to the relations obtaining among items constituting or drawn from some lexical domain. Since each procedure interprets proximity data in terms of a different conception of structure and hence, necessarily, reveals only certain aspects of structure, neither provides a complete and "neutral" account of the nature of that structure. Considering pure typal and pure dimensional structures as representing two extremes on a continuum of possible data structures, Degerman (1968) has attempted a more extensive treatment of structure by considering a class of structures containing both typal and dimensional variation, focusing on "structures representing discrete classes which contain internal quantitative variation (p. 3)." In Degerman's formulation, configurations are assumed to be composed of two orthogonal subspaces, a class subspace in which systematic variation is assumed to reflect differences due to cluster membership only, and a complementary dimension subspace assumed to display variation in a continuous manner along quantitative dimensions. His technique "is similar to the standard approaches in attempting to determine natural clusters in the data and in assigning each element to a single cluster. It is different in the sense that it allows solutions for a wider range of structures, while offering a meaningful interpretation in terms of clusters containing internal quantitative variation (p. 8)." Starting with a symmetric proximity matrix of order N, the technique first applies any of the current programs for metric or nonmetric MDS to the proximity data to obtain the spatial coordinates for the N stimulus objects in m dimensions. The resulting coordinates are then used as input for a metric *multidimensional cluster analysis* computer program, and, finally, the original m-dimensional configuration is rotated orthogonally so that the first $m-q$ dimensions, $q = 1, 2, \ldots, m-1$, display the clusters, and the last q dimensions represent quantitative variation.

Degerman's formulation as well as any other approach which considers configurations containing both structural and typal variation is attractive and potentially useful, especially for studies attempting to reveal structural properties of ill-defined, unexplored domains. One should not adopt such approaches uncritically, however, or apply blindly the computer programs that they produce. Rather, one should carefully examine the assumptions of such procedures and their properties before too much time and effort is invested in them. Degerman's procedure which, like Peay's method, came to our attention when the bulk of our work was already completed, seems to have its limitations. Two of its assumptions, namely, (1) that the dimension and class subspaces are orthogonal, and, more seriously, (2) that the proximity data which are input to the multidimensional cluster analysis have interval properties, are too strong for the purposes of our work. Moreover, the procedure has been tested by Degerman only, and when tested the stimulus objects which were selected were known *a priori* to vary in combinations of class and quantitative aspects. As Degerman has himself noted, "for stimulus sets which can be considered to contain both quantitative variation and variation due to class membership, a number of questions arise concerning the production of similarity judgments by subjects (p. 22)." Can subjects make reliable judgments in such cases? Will their judgments reflect the qualitative difference between the types of variation, and if so, will the multidimensional similarity space be partitioned as postulated, or will one or the other source of variation predominate in determining the judgments? These questions can and should be answered by carefully designed methodological studies, Degerman's dissertation being the first step in this direction, before the procedure is applied widely. There is one more problem, probably only minor, with Degerman's two-step procedure. After conducting a MDS analysis, the procedure clusters the resulting spatial coordinates rather than the original proximity measures, thus introducing distortions depending upon the type of metric chosen for the MDS analysis, and goodness of fit. As we remarked before, very little is presently known about the effects of the particular metric chosen and the statistical properties of the measure of goodness of fit on the adequacy of the MDS model.

Rather than applying a "class-quantitative" model, we treated the MDS and the hierarchical clustering methods as two different, independent models, applied them separately to our proximity data, and then compared their results to each other. It should be noted that the hierarchical clustering method, in addition to providing a further and possibly different insight into the structure of a semantic domain, may also provide a check upon the adequacy of the MDS model, i.e., upon the adequacy of a truly dimensional configuration. A check is needed only if a spatial representation, forced into low dimensionality, has so badly distorted the underlying configuration as to result in a misleading picture. But how does one know when the underlying configuration has been badly distorted? Clearly, the null hypothesis that the proximity data are randomly generated is very weak and rejection of this hypothesis may still leave us with a representation that severely distorts the underlying configuration. Moreover, any global measure of goodness of fit, such as Kruskal's "stress," does not tell whether the departure from perfect fit is systematic or whether it only represents the averaging out of random errors (Shepard, 1969).

The checking technique that we have employed "is that of embedding a dimension-free representation into a dimensional one (Shepard, 1969, p. 41)," and concluding that the spatial representation does not distort the true underlying structure if it is (1) *interpretable*, and (2) *consistent* with the hierarchical clustering results. By "consistent" we mean, very loosely, that the closed curves drawn around each group of points that forms a significant cluster in a two-dimensional spatial representation are simple and compact, that the location of the curves in the two-dimensional representation is relatively stable and unaffected by the methods used to gather the data, and that only points that are close together in the two-dimensional representation are also clustered together. Clearly, the notion of "consistency" is ill-defined, since no criteria are given for determining which points are close together in the dimensional representation. Therefore, to determine whether or not the underlying configuration had been distorted by the MDS analysis we relied mainly on interpretability of the results and a visual inspection of the representations.

Beyond simply comparing the fit of different kinds of solutions, there are additional independent grounds for evaluating the appropriateness or adequacy of a structural representation. One may assess the compatibility between a particular structural solution and what is required by some theoretical model. Indeed one of the criteria guiding our selection of domains for study was precisely the availability of some independent structural account for each of these domains, see, e.g., kinship terms, pronouns, color names, etc. Even in cases where such accounts are partial and poorly articulated, as, e.g., prepositions, HAVE verbs, and verbs of judging, they are of considerable heuristic value when it comes to judging the interpretability of a particular structural solution. In addition, one may attempt to validate a particular solution by determining whether or not one can use it to predict performance on some quite different sort of cognitive or learning task. We sought to do this, e.g., by considering the results of a sentence completion task for conjunctions and by examining errors during learning of pronouns in a paired-associate task. For some general comments on the structure of long-term memory, and on the ways in which learning data may be relevant to matters of underlying semantic structure see, e.g., Kintsch (1970) which sketches a "marker theory of memory."

Chapter 3   COLOR NAMES

We know that color space can be represented in terms of a three-dimensional system, and we can specify the relation between these dimensions and certain physical variables. Colors can be described in terms of their variation in hue (the reflection of light of different wavelengths), brightness (the reflection of more or less light, commonly referred to by terms such as "light" and "dark"), and saturation (the degree of freedom from dilution with white, commonly referred to by words such as "weak" or "strong", "pale" or "deep"). Colors are usually specified according to all three dimensions of variation; e.g., PINK refers to a range of color that is reddish in hue, of fairly high brightness, and fairly low saturation, and BROWN refers to a range of color between RED and YELLOW in hue, of fairly low saturation and brightness. The ranges of color denoted by BLACK, GREY, and WHITE, on the other hand, differ mainly with respect to one dimension, viz. brightness.

But, of itself, this says nothing regarding the nature of the color name space (CNS), or the relation between this and the color space. Different languages segment the color continuum in different ways: category boundaries may fall at different places, the number of terms available for describing a particular color range may differ, and the very basis for making distinctions may differ among languages. It is well known that color names of different languages cannot always be brought into one-to-one correspondence with one another. For example, the English word BLUE has no equivalent in Russian, and there is no equivalent to BROWN in French. The substance of the vocabulary of color may therefore be thought of as "a physical continuum within which languages may draw either the same or a different number of boundaries and with which they may draw the boundaries at the same or different places (Lyons, 1968, p. 58)."

Now for a given language, specifically English, what might one expect to be the relation between the color space and the color name space? Assuming that the three dimensions of color are relevant to our naming behavior, what about the different weights that should be assigned to these dimensions in order to account for the locations of the principal color names in the color name configuration? Chapanis has suggested that "Hue is perhaps the most important of the three fundamental variables of color as a mental phenomenon. It is the main *quality* factor in color and is what the ordinary person means when he says color (Chapanis, 1965, p. 330)." It seems reasonable to assume that, unless BLACK, GREY, and WHITE are included in the color name list, variations in brightness will have little or no effect on the configuration. Saturation will probably appear in the representation, particularly when the color name list includes words such as BEIGE, TAN, BRONZE—all three terms referring to weakly saturated colors.

Note that even if there are individual differences between speakers of English in the absolute location of their color terms, i.e., with regard to the locations of the referents of these terms, as long as relations of betweenness or adjacency are appropriately maintained the CNS results for different individuals should be quite similar. We are interested in the CNS (1) for its own sake, i.e., as revealing the semantic structure of a set of lexical items in terms "of the network of semantic relations that hold among the items (Lyons, 1968)," and (2) with regard to its relation or mapping onto the color space, some sectors of which constitute the referents of the color names under consideration.

METHOD

There were four groups of subjects; two of these (Groups CTM[1] and CTF) constructed labeled trees; the other two (Groups CCS and CCD) constructed complete graphs. Groups CTM and CTF consisted of 17 male and 17 female students, respectively, enrolled at the University of North Carolina. (Originally there were 41 subjects; seven of these, who were not familiar with at least one of

---

[1] A word might be said with regard to the principle governing the use of abbreviations in naming the various experimental groups. The first letter always refers to the domain studied, as K (kinship terms), E (emotion names) etc.; the next letter or letters index the way in which data were gathered, as T (tree method), DG (direct grouping), etc.; finally, if a distinction between male and female subjects is maintained, the last letter will be M (male) or F (female). The only exceptions to the above are to be found, first, in the case of pronouns where the groups are labeled PR, and where PRC identifies the subjects who learned pronouns as response members in a paired-associate task, and, second, in the case of kinship terms where subjects using an "affection or love" criterion are labeled KLTM and KLTF, respectively.

the color names, were discarded.) The subjects in Groups CCS and CCD were 26 male and female American students at the Hebrew University of Jerusalem, all of them native speakers of English.

Groups CTM and CTF were run separately. Every subject received upon arrival a list of 24 color names arranged alphabetically, a blank sheet, and written instructions for the tree construction method (see Chapter 2). After he had read the instructions, the experimenter exemplified them by constructing a tree on the blackboard and answered questions. The subjects were allowed up to two hours to complete the task, but most of them completed it in less than one hour. All subjects received course credit for their participation.

The list of 24 color names, presented in Table 3-1, includes words that were assumed to be known by all the subjects and which were judged to provide a wide coverage of the color circle. Several color names such as IVORY and SILVER were deliberately introduced to see whether they would require an additional dimension in the MDS analysis.

TABLE 3-1   Color Names Presented to Subjects

1. BEIGE	9. IVORY	17. *RED
2. *BLUE	10. *KHAKI	18. RUST
3. *BRONZE	11. MAGENTA	19. *SCARLET
4. *BROWN	12. MUSTARD	20. SILVER
5. CHARTREUSE	13. *OLIVE	21. *TAN
6. *CRIMSON	14. *ORANGE	22. *TURQUOISE
7. GOLD	15. PINK	23. *VIOLET
8. *GREEN	16. *PURPLE	24. *YELLOW

The subjects in Groups CCS and CCD were run together in one session that lasted about 90 minutes. Upon arrival, each subject received a list of 15 color names (the starred words in Table 3-1) arranged alphabetically, a second list with all 105 pairs of words arranged randomly, and the standard instructions for constructing a complete undirected graph (see Chapter 2). The instructions for the two groups were identical with the exception of two words; "more" and "most" were substituted in Group CCS for "less" and "least," respectively, in Group CCD. That is, subjects in Groups CCS were required to rank-order all 105 pairs in terms of similarity while subjects in Group CCD were asked to use a criterion of dissimilarity.

After a month, six randomly selected subjects, four from Group CCS and two from Group CCD, were recalled to do the same task once more, using the same procedure.

RESULTS

Graph Analysis

By tracing the labeled links, the number of subtrees were counted separately for each subject. The mean number of subtrees was 4.76 and 4.94 for Groups CTM and CTF, respectively. With only three exceptions, the subjects used all three options. The labeling of the links shows that subtrees were typically connected toward the end of the task; the subjects tended to sort the nodes into separate clusters, and after exhausting the whole list of color names they merged these clusters together. The difference between males and females in terms of the mean number of subtrees was nonsignificant.

The first property examined in comparing random and observed labeled trees is the distribution of node degree. This distribution was obtained for each subject and then summed over subjects within each of the two groups. Table 3-2 compares the observed distributions for Groups CTM and CTF to the Poisson distribution predicted from equation 4. The difference was highly significant in each case ($p < 0.001$, by the one-sample Kolmogorov-Smirnov test). The difference between the two observed distributions, tested by the two-sample Kolmogorov-Smirnov test, was nonsignificant.

TABLE 3-2   Observed and Predicted Frequency Distributions of Node Degree
(Groups CTM and CTF)

Degree	Predicted	Observed	
		Group CTM	Group CTF
1	156	118	105
2	150	222	242
3	72	55	52
4	23	10	8
5+	7	3	1

Inspection of Table 3-2 shows that the observed trees had more nodes with degree $r = 2$, and fewer nodes with degree $r > 2$ or $r = 1$. The observed means for nodes with degree 1 were 6.94 and 6.18 for Groups CTM and CTF, respectively. The expected number of nodes with degree 1, computed from equation 5, is 9.40, and the standard deviation, computed from equation 6, is 1.42. The difference between observed and predicted mean number of nodes with degree 1 was significant for both groups.

Since trees were not constructed randomly, differences may be expected in the "popularity bias" of various pairs of adjacent nodes. Table 3-3 presents the distribution of the number of pairs of adjacent nodes connected y times, $y = 0, 1, \ldots, 17$; results are presented separately for the two groups. Using the method of moments to estimate the parameters of the predicted negative

TABLE 3-3   Observed and Predicted Frequency Distribution of Selected Pairs of Adjacent Nodes (Groups CTM and CTF)[a]

y	Group CTM		Group CTF	
	Predicted	Observed	Predicted	Observed
0	163	171	181	198
1	41	40	33	23
2	22	16	17	13
3	14	12	11	8
4	9	7	8	4
5	7	5	6	3
6	5	5	4	3
7	4	3	3	2
8	3	4	2	4
9	2	4	2	2
10	2	2	2	3
11	1	2	1	2
12	1	2	1	4
13	1	0	1	2
14+	2	3	4	5

[a]Parameters:

	p	s
CTM	0.176	0.303
CTF	0.127	0.206

binomial distribution, p and s, equation 7 was used to generate the predicted distributions, which are also presented in Table 3-3.

Inspection of the table shows a fair agreement between the observed and predicted distributions, with minor but consistent discrepancies. For both groups the predicted frequency is smaller than the observed frequency when $y = 0$, and larger when $y = 1, 2, \ldots, 5$. These discrepancies, however, are nonsignificant ($p > 0.20$) by the one-sample Kolmogorov-Smirnov test, lending support to the assumption that the popularity bias is gamma distributed in the population of pairs of color names. Values of s for Groups CTM and CTF are presented in the lower part of Table 3-3, suggesting that when the color name space of college students is investigated, the popularity bias is stronger in women than in men.

The results reported thus far reject the hypothesis of random construction of trees. The small values of s suggest that certain pairs of color names are considerably more "popular" than others, and this is more so for females than for males. The small frequency of nodes with degree 1 and the large frequency of nodes with degree 2, relative to the expected frequencies in a random graph, suggest "loose" structures such as a straight line, a curve, or a circle. The difference between the observed distributions of pairs of nodes indicates that results for males and females should be kept separate in further analyses of the data. Before undertaking such analyses, properties of the complete undirected graphs constructed by Groups CCS and CCD will be examined.

Since rank-ordering 105 pairs of words is a demanding task, six subjects were run twice to assess the reliability of the procedure. A Spearman rank-order correlation, computed for each subject between the two separate orderings of the 105 pairs, resulted in correlations of 0.432, 0.641, 0.782, and 0.635 for the four subjects in Group CCS, and 0.901 and 0.792 for the two subjects in Group CCD. All correlations are highly significant, showing a surprisingly high reliability for the procedure.

TABLE 3-4   Observed and Predicted Cumulative Probability that G_{N,v_N} is Completely Connected (Groups CCS and CCD)

v_N	Predicted	Observed		v_N	Predicted	Observed	
		CCS	CCD			CCS	CCD
14	0.0320	0	0.0769	29	0.6624	0.6154	0.9230
15	0.0689	0	0.2307	30	0.6893	0.7692	0.9230
16	0.1102	0	0.2307	31	0.7137	0.7692	0.9230
17	0.1550	0	0.2307	32	0.7357	0.7692	0.9230
18	0.2025	0	0.3076	33	0.7554	0.8462	0.9230
19	0.2512	0	0.3076	34	0.7731	0.8462	0.9230
20	0.3003	0.1538	0.3846	35	0.7888	0.8462	1.0000
21	0.3490	0.2307	0.3846	36	0.8028	0.8462	1.0000
22	0.3965	0.2307	0.3846	37	0.8153	0.8462	1.0000
23	0.4422	0.3076	0.5385	38	0.8264	0.9230	1.0000
24	0.4857	0.3076	0.5385	39	0.8362	0.9230	1.0000
25	0.5266	0.3846	0.5385	40	0.8449	1.0000	1.0000
26	0.5649	0.3846	0.6923	50	0.8905	1.0000	1.0000
27	0.6002	0.4614	0.8462	60	0.9028	1.0000	1.0000
28	0.6327	0.5385	0.8462				

Equation 1 was used to compute the cumulative probability, shown in Table 3-4, that a random graph G_{N,v_N} is completely connected. The first column gives the predicted cumulative probabilities for $v_N = 14, 15, \ldots, 40, 50, 60$, and the second and third columns show the cumulative proportions of the observed graphs that were completely connected by the first w links, $w \leqslant v_N$, for Groups CCS and CCD, respectively.

The cumulative proportion of completely connected graphs in Group CCS was smaller than predicted for $w < 30$, but larger than predicted for $w \geqslant 30$. As for Group CCD, the observed cumulative proportion was almost always larger than predicted. The difference between the predicted and each of the observed distributions, tested by the one-sample Kolmogorov-Smirnov test, and the difference between the two observed distributions, tested by the Mann-Whitney two-tailed test, was nonsignificant ($p > 0.05$). The results suggest either that subjects in both groups constructed the graphs randomly, or, more plausibly, that, because of the very small number of subjects, the comparison between predicted and observed distributions is insensitive to biases operating in the construction of the graphs and insensitive to the differences between the two groups.

The next property of random graphs that we examined was the probability distribution of node degree in a random undirected graph. Table 3-5 shows the predicted number of nodes with degree r, obtained from equation 2, for 13 random graphs with $N = n = 15$. Presented in the next two columns are the frequency distributions of node degree for the first 15 links summed separately over the subjects in Groups CCS and CCD.

TABLE 3-5   Observed and Predicted Frequency Distributions of Node Degree for Thirteen Graphs with $n = 15$ (Groups CCS and CCD)

r	Predicted	Observed	
		Group CCS	Group CCD
0	19	24	31
1	52	45	41
2	61	60	69
3	40	44	28
4	17	17	11
5	5	5	10
6	1	0	3
7	0	0	1
8	0	0	1

The difference between predicted and observed frequencies was tested by chi square. For $n = 15$ the difference was not significant for Group CCS, $\chi^2(5) = 2.655$, $p > 0.70$, but highly significant for Group CCD, $\chi^2(5) = 34.070$ $p < 0.001$. Table 3-5 shows that the graphs of Group CCD included more nodes with a high degree than expected by chance alone.

Since the distribution of node degree discriminates between the two groups, one may seek other properties of linear graphs that are also sensitive to the differences between the groups. We next turn to another property of random undirected graphs—the number of cycles of order k. Since the particular color names used in the study may predispose the subject to the early construction of "triangular" cycles, such as RED-SCARLET-CRIMSON, or "rectangular" cycles such as BRONZE-BROWN-TAN-KHAKI, only the cases $k = 3$ and $k = 4$ are investigated. For $n = N = 15$ equation 3 yields $M(g_3) = 1.105$ and $M(g_4) = 1.141$. Table 3-6 presents the number of observed graphs with C cycles, $C = 0, 1, \ldots$, of order k for each of the two groups.

The means of the observed numbers of "triangular" cycles are 5.231 and 0.231

TABLE 3-6   Number of Observed Cycles of Order k with $n = 15$ (Groups CCS and CCD)

C	$k = 3$		$k = 4$	
	Group CCS	Group CCD	Group CCS	Group CCD
0	0	11	1	4
1	0	1	2	1
2	1	1	1	1
3	3	0	3	0
4	1	0	4	2
5	3	0	0	2
6	2	0	0	1
7	1	0	1	0
8	1	0	0	0
9	0	0	0	1
10	0	0	0	1
11	1	0	0	0
12	0	0	0	0
13	0	0	0	0
14	0	0	0	0
15	0	0	1	0
Mean	5.231	0.231	3.923	3.538
SD	2.358	0.576	3.407	3.297

for Groups CCS and CCD, respectively. The difference between each of the observed means and $M(g_3)$ is significant [$t(12) = 6.06$, $p < 0.001$, for Group CCS and $t(12) = 5.25$, $p < 0.001$, for Group CCD]. As Table 3-6 shows the two groups differ from each other with respect to the number of cycles of order 3. Group CCS shows a strong "triangular" bias, while Group CCD shows an opposite bias in the early construction of the graphs. The results show clearly that both groups did not perform the task randomly, but that subjects in Group CCS, who rank-ordered similarities, had a predisposition to grouping color names into groups of three, while subjects in Group CCD had an opposite predisposition.

The two groups did not differ from each other with respect to the mean of the observed cycles of order 4 [$t(24) = 0.27$, $p > 0.70$]. The means for both groups were, however, significantly greater than expected by chance alone [$t(12) = 2.83$, $p < 0.02$, for Group CCS, and $t(12) = 2.52$, $p < 0.05$, for Group CCD]. Thus, a "rectangular" bias operated in both groups in the early part of the task.

Cluster Analysis

The graph analysis of the group results shows that the proximity data were not generated randomly. Moreover, the fact that subjects in Groups CTM and CTF used options 2 and 3 in constructing subtrees later merged into a tree, and the discovery of a popularity bias for color names (Table 3-2) and pairs of color names (Table 3-3), suggests that a cluster analysis of the proximity data is in order.

Applying the two clustering methods to the mean proximity matrices of Groups CTM and CTF resulted in two HCSs for each group, one for each clustering method. If the proximity data satisfy the *ultrametric inequality*, i.e., $s_{i,j} \leqslant \max(s_{i,k}, s_{k,j})$, the two HCSs should be identical. A wide discrepancy between the two solutions indicates that either we are not dealing with a hierarchical conceptual system, or that the proximity data are too noisy for a precise analysis (Miller, 1969). To assess the similarity between the two HCSs, taking into account the significance of the clusters, we measured the distance between the two MAXC clusterings obtained for each group by the two clustering methods. The distances were 0.103 and 0.257 for Groups CTM and CTF, respectively, indicating a fair similarity.

Since the results of the Diameter method are more meaningful or interpretable, we prefer to present them. Figures 3-1 and 3-2 present the HCSs obtained by the Diameter method for the mean proximity matrices of Groups CTM and CTF, respectively. The lines connecting the x's in the two plots denote significant clusters.

The MAXC clustering for Group CTM included the following significant clusters:

1. A GREEN-VIOLET cluster [CHARTREUSE, GREEN, OLIVE, BLUE,

```
                      C
                      H
                      A
                      R
                      T
                    S R
                  I L E         V            S       V
                  V I U G O B   I   C     S M U   B   R K B   O   M Y
                  O L S R L L   O P R   R C A I P I R R U H E T R G U E
                  R V E E I U   L I I   E A G O U O O W S A I A A O S L
              L e Y E U E V E   E N S   D R E L R L N N T K G N N L T L
              v e l R S N V T   T K O   . L N E P E Z . . I E . G D A L
Level                                   N T A T L T E                 O W   α
  1           .  .  .  .  .  .  . XXX .  .  .  .  .  .  .  .  .  .  .  .  .   2.19
  2           .  .  .  .  .  .  . XXX .  .  .  .  .  .  . XXX .  .  .  .      2.75
  3           .  .  . XXX .  .  . XXX .  .  .  .  .  .  . XXX .  .  .  .      2.76
  4           .  .  . XXX .  .  . XXXXX . XXX .  .  .  . XXX .  .  .  .       2.97
  5           .  .  . XXX .  .  . XXXXX . XXX .  .  .  . XXX .  . XXX         3.35
  6           .  .  . XXX .  .  . XXXXX . XXX XXX .  . XXX .  . XXX           3.44
  7           .  .  . XXX XXX . XXXXX . XXX XXX .  . XXX .  . XXX             3.51
  8           .  .  . XXX XXX . XXXXX . XXX XXX .  . XXX . XXXXX              4.14
  9           .  .  . XXX XXX . XXXXX . XXX XXXXX . XXX . XXXXX               4.59
 10           XXX . XXX XXX . XXXXX . XXX XXXXX . XXX . XXXXX                 5.21
 11           XXX . XXX XXX . XXXXX XXXXX XXXXX . XXX . XXXXX                 6.72
 12           XXX . XXX XXX . XXXXX XXXXX XXXXX XXXXX . XXXXX                 7.16
 13           XXX . XXX XXX . XXXXX XXXXX XXXXX XXXXX XXXXXX                  7.41
 14           XXX XXXXX XXX . XXXXX XXXXX XXXXX XXXXX XXXXXXX                 8.53
 15           XXX XXXXX XXX . XXXXXXXXXXX XXXXX XXXXX XXXXXXX                 8.80
 16           XXX XXXXX XXX . XXXXXXXXXXX XXXXXXXXXXX XXXXXXX                 9.01
 17           XXX XXXXX XXX XXXXXXXXXXXX XXXXXXXXXXX XXXXXXX                  9.93
 18           XXX XXXXXXXXXX XXXXXXXXXXXX XXXXXXXXXXX XXXXXXX                11.43
 19           XXX XXXXXXXXXX XXXXXXXXXXXX XXXXXXXXXXXXXXXXXX                 12.20
 20           XXX XXXXXXXXXXXXXXXXXXXXXXXX XXXXXXXXXXXXXXXXXXX              14.74
 21           XXX XXXXXXXXXXXXXXXXXXXXXXXXXXXXXXXXXXXXXXXXXXX               16.98
 22           XXXXXXXXXXXXXXXXXXXXXXXXXXXXXXXXXXXXXXXXXXXXXXXXX             19.01
```

Fig. 3-1. HCS for Group CTM (Diameter method).

```
                    ш
                    ш
                    S
                    Ш
                    œ
                  ≥         ш
              >   œ         S
              œ   ≥         O
              O   ⊢   z  ш  ⊃  z
              ≥   œ  шш> O  O ш  Оz
          > œ  ≤шz<O≥шш⊃  О⊢≥≤œ⊃ш⊢>шz⊢  ≤Оœ⊃⊢œО   Ош> ш  ⊢шœ⊢œ
   Level                                                              α
     1    . . . . . .  . . . . . . XXX . . . . . . . . .            0.79
     2    . . . . XXX . . . . . . . XXX . . . . . . . . .           1.27
     3    . . . . XXX . . . . . . XXXXX . . . . . . . .             1.43
     4    . . . . XXX . . . . . . XXXXX . XXX . . . . . .           1.56
     5    . . . . XXX . . . . . . XXXXX . XXX . . . . XXX           2.02
     6    . . . XXXXX . . . . . . XXXXX . XXX . . . . XXX           2.29
     7    . . . XXXXX . XXX . . . XXXXX . XXX . . . . XXX           2.56
     8    . . . XXXXX . XXX XXX . XXXXX . XXX . . . . XXX           2.62
     9    . . . XXXXX . XXX XXX . XXXXX . XXX . . . XXXXX           2.88
    10    . . XXXXXXX . XXX XXX . XXXXX.. XXX . . . XXXXX           3.76
    11    . . XXXXXXX . XXX XXX XXXXXX . XXX . . . XXXXX            5.30
    12    . . XXXXXXX . XXX XXX XXXXXX . XXX . XXX. XXXXX           5.36
    13    . . XXXXXXX XXXXX XXX XXXXXX . XXX . XXX XXXXX            5.78
    14    . . XXXXXXX XXXXX XXX XXXXXX XXXXX . XXX XXXXX            6.69
    15    . . XXXXXXX XXXXX XXX XXXXXX XXXXX XXXXX XXXXX            6.82
    16    XXX XXXXXXX XXXXX XXX XXXXXX XXXXX XXXXX XXXXX            6.89
    17    XXX XXXXXXX XXXXX XXX XXXXXXXXXXXX XXXXX XXXXX            8.50
    18    XXX XXXXXXX XXXXX XXX XXXXXXXXXXXX XXXXXXXXXX             9.29
    19    XXX XXXXXXX XXXXXXXXX XXXXXXXXXXXX XXXXXXXXXX            10.66
    20    XXXXXXXXXXX XXXXXXXXX XXXXXXXXXXXX XXXXXXXXXX            11.93
    21    XXXXXXXXXXX XXXXXXXXX XXXXXXXXXXXXXXXXXXXXXXX            17.14
    22    XXXXXXXXXXX XXXXXXXXXXXXXXXXXXXXXXXXXXXXXXXXX            18.97
    23    XXXXXXXXXXXXXXXXXXXXXXXXXXXXXXXXXXXXXXXXXXXXX            23.48
```

Fig. 3-2. HCS for Group CTF (Diameter method).

TURQUOISE, PINK, CRIMSON, RED, SCARLET, MAGENTA, PURPLE, VIOLET].

2. A BROWN cluster [BRONZE, BROWN, RUST, KHAKI, BEIGE, TAN].

3. An ORANGE-YELLOW cluster [ORANGE, GOLD, MUSTARD, YELLOW].

The MAXC clustering for Group CTF included the following four significant clusters:

1. A BROWN cluster [IVORY, SILVER, BROWN, KHAKI, BEIGE, TAN].

2. A RED-VIOLET cluster [PINK, RED, CRIMSON, SCARLET, MAGENTA, PURPLE, VIOLET].

3. An ORANGE-YELLOW cluster [ORANGE, BRONZE, RUST, GOLD, MUSTARD, YELLOW].

4. A GREEN-BLUE cluster [CHARTREUSE, GREEN, OLIVE, BLUE, TURQUOISE].

The two clusterings are essentially the same. Cluster 1 in Group CTM is split into two clusters, 2 and 4, in Group CTF, with color names arranged in the same order. Clusters 2 and 3 in Group CTM are the same as clusters 1 and 3 in Group CTF, with the exception of BRONZE and RUST, which fall in the BROWN cluster in Group CTM and in the ORANGE-YELLOW cluster in Group CTF, and IVORY and SILVER, which are not included in the Group CTM MAXC clustering. The distance between the two MAXC clusterings is 0.217.

The proximity matrices of eight randomly selected subjects, four from each group, were also analyzed by the Diameter method, which identified two or three clusters in every MAXC clustering. With few exceptions, the individual MAXC clusterings resembled the group MAXC clusterings. The distances between individual and group MAXC clusterings were 0.420, 0.398, 0.406, and 0.431 for the four randomly selected male subjects, and 0.130, 0.424, 0.120, and 0.341 for the four randomly selected female subjects. The difference between Groups CTM and CTF in terms of the distances between individual and group MAXC clusterings is consistent with the difference between the distributions of node degree (Table 3-3) and the s values, showing a stronger popularity bias for females than for males.

The results yielded by cluster analysis for Groups CCS and CCD add very little information and will not be presented here. The main reason for this is that the relevance of clustering information can best be judged only in terms of the theoretical model(s) that the investigator has in mind, or in terms of practical purposes for which the classification is intended. Although we have shown that clustering information can be used to differentiate between populations of subjects, additional results and further interpretation of the clusters will serve no theoretical purpose since the obvious model to investigate is a spatial model, postulating that color names lie on the color circle or the color solid. Indeed, as Figs. 3-1 and 3-2 show, the two HCSs for Groups CTM and CTF seem consistent with a circular representation if clusters are properly rearranged. We turn, therefore, to an MDS analysis of the proximity data.

Multidimensional Scaling Analysis

If the semantic structure of color names has a close functional relation to the color space, with physical properties of colors reflected in some orderly way in the semantic space, then regardless of where the boundaries between color names are drawn, the discussion at the beginning of this chapter leads us to expect a two-dimensional representation for the mean or individual proximity data, with hue having a greater effect than saturation, and brightness having little or no effect at all. Moroever, if the effect of saturation is very small relative to that of hue, the color names may be expected to lie, in a prespecified order, on the circumference of a circle, whose "intrinsic" dimensionality, to use Shepard's (1969) somewhat vague concept, is not two, but one. Because of the difference between the two color name lists (see Table 3-1), the items of the second list being selected so as to be more homogeneous in terms of saturation, a spatial representation whose intrinsic dimensionality is two is expected for Groups CTM and CTF, and a spatial representation whose intrinsic dimensionality is one is expected for the other two groups.

The Young-Torgerson nonmetric MDS program was applied to the proximity matrices of 16 randomly selected subjects, four from each group, and to the four mean proximity matrices. Solutions were obtained in one, two, and three dimensions, for both the Euclidean and City Block metrics. The stress values for the Euclidean solutions, which were always smaller than the corresponding values for the City Block solutions, are presented in Table 3-7.

TABLE 3-7   Stress Values for Euclidean Representations

Dimensions	No. 1	No. 5	No. 9	No. 13	Mean
			Group CTM		
3	0.050	0.028	0.015	0.096	0.064
2	0.079	0.053	0.021	0.169	0.156
1	0.206	0.141	0.059	0.356	0.280
			Group CTF		
Dimensions	No. 1	No. 5	No. 9	No. 13	Mean
3	0.027	0.024	0.015	0.021	0.024
2	0.045	0.032	0.022	0.041	0.071
1	0.154	0.070	0.051	0.129	0.208
			Group CCS		
Dimensions	No. 3	No. 6	No. 7	No. 10	Mean
3	0.138	0.107	0.104	0.121	0.040
2	0.233	0.167	0.147	0.168	0.078
1	0.403	0.355	0.321	0.352	0.384
			Group CCD		
Dimensions	No. 1	No. 6	No. 9	No. 11	Mean
3	0.067	0.092	0.107	0.083	0.045
2	0.096	0.182	0.197	0.120	0.085
1	0.293	0.415	0.362	0.324	0.339

Considering first the stress values for the mean proximity data, a sharp break between $m = 1$ and $m = 2$ is noted for all groups, with the possible exception of Group CTM. Combined with the theoretical reasons discussed above and the significant departures of the stress values from the critical cut-off points that we have established, the stress values suggest that the color names can be adequately represented in a two-dimensional Euclidean space.

Figures 3-3 to 3-6 portray the two-dimensional Euclidean representations for the mean proximity matrices of each of the four groups. The solutions for Groups CCS and CCD show a very orderly picture. They are circular in shape, very similar to each other, and closely related to the color circle. The qualitative agreement between the circular arrangement of the color names in each of the representations and the arrangement of colors on the color circle is almost perfect. The representations for Groups CTM and CTF are less orderly, though

Fig. 3-3. Two-dimensional Euclidean representation for Group CTM.

Fig. 3-4. Two-dimensional Euclidean representation for Group CTF.

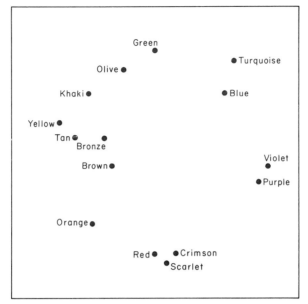

Fig. 3-5. Two-dimensional Euclidean representation for Group CCS.

Fig. 3-6. Two-dimensional Euclidean representation for Group CCD.

the somewhat distorted color circle can be clearly identified. There seems to be a small effect of saturation, with "weakly saturated" color names such as SILVER, IVORY, PINK, BEIGE, and TAN lying away from the centers of the representations.

With the exceptions of Subject 3 in Group CCS and Subject 9 in Group CCD, the two-dimensional representations of the other six subjects resemble the color circle very closely. The solutions for the two exceptional subjects could not be interpreted. Table 3-7 shows that the stress values for the individual subjects in Groups CCS and CCD are always larger than the corresponding stress values for the mean proximity data. This discrepancy does not affect the shape of the representations, the larger stress values for individual subjects are probably due to random errors, resulting from the difficulty of the task, which errors are mostly cancelled out when the proximity data are averaged over subjects.

No attempts were made to interpret the two-dimensional solutions of the individual subjects in Groups CTM and CTF. Since the tree construction method does not permit subjects to form circles, two-dimensional circular representations cannot be obtained for individual subjects. When circular, triangular, or other closed configurations are expected on some theoretical grounds, the tree construction method should be avoided when semantic spaces of individual subjects are investigated. Since the restriction imposed by the method amounts to breaking closed representations at some arbitrary point, the method is still serviceable for studying group results as Figs. 3-3 and 3-4 clearly demonstrate.

DISCUSSION

We shall concentrate attention on the results yielded by the method of complete undirected graphs since the results it yields are particularly clear. Considering such statistics as the distribution of node degree and the popularity bias of pairs of color names, it is clear that, for both male and female subjects, trees were not constructed at random. Similarly, the analysis of graphs obtained by the method of complete undirected graphs revealed that in the early and, therefore, most meaningful part of the task, pairs of color names were not ranked randomly, whether a similarity or dissimilarity criterion was employed. These results provide partial justification for applying nonmetric MDS techniques to the data.

It is reassuring to find strikingly similar dimensional representations, whether a similarity or a dissimilarity criterion is used in making the rankings. From the perspective of the subject, the former criterion may make for an easier and more manageable task. If a similarity criterion is employed the subject, especially in his early rankings which may be the most meaningful and reliable ones, must be sensitive to small differences in "distance" where all the "distances" are relatively small, while if a dissimilarity criterion is employed, he must be sensitive to small differences in "distance" where all the "distances" are relatively large. Given that, in fact, the two procedures yield the same outcomes, the former is surely to be preferred as making less strenuous demands on the subject.

In continuing the examination of results obtained by the method of undirected graphs note that while the placement of colors by individual subjects follows in general the hue circle, the fit in two dimensions is characteristically only fair. However, the two-dimensional color name spaces (CNSs) based on the *mean* proximity matrices yield very similar orderly arrays with almost perfect correspondence between the arrangement of the color names in the CNSs, the space of perceived similarities among colors, and the hue circle (see Chapanis, 1965, p. 341 for a discussion of the hue circle, and Shepard, 1962b, Fig. 13, for a reanalysis of some of Ekman's results based on similarity judgments among colors). The principal determinant of the placement of the color names appears to be hue, most of the items falling, as it were, on or near the rim of a circle. There is some slight saturation effect because, as can be seen in Figs. 3-5 and 3-6, BROWN, BRONZE, and TAN, which refer to relatively desaturated colors, are displaced somewhat toward the center of the CNS. There are very few common, single word names which refer to desaturated colors, e.g., pastels. Other than those listed above, PINK is perhaps the only obvious candidate. Given this fact, it is almost inevitable that any study using only common, unqualified single word color names will provide little evidence regarding the saturation dimension, or for that matter, regarding the brightness dimension. Thus, necessarily, the CNS can only be in partial correspondence to the color space, and, indeed, has to be a collapsed or degenerate version of such a space insofar as common color names principally index the hue of the simply named colors. To discover more complex structures, it might be of interest to determine the CNSs of sophisticated users of a richly differentiated color vocabulary, e.g., interior decorators, painters, etc.

As pointed out earlier, the tree construction method imposes certain constraints on the data, namely: cycles are not allowed, circular representations cannot be obtained for individual subjects, and weights are assumed to be additive. An examination of the two-dimensional representations for male and female subjects (Figs. 3-3 and 3-4) indicates that the general arrangement of the 15 common color names is roughly similar to that obtained by the other graph construction method, although the arrays are hardly circular. For these arrays note how terms like IVORY and SILVER, whose referents do not fall anywhere on the color circle, are displaced away from the other terms in the array and distort its circular shape.

One can hardly evade the very basic question as to how judgments of similarity can be made at all on color names, and whether the basis for such judgments is the same for color names as for colors. It has been argued (Shepard, 1964, Torgerson, 1965) that one should distinguish between (1) similarity as a basic perceptual relation between instances of a multidimensional attribute where the stimuli are "unitary" and (2) similarity as a derivative cognitive relation between "analyzable" stimuli varying in several distinct components or attributes, and it has been suggested that similarity in the latter case may be particularly "sensitive to all of the delicate problems of attitude, stimulus context, etc.," and that the form of the metric may depend upon "the extent to which the different dimensions of the stimuli are perceptually distinct" with the Euclidean metric more appropriate for case (1) and a City Block metric more appropriate for case (2).

There seems to be agreement that colors fall under case (1) and tend to be reacted to "as homogeneous unanalyzable wholes." But what about color names? When a subject is required to make similarity judgments for a set of color names, one way in which he could proceed might be to call up appropriate (generic) color images and make his judgments on these, or to think of common objects which are in the named colors and compare their colors. If this is how he proceeds, then, in principle, similarity judgments based on color names are no different from those based on colors and fall under case (1), and, in these circumstances, it should perhaps not be surprising that CNS is functionally related to the color space. On the other hand, for at least some colors, it is possible that the subject may proceed in a more analytic fashion, defining a given color name in terms of some combination of more primitive color names. Thus, BRONZE might be defined roughly, as, for example, in Webster's dictionary, as "a brown yellowish red-yellow" or, even verbally located in a color space in terms analogous to those in the rest of the definition "of low saturation and medium brilliance." If a subject proceeded in some such fashion, a common set of dimensions could hardly be used in the judgment of all the color names, even if a small set of primitive color names were used as a reference set, and in any case this could not be the basis of judgment for whatever terms constituted the primitive reference set. Certainly, some such procedure as the above might well be used when the color name to be judged is a relatively *rare term* whose referent is "seen" as an amalgam or mix of the referents of some common color names, but this hardly seems likely for more than a few of the color names used in the present study. Thus, it would appear very unlikely that judgments of similarity of color names could constitute a pure case of (2), where all the stimuli are "analyzable," although to some extent there may be some admixture or trace of the (2) case, at least for the rarer color names. As far as our results go, it appears that even if there is some admixture of "analyzable" stimuli, the CNS is very similar to the space of perceived similarity judgments of colors, and that both are very similar to the hue circle.

Chapter 4   *KINSHIP TERMS*

Another example of a highly structured, well defined semantic domain is that of kinship terms. We said in Chapter 1 that one of the reasons for studying the structure of the semantic relations that hold between kinship terms was to test two componential analyses of kinship terms due, respectively, to Wallace and Atkins (1960) and Romney and D'Andrade (1964). To explain what is meant by the terms "componential analysis" and "semantic components" we use a simple example from Lyons (1968).

Consider the following "proportional equation:"

man : woman : child : : bull : cow : calf.

> This equation expresses the fact (and for the moment we may assume that it is a fact) that, from the semantic point of view, the words *man, woman*, and *child*, on one hand, and *bull, cow*, and *calf*, on the other, all have something in common; furthermore, that *bull* and *man* have something in common, which is not shared by either *cow* and *woman* or *calf* and *child*; that *cow* and *woman* have something in common, which is not shared by either *bull* and *man* or *calf* and *child*; that *calf* and *child* have something in common that is not shared by either *bull* and *man* or *cow* and *woman*. What these different groups of words have in common we will call a *semantic component*. (Other terms have also been used in the literature: "plereme," "sememe," "semantic marker," "semantic category," etc.) (Lyons 1968, pp. 470–471.)

Semantic relations among lexical items can be expressed in a theory in terms of semantic markers, which, when assigned to a lexical item in a dictionary entry, "are intended to reflect whatever systematic semantic relations hold between that item and the rest of the vocabulary of the language (Katz and Fodor, 1963, p. 187)." Once a theory proposes a set of semantic markers for a restricted semantic domain, the theory can be tested by studying the semantic relations that hold among the terms constituting this domain. The most interesting work so far in the field of componential semantics has been done by anthropologists analyzing the vocabulary of kinship. It has been shown by Romney and D'Andrade (1964), Wallace and Atkins (1960), and Wexler and Romney (1969) that the most common kinship terms in English can be analyzed in different ways. Moreover, claims have been made that componential analyses of kinship terms, "in addition to representing the data in an abstract, structural, and elegant manner, uncover and represent psychological reality for the native users of these systems (Romney and D'Andrade, p. 146)."

We shall describe in this chapter two alternative componential analyses of American-English kinship terms, and then present proximity data to test their "psychological reality" for users of the language. The first componential analysis of kinship terms to be described here was presented by Wallace and Atkins, and further discussed and tested by Romney and D'Andrade, and Wexler and Romney. This analysis, referred to hereafter as Model WA, is portrayed paradigmatically in Fig. 4-1. The rows and columns in Fig. 4-1 represent different dimensions of meaning (semantic components). Dimension a is a sex dimension with two levels: male (a_1) and female (a_2). Dimension b is a generation dimension with five levels: two generations above ego (b_1), one generation above ego (b_2), ego's own generation (b_3), one generation below ego (b_4), and two generations below ego (b_5). Lineality is the third dimension, dimension c, with three levels: lineal (c_1), colineal (c_2), and ablineal (c_3). "Lineals are persons who are ancestors or descendants of ego; colineals are non-lineals all of whose ancestors include, or are included in, all the ancestors of ego; ablineals are consanguineal relatives who are neither lineals nor colineals

	c_1		c_2		c_3
	a_1	a_2	a_1	a_2	a_1 a_2
b_1	GRANDFATHER (GF)	GRANDMOTHER (GM)	UNCLE	AUNT	COUSIN
b_2	FATHER	MOTHER			
b_3	[EGO]		BROTHER	SISTER	
b_4	SON	DAUGHTER	NEPHEW	NIECE	
b_5	GRANDSON	GRANDDAUGHTER			

Fig. 4-1. Model WA.

(Romney and D'Andrade, p. 147)." Note that all but one (COUSIN) of the 15 terms in Fig. 4-1 specify sex of relative; all terms specify whether or not the relative is lineally related to ego; and that some terms (UNCLE, AUNT, NEPHEW, NIECE, and COUSIN) do not specify generation uniquely. Moreover, "no term overlaps or includes another; every component is discriminated by at least one term; and all terms can be displayed on the same paradigm (Romney and D'Andrade, p. 147)."

| | c_1 Direct | | c_2 Collateral | |
	a_1	a_2	a_1	a_2
$b\pm2$	GRANDFATHER (GF)	GRANDMOTHER (GM)		
	GRANDSON (GS)	GRANDDAUGHTER (GD)		
$b\pm1$	FATHER	MOTHER	UNCLE	AUNT
	SON	DAUGHTER	NEPHEW	NIECE
b	BROTHER	SISTER	COUSIN	

Fig. 4-2. Model RD.

An alternative componential analysis of kinship terms was presented by Romney and D'Andrade, and further tested by Wexler and Romney. That analysis, referred to hereafter as Model RD, is portrayed paradigmatically in Fig. 4-2. Dimension a is defined as before. Dimension b has only three levels: ego's own generation (b), one generation above or below ego ($b \pm 1$), and two generations above or below ego ($b \pm 2$); differences between, say, grandfather and grandson, are marked by their difference on a third dimension called the "reciprocal" dimension. Finally, there is a contrast between direct (c_1), and collateral (c_2) terms. Note that in Fig. 4-2 we follow the practice of Wexler and Romney (1969) rather than that of Romney and D'Andrade (1964, Fig. 2, p. 153) in locating UNCLE/AUNT and NEPHEW/NIECE on levels +1 and −1, respectively, of the generation dimension.

The dotted lines in Fig. 4-2 arise from analytical procedures and represent the relations between kinship terms obtained with simple operations on a notation scheme developed by Romney and D'Andrade. "Since the notation scheme represents the genealogical elements, it may be assumed that terms joined by dotted lines are somehow 'closer' than terms separated by solid lines (Romney and D'Andrade, p. 153)." Terms within solid lines are defined as constituting a *range set*. It is seen that Fig. 4-2 has five range sets. The dotted lines in Fig. 4-1 do not represent range sets in the same sense, because while "Wallace and Atkins use dotted lines between sex pairs, e.g., mother and father, they are not derived from steps in the analysis (Romney and D'Andrade, p. 153)."

The two models suggest alternative structures for the semantic space of American-English kinship terms. They differ from each other in their motivation and cognitive implications, which, because predictions are made on a qualitative level only, are not easily testable. Assuming that the semantic components of a kinship term constitute its meaning, and that the more components two terms have in common the more similar their meaning, the theories make different predictions as to the similarity relations among terms. These predictions will be tested below.

METHOD

There were five groups of subjects: four of these constructed labeled trees and one formed complete undirected graphs. Groups KTM and KTF ("K" for "kinship", "T" for "tree", and "M" and "F" for "male" and "female," respectively) consisted of 13 males and 13 females, who were enrolled at the University of North Carolina. Both groups received the standard instructions for constructing a labeled tree (see Chapter 2) and employed a criterion of similarity in meaning. They were told that "all the words refer to related persons; however some of the words are more similar than others, i.e., some of the persons referred to by these words are more closely related than others;" thus attention was directed to degree of closeness in family relation.

Groups KLTM and KLTF ("L" for "love") consisted of nine males and nine females, respectively, sampled from the same population of students. The subjects in these groups were also required to construct labeled trees, but similarity was defined in terms of mutual affection. In particular, the instructions for the tree construction method for these two groups were preceded by the following two paragraphs:

> In this experiment we are interested in mutual relations of affection or love among people. As you know, these relations are stronger between some persons than others. Your task in this experiment is to evaluate the strength of mutual love between persons.
>
> You will be given a list of 15 words. You are to consider mutual love as defining similarity, the stronger the mutual love between two persons the greater the similarity between the words referring to these persons. You will have to decide which is the most similar pair of words, etc. The experiment will proceed as follows.

Group KC consisted of 24 male undergraduates enrolled at the University of

North Carolina. These subjects received the standard instructions for constructing a complete undirected graph (see Chapter 2) employing the same similarity criterion as Groups KTM and KTF, a list of all pairs of kinship terms, and a list of the kinship terms arranged alphabetically. The latter list, which was also given to the other four groups, included the 15 terms appearing in Figs. 4-1 and 4-2.

RESULTS

The five groups of subjects differed from each other in terms of at least one of the following respects: sex of subjects, definition of similarity, and method for constructing graphs. To test whether these affected the structure of the semantic space of kinship terms, the five groups will be kept separate in the analysis, which will follow the same sequence of steps as in the preceding chapter.

Graph Analysis

To check whether Groups KTM and KTF used all three options in constructing labeled trees, the number of subtrees was counted for each subject separately. The mean number of subtrees was 3.846 and 3.923 for Groups KTM and KTF, respectively. The difference between the two means was not significant. With the exception of four subjects, three in Group KTM and one in Group KTF, the subjects used all three options in constructing the trees. Subtrees were typically merged together toward the end of the task.

Investigated next is the distribution of node degree summed over all subjects within a group. Table 4-1 presents the predicted (Poisson) and observed frequency distributions of node degree for the two groups. The difference between the predicted and observed distributions is not significant in both cases, suggesting either that the hypothesis of random construction of trees should not

TABLE 4-1   Observed and Predicted Frequency Distributions of Node Degree
(Groups KTM and KTF)

| | | Observed | |
| | | --- | --- |
Degree	Predicted	Group KTM	Group KTF
1	77	79	81
2	72	76	68
3	33	28	38
4	10	11	7
5+	3	1	1

be rejected, or that the distribution of node degree, which does not take account of the labeling of the nodes, is not a sufficiently sensitive statistic to detect significant differences.

Table 4-2 presents the frequency distribution of the number of pairs of adjacent nodes selected y times, $y = 0, 1, \ldots, 13$. Results are presented separately for males and females. The parameters of the predicted negative

TABLE 4-2   Observed and Predicted Frequency Distributions of Selected Pairs of Adjacent Nodes (Groups KTM and KTF)[a]

y	Group KTM		Group KTF	
	Predicted	Observed	Predicted	Observed
0	48	54	53	57
1	20	16	18	21
2	12	11	10	6
3	8	6	7	4
4	5	3	4	2
5	4	2	3	2
6	2	2	2	0
7	2	5	2	1
8	1	1	1	3
9	1	3	1	5
10	0	0	1	2
11+	2	2	3	2

[a]Parameters:

	p	s
KTM	0.239	0.543
KTF	0.190	0.406

binomial distribution, p and s, estimated by the method of moments, are presented below the table, and the predicted frequency distributions, obtained from equation 7, are given in columns 2 and 4. There is good agreement between the predicted and observed frequency distributions, with small but consistent discrepancies similar to the ones observed in the previous chapter. For both groups, the predicted frequency is smaller than the observed frequency for $y = 0$, but larger for $y = 2, 3, \ldots, 5$. These discrepancies, however, are nonsignificant ($p > 0.20$) by the one-sample Kolmogorov-Smirnov test, lending further support to the assumption that the "popularity bias," discussed in Chapter 2, is gamma distributed in the population of kinship terms. The small values of s and the difference between the s values of the two groups suggest that certain pairs of kinship terms are significantly more "popular" than others, and that this is more so for females than for males. Inspection of the individual graphs show that, not surprisingly, the most popular pairs of terms are MOTHER-FATHER, SISTER-BROTHER, AUNT-UNCLE, GRANDMOTHER-GRANDFATHER, and GRANDDAUGHTER-GRANDSON.

In studying the distribution of node degree the labeling of the nodes has so far been ignored. No distinction has been made between unlabeled (topological) trees and labeled trees. Formally, two labeled trees are equivalent if, and only if, they include the same set of labeled nodes, and a node which is labeled in the same way in both trees has the same node degree. Clearly, two labeled trees may be considered distinct even though the two corresponding unlabeled trees are isomorphic. In discussing the distribution of node degree a node could represent a color name, a kinship term, or any symbol whatsoever, without affecting the results of the analysis. Thus, despite the finding that the distributions of node degree for Groups KTM and KTF did not differ from randomness, a particular kinship term might still have a larger number of links affixed to it than another. Were labeled trees constructed randomly, the mean node degree taken over a relatively large number of subjects should be approximately the same for every labeled node.

If labeled trees are not constructed randomly, certain labels will be assigned to nodes occupying a central position in the tree, and other labels will be assigned to peripheral nodes. The degree of a labeled node (the kinship degree) relative to the selected set of kinship terms may then be interpreted as a measure of centrality or relatedness in meaning of this term. The smaller the degree of a kinship term, the less it is related in meaning to other terms. One may expect terms such as MOTHER and FATHER to be more related to other terms than COUSIN, NEPHEW, and NIECE, and hence to have a higher degree.

The number of links affixed to each kinship term was summed over all subjects in each group separately. The distributions of kinship mean degree for Groups KTM and KTF are presented in columns 1 and 2 of Table 4-3, respectively. The table shows that the two distributions are very similar to each other. Indeed, the product-moment correlation between the two is 0.87 ($p < 0.01$). The table further shows that, as might have been expected, MOTHER and FATHER have the highest mean degrees, while GRAND-DAUGHTER, COUSIN, and NIECE have the lowest. We shall defer further discussion of these results to a later section and turn next to the graph analysis of the data of Groups KLTM and KLTF, both using the tree construction method and the "mutual affection" instructions.

The mean number of subtrees for Groups KLTM and KLTF was 3.666 and 3.111, respectively. With the exception of only one subject in Group KLTM, the subjects used all three options in constructing the trees. The difference between the two groups in the mean number of subtrees was not significant.

Table 4-4 presents the observed and predicted frequency distributions of node degree for the two groups. The observed distributions differ significantly from each other, and both differ significantly from the predicted Poisson distribution ($p < 0.05$ and $p < 0.01$ for Groups KLTM and KLTF, respectively, by the one-sample Kolmogorov-Smirnov test).

TABLE 4-3   Distribution of Kinship Mean Degree

Term	Group				
	KTM	KTF	KLTM	KLTF	KC
AUNT	1.846	2.231	1.556	2.222	2.250
BROTHER	2.000	1.769	1.778	1.889	1.875
COUSIN	1.077	1.231	1.222	1.111	0.583
DAUGHTER	2.077	1.769	1.556	1.333	1.833
FATHER	2.615	2.615	2.444	2.667	4.291
GD	1.000	1.077	1.111	1.444	0.833
GF	2.000	2.000	2.222	2.222	2.416
GM	2.000	2.385	3.000	2.222	2.333
GS	1.308	1.462	1.222	1.444	1.083
MOTHER	3.077	2.769	3.444	2.667	4.500
NEPHEW	1.538	1.308	1.556	1.333	0.917
NIECE	1.231	1.769	1.111	1.444	0.833
SISTER	1.846	1.692	1.333	1.778	1.791
SON	2.000	2.000	2.333	1.667	2.541
UNCLE	2.385	2.077	2.111	2.556	1.875

TABLE 4-4   Observed and Predicted Frequency Distributions of Node Degree
(Groups KLTM and KLTF)

Degree	Predicted	Observed	
		Group KLTM	Group KLTF
1	53	70	48
2	50	26	61
3	23	28	23
4	7	9	2
5+	2	2	1

The observed and predicted frequency distributions of pairs of adjacent nodes are presented in Table 4-5. The parameters p and s of the predicted distributions, estimated by the method of moments from the mean and variance of the observed distributions, are shown beneath the table. Similar to the corresponding results of Groups KTM and KTF (Table 4-2), the negative binomial distribution provides a good fit for each group ($p > 0.20$ by the one-sample Kolmogorov-Smirnov test). Also, the popularity bias is seen to be somewhat stronger for females than for males.

The mean kinship degree for each term is presented next in columns 3 and 4 of Table 4-3 for Groups KLTM and KLTF, respectively. The results of the two groups are very close to each other (the product-moment correlation is 0.76,

TABLE 4-5   Observed and Predicted Frequency Distributions of Selected Pairs of Nodes (Groups KLTM and KLTF)[a]

y	Group KLTM		Group KLTF	
	Predicted	Observed	Predicted	Observed
0	54	53	54	55
1	22	28	22	25
2	12	7	12	8
3	7	5	7	6
4	4	2	4	1
5	2	4	2	1
6	1	3	1	6
7	1	1	1	2
8+	2	2	2	1

[a]Parameters:

	p	s
KLTM	0.3435	0.6279
KLTF	0.3326	0.5980

$p < 0.01$). Indeed, the frequency distributions presented in the first four columns of Table 4-3 are all very similar to one another; none of the six correlations among them being lower than 0.76.

We turn next to examination of the results for Group KC, which constructed complete undirected graphs. Table 4-6 presents the cumulative probability that a random graph G_{N,V_N} is completely connected, for $N = 15$, and

TABLE 4-6   Observed and Predicted Cumulative Probability that G_{N, V_N} is Completely Connected (Group KC)

V_N	Predicted	Observed	V_N	Predicted	Observed
14	0.0320	0.0417	29	0.6624	0.2500
15	0.0689	0.0417	30	0.6893	0.2917
16	0.1102	0.0417	31	0.7137	0.3333
17	0.1550	0.0417	32	0.7357	0.3750
18	0.2025	0.0417	33	0.7554	0.3750
19	0.2512	0.0417	34	0.7731	0.4167
20	0.3003	0.0417	35	0.7888	0.4583
21	0.3490	0.0417	36	0.8028	0.5417
22	0.3965	0.0417	37	0.8153	0.5417
23	0.4422	0.1250	38	0.8264	0.5417
24	0.4857	0.1250	39	0.8362	0.5417
25	0.5266	0.1250	40	0.8449	0.5833
26	0.5649	0.1667	50	0.8905	0.7917
27	0.6002	0.1667	60	0.9028	0.8333
28	0.6327	0.2500			

V_N = 14, 15, . . ., 40, 50, 60, and the cumulative proportions of observed graphs completely connected by the first w links. The discrepancy between predicted and observed proportions is noticeable. With the exception of V_N = 14, the observed cumulative proportion is smaller than predicted. The difference between the distributions is highly significant ($p < 0.01$) by the one-sample Kolmogorov-Smirnov test.

The departure from the predicted distribution may be attributed to one or more "biases" operating in the construction of the graphs. In the early, most meaningful part of the task, when the first 30 or so pairs of adjacent nodes were rank-ordered in terms of similarity, the subjects might tend to leave one or more terms unconnected. Another, more likely alternative, is that the subjects constructed several completely connected subgraphs, exhausting all 15 nodes, but merged these subgraphs into a completely connected graph at a rather late stage of the task. To discover such "biases" further analysis is needed.

TABLE 4-7   Observed and Predicted Frequency Distributions of Node Degree for 24 Graphs with n = 15 (Group KC)

r	Predicted	Observed
0	35	77
1	97	83
2	113	72
3	74	66
4	31	29
5	8	24
6+	2	9

Table 4-7 shows the predicted frequency of nodes with degree r, obtained from equation 2, for 24 random graphs and $N = n = 15$. The last column in this table shows the observed frequency distribution of node degree summed over all subjects. The difference between predicted and observed frequency distributions is highly significant ($p < 0.01$). Inspection of the table shows that, as conjectured earlier, subjects left more nodes unconnected ($r = 0$) and had more nodes with a high degree than expected by chance alone.

To complete the analysis we examine next the degree of labeled nodes. As suggested earlier, the degree of a labeled node can be interpreted as a measure of centrality or relatedness in meaning, relative to the set of labeled nodes under study. Presented in the last column of Table 4-3 is the distribution of mean kinship degree for Group KC. Inspection of the table suggests that the means, rather than assuming the same value under the hypothesis of random construction of graphs, differ considerably from one another. One-way analysis of variance resulted in significant differences among the means, $F(14, 345) = 22.2, p < 0.001$.

Table 4-3 shows that the most "central" terms in Group KC, the ones judged earlier in the task to be related to the largest number of terms, are MOTHER and FATHER. COUSIN, NIECE, NEPHEW, GRANDDAUGHTER, and GRAND-SON are the most isolated terms. These results are very close to the ones presented in columns 1 through 4 of the same table; indeed, none of the four correlations between Group KC and the other four groups is less than 0.83.

In summary, the graph-theoretic results reject the null hypothesis of random construction of graphs; significant discrepancies between certain predicted and observed statistical properties of graphs have been found for each of the five groups. Moreover, several "biases" or processes operating in the construction of the graphs seem to be shared by all groups. Subjects in all groups constructed separate subtrees or completely connected subgraphs and merged them together at a very late stage of the task. The cluster analysis presented in the immediately following section should tell whether these subgraphs correspond to the semantic components or range sets postulated by one or the other of the two models. Further, and perhaps not surprisingly, the graph analysis shows that certain pairs of kinship terms, e.g. MOTHER-FATHER, GRANDMOTHER-GRANDFATHER, BROTHER-SISTER, and AUNT-UNCLE, are more popular than others. This result should also be reflected in the analyses carried out in the next two sections. Finally, approximately the same distribution of mean kinship degree has been observed in all five groups. We shall try later to determine whether mean kinship degree may be interpreted in terms of the distance from the (0, 0) point in the two-dimensional representation yielded by the MDS analysis.

Cluster Analysis

Johnson's two clustering methods were applied to the mean proximity matrix of each group, as well as to the data from several subjects selected randomly from each of the five groups. Since the differences between the HCSs yielded by the two methods, particularly for the mean proximity data, were rather small, we present only the results of the Diameter method. Figures 4-3 through 4-7 show the HCSs for the mean proximity data of Groups KTM, KTF, KLTM, KLTF, and KC, respectively. As in Chapter 3, the lines connecting the x's denote clusters that are significant by our (rather strict) criterion, and the last column in each figure gives the value of each of the clusterings. Each figure, with the exception of Fig. 4-5, shows $N-1 = 14$ clusterings. There are only 13 clusterings in Fig. 4-5, since on level 6 the cluster BROTHER-SISTER was formed and, on the same level, GRANDDAUGHTER was added to the cluster GRANDSON-GRANDFATHER-GRANDMOTHER.

Since subjects in Groups KTM, KTF, KLTM, and KLTF used the same tree-construction method, the α measures of Figs. 4-3 to 4-6 are comparable. It can be seen that the α measures of the four groups are approximately of the same size with one exception, namely, the values of the first five clusterings (levels 1–5) of Groups KLTM and KLTF are always smaller than the corresponding values for Groups KTM and KTF. Recalling that the value of a clustering under the Diameter method is the smallest diameter (the largest intracluster proximity measure) for the corresponding level, the four figures show that the first five clusterings formed by Groups KLTM and KLTF, which used the "mutual affection" instructions, are somewhat tighter than the first five clusterings formed by Groups KTM and KTF. In particular, the diameter of the cluster FATHER-MOTHER-SON-DAUGHTER, which was formed by all four groups on either level 4 or 5, is smaller for the former two groups than for the latter. The results indicate that FATHER, MOTHER, SON, and DAUGHTER are judged to be closer when "mutual affection," rather than "similarity" emphasizing closeness of kin relation, is considered by the subjects.

A further inspection of Figs. 4 3 through 4-7 shows a remarkable similarity among all the five HCSs. With only three minor exceptions, the columns of each HCS are labeled in the same order. In terms of Model WA, presented from left to right are all the lineal terms, then all the colineal terms, and, finally, on the right, is the one ablineal term, i.e., COUSIN. In the terminology of Model RD, the direct terms are presented on the left-hand side of each HCS and the collateral terms on the right-hand side. Moreover, the terms are arranged in perfect order according to the three generation levels postulated by Model RD. For each of the two levels of the Reciprocal dimension the $b \pm 2$ terms are presented on the left, the $b \pm 1$ terms in the middle, and the b terms on the right. The three minor exceptions mentioned above are MOTHER and DAUGHTER in Fig. 4-4,

```
                                  MOTHER
                                  FATHER
                                  DAUGHTER
                                  SON
                                  BROTHER
                                  SISTER
                                  NEPHEW
                                  NIECE
                                  UNCLE
                                  AUNT
                                  COUSIN
          GD
          GS
          GF
          GM
Level                                                        α
  1       . . . . XXX . . . . . . . . .                      5.0
  2       . . . . XXX . . XXX . . . . .                      8.3
  3       . . . . XXX XXX XXX . . . . .                      8.8
  4       . . . . XXX XXX XXX . . XXX .                      9.6
  5       . . . . XXXXXXX XXX . . XXX .                     10.3
  6       . . XXX XXXXXXX XXX . . XXX .                     10.6
  7       . . XXX XXXXXXXXXXX . . XXX .                     18.1
  8       . . XXX XXXXXXXXXXX XXX XXX .                     22.8
  9       . XXXXX XXXXXXXXXXX XXX XXX .                     24.7
 10       . XXXXX XXXXXXXXXXX XXXXXXX .                     25.8
 11       XXXXXX XXXXXXXXXXX XXXXXXX .                      27.2
 12       XXXXXXXXXXXXXXXXX XXXXXXX .                       29.5
 13       XXXXXXXXXXXXXXXXXX XXXXXXXXX                      37.2
 14       XXXXXXXXXXXXXXXXXXXXXXXXXXXXXXX                   51.5
```

Fig. 4-3. HCS for Group KTM (Diameter method).

```
                              DAUGHTER
                              FATHER
                              MOTHER
                              SON
                              BROTHER
                              SISTER
                              NEPHEW
                              NIECE
                              UNCLE
                              AUNT
                              COUSIN
 Level     GD GS GF GM                                         α

   1     .  .  .  . XXX .  .  .  .  .  .  .  .  .  .          5.1
   2     .  .  .  . XXX XXX .  .  .  .  .  .  .  .  .         5.2
   3     .  . XXX XXX XXX .  .  .  .  .  .  .  .  .          8.7
   4     .  . XXX XXX XXX XXX .  .  .  .  .  .  .            9.0
   5     .  . XXX XXXXXX XXX .  .  .  .  .  .              10.8
   6     .  . XXX XXXXXX XXX .  . XXX .                    12.5
   7     .  . XXX XXXXXXXXXX .  . XXX .                    16.1
   8     . XXXXX XXXXXXXXXX .  . XXX .                     18.8
   9    XXXXXXX XXXXXXXXXX .  . XXX .                      20.7
  10    XXXXXXX XXXXXXXXXXX XXX XXX .                      23.5
  11    XXXXXXX XXXXXXXXXXX XXXXXXX .                      26.3
  12    XXXXXXXXXXXXXXXXXXX XXXXXXX .                      31.6
  13    XXXXXXXXXXXXXXXXXXX XXXXXXXXX                      38.5
  14    XXXXXXXXXXXXXXXXXXXXXXXXXXXXXX                     48.5
```

Fig. 4-4. HCS for Group KTF (Diameter method).

```
                              MOTHER
                              FATHER
                              DAUGHTER
                              SON
                              BROTHER
                              SISTER
                              NEPHEW
                              NIECE
                              UNCLE
                              AUNT
                              COUSIN
 Level     GD GS GF GM                                         α

   1     .  .  .  . XXX .  .  .  .  .  .  .  .  .  .          1.7
   2     .  . XXX XXX .  .  .  .  .  .  .  .  .  .           4.6
   3     .  . XXX XXX XXX .  .  .  .  .  .  .              7.0
   4     . XXXXX XXX XXX .  .  .  .  .  .  .               8.9
   5     . XXXXX XXXXXXX .  .  .  .  .  .                 10.1
   6    XXXXXX XXXXXXX XXX .  .  .  .                     12.8
   7    XXXXXX XXXXXXX XXX .  . XXX .                     15.2
   8    XXXXXX XXXXXXX XXX XXX XXX .                      22.8
   9    XXXXXXXXXXXXX XXX XXX XXX .                       23.7
  10    XXXXXXXXXXXXX XXX XXXXXXX .                       27.1
  11    XXXXXXXXXXXXX XXXXXXXXXX .                        34.7
  12    XXXXXXXXXXXXX XXXXXXXXXXXX                        39.8
  13    XXXXXXXXXXXXXXXXXXXXXXXXXXXX                      43.7
```

Fig. 4-5. HCS for Group KLTM (Diameter method).

```
                              DAUGHTER
                              MOTHER
                              FATHER
                              SON
                              BROTHER
                              SISTER
                              NEPHEW
                              UNCLE
                              NIECE
                              AUNT
                              COUSIN
 Level     GS GD GF GM                                         α

   1     .  .  .  . XXX .  .  .  .  .  .  .  .  .  .          1.6
   2     .  .  .  . XXXXX .  .  .  .  .  .  .  .            4.3
   3     .  . XXX XXXXX .  .  .  .  .  .  .                5.6
   4     .  . XXX XXXXXX .  .  .  .  .  .                  8.8
   5     .  . XXX XXXXXX XXX .  .  .  .                    9.9
   6     . XXXXX XXXXXX XXX .  .  .  .                    10.6
   7     . XXXXX XXXXXX XXX XXX .  .  .                   12.7
   8     . XXXXX XXXXXX XXX XXX XXX .                     14.4
   9    XXXXXX XXXXXX XXX XXX XXX .                       15.4
  10    XXXXXX XXXXXXXXXXX XXX XXX .                      19.3
  11    XXXXXX XXXXXXXXXXX XXXXXXX .                      24.7
  12    XXXXXXXXXXXXXXXXXXX XXXXXXX .                     37.8
  13    XXXXXXXXXXXXXXXXXXX XXXXXXXXX                     38.2
  14    XXXXXXXXXXXXXXXXXXXXXXXXXXXXXX                    53.2
```

Fig. 4-6. HCS for Group KLTF (Diameter method).

```
                          R   R         R
                        E   E         E   R
                      T   T   R       W   E
                    H   H   E     R   E   T
                  T   T   T   S   E   H   S
                O   O   N   H   O   P   U   U
              M   M   O   G   T   E   E   O   N
            F   F   A   U   O   N   I   C   I
          D   S   F   M   R   A   R   B   S   N   N   U   A   S
    Level G   G   G   G   (MOTHER FATHER SON DAUGHTER BROTHER SISTER NEPHEW NIECE UNCLE AUNT COUSIN)   α

      1   .   .   .   .   .   .   .   XXX   .   .   .   .   .    10.2
      2   .   .   .   .   XXX   .   .   XXX   .   .   .   .   .    12.3
      3   .   .   .   .   XXXXX   .   XXX   .   .   .   .   .    18.5
      4   .   .   .   .   XXXXX   .   XXX   .   .   XXX   .    19.4
      5   .   .   XXX   XXXXX   .   XXX   .   .   XXX   .    19.7
      6   .   .   XXX   XXXXXXX   XXX   .   .   XXX   .    29.1
      7   XXX   XXX   XXXXXXX   XXX   .   .   XXX   .    31.3
      8   XXX   XXX   XXXXXXX   XXX   XXX   XXX   .    37.0
      9   XXX   XXX   XXXXXXX   XXX   XXX   XXXXX    47.1
     10   XXX   XXX   XXXXXXXXXXX   XXX   XXXXX    47.7
     11   XXXXXXX   XXXXXXXXXX   XXX   XXXXX    53.2
     12   XXXXXXX   XXXXXXXXXX   XXXXXXXXX    71.8
     13   XXXXXXXXXXXXXXXXXX   XXXXXXXXX    77.7
     14   XXXXXXXXXXXXXXXXXXXXXXXXXXXXXX    94.2
```

Fig. 4-7. HCS for Group KC (Diameter method).

GRANDSON and GRANDDAUGHTER in Fig. 4-6, and SON and DAUGHTER in Fig. 4-7. All three exceptions involve terms which fall within the same range set, and hence are also consistent with the RD model.

The arrangement of the terms in each HCS is, of course, not unique. Certain terms may be interchanged without affecting the results. For example, the following terms may be interchanged in Fig. 4-3 without changing the cluster analysis results: GRANDFATHER and GRANDMOTHER, MOTHER and FATHER, SON and DAUGHTER, BROTHER and SISTER, NEPHEW and NIECE, and UNCLE and AUNT. Furthermore, the two clusters GRAND-DAUGHTER-GRANDSON-GRANDMOTHER-GRANDFATHER and MOTHER-FATHER-DAUGHTER-SON-BROTHER-SISTER in Fig. 4-3 may be interchanged without affecting the HCS. Despite the many degrees of freedom available in arranging the columns of each HCS, the cluster analysis results can be shown to be inconsistent with Model WA. In particular, the assumption of five generation levels implies that GRANDMOTHER and GRANDFATHER, located on level b_1, are closer to FATHER and MOTHER on level b_2 than to GRANDSON and GRANDDAUGHTER on level b_5, and that the latter two terms are closer to SON and DAUGHTER than to FATHER and MOTHER. Figures 4-3 through 4-7 show that this is not the case. In all five figures the cluster GRANDDAUGHTER-GRANDSON-GRANDFATHER-GRAND-MOTHER is first formed and only later, around level 12 or so, is it merged with a cluster including the terms FATHER, MOTHER, SON, and DAUGHTER. Another prediction of Model WA is that BROTHER and SISTER are closer in meaning to AUNT, UNCLE, NEPHEW and NIECE, than to the eight lineal terms. With the exception of the HCS for Group KLTM, this prediction is also rejected by the data.

There are few terms constituting significant clusters in the five HCSs. Thus,

Fig. 4-3 has no significant clusters at all and Fig. 4-7 has one significant cluster with only six terms. Since there are so few terms constituting significant clusters, primarily because the total number of terms, $N = 15$, is small, significance of the clusters will not be employed in comparing the five HCSs. Rather, we shall fix an arbitrary level, yielding the same number of clusters for each group, and then compare the five clusterings on this level. Since the results reported so far support Model RD, one may expect to find a clustering with five clusters in each HCS corresponding to the five range sets postulated by Model RD. We shall therefore compare the clusterings C_{10} (C_9 for Group KLTM), each of which has five clusters, to one another, and attempt to relate these clusterings to the range sets of Model RD.

TABLE 4-8   Interclustering Distances for All Five Groups

Group	Group				
	KTM	KTF	KLTM	KLTF	KC
KTM	—	0.067	0.295	0.067	0.076
KTF	0.067	—	0.229	0.038	0.057
KLTM	0.295	0.229	—	0.267	0.286
KLTF	0.067	0.038	0.267	—	0.095
KC	0.076	0.057	0.286	0.095	—

Table 4-8 presents the 10 distances, $d(C_{10}, C_{10})$, among all five clusterings. Four of the distances involving Group KLTM are large; the other distances are judged to be very small relative to the magnitude of distances reported in Chapter 3. Clustering C_9 of Group KLTM differs from clusterings C_{10} of the other groups in two major ways: GRANDDAUGHTER, GRANDSON, GRANDFATHER, and GRANDMOTHER on the one hand, and FATHER, MOTHER, DAUGHTER, and SON, on the other hand, make one, rather than two clusters, and BROTHER-SISTER forms a separate cluster. Note, also, that the cluster BROTHER-SISTER in this group is merged (on level 11) with the other colineal terms and not with the lineal terms. In this sense, the HCS of Group KLTM supports neither the predictions of Model WA nor those of Model RD.

None of the five C_{10} clusterings, with five clusters each, corresponds exactly to the five range sets assumed by Model RD. In four cases, the discrepancies are only minor. There are two differences in Fig. 4-3: GRANDDAUGHTER makes a separate cluster (merged with the other $b \pm 2$ terms on the next level), and the $b \pm 1$ plus the b terms are clustered together. It is seen that the $b \pm 1$ and the b terms are clustered together in all figures with the exception of Fig. 4-6. Other differences occur in Figs. 4-4, 4-5, and 4-7, in which NEPHEW-NIECE and

AUNT-UNCLE make two separate clusters, and in Fig. 4-7, in which GRANDDAUGHTER-GRANDSON and GRANDFATHER-GRANDMOTHER make two separate clusters (merged together on the next level). To better study the correspondence between Model RD and our results, and to study the adequacy of a dimensional representation of the kinship space, we turn to a MDS analysis in the next section.

Multidimensional Scaling Analysis

The Young-Torgerson MDS program was applied to the individual proximity matrices of 20 subjects, randomly selected from all five groups, and to the five mean proximity matrices, the cluster analytic results for which were reported in the preceding section. Solutions were obtained in one, two, and three dimensions for both the Euclidean and City Block metrics. With only few exceptions (Subject No. 3, Group KTM, $m = 2$; Subject No. 9, Group KTM, $m = 1$; Subject No. 8, Group KLTM, $m = 2$; and Subject No. 1, Group KLTF, $m = 2$) the stress values for the Euclidean solutions were smaller, and in the case of the mean proximity matrices considerably smaller, than the corresponding stress values for the City Block solutions. The former stress values are shown in Table 4-9.

The stress values can be seen to be much smaller than the critical cut-off point values established in Chapter 2 for $m \geqslant 2$. Parsimony, interpretability of the MDS results, and the sharp break noted in the stress values between $m = 1$ and $m = 2$ suggest an adequate representability of the kinship terms in a two-dimensional Euclidean space. Figures 4-8 to 4-12 portray the two-dimensional Euclidean representations for the mean proximity matrices of each of the five groups.

In the last section of Chapter 2 we discussed the problem of comparing the results of an MDS analysis with those of a hierarchical clustering analysis; these represent two different structural models about the relations that hold among terms constituting some semantic domain. The checking procedure that we have adopted is that of embedding a dimension-free representation into a dimensional one, and then considering the interpretability of the results of each analysis and the consistency between them. To embed an HCS in the two-dimensional spatial representation of the same proximity data we drew, in each of Figs. 4-8 to 4-12, a closed convex curve around each group of points that was clustered together at some specified level in the hierarchical clustering. In particular, we drew the curves corresponding to levels 9 through 13 (8 through 12 for Group KLTM) in the HCSs presented in Figs. 4-3 to 4-7. The lower six levels of each HCS may be reconstructed from Figs. 4-8 to 4-12.

In interpreting the MDS scaling analysis of the kinship data, two quite separate questions have to be answered, one partly methodological, partly

TABLE 4-9   Stress Values for Euclidean Representations

Dimensions	No. 3	No. 6	No. 9	No. 12	Mean
			Group KTM		
3	0.020	0.068	0.065	0.044	0.057
2	0.042	0.105	0.110	0.118	0.105
1	0.211	0.203	0.242	0.279	0.203

Dimensions	No. 4	No. 7	No. 10	No. 13	Mean
			Group KTF		
3	0.046	0.028	0.021	0.015	0.033
2	0.083	0.075	0.036	0.016	0.060
1	0.148	0.264	0.107	0.065	0.206

Dimensions	No. 2	No. 8	Mean
	Group KLTM		
3	0.023	0.021	0.043
2	0.051	0.045	0.113
1	0.115	0.232	0.256

Dimensions	No. 1	No. 4	No. 7	Mean
		Group KLTF		
3	0.024	0.016	0.059	0.034
2	0.046	0.044	0.087	0.067
1	0.125	0.231	0.159	0.167

Dimensions	No. 2	No. 6	No. 10	No. 14	No. 18	No. 22	Mean
			Group KC				
3	0.077	0.126	0.178	0.132	0.119	0.134	0.062
2	0.134	0.172	0.242	0.189	0.191	0.201	0.124
1	0.259	0.357	0.369	0.292	0.403	0.368	0.234

substantive, the other substantive: (1) how do the MDS results compare with the graph and hierarchical clustering analyses of the same data? (2) do the MDS results support the componential models? With respect to the second question, the predictions made by the componential models must be specified before the models can be adequately tested. Recall that Model RD, the only model to be tested in this section, predicts that terms lying within each of the five range sets portrayed in Fig. 4-2 will be closer to one another than to any other term outside the range set, and that the $b \pm 2$ "direct" (level c_1 in Fig. 4-2) terms will be closer to the $b \pm 1$ terms than to the b terms. We shall take the second question first, ignore the closed curves in the two-dimensional representations, and test the above predictions in terms of the MDS results for each group.

Consider Fig. 4-8 first, which portrays the two-dimensional representation for Group KTM. With regard to the direct terms, it is seen, indeed, that the $b \pm 1$

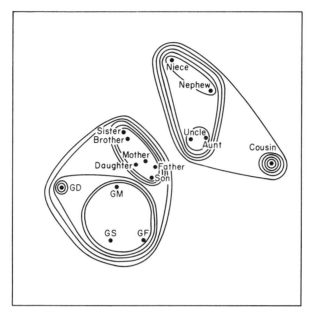

Fig. 4-8.   Two-dimensional Euclidean representation for Group KTM.

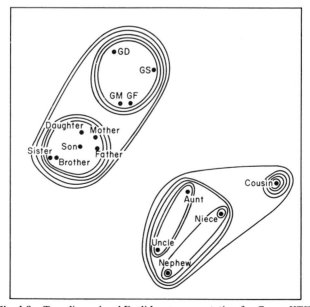

Fig. 4-9.   Two-dimensional Euclidean representation for Group KTF.

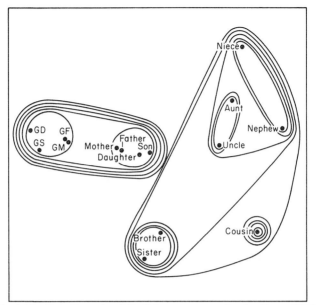

Fig. 4-10. Two-dimensional Euclidean representation for Group KLTM.

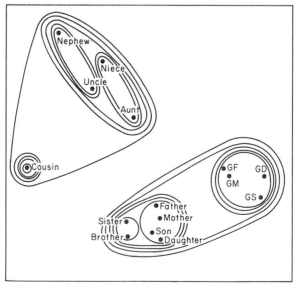

Fig. 4-11. Two-dimensional Euclidean representation for Group KLTF.

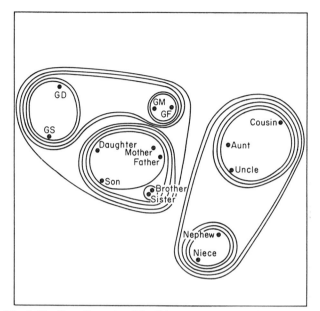

Fig. 4-12. Two-dimensional Euclidean representation for Group KC.

and b terms are closer to one another than to terms in other range sets. This is not the case for the $b \pm 2$ terms; GRANDMOTHER is closer to the $b \pm 1$ terms than to GRANDFATHER, GRANDSON, and GRANDDAUGHTER. Another violation of the model is provided by AUNT and UNCLE, which are closer to FATHER, MOTHER, SON, and DAUGHTER, than to NIECE and NEPHEW, despite the fact that the latter terms fall in the same range set.

Figure 4-9 portrays a picture which is almost completely consistent with Model RD. The $b \pm 2$, $b \pm 1$, and b terms on level c_1 are arranged from top to bottom in this order, and the terms on each b-level are closer to one another than to other terms. The "collateral" terms (level c_2), also behave as expected, with the exception of NIECE which is somewhat closer to COUSIN than to NEPHEW, and COUSIN, which should be placed between the other collateral terms and BROTHER and SISTER. Note the large separation between the direct and collateral terms.

Figure 4-10 presents a similar representation, almost entirely consistent with Model RD. The only exception is UNCLE, which is somewhat closer to FATHER, MOTHER, SON, and DAUGHTER than BROTHER and SISTER are to these four terms. Note the similarity between Figs. 4-2 and 4-10. Figure 4-11 is also very similar to Fig. 4-2, if the direct and collateral terms in the latter figure are interchanged. The MDS results of the two "mutual affection" groups thus are consistent with Model RD.

The MDS results of Group KC are less consistent with Model RD than are the results from any other group. One can almost, but not quite, detect five rather than three generation levels in the direct terms, lying on a curve rather than a straight line. The distances between FATHER and MOTHER on the one hand and SON and DAUGHTER on the other hand, and between GRANDMOTHER and GRANDFATHER on one hand and GRANDSON and GRANDDAUGHTER on the other hand are large relative to the tight $b \pm 2$ and $b \pm 1$ clusters observed in Figs. 4-8 to 4-11. Note, also, that AUNT and UNCLE are closer to COUSIN on one hand and MOTHER and FATHER on the other hand than to NEPHEW and NIECE, in strict violation of the RD model. This latter result was also observed in Fig. 4-8.

In summary, Model RD seems to be fairly well supported by the MDS scaling analysis of the mean kinship data. Inconsistencies with the model may possibly be attributed to the data collection methods, with the tree construction method supporting the model and the method of complete undirected graphs yielding somewhat inconsistent results. The definition of the similarity relation (closeness in kinship versus mutual affection) may also have had some slight effect on the results, with Group KLTM and KLTF providing slightly better support of the model.

We turn next to a comparison of the results of the MDS and cluster analyses. It may be recalled that the notion of consistency between these two models was defined, more or less intuitively, in terms of the simplicity and compactness of the curves enclosing the points in the two-dimensional representation that were clustered together at a certain level of the HCS representing the same data. Certainly, convexity is a necessary, though not a sufficient, condition for compactness. And, indeed, all the closed curves in Figs. 4-8 to 4-12 are convex, and most of them appear to us to be quite simple. With few exceptions, interpoint distances among terms that were clustered together in the last six levels are quite small. This is particularly true for the direct terms, especially the b and $b \pm 1$ terms, which form very tight clusters. Most of the exceptions occur in the collateral terms. While the distances between AUNT and UNCLE and between NEPHEW and NIECE are usually small (the distances between the former two terms are always smaller than the distances between the latter two terms), the distances between the two pairs of terms, and the distances between these four collateral terms and COUSIN, are relatively large.

Another discrepancy between the hierarchical clustering and the MDS scaling results occurs in Fig. 4-10. Although BROTHER-SISTER is closer to FATHER-MOTHER-SON-DAUGHTER than to NEPHEW-NIECE-UNCLE-AUNT, it is clustered together with the latter four collateral terms. Since, in all four other figures, the terms BROTHER and SISTER are closer to the $b \pm 1$ direct terms than to any other term, one may regard the HCS for Group KLTM as an exception, and accept the MDS scaling results as a more adequate representation of the underlying structure of Group KLTM.

The consistency of the MDS scaling and the graph results may be assessed by comparing for each node its mean kinship degree (see Table 4-3) and its Euclidean distance from the (0,0) point of the two-dimensional representation. We suggested that mean kinship degree, a dimension-free statistic, be interpreted as a measure of centrality or relatedness in meaning, such that the larger the mean degree of a given term the more central is its meaning relative to the other terms in the set. Since the (0,0) point in a two-dimensional representation is fixed, and the Euclidean distance of each point from the (0,0) point is unique up to multiplication by a constant, a high correlation between mean kinship degree and the Euclidean distance will support our interpretation and indicate a high consistency between the two analyses. The Euclidean distance of each point from the (0,0) point was computed for each group separately and then correlated with the mean kinship degrees presented in Table 4-3. The correlations were negative, as expected, and highly significant: -0.90, -0.81, -0.63, -0.66, and -0.71, for Groups KTM, KTF, KLTM, KLTF, and KC, respectively.

DISCUSSION

What can one mean by speaking about the "psychological validity" of a componential analysis, and how may one proceed in trying to assess the validity of such an analysis? In attempting any psychologically valid semantic description we seek to discover the intensional meanings of a set of terms for their native users, to discover the criteria by which native speakers classify the denotata in a particular domain, and to determine how such native speakers "reckon," to use Wallace's term (1965). It is clear that "psychological validity must be established by means independent of the mechanics of componential analysis itself (Wallace, 1965, p. 231)," and that given two or more componential analyses one seeks to determine which best fits the data, and whether or not the fit of the better model is a good one. One way to proceed in the task "is to supply different sets of terms, in series or simultaneously, in order to discover what dimensions of information the native speakers can infer from the terms (Wallace, 1965, p. 236)." This is precisely what we have attempted to do except that rather than requiring "the native speaker to make manifest his reckoning procedures" directly, we have attempted to infer these by means of various sorts of structural analyses of the proximity data that he has provided for us. The rationale for this is, in large part, that the speaker may not be able to state explicitly the principles upon which he is operating even though these may be revealed by appropriate analyses of his similarity judgments.

The principal burden of our results is quite clear, the findings in general being consistent over the different methods for obtaining data—not only does the RD model fit the data better than the WA model but, in fact, it fits them rather well, overall. These findings are consistent with previous findings. Romney and D'Andrade (1964) used a number of different tasks including direct similarity judgments obtained by means of the method of triads and, upon using a metric multidimensional scaling analysis, found that the results were better fitted by their model, i.e., the RD model, than by the WA model. Repeating the earlier study, which had been carried out using high school students with a large group of college students, and analyzing both sets of results by means of a process model in which the distance between any two items is computed essentially in terms of the number of steps on the componential grid needed to get from the one to the other, Wexler and Romney (1969) compared the obtained results with those predicted by the RD and WA models. They found that the RD model provided a distinctly better fit; for the two samples the product moment correlations between obtained and predicted values were 0.87 and 0.81, given model RD, and only 0.26 and 0.40, given model WA. A number of additional analyses only served to confirm and corroborate the above findings.

It is worth noting that there is a close agreement between our results and those of Romney and his associates, even with differences in methods of data collection and techniques for evaluating the fit of the results to the theoretical models. In evaluating the fit of the models, Wexler and Romney make a number of assumptions concerning the theoretical consequences for judgment of differences in distance between every pair of items in a triad, and concerning the consequences of the introduction of an error or random process. These assumptions permit them to derive theoretically expected values for each model, and then to provide an overall statistical index of closeness of fit between such values and those actually obtained. We, on the other hand, assess the adequacy of each model by a direct inspection of the cluster analytic and MDS results, comparing the clustering and relative locations of the items with what was to be expected on the basis of each of the models. While this does not allow us to derive any overall measure of closeness of fit, it does make it possible, in a more detailed way, to determine where the relations obtained fit each model, and to identify the locus or loci of discrepancies between the models and the data. Thus we may observe, to take one example which has also been noted on a more casual basis by Wexler and Romney, that terms such as GRANDFATHER (GF), and GRANDSON (GS), which are distant from each other on the WA model, which has five generation values, are relatively close on the RD model, which marks their difference in terms of the differences on a reciprocity dimension. We can also observe that these terms are, indeed, judged close together both in our studies and those of Romney; this would argue for the importance and psychological validity of something like the reciprocity dimension.

With reference to individual differences in the cognitive structure representing the relations among English kin terms, one possible difference between the present data and the results obtained by Wexler and Romney (1969) should be mentioned. Our results for the averaged data strongly support the model offered by Romney and D'Andrade over that suggested by Wallace and Atkins, as do the findings of Wexler and Romney. These latter authors, however, upon applying a MDS analysis to indices of similarity among individual subjects, found a tight cluster comprised of more than half the subjects, who appeared to regard the lineality dimension as of considerable importance since they seldom classified together items differing in that dimension. The remaining subjects were more diffusely spread over the two-dimensional space of the solution. This led Wexler and Romney to speculate that "there is one structural type to which a relatively large (over half) proportion of subjects agree, and that the other subjects who do not follow this pattern differ in many, possibly idiosyncratic, ways (p. 7)." In the present case there is no particular evidence for such differences with regard to the importance or salience of the lineality dimension. However, given a rather haphazard examination of only a handful of individual cases, it is quite possible that even if there were such evidence, it might well have escaped notice. For another approach to the study of American-English kin terms with some attention to possible individual and subcultural differences in regard to information processing strategies, see Sanday (1968).

The RD model, and for that matter the WA model and any paradigmatic model which involves cross-classification in terms of a number of orthogonal components, implies that a spatial representation, perhaps in somewhat degenerate form since some regions of the space will be empty, should be more appropriate than a hierarchic one for the set of kinship terms used in the present study (although this does not hold with complete generality for any set of kinship terms since presumably terms such as FATHER and MOTHER are nested under PARENT, HUSBAND and WIFE under SPOUSE, etc.). Following Shepard's (1969) suggestion, we have attempted to check on the appropriateness of the Euclidean representation by embedding the results obtained by a cluster analysis within the dimensional representation. Insofar as the closed contours yielded by the dimension-free analysis are simple and compact with points close in the spatial representation clustered together, we have some support for the belief that the two-dimensional Euclidean representation is an adequate one. In general this condition appears to be met in our data, so there are some grounds for faith in the adequacy or appropriateness of the spatial solution. The dimensions involved in the spatial solution cannot be readily interpreted, except insofar as direct terms are always set off from collateral ones. Nevertheless, we prefer a spatial representation to a clustering representation, even though there are perhaps no absolutely compelling grounds for either preference within the data proper, because all models whatsoever that have been proposed for the subset of kin terms considered in the present study have been cross-classificatory models, implying or requiring some sort of dimensional or spatial representation rather than a hierarchic clustering representation appropriate to a taxonomic structure. It is very difficult to see how any structure of the latter sort could provide a coherent, intelligible account for the domain or sub-domain under consideration. Thus given data at least equally compatible with a spatial and with a hierarchic cluster solution, the former is to be preferred.

Given the present outcome we can, in a sense, extend or go beyond the model, which gives equal weight to all putative components, and use the results of the MDS analysis to assign differential weights to the various components noting, e.g., that terms differing only with regard to sex characteristically fall very close together, while collaterals are usually considerably displaced from the direct terms, etc. It should be pointed out that on the assumption that the distance between any two items is evaluated in terms of the number of common components by a sort of stepping off procedure on the componential grid, one might perhaps expect a City Block space to provide a better representation than a Euclidean space. However, there is no support for this in the data for, as was noted earlier, stress values for the Euclidean solutions were generally lower than those for the City Block solutions, and the latter configurations were not any more interpretable than the former.

It will be recalled that, on the whole, results are very similar whether subjects use a "mutual affection" criterion or one where attention is simply drawn to the fact that "some of the persons referred to by these words are more closely related than others," i.e., one where the fact of kin relationships is made salient. How may one interpret these findings? Presumably in making their judgments regarding "mutual affection" subjects must identify the persons referred to by the kin terms, and use the information they have concerning family relations obtaining among specified kinfolk to guide their judgments. Our data suggest that degree and nature of relation among kinfolk is the principal determinant of judgments of mutual affection, essentially they represent a rather simple generalization concerning the sociological or social psychological determinants of affection. It is interesting to note that the nuclear terms FATHER-MOTHER-SON-DAUGHTER are more tightly clustered both for male and female subjects when the mutual affection criterion is employed than when the other criterion is used. *A priori* one might, perhaps, have expected greater agreement or consensus regarding the structure of family relations than regarding the structure of affectional relations, since the former constitutes a general social fact, whereas the latter would appear to be more subject to the vicissitudes of idiosyncratic experience. However, to the extent that our data have anything to say on this issue, there seems to be no systematic difference as a function of the similarity criterion governing the judgments.

While differences in the similarity criterion employed made very little difference in the results, there were some differences in results as a function of the method of data collection. The findings for Group KC, where subjects were required to construct a complete undirected graph, were somewhat different from those obtained by the tree construction method, and the MDS results from this group were less consistent with model RD than those from any other group. It should be noted that kinship terms are inherently *relational* terms and this may make considerable difficulties for the subject, perhaps even make the task systematically ambiguous, when the method of undirected graphs is used to obtain similarity data. Consider, for example, a pair such as UNCLE-SON. Is this to be interpreted as UNCLE and (his) SON, in which case presumably it reduces to MAN-SON, and in which case presumably the reordered pair SON-UNCLE would reduce to the quite different MAN-UNCLE, or is some tacit reference to be made to EGO, in which case the order of terms become irrelevant? If the latter interpretation is made, then to be consistent, should not the subject consider the pair MOTHER-DAUGHTER as really referring to the relation between a woman and her granddaughter rather than the relation between a woman and her daughter? It is our impression from speaking with subjects after the experiment that for closely related terms which in some sense are complementary (such as MOTHER-DAUGHTER) they characteristically considered the relation without any reference to EGO, but that for more distantly related terms (as UNCLE-SON) sometimes, perhaps predominantly, they did make tacit reference to EGO. To the extent that different subjects use different criteria, or that the same subject uses different criteria for different pairs, any results will be hard to interpret. The above clearly implies that the method of undirected graphs may have severe disadvantages when the terms involved are inherently relational. These problems are distinctly lessened if a tree construction method is used, for with such a procedure the subject needs to link only the most closely related items.

With regard to the methodological implications or consequences of using a number of different data analysis procedures concurrently, it can be seen that the graph theoretic analysis not only serves to establish that the data are nonrandom, thus justifying the application of the other techniques, but that in at least one respect it also allows for substantive interpretation. As we have noted, the mean kinship degree of a labeled node may be taken as a measure of relatedness or centrality of meaning, and this index is substantially related to the distance of a term from the origin of the Euclidean space yielded by a MDS analysis; the greater the kinship degree of a node, the closer its location to the origin of the space. The clustering and MDS procedures involve rather different substantive hypotheses as to the nature of the system underlying the relations obtaining among the terms in a particular domain, and in the present case, consistent with what is to be expected given a paradigmatic model, the dimensional or spatial representation appears to be somewhat more appropriate to the data.

What of the substantive yield of the present study? Insofar as our principal concern is with a description of the structure of a subset of the domain of English kin terms and the testing of the psychological validity or reality of two componential analyses that have been offered for this domain, we have obtained rather clear-cut results. Consistent with other work, our results decisively support one of the models, and permit us to provide some weighting as to the importance of the postulated components, and, to the extent that there are still discrepancies between the data and the model, they may have some implications regarding ways in which the model might be modified. While "Ideally, the best test of the psychological reality of a proposed semantic paradigm is to observe whether the subject can apply the kinship terms correctly when he is supplied only with information implying the dimensions and values of the space on which the proposed paradigm is mapped (Wallace, 1965, p. 242)," it must be obvious that there are severe methodological difficulties associated with using the preceding as a model for a *data gathering* procedure. "A safer procedure," as Wallace puts it, may be "instead to ask the informant to apply his own concepts to the sorting of the terms themselves (p. 243)." This is exactly what we have attempted to do using a tree construction method and the method of undirected graphs, with results as reported above.

Chapter 5   *PRONOUNS*

As described in the preceding chapter, a componential analysis is an analysis of a set of terms, some members of which share features not shared by other terms in the set, with regard to defining features or "criterial attributes." The procedure is to search for minimal features of meaning which differentiate the terms in the set. Personal pronouns clearly constitute a delimited, structured set of terms which may be subjected to such an analysis, and some instances of this sort of analysis of pronominal paradigms are surveyed in Sturtevant (1964); see particularly the work of Roger Brown and his associates (e.g., in Brown, 1965) with regard to two basic semantic oppositions, status-power and solidarity-intimacy, which govern the use of the familiar *T* (du, tu, etc.) or the polite *V* (vous, sie, etc.) as terms of address. Pronouns are particularly of interest because the distinctions among them are syntactically governed, in that, e.g., there are distributional constraints on their occurrence such that any particular pronoun "stands for" a (usually preceding) noun or noun phrase, and in that syntactic categories, such as that of case, serve to differentiate them, while at the same time at least some of the distinctions among them, e.g., that between singular and plural terms, clearly have semantic import. Further, while at least one of the features that differentiates pronouns, viz. that of person, is deictic, referring to "orientational" features relative to the occasion or situation of utterance, other features, such as that of number mentioned above, are absolute and situationally independent. In addition, the system governing English pronouns is such that items falling into different categories or subcategories are not all morphologically distinct, e.g., consider YOU which may function either as a singular or plural term in either the nominative or accusative case, and such that certain distinctions overtly made for singular terms may be neutralized in the plural, e.g., consider the distinction in gender for the third person singular (HE, SHE, IT) which is neutralized in the plural THEY.

There are a number of obvious candidates with regard to the features or components involved in the system governing the use of English pronouns, namely: *person, gender, number,* and *case.* With regard to person, the obvious differentiation is that between "first," "second," and "third" person, but it has been argued that the primary distinction may be "between 'first'–and 'not first'–and that the distinction of 'second' and 'third' is secondary (Lyons, 1968, p. 278)." Gender (male, female, neuter) may be considered to constitute a subclassification of the third person singular (unless one takes the rather extreme position of considering it as an independent cross-classifying factor, distinctions in which are neutralized in all cases except the third person singular). With regard to number, there is the gross distinction between singular and plural, and with regard to case, one may distinguish nominative, accusative, and genitive (the last functioning principally as a possessive). As for the system in which such features may be organized, it is clearly not a simple, complete, cross-classification, since even if one were to make the extreme assumption that gender constitutes an independent cross-classifying factor, there would still be a number of distinct cells in the matrix filled by identical items; indeed that assumption would extravagantly increase the number of such cells. Rather, the system would appear to constitute some sort of a cross-classification: person x number x case, with a taxonomic component or components embedded in this cross-classification. On the more commonplace assumption of equal differences in status between first, second, and third persons, there would simply be a subclassification of the third person singular with regard to gender, constituting just two levels. Following the suggestion of Lyons (see above) one would first distinguish between "first" and "nonfirst" person, then subcategorize the latter into "second" and "third" persons, and then subcategorize the last, as above, with regard to gender, resulting in three taxonomic levels.

Deese (1965), analyzing some association data obtained by Jones and Fillenbaum (1964), has already shown that pronouns appear to be organized in a way that can be described "by ordinary grammatical statements." Carrying out a factor analysis of the intersection coefficients obtained from the associations to a set of personal pronouns, he found factors that differentiated the pronouns roughly in terms of number, case, and person. We shall attempt to determine whether recourse to underlying properties of the sort detailed above will permit us efficiently to interpret the data we obtain, to use the data to assess the weight or cognitive salience of the various putative features, and to evaluate the data with regard to their implications for the nature of the system into which these features may be organized.

As usual we shall obtain direct similarity data by means of a tree building technique, and subject these data to graph, cluster, and MDS analysis. In addition, we shall examine errors or confusions during learning in a paired-associate task where personal pronouns constituted the response items. We shall be interested in determining whether terms differing in fewer putative features tend to be more confused with each other than terms differing in more such features, and in juxtaposing the results yielded by the direct similarity procedure with those yielded on the learning task, to see whether the results of the former task help in the interpretation of the results of the latter task. Thus, if some component turns out to have little weight in differentiating terms on the direct similarity task, we shall seek to discover whether terms differing only in that component tend to be particularly frequently confused in the learning task. Insofar as confusions during learning are an orderly function of similarities in underlying putative features, this may perhaps be taken as evidence that pronouns really are coded in memory as complexes of such features, errors occurring when information on some feature(s) is lost. On the hypothesis that information on one feature is more likely to be lost than information on two features, and that information on two features is more likely to be lost than information on more than two features, we should expect, *ceteris paribus*, that two terms would be more likely to be confused, the fewer the underlying features that distinguish the one from the other (for some relevant evidence on this point see, e.g., Anisfeld and Knapp, 1968; Fillenbaum, 1969). Consistency between the results obtained in a direct similarity task and those obtained by a more indirect procedure, as, say, a memory task, would be of importance in suggesting that the presumptive underlying features are not just imposed by (or artifacts of) the conditions of directed scrutiny of similarities and differences among terms, but that they are relevant and consequential even when the subject is involved with a quite different (learning) task, i.e., that these distinctions have some cognitive reality even when the subject is not explicitly concerned to make them, or attend to them.

METHOD

Two groups of subjects, all of them University of North Carolina undergraduates, participated in the experiment. Group PRT consisted of 32 subjects (18 males and 14 females), who constructed labeled trees, using the standard instructions for this method (see Chapter 2) and the list of 16 pronouns presented in Table 5-1. Group PRC consisted of 138 male and female subjects participating in a typical paired-associate task, which was conducted as follows: 16 two-digit numbers, randomly selected from the numbers 10, . . ., 98, (with the constraint that no number consisted of the same two digits) were assigned to the 16 pronouns. The resulting 16 pairs (a number followed by a pronoun) were

TABLE 5-1   Distribution of Pronoun Mean Degree (Group PRT) and Proportions of Correct Responses (Group PRC)

Term	Mean degree for group PRT	Proportions of correct responses			
		Block 1	Block 2	Block 3	Block 4
HE	2.406	0.116	0.268	0.312	0.435
HER	1.625	0.145	0.261	0.399	0.522
HIM	1.906	0.145	0.304	0.478	0.536
HIS	1.500	0.130	0.181	0.188	0.464
I	1.875	0.594	0.855	0.928	0.928
ME	2.062	0.420	0.572	0.696	0.754
MY	1.500	0.188	0.283	0.449	0.464
OUR	1.719	0.123	0.283	0.384	0.616
SHE	1.781	0.420	0.536	0.703	0.754
THEIR	1.875	0.246	0.312	0.391	0.507
THEM	1.719	0.167	0.145	0.261	0.362
THEY	2.156	0.101	0.203	0.203	0.377
US	1.844	0.225	0.348	0.406	0.486
WE	2.219	0.065	0.232	0.420	0.391
YOU	2.062	0.210	0.413	0.674	0.746
YOUR	1.750	0.283	0.384	0.435	0.514
Mean		0.224	0.349	0.458	0.554

then read at a rate of five seconds per pair, and recorded on tape. A learning trial consisted of the presentation of all 16 pairs, one after another; on a test trial only the numbers were presented (at the same rate of five seconds per number). The subjects were run in groups of approximately 10. They were told that "on a test trial you will be given the two digit numbers one at a time and will be required to write down each number together with whatever was paired with it." There were, altogether, four blocks, each of which consisted of two learning trials followed by one test trial. The order of the items (pairs in the eight learning trials and numbers only in the four test trials) was randomized within trials. The subjects were instructed not to leave out any of the items, and were asked to guess if they did not recall the correct response.

RESULTS

Graph Analysis

We began the analysis by subjecting the direct similarity data of Group PRT to graph, cluster, and MDS analyses, in that order, and then examined the paired-associate data of Group PRC in light of the results of these analyses. The first property to be examined was the number of distinct subtrees constructed by Group PRT. Tracing over the labeled links in each tree, counting the number of distinct subtrees, and then averaging over subjects resulted in a mean of 5.063 and a standard deviation of 1.217. (The mean number of subtrees and the standard deviation were 5.167 and 1.258, respectively, for the male subjects, and 4.929 and 1.163 for the female subjects. Since the difference between males and females with regard to the mean number of trees and all other statistics that were examined was nonsignificant at the 0.20 level, these two subgroups were combined.) With no exception, the subjects in Group PRT used all three options in constructing trees, typically building 5–6 subtrees (26 out of the 32 subjects constructed exactly either five or six subtrees) and merging these in the final stages of the task.

Examined next is the distribution of node degree. Table 5-2 presents the predicted (Poisson) and observed frequency distribution of node degree summed over all subjects in Group PRT. Unlike the results for the kinship data reported in the preceding chapter, the difference between the predicted and observed distributions is highly significant ($p < 0.01$ by the one-sample Kolmogorov-Smirnov test), rejecting the hypothesis of a random construction of trees. Table 5-2 shows the same type of discrepancies between observed and predicted frequencies as the ones observed in Chapter 3, i.e., the observed trees had more nodes with degree $r = 2$ and fewer nodes with degree $r = 1$ or $r > 2$ than predicted by the Poisson distribution.

TABLE 5-2 Observed and Predicted Frequency Distributions of Node Degree (Group PRT)

Degree	Predicted	Observed
1	201	179
2	188	234
3	88	86
4	28	10
5+	7	3

Table 5-3 presents the observed and predicted distributions of pairs of (adjacent) nodes chosen by y subjects, $y = 0, 1, \ldots, 32$. The parameters of the predicted negative binomial distribution, p and s, estimated by the method of moments from the mean and variance of the observed frequency distribution, are shown below the table. The difference between the observed and predicted distributions, tested by the one-sample Kolmogorov-Smirnov test, was nonsignificant ($p > 0.20$), supporting the assumption of a gamma distributed popularity bias in the population of pairs of pronouns. Table 5-3 shows that the discrepancies between observed and predicted frequencies differ from the ones reported in the preceding two chapters. The predicted frequency for the color and kinship data was smaller than the observed frequency for $y = 0$ but larger for

TABLE 5-3   Observed and Predicted Frequency Distributions of Pairs of Adjacent Nodes
(Group PRT)[a]

y	Predicted	Observed
0	61	55
1	14	17
2	8	13
3	6	6
4	4	2
5	3	1
6	3	3
7	2	4
8	2	2
9	2	0
10	1	1
11	1	1
12	1	2
13	1	2
14	1	0
15	1	0
16	1	0
17+	8	11

[a]Parameters:

	p	s
PTR	0.056	0.236

$y = 2, 3, 4, 5$, whereas opposite results were obtained for the pronoun data. Table 5-3 further shows that the value of s is considerably smaller than the s values obtained for the tree construction groups in the preceding chapter, indicating a stronger popularity bias for pronouns than for kinship terms.

The ten most popular pairs of pronouns (connected by one link only), all of which were selected by more than half of the subjects, are presented below, where the number in the parentheses following each pair shows the number of subjects (out of 32) selecting it: THEY-THEM (32), WE-US (31), YOU-YOUR (30), HE-HIM (30), SHE-HER (30), I-ME (28), ME-MY (24), HIM-HIS (19), US-OUR (17), and THEM-THEIR (17). It can be noticed that all the members of the ten pairs differ from each other with respect to only one component, viz. case, and have the same values with regard to the other components, i.e., person, number, and gender. More interestingly, the ten pairs are nicely arranged in a decreasing order of popularity (reflected by the decreasing order of the frequencies) with respect to contrasts within "case." Three such contrasts can be distinguished in the set of pronouns we used: nominative-accusative, accusative-genitive, and nominative-genitive, and 12 out of the 120 possible pairs of pronouns can be classified unambiguously in terms of just these contrasts: Nominative-Accusative: I-ME, WE-US, HE-HIM, THEY-THEM. Accusative-

Genitive: ME-MY, US-OUR, HIM-HIS, THEM-THEIR. Nominative-Genitive: I-MY, WE-OUR, HE-HIS, THEY-THEIR. One pair, viz., SHE-HER, may fall either into the first or third class, since HER may be either an accusative or genitive. Another pair, viz., YOU-YOUR, may fall either into the second or third class, since YOU may be either a nominative or accusative. It can be seen that, with the exception of YOU-YOUR, the first six most popular pairs reveal a nominative-accusative contrast, and the next four pairs represent the accusative-genitive contrast. Indeed, all eight members of the first and second classes above are included among the ten most popular pairs. A further inspection of the data of Group PRT shows the frequency with which the remaining four pairs, falling in the third class above, were chosen: THEY-THEIR (13), WE-OUR (13), HE-HIS (12), and I-MY (8). Thus 13 out of the 14 pairs of pronouns differing only in case were included among the 15 most popular pairs.

To sum up: the graph analysis of the similarity data shows clearly that trees were not constructed randomly. Rather, it suggests that the most prominent component determining proximities between pronouns was case and that within case proximities were smallest for nominative-accusative pairs, and largest for nominative-genitive pairs, with accusative-genitive pairs falling in between. The modal number of subtrees (6) and the similarity of pronouns differing only in case, suggests a structure consisting of about six tight clusters, each of which includes two or three terms.

Cluster Analysis

The Connectedness and Diameter methods were both applied to the mean proximity matrix of Group PRT. Unlike the clustering results for the color and kinship data reported in the preceding two chapters, the ultrametric inequality was completely satisfied, i.e., the two clustering methods yielded the same HCS—the one portrayed in Fig. 5-1. Inspection of Fig. 5-1 seems to suggest six distinct clusters, a suggestion further supported by the large jump in the α value between row 10 and row 11. These clusters are:

1. First person, singular [I, ME, MY].
2. First person, plural [WE, US, OUR].
3. Third person, singular, male [HE, HIM, HIS].
4. Third person, singular, female [SHE, HER].
5. Third person, plural [THEY, THEM, THEIR].
6. Second person [YOU, YOUR].

In terms of the MAXC clustering, there are only four (significant) clusters: [1], [2], [3], and [4, 5, 6]. It should be noted, however, that the only reason clusters 4 and 6 are not significant is because each of them includes two terms only. The MAXC criterion does not yield significant clusters with only two

```
Level    I ME MY WE US OUR HE HIM HIS SHE HER THEY THEM THEIR YOU YOUR     α

  1    XXXX  .   .   .   .   .   .   .   .   .   .   .   .   .   .   .     4.28
  2    XXXX  .   .   .   .  XXXX  .   .   .   .   .   .   .   .   .        5.41
  3    XXXX  .  XXXX  .  XXXX  .   .   .   .   .   .   .   .   .           7.19
  4    XXXX  .  XXXX  .  XXXX  .  XXXX  .   .   .   .   .                  7.78
  5    XXXX  .  XXXX  .  XXXX  .  XXXX XXXX  .   .   .                     9.56
  6   XXXXXXX XXXX  .  XXXX  .  XXXX XXXX  .   .   .                       9.97
  7   XXXXXXX XXXX  .  XXXX  .  XXXX XXXX  .  XXXX                        11.22
  8   XXXXXXX XXXX  .  XXXXXXX XXXX XXXX  .  XXXX                         11.94
  9   XXXXXXX XXXXXXX XXXXXXX XXXX XXXX  .  XXXX                          13.66
 10   XXXXXXX XXXXXXX XXXXXXX XXXX XXXXXXX XXXX                           14.72
 11   XXXXXXX XXXXXXX XXXXXXXXXXXX XXXXXXX XXXX                           26.25
 12   XXXXXXXXXXXXXXXX XXXXXXXXXXXX XXXXXXX XXXX                          30.47
 13   XXXXXXXXXXXXXXXX XXXXXXXXXXXX XXXXXXXXXXXX                          39.16
 14   XXXXXXXXXXXXXXXX XXXXXXXXXXXXXXXXXXXXXXXXXXXX                       53.84
 15   XXXXXXXXXXXXXXXXXXXXXXXXXXXXXXXXXXXXXXXXXXXXXXXX                    55.75
```

Fig. 5-1.   HCS for Group PRT.

terms unless the size of the proximity matrix or the number of subjects is considerably larger than 16 and 32, respectively.

Inspecting Fig. 5-1 from bottom to top suggests an ordering of the components governing similarity judgments between pronouns in terms of their prominence or differential weighting. The most prominent component is "person" with the primary distinction being between "first" (clusters 1 and 2) and "not first" (clusters, 3, 4, 5, and 6). The second most prominent component is "number," differentiating (1) between clusters 1 and 2, and (2) between clusters 3 and 4 on one hand and clusters 5 and 6 on the other hand. Next, clusters 5 and 6 are split (row 12) in terms of the distinction of "second" versus "third" person, and "gender" splits clusters 2 and 3 (row 10). Consistent with the results of the graph analysis, "case" is by far the least prominent component in terms of distinguishing between terms; pronouns differing from one another in case are always the first to be clustered. The consistency between clustering and graph results extends even further. Not only does the cluster analysis identify the six clusters suggested by the graph analysis, but as Fig. 5-1 shows, the first terms to be clustered within each of the four clusters with three terms each fall under the nominative and accusative cases. Terms falling under the genitive case are clustered later.

The proximity matrices of five subjects, randomly selected from Group PRT, were also subjected to the Diameter method. The HCSs of three out of these five subjects are very similar to the HCS for the mean data portrayed in Fig. 5-1; the distances between the C_{10} clusterings in the HCSs for individual and mean data range between 0 and 0.1. The HCSs of the remaining two subjects are uninterpretable.

Multidimensional Scaling Analysis

We applied the Young-Torgerson MDS method to the five randomly selected proximity matrices and to the mean proximity matrix of Group PRT. Solutions were obtained again in one, two, and three dimensions, in both City Block and Euclidean spaces. Since the stress values for the Euclidean representations were always the smallest, they are presented in Table 5-4. Inspection of Table 5-4 suggests an adequate representability of the proximity data in a two-dimensional Euclidean space—the break in the stress values between $m = 2$ and $m = 1$ is sharp, and a comparison of the stress values with the critical cut-off points presented in Chapter 2 clearly rejects the hypothesis of randomly generated proximity data.

TABLE 5-4   Stress Values for Euclidean Representations

| Dimensions | Group PRT | | | | | |
	No. 5	No. 11	No. 20	No. 25	No. 29	Mean
3	0.046	0.015	0.030	0.046	0.022	0.015
2	0.080	0.057	0.051	0.106	0.034	0.075
1	0.198	0.167	0.111	0.248	0.091	0.274

Figure 5-2 portrays the two-dimensional Euclidean representation for the mean data. We followed the procedure discussed in the previous chapter and embedded the clustering results in the representation by drawing closed convex curves around clusters of points that were identified as such on levels 9–14 of the HCS (Fig. 5-1). Figure 5-2 shows a very orderly picture and indicates an excellent agreement between the clustering and MDS results. Terms differing in case only fall closer to each other than any other terms; the six clusters obtained by the Diameter method appear as highly compact clusters on the representation. The clusters may further be classified in terms of the two axes, though by this we do not wish to imply a quantitative, dimensional interpretation. The major distinction, as suggested by the clustering results, is in terms of the "person" component, with "first person" terms located in the lower part of the representation and the remaining terms located in the upper part. A second way to classify the terms is in terms of "number," with singular terms residing in the right-hand part of the figure, and plural terms falling on the left-hand side. "Gender" and "person" further divide the third person singular terms and the "not first person" plural terms, respectively.

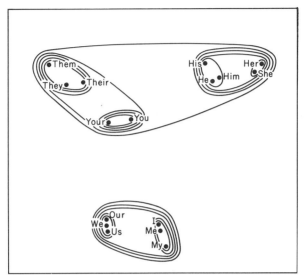

Fig. 5-2.   Two-dimensional Euclidean representation for Group PRT.

Figure 5-2 further indicates that the distances between pronouns differing in three components (e.g., I-THEM, MY-THEY, WE-HIS) are somewhat larger than the ones between pronouns differing in two components (e.g., ME-WE, HE-THEIR, WE-HE), and that the latter are slightly larger in general than the distances between pronouns differing in one component only. Furthermore, the figure shows that pairs of pronouns differing in one component only may be subdivided in terms of the distances between their members into (1) pairs of terms differing in case only (e.g., I-ME, THEY-THEIR, HE-HIM) and (2) pairs of terms differing in either person, number, or gender (e.g., ME-HIM, MY-OUR, HE-SHE), and that the distances between terms belonging to the first group are considerably smaller than the ones between terms falling in the second group. In short, Fig. 5-2 suggests that terms can be classified in terms of the distances between them into four groups: terms differing in case only; terms differing in either person, number, or gender; terms differing in two components; and terms differing in three components. If confusability between pronouns in a paired-associate task is some monotonic function of the semantic distance between them, one would expect to find the same order in the four groups of pairs of pronouns, arranged in terms of some measure of confusability. This hypothesis will be tested in the immediately following section.

Group PRC

The data of Group PRC, participating in the paired-associate task, were summarized in four 16 x 16 confusion matrices, one for each block of trials, where an entry (i,j) shows the proportion of subjects (out of 138) responding with term j on a test trial when i is the correct response. The four columns in the right-hand side of Table 5-1 present the diagonal elements of these four confusion matrices, i.e., the proportion of correct responses for each term and for each block. The table shows clearly that paired-associate performance improved with practice; with only two minor exceptions (THEM on blocks 1 and 2, and WE on blocks 3 and 4) the proportions of correct responses for each term either remained the same or increased with blocks. Perfect learning was not achieved, however, even after four blocks. The mean proportions of correct responses were 0.224, 0.349, 0.458, and 0.554 for blocks 1, 2, 3, and 4, respectively. The table further shows large individual differences among pronouns. The term I was the easiest to learn; the proportions of correct responses for I ranged between 0.594 for block 1 to 0.928 for blocks 3 and 4. The most difficult terms to learn were THEY and THEM; the proportions of correct responses for these terms on block 4 were 0.362 and 0.377, respectively. We have found no simple way to account for the observed order of the pronouns arranged in terms of the proportion of correct responses.

To check whether the number of component values differing between any two pronouns had any effect on the number of incorrect responses (errors) made, the entries (i,j) and (j,i) in the original 16 x 16 confusion matrices were averaged, and then the 120 entries of the resulting half matrix were classified into four groups, depending whether i and j differed in (1) case only (14 entries); (2) either person, number, or gender (36 entries); (3) two components (55 entries); (4) three components (15 entries). In cases of ambiguity, e.g., consider the terms YOU and HER, the smallest number of components differentiating between any of these terms and some other term was always taken (thus the number of components differentiating either YOU or HER from some other term could not be larger than two).

Table 5-5 presents the means and standard deviations of the number of errors per term for each of the four groups and each of the four blocks of trials. The block effect for each group is, with two minor exceptions, consistent with the results shown in Table 5-1—the mean number of errors decreases with practice for each group. The group effect for each block confirms the hypothesis stated at the end of the preceding section. With only two minor exceptions, the mean number of errors decreases as the number of components differentiating between two pronouns increases. (We have not employed any standard statistical test because of the dependence between the means. It is noted, however, that since there are only 24 different ways to arrange four numbers, the probability of obtaining a prespecified order is equal to 1/24.) Table 5-5 shows clearly that the main difference is between pronouns differing in case only and pronouns differing in some other component. The differences between the latter means and

TABLE 5-5   Means and Standard Deviations of Confusion Errors

Block	Difference in number of component values			
	1		2	3
	Case	Other		
1 Mean	8.786	6.333	5.864	4.833
S.D.	4.020	3.994	4.093	3.257
2 Mean	9.000	5.667	4.927	3.667
S.D.	5.849	4.186	4.129	1.954
3 Mean	7.429	4.431	4.064	4.167
S.D.	5.280	4.098	4.476	3.077
4 Mean	6.964	3.750	3.227	3.267
S.D.	5.068	3.566	3.440	2.999

the means for pronouns differing in either two or three components almost vanish on the third and fourth blocks.

Both Tables 5-1 and 5-5 indicate a high level of consistency among blocks in the paired-associate learning and the type of errors made. This is further supported by the pair-wise correlations computed between the four confusion (half) matrices. All six correlations were moderately large, ranging between 0.60 and 0.75, and highly significant ($p < 0.001$). To compare the results of Groups PRT and PRC, correlations were computed between each of the four confusion matrices and the mean proximity matrix of Group PRT. As expected, all four correlations were negative (since the confusion matrices consist of similarities and the mean proximity matrix of dissimilarities) but the values were disappointingly low, ranging between -0.11 and -0.26. Only the correlation between the confusion matrix on the fourth block and the mean proximity matrix reached the 0.01 level of significance, and this accounted for less than 7% of the total variance. The low correlations suggest that clustering and MDS analyses performed on the confusion matrices would yield entirely different results from the ones obtained for Group PRT. Indeed, the clustering analysis yielded results which were hardly interpretable, and the stress values for the two- and three-dimensional representations came very close to the cut-off points established in Chapter 2. Hence no attempt has been made to present or interpret these results.

DISCUSSION

Considering the direct similarity data, one might perhaps argue that while these results are very clear and plausible, in that some obvious candidate features do emerge as relevant, they are, nevertheless, of little interest, just because the pronominal system constitutes such a straightforward and transparent case, that we have gone to great labor to produce a truism. Such an argument is in part misguided, in part simply wrong. The argument is misguided since even if it were the case that the results constitute simply a documentation of the obvious, it might be noted that even the obvious needs empirical substantiation, and on occasion does not survive when this is attempted. More important, results of the present sort may be considered as methodologically significant in that they validate the techniques we have employed for gathering and analyzing similarity data in a clear case, and thus provide some warrant for the application of such techniques to other domains where the underlying relations are very far from clear (as in some of the domains investigated in subsequent chapters of this work).

The argument is wrong in that the direct similarity data yield substantive results with regard to (1) the *weighting* of the importance of the various underlying features, and (2) the nature of their structural *organization*. Thus, *a priori* there are no compelling reasons arguing that differences in case would be regarded as cognitively less significant than differences in person or number, yet this was found to be true, very consistently. Further, with regard to the underlying organization of these features, consider the significance of differences in "person." Certainly the most obvious analysis would require a straightforward differentiation between "first," "second," and "third" persons, treating these differences as all on a par with each other. Yet the present results showing first person terms compactly clustered together and set apart from the other terms do not really support such an analysis, but are distinctly more consistent with the analysis suggested by Lyons (1968), which requires a primary distinction between "first" person and "other," and a subsequent differentiation of "other" into "second" and "third" persons. Thus, these results permit a choice between two hypotheses concerning the organization of the feature "person," supporting an account which regards this feature as hierarchically organized on two levels.

The results of the cluster analysis and of the MDS analysis of the direct similarity data are consistent in revealing the preponderant influence of the "person" and "number" components in differentiating among the various terms. It is interesting to find that, in the spatial solution, YOU and YOUR fall intermediate between the singular and plural nonfirst person terms, since these pronouns can, in fact, be regarded as either singular or plural terms. Both kinds of analysis agree in giving much less weight to the "case" component, for terms differing only in case are clustered together and are contiguous in the spatial solution. Here the graph analysis turns out to be particularly useful in indexing differences among these closely related terms, showing that when the difference between terms involves a nominative-accusative contrast they are more likely to be closely associated than when the difference involves an accusative-genitive contrast, and that terms differing in either of these respects are more closely linked than terms differing with regard to a nominative-genitive contrast. In general, the present results strongly support a model of the pronominal system (personal pronouns) which requires such features as person, number, gender, and case (the last of distinctly less weight than the others), and where these features are organized in some sort of a cross-classificatory system (with regard to person and number and case), with a taxonomic component embedded in this cross-classification (with regard to person and gender).

Examining errors or confusions during learning in the paired-associate task we find, indeed, that, with only minor exceptions, the mean number of confusions decreases as the number of components differentiating between two items increases (see Table 6-5). Distinctly more errors occurred for terms differing in only one component than for terms differing in two or three components—the mean numbers of confusion errors taken over all one component differences are 7.02, 6.60, 5.27, and 4.65 for Blocks 1, 2, 3, and 4, respectively. On the direct similarity task, terms differing only in "case" were clustered very closely together; insofar as differences in this regard are not cognitively salient, we should expect that such pairs of terms would be particularly prone to confusion. We therefore divided the pairs of terms differing in only one component into those differing with regard to case only, and all others. An examination of the confusion results for these two groupings (see Table 5-5) shows that, in fact, terms differing only in case were much more frequently mutually confused than terms differing in some other single component. This finding thus reveals a strong consistency between the direct similarity results and the learning results, and indicates how use of the former results may clarify the latter. Although the "case" feature or variable is clearly relevant to an analysis of errors or confusions during learning, the paired-associate results are otherwise somewhat disappointing. While there is some tendency for confusion errors to decrease as the number of components differentiating terms increases, this tendency is moderate at best even for Blocks 1 and 2, and just about disappears for the last two blocks. How can one account for this? One might perhaps note that the level of learning on the paired-associate task is low, reaching only a little over 50% even on the last block, which was indeed the only block for which the correlation between the confusion matrix and the similarity matrix reached significance, and speculate that a closer fit between the direct similarity data and the learning data might have been obtained had learning been permitted to progress further. On the whole, this speculation does not seem very convincing. We have seen already that, putting aside results associated with the "case" feature, differences in confusion frequency as a function of number of component differences between pairs of terms are minimal on Blocks 3 and 4. Further, and more important, note that confusion errors can only be revealing as to possible similarities among terms just so long as many such errors are being made; as performance approaches criterion there will be too few errors to provide any reliable basis for assessing similarities among terms, and these errors are likely to be due to all sorts of idiosyncratic or random factors. The above argues that confusion data at a relatively early stage of learning, but not at the very start where little is known about the terms, may in fact be most revealing of underlying similarities among terms. To some extent, the present data are consistent with this analysis for, indeed, the confusion results are most orderly on Blocks 1 and 2, with differences in errors between the different cases somewhat greater on Block 2 than on any other block.

One must distinguish between two questions: (1) What is the underlying system governing the use of a particular set of related terms? (2) How may such a set of terms be learned, or remembered? The answers to these two questions need not be identical. With regard to the second question, there is indeed evidence that words may be learned as feature complexes (see e.g., Anisfeld and Knapp, 1968, and Fillenbaum, 1969, with regard to false recognition of synonyms, and synonyms and antonyms, respectively) but these experiments have characteristically focused on relations obtaining just between discrete pairs of words, or very limited subsets of terms (as in Henley, Noyes, and Deese, 1968, dealing with short-term memory for triads drawn from eight kin terms differing with regard to either two or three underlying features). In the present study a larger set of terms involving a distinctly more complex system was involved, and there is rather direct evidence that the number of features distinguishing between two terms was not the principal determinant of confusions among them, in that entries in the confusion matrix characteristically were not symmetric, i.e., even though the componential difference between items i and j is necessarily identical with that between items j and i, the relative frequency with which erroneous j responses were made when i would have been the correct response was generally not the same as that with which erroneous i responses were made when j would have been the correct response. Thus, while there is fairly good evidence that terms were analyzed with regard to "case", and that differences in this regard were often lost during learning, evidence with regard to the significance of the other presumptive components is very sparse at best, and we cannot say very much as to how these terms were coded and processed. One might note some work by Henley (1969) on the semantics of animal names, which yielded rather similar findings. While a fairly clear structure involving such dimensions as size and ferocity emerged from an analysis of free listing data, pairwise and triad ratings, etc., the results of a paired-associate study were essentially quite distinct and unrelated to the other results.

Chapter 6   *EMOTION NAMES*

The attempt to provide a structural description of the emotions has a long history. There have been all sorts of suggestions as to the nature of the primary, elementary, or pure emotions from which the other, secondary, or mixed emotions might be derived. Thus, e.g., Descartes distinguished six primary passions, viz. Love, Hatred, Desire, Joy, Sadness, and Admiration, and Hobbes seven, dropping Sadness and Admiration from the list and substituting Appetite, Aversion, and Grief. More recently, in this century, McDougall distinguished between a dozen or so properties and the affective or emotional quality associated with each. On the other hand, there is an equally long intellectual tradition which seeks to account even for the primary emotions in terms of a more elementary set of principles, with a Pleasure-Pain dimension indexing differences in pleasantness and unpleasantness, perhaps being most commonly used as a, or even the basic dimension. In a sense, then, one may differentiate between dimensional and typological approaches to the study of emotions. Of the former kind is Wundt's formulation of a three-dimensional theory of feeling in terms of Pleasantness-Unpleasantness, Excitement-Quiet, and Tension-Relaxation or, more recently, Schlosberg's analysis of emotional expressions first in terms of the two dimensions of Pleasantness-Unpleasantness and Attention-Rejection (1952), and then in terms of a three-dimensional scheme adding an activation dimension of Sleep-Tension (1954). As examples of the latter kind, in addition to the historical examples noted above, one may cite F. H. Allport's list of six normal types of expression, viz. pain-grief, suspense-fear, anger, disgust, pleasure, and attitudinal group (1924), or, to take a recent instance, Tomkins and McCarter's classification of nine primary affects, viz. enjoyment, interest, surprise, fear, anger, disgust, shame, distress, and neutrality (1964).

To provide some concrete exemplifications of work which attempts to bridge the gap between dimensional and typological approaches, we shall briefly comment on a recent study by Osgood (1966a), which seeks by means of factor analysis to provide information concerning underlying dimensional structure, and by means of a cluster analytic approach attempts to identify some primary affects as densely populated regions within the dimensional space. Facial expressions posed by students were labeled by student judges using the same set of terms as that provided for the actors. A number of factor analyses of the resulting data provided evidence for three principal dimensions, which Osgood named Pleasantness, Activation, and, with some awkwardness, Control (this last factor being defined by DISGUST, CONTEMPT, LOATHING at one end and SURPRISE and AMAZEMENT at the other). The hypothetical space of emotional expression was modeled by a "pyramid truncated at the rear end." Cluster analyses of the results confirmed "the existence of some seven or ten regions within this space, densely populated with quasi-synonymous states which warrant identification as 'primary affects' (p. 1)." Thus Osgood's results appear to require both a dimensional representation, largely consistent with that proposed by Schlosberg (1954), and also to reveal the existence of clusters, which agree largely with the affect types suggested by Tomkins and McCarter (1964), with the exception only of the DISTRESS, SHAME, and NEUTRAL categories. As Osgood puts it in discussing dimensions versus types of expression "the distinction is not a matter of *either-or* but of *both*." He suggests, indeed, that "the major dimensions and shape" of the space of expressed emotions will be common across cultures as indexing basic affective components, while the clusters or types found in this common space will vary with language and culture as a function of differences in referential or denotative meanings.

It should, however, be noted that it is by no means clear how clusters were identified in the study, and that, in a sense, the dimensional representation is simply considered as primary with clusters merely being taken as "densely populated" regions in the dimensional space. Clearly, this view is very different from any characterization of "primary" affects as different nominal types with secondary or mixed emotions regarded as composites or hierarchically organized derivatives. Finally, it is in no way obvious why dimensional analysis should reveal affective properties and typal analysis referential aspects, even when emotion names are considered, but particularly in the present case concerned with the facial expression of emotions.

In any study of the emotions, a number of significant methodological decisions must be made before work can begin. These concern questions regarding (1) the objects or domain of study, whether facial expressions of emotion, or emotion names, or whatever are to be considered, (2) the identity and number of items selected and their distribution within the domain, (3) the methods of data collection, whether constrained by having subjects label the items or rate them in terms of a number of specified scales or dimensions, or free, with subjects only required to assess the similarities among the items letting whatever structure obtains emerge from the analysis of the data, and (4) methods of data analysis, whether to use correlational and factor analytic techniques, MDS scaling techniques, or typal-clustering techniques. Decisions with regard to any or all of the above will be governed by theoretical interests and presuppositions, and may make for very considerable differences in the findings and their interpretation, e.g., we shall show below that the same data, those of Block (1957), may appear in a very different light when analyzed by factor analytic and nonmetric multidimensional scaling techniques, respectively.

Let us distinguish between two classes of studies of the emotions, which will be discussed in more detail below. One popular approach has involved an examination of the structural relations among expressed emotions by means of the study of (usually posed) facial expressions, see, e.g., the work of Osgood above and particularly the work of Schlosberg and his students (Schlosberg, 1952, 1954; Engen, Levy, and Schlosberg, 1957, 1958). Another approach to the phenomenology of the emotions bases itself on an analysis of the relations among emotion names or terms. While it might be nice if one were to discover an isomorphism between the structure of expressed and that of named emotions, such a result is surely by no means guaranteed or even conceptually necessary, for these two classes of studies may be addressed to rather different aspects of emotion. It is not only that "the language of emotions appears to be much richer than the territory it is designed to cover" and that facial expressions may primarily communicate affective meaning whereas emotion terms may more readily tap both affective and denotative components (Osgood, 1966a), but that the study of each domain introduces further problems of its own. In studies of facial expression of emotions there are special problems with regard to the representation or encoding of emotional state by the actor, whether or not the expression is specially posed, and the extent to which different emotional states can be, or are, in fact, differentially encoded in momentary facial expression, and with regard to the abilities of the observer in decoding or deciphering these, and the cues he utilizes in doing this. All this is exacerbated by the fact that conventional procedures in this area eliminate situational context, providing only an instantaneous, snapshot view of the face. While these sorts of problems are avoided when one studies emotion names, others are introduced. Perhaps the principal difficulty is that the structural relations obtaining among emotion names may only tell us something about the meaning relations obtaining among these terms without neccessarily saying anything about the relations among their referents (whatever these may be as feeling states). Essentially, when one studies emotion names one is dealing with a semantic domain, and the relation between it and the facts to which it refers may be a contingent and arbitrary one. We shall recur to this point later.

Studies of Facial Expressions

Now we shall briefly review some of the studies on the facial expression of emotions, noting differences in methods of obtaining and analyzing data, and indicating the general burden of the findings. Following up some analyses of Woodworth, Schlosberg (1941) discovered that posed faces could be arranged in a circular array and proposed a two-dimensional model in terms of a Pleasant-Unpleasant and an Attention-Rejection dimension. Subsequently (1954), he added an Activation dimension (Sleep-Tension) and, together with his students (Engen, Levy, and Schlosberg, 1957, 1958), showed that subjects could reliably locate posed expressions with regard to position on each of these three dimensions. In the preceding studies, emotion names or dimensions were always specified for the subjects and, thus, as Abelson and Sermat (1962) put it, "no direct account is taken of the dimensions operative for the judges; E imposes particular dimensions of his own choosing and is arbitrarily required to give them equal weight (p. 546)." To escape from this constraint, these authors used a selection of 13 of Schlosberg's stimuli, but required subjects simply to make similarity-dissimilarity ratings for the $\binom{13}{2}$ pairs of facial poses. These ratings were converted to interstimulus distances and then analyzed by means of a metric MDS scaling procedure, which yielded two principal dimensions identified as a Pleasant-Unpleasant and a sort of Activation dimension close to Schlosberg's Tension-Sleep dimension, but in some respects a compromise between this and the Attention-Rejection dimension. Reanalyzing these data by means of a nonmetric MDS scaling procedure, which "makes substantially weaker demands upon the input data," Shepard (1962a) obtained essentially the same pattern of results, lending some support to our use of nonmetric MDS procedures in the present study. Carrying out a very similar study, again using nonmetric MDS procedures in the analysis of data, Cliff and Young (1968) obtained a two-dimensional solution very similar to that yielded by Shepard's reanalysis of the Abelson and Sermat data.

All the studies mentioned above have attempted to provide some dimensional representation for the structure of facially expressed emotions. In another study conducted by Stringer (1967), a typal or cluster analytic procedure was applied to data obtained when subjects grouped directly, into as many piles as they wished, 30 photographs depicting various emotions. Stringer's data were analyzed by a variant (Cluster 3) of a general purpose clustering program developed by Constantinescu (1966, 1967). The method operates on the same input information as Johnson's two methods—a symmetric proximity matrix whose elements are measured on an ordinal scale, but the principles underlying the clustering are entirely different. In particular, Constantinescu's method does not yield a unique solution to the clustering problem, and, like Peay's (1970) work, the system of clusters which fulfils its three conditions is not a partition of the set of elements, i.e., the clusters are not necessarily disjoint. The analysis yielded five principal clusters characterized by the author as Worry, Disgust-Pain, Suspense, Thoughtfulness, and Happiness, in terms of an examination of the labels that subjects had provided for their clusters after completing the grouping procedure. While making a few remarks concerning the identifiability of something like the commonly found Pleasantness-Unpleasantness dimension, Stringer basically limits himself to a careful description of the composition of each of the clusters obtained.

We reanalyzed Stringer's data using Johnson's Diameter method and obtained five significant clusters corresponding exactly to those obtained by use of Constantinescu's method, except that in our case all clusters were, of course, disjoint, while use of the other procedure yielded a couple of items (6 and 17), out of 30, which appeared in two clusters. We also performed an MDS analysis of these data, the two-dimensional solution, which had an acceptable stress value of 0.201, is shown in Fig. 6-1, with the cluster results embedded in the spatial representation. The 30 photograph numbers appearing in the representation and the labeling of the clusters correspond to Stringer's use. While the clusters are compact (with the exception of picture 28 in the DISGUST-PAIN cluster), and there is some suggestion of a circular structure, no obvious dimensional interpretation of these findings seems possible.

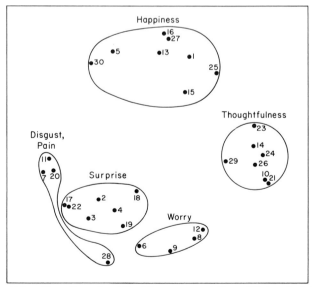

Fig. 6-1.   Two-dimensional Euclidean representation of Stringer's data.

To summarize the dimensional findings, it seems clear that a Pleasantness-Unpleasantness dimension emerges from all the studies cited, as well as others that might have been cited, and that some sort of Activation dimension is also often obtained. There may perhaps be an additional dimension corresponding to what Osgood (1966a) calls the Control dimension, but, with regard to this, results are not very consistent across studies, and, beyond this, results of different studies are quite unclear and inconsistent.

Studies of Emotion Names

We turn now to the study of emotion names. This work appears to be based on the assumption "that the more general properties of language habit systems, to the extent that they do operate, seem to reflect experiential qualities—the S can only turn inward for the basis of his report and what is inward is by implication his private emotional experience (Block, 1957, p. 358)." We have already noted that the basis for such an assumption is not at all clear, and it is obviously essential to avoid confusing "propositions about the world with propositions about language (D'Andrade, 1965)." Consider the related case from trait psychology. D'Andrade (1965) has demonstrated, for at least two examples, that the factor structure and loadings emerging in trait rating studies, where in the one instance subjects rated other persons and, in the second, themselves, could essentially be reproduced by an analysis of ratings of similarity of meaning among the trait names employed.

Consider the first example in a little more detail. Basing himself on previous studies, Norman (1963) "selected 20 sets of bipolar adjectives that attempt exhaustiveness and independence in the domain of natural language description of personality characteristics (D'Andrade, p. 216)" and had subjects use these in rating their acquaintances. The resulting scores were correlated and factored yielding five clear, interpretable dimensions, labeled Extraversion, Agreeableness, Conscientiousness, Emotional Stability, and Culture. Suspecting that the correlations and factors obtained in Norman's study might result from partial overlaps in the meanings of sets of terms from the rating scales used, D'Andrade selected one polar term for each of the 20 bipolar scales and had subjects rate "the degree of similarity in *meaning* between all possible pairs of terms." He correlated and factored the resulting scores, obtaining results very similar to those of Norman. The analogy between the trait case and that of emotion names is actually a close one, and, indeed, even a fair number of the terms used to describe personality traits are just adjectival versions of emotion names. Note that even the case of judged facial expressions may be a conceptually equivalent one, insofar as subjects label or name the expressions to themselves (and many say that they do just this) and such labels mediate their judgments. Therefore even these sorts of findings may be open to the same question as to whether the findings are about the world or, again, findings largely concerning linguistic organization.

It should be recognized that the argument and results presented above do not require the conclusion that all along we have been dealing only with facts of linguistic organization, for, as D'Andrade put it, "it is possible that the so-called psychological traits dealt with in this paper exist both as components in the terms used to describe the external world and in the external world as well (p. 227)," and, thus that there is some kind of isomorphism between these domains. What the above argument does entail is the recognition that the issue is confounded and that the conceptual status of the data is not clear in cases of this sort. Even if the analysis of emotion names does not reveal the structure of the interior world of emotions (it is not obvious that there is any technique available which will do that), yielding only semantic information, it is of considerable interest in its own right as revealing something about the organization of the semantic domain of emotion names.

The issue of possible isomorphism warrants some further discussion. It has been argued (Shepard and Chipman, 1970) that "while there is no structural resemblance between an individual internal representation and its corresponding external object an approximate parallelism should nevertheless hold between the *relations* among different internal representations and the *relations* among their corresponding external objects (p. 1)." Supporting this position, these investigators showed that subjective judgments of the similarities among the shapes of 15 states of the U.S. were very much the same, whether the states to be compared were presented as outline forms or whether only the names of the states were presented for judgment. This was taken as demonstrating that "judgments of similarity can be more strongly determined by visual features of the shapes named than by any features of the name themselves. And this is taken as indicating that the inferred representations studied here were more isomorphic to the unpresented shapes than to the explicitly presented names (p. 14)." We have presented results having similar implications in Chapter 3, where we showed that the circular configuration resulting from an analysis of the similarities among color names was very similar to that yielded by an analysis of the similarities among the colors themselves (Shepard, 1962a).

While results of the sort noted above are very intriguing, they may well be limited to cases where there is some relatively direct relation between a name and its referent, such that given a state name or color name one may conjure up some sort of corresponding, probably visual, mental image. Further, note that these are cases where one can present for judgment the "external objects" whether colors or outline shapes of states, while in the case of emotions the "external objects" are, or refer to, interior experiential states or facts. Hence, it is not possible in this sort of case to provide the sort of validating evidence that can be, and has been, provided for the cases described above. Indeed, in those cases the previous availability of external objects for perception may be what permits the "direct" relation between name and image. One can make the assumption that emotion names tap the internal representations of the emotions, which representations in a sense are the emotions as experiential states. One can further assume that the relational structure obtaining among emotion names will therefore reveal something as to the relations obtaining among the emotions. Under these assumptions, if one is interested in the richest and fullest description of these states and their relationships, there is perhaps some argument for using as subjects persons who are sophisticated users of a richly differentiated emotional vocabulary, e.g., novelists, or maybe phenomenologists. We have previously (Chapter 3) made a similar suggestion with regard to the study of people who use a highly differentiated color vocabulary. Be that as it may, it should be clear that while the sort of isomorphism argument offered by Shepard and Chipman in some measure provides motivation for the present study of emotion names, and while indeed such a study may reveal something as to the structure of emotions *per se*, and may better serve that purpose than any other technique, all one can justifiably claim for it is that it will provide information regarding the semantic domain of emotion names.

We now turn to a consideration of some prior studies of emotion names. Ekman (1955) had subjects rate the qualitative similarity between all pairs drawn from a set of 23 Swedish words chosen so as to cover a wide range of emotions. He factored the resulting matrix of similarity scores, extracted 11 factors, and attempted interpretation of nine of these. It should be noted that the factoring technique he employed spuriously increases the dimensionality of the solution and that Shepard (1962a) has shown that some data on similarities among colors, which Ekman (1954) obtained and analyzed in a similar way, and for which he found five factors, could be satisfactorily analyzed by nonmetric MDS and described by a circular array very much like the conventional color circle. A reanalysis of Ekman's data by Dietze (1963), using some clustering techniques developed by McQuitty (1957), yielded a more economical typal solution revealing some seven clusters, and seemed to better capture some relevant aspects of the data.

We also reanalyzed Ekman's data using both MDS and Johnson's clustering procedures. The two-dimensional solution is shown in Fig. 6-2. While the fit in two dimensions was adequate with a stress value of 0.133, the three-dimensional fit being only slightly better with stress of 0.093, no simple or obvious dimensional interpretation of the configuration seems possible. What the results do suggest, however, is that a solution that requires eleven or nine factors is an inappropriate one, very likely stemming from inadequacies in procedures used for data analysis. Cluster analysis, using Johnson's Diameter method, yielded results very similar to those obtained by Dietze. Considering only significant clusters we find that the first two clusters yielded by our analysis correspond

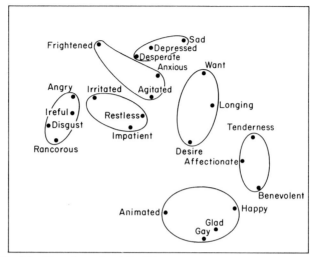

Fig. 6-2. Two-dimensional Euclidean representation of Ekman's data.

exactly to his, that we have one cluster which combines three clusters in his solution, and that our fourth cluster corresponds to the hierarchic union of his remaining two clusters. If we relax our rather conservative significance criterion, using a value of 3.5 rather than of 4.0, then our clusters correspond almost exactly to those obtained by Dietze. The clusters found using this more relaxed criterion are indicated in Fig. 6-2. Following Dietze's terminology we find a JOY cluster: HAPPY-GLAD-GAY-ANIMATED; a LOVE cluster: AFFECTIONATE-TENDERNESS-BENEVOLENT, these being subsumable under an ACCEPT-ANCE rubric; two clusters: AGITATED-ANXIOUS-FRIGHTENED, and RESTLESS-IMPATIENT-IRRITATED, which come together in Dietze's analysis and which he describes with the title UNREST; a DISCOMFORT cluster: SAD-DEPRESSED-DESPERATE; a LONGING cluster: LONGING-WANT-DESIRE, the last three clusters he subsumes under the rubric DISTURBANCE; and a REJECTION cluster: ANGRY-IREFUL-DISGUST-RANCOROUS, which corresponds to the two sub-clusters of ANGRY-IREFUL and DISGUST-RANCOROUS distinguished by Dietze. It would appear that a typal or hierarchic representation allows us to make rather more sense of Ekman's data than does a dimensional one.

Block (1957) selected some 15 emotion names with the intention of providing a relatively "comprehensive coverage of the affective sphere" and had subjects rate each of these in terms of 20 semantic differential scales. He correlated and factored the resulting score matrix extracting three factors, a Pleasantness-Unpleasantness dimension, a factor corresponding to an Activation dimension, and, finally, a unipolar factor defined by SYMPATHY,

NOSTALGIA, and GRIEF, which he termed Interpersonal Relatedness. We reanalyzed these data using MDS and cluster procedures. The two-dimensional solution yielded by the MDS analysis is shown in Fig. 6-3; the fit here is excellent with stress value of only 0.037. (The stress values for the three-dimensional and one-dimensional solutions are 0.016 and 0.273, respectively.) The emotion names arrange themselves rather neatly on the

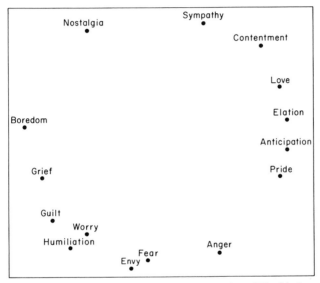

Fig. 6-3. Two-dimensional Euclidean representation of Block's data.

circumference of a circle. While an inspection of the plot indicates the presence of some sort of a Pleasantness-Unpleasantness contrast, there is little evidence for an Activation dimension, and even less for Block's third factor of Interpersonal Relatedness.

The methodological implication of this reanalysis is quite clear, namely, that different techniques of data analysis may result in what appear to be different substantive outcomes. Our reasons for preferring the configuration yielded by the MDS analysis derive from the fact that this analysis is based on weaker assumptions and yet yields a more interesting structure, and a more parsimonious solution with excellent fit. Substantively, however, we are hard put to provide any coherent interpretation for the putative single dimension that appears to have generated this circular array. The results of the cluster analysis were not very revealing, the terms falling into two significant clusters: LOVE*, PRIDE*, CONTENTMENT, SYMPATHY, ELATION and ANTICIPATION* falling into one cluster, and ANGER*, ENVY*, HUMILIATION*, NOSTALGIA, BOREDOM, GRIEF*, FEAR*, WORRY* and GUILT* into the other, indicating a Pleasantness-Unpleasantness contrast, but revealing little more than that. The ten terms with asterisks are ones whose Hebrew translation equivalents occurred among the 15 emotion terms employed in the present study; the other terms we used are (in translation) CONTEMPT, DISGUST, SADNESS, JOY and SURPRISE. The ten common terms lie on roughly half of a circle in Fig. 6-3, and we shall be interested in seeing whether these points will fall in a more or less circular configuration in our data, or whether their arrangement will be substantially altered as a function of the other terms in the set being judged, since there is only overlap for two-thirds of the terms used in the two studies (not to speak of differences between Hebrew and English).

It seems obvious that beyond the ubiquitous Pleasantness-Unpleasantness contrast, the studies of emotion names we have cited, as well as one or two others that might have been cited, e.g., Plutchik (1962), and Nummenmaa (1964), referred to in Osgood (1966a), have not yielded any very clear results either with regard to whether a dimensional or typal model is the more appropriate one, or as to the nature of the underlying dimensions or types. And we can hardly expect that the present study will resolve the substantive issues involved, especially considering the fact that only 15 names were sampled from the vast potential array of emotion names. Our purpose in carrying out this study is principally methodological. Wishing to minimize constraints on judgment, we used four different techniques to elicit similarity judgments, requiring subjects to rank pairs of emotion names with regard to a similarity or dissimilarity criterion, to build a similarity tree using the names (all techniques we have also used in other studies, see, e.g. Chapter 3), as well as requiring subjects to rate directly the similarity between every pair of terms, a procedure in very common use among psychologists. Our main interest then is to see whether the results would remain more or less invariant, given differences in techniques of data collection. Further, these results were analyzed concurrently by means of MDS and clustering procedures (as well as by graph techniques) in an attempt to provide some basis for choosing between dimensional and hierarchical-typological models. We were interested in seeing what sorts of structure might emerge from an analysis of the present data, in how these results might compare with the findings of previous studies, and what relation there might be between such results obtained for the semantic domain of emotion names and results yielded by an analysis of the relations among emotions judged to be present in facial expressions. Direct comparison with earlier results will not be possible, however, since, to the best of our knowledge, there are no previous studies based on similarity judgments of emotion names which have employed the same techniques for data collection and analysis, and since, in any case, the sampling of emotion names has varied considerably from study to study, e.g., there is hardly any overlap between the 15 terms employed by Block and the 23 terms used by Ekman.

METHOD

The subjects were 60 male and female Israeli undergraduates enrolled at the Hebrew University of Jerusalem, who volunteered to participate in a language experiment and were paid IL3 (approximately $1) for their participation. There were four groups, each comprising 15 randomly selected subjects. The subjects in Group ET constructed labeled trees, employing the criterion of similarity in meaning, while the subjects in Groups ECS and ECD constructed complete undirected graphs. Printed on one page and presented to the latter two groups were 105 pairs of emotion names arranged in a random order. The subjects in Group ECS were required to rank order all pairs in terms of similarity in meaning, and the subjects in Group ECD rank ordered the pairs in terms of dissimilarity in meaning. The subjects in Group ER were presented with all 105 pairs of emotion names in the same random order as Groups ECS and ECD, and were asked to rate each pair with regard to dissimilarity on a 1–19 rating scale.

Fifteen emotion names were selected with the intention of obtaining a coverage of the sphere of emotions and partial overlap with the emotion names employed by Block. As noted in the preceding section, the original list used by Block was not employed since some of the terms (such as NOSTALGIA and SYMPATHY) are difficult to translate into Hebrew.

RESULTS

Graph Analysis

Since our main purpose in this study is methodological, we shall only investigate properties that may differentiate between randomly and non-randomly constructed graphs, and then move to the more interesting cluster and MDS analyses. Starting with Group ET, we first checked whether subjects in this group employed all three options in constructing trees, tracing the labeled links in each tree and counting the number of subtrees for each subject. The mean number of subtrees was 3.60, and was of the same order of magnitude as in Groups KTM and KTF in Chapter 3. With only one exception, the subjects in Group ET constructed several subtrees and merged them into one tree toward the end of the task.

Table 6-1 presents the predicted and observed frequency distributions of node degree. The difference between the two distributions is significant ($p < 0.05$, by the one-sample Kolmogorov-Smirnov test), indicating that trees were not constructed randomly. Moreover, the differences between predicted and observed frequencies are similar to the ones observed in previous chapters—there are fewer nodes with degree $r = 1$ and more with degree $r = 2$ than predicted by the Poisson distribution.

TABLE 6-1   Observed and Predicted Frequency Distributions of Node Degree (Group ET)

Degree	Predicted	Observed
1	89	69
2	83	123
3	38	28
4	12	4
5+	3	1

Table 6-2 shows the observed distribution of the number of pairs of adjacent nodes chosen by y subjects from Group ET, $y = 0, 1, \ldots, 15$. The parameters of the negative binomial distribution, p and s, are presented in the lower part of the table, and the predicted frequencies are shown in the last column. The results are consistent with those reported in Chapters 3, 4 and 5—the negative binomial distribution provides a very good fit to the data ($p > 0.20$, by the one-sample Kolmogorov-Smirnov test). The results thus provide additional evidence refuting the hypothesis of a random construction of graphs, and supporting the assumption that the popularity of pairs of emotion names is gamma distributed. The most popular pairs of nodes, all of which were selected by the majority of the subjects in their first three choices, are SADNESS-GRIEF, FEAR-WORRY, and JOY-LOVE; the first two pairs are "unpleasant," whereas the last pair is "pleasant."

TABLE 6-2   Observed and Predicted Frequency Distributions of Selected Pairs of Adjacent Nodes (Group ET)[a]

y	Predicted	Observed
0	49	51
1	18	21
2	11	7
3	7	6
4	5	5
5	4	1
6	3	3
7	2	2
8	1	1
9	1	1
10	1	3
11+	3	4

[a]Parameters: p s
                0.182   0.445

We turn next to the graph analysis of Groups ECS and ECD. Table 6-3 shows the predicted cumulative probability that a random graph is completely connected. Presented also are the observed cumulative proportions of the graphs constructed by Groups ECS and ECD, completely connected by the first w links. The difference between the observed proportions and predicted probabilities, tested by the one-sample Kolmogorov-Smirnov test, is not significant for either group ($p > 0.20$), suggesting, as in Chapter 3, that either the graphs of Groups ECS and ECD were constructed randomly, or that the statistic investigated here is not sufficiently sensitive to the biases operating in the construction of the graphs. The observed and predicted frequencies of nodes with degree r (for $N = n = 15$) are presented in Table 6-4. These results duplicate the ones obtained

TABLE 6-3   Observed and Predicted Cumulative Probability that G_{N,v_N} is Completely Connected (Groups ECS and ECD)

v_N	Predicted	Observed ECS	Observed ECD	v_N	Predicted	Observed ECS	Observed ECD
14	0.0320	0.066	0.066	29	0.6624	0.733	0.800
15	0.0689	0.133	0.133	30	0.6893	0.800	0.800
16	0.1102	0.133	0.133	31	0.7137	0.866	0.800
17	0.1550	0.266	0.133	32	0.7357	0.933	0.800
18	0.2025	0.333	0.133	33	0.7554	0.933	0.866
19	0.2512	0.400	0.200	34	0.7731	0.933	0.866
20	0.3003	0.400	0.200	35	0.7888	0.933	0.866
21	0.3490	0.400	0.266	36	0.8028	0.933	0.866
22	0.3965	0.400	0.266	37	0.8153	0.933	0.933
23	0.4422	0.400	0.266	38	0.8264	1.000	0.933
24	0.4857	0.400	0.466	39	0.8362	1.000	0.933
25	0.5266	0.466	0.533	40	0.8449	1.000	0.933
26	0.5649	0.666	0.666	50	0.8905	1.000	1.000
27	0.6002	0.666	0.733	60	0.9028	1.000	1.000
28	0.6327	0.733	0.800				

TABLE 6-4   Observed and Predicted Frequency Distributions of Node Degree for 15 Graphs with $n = 15$ (Groups ECS and ECD)

r	Predicted	Observed ECS	Observed ECD
0	22	20	32
1	61	63	71
2	71	75	58
3	46	40	26
4	19	20	23
5	5	7	6
6+	1	0	9

with Groups CCS and CCD in Chapter 3, i.e., the difference between observed and predicted frequencies is nonsignificant for Group ECS but highly significant for Group ECD.

We turn next to an examination of another property of undirected graphs—the number of cycles of order k—which seems to be more sensitive than other graph statistics to the existence of discrepancies between observed and predicted results, and to differences between groups using different criteria for constructing complete undirected graphs. Presented in Table 6-5 is the number of observed graphs with C cycles of order $k = 3$ and $k = 4$; the means are presented in the bottom of the table. The difference between the two means and $M(g_3)$, obtained from equation 3, is significant ($p < 0.05$) for Group ECS, but nonsignificant for Group ECD, showing a strong "triangular bias" for the former group in the early part of the task, and none for the latter. The opposite result was obtained when cycles of order $k = 4$ were examined—subjects in Group ECD showed a strong "rectangular bias" in the early part of the task, while Group ECS showed no such bias.

TABLE 6-5   Number of Observed Cycles of Order k for $n = 15$ (Groups ECS and ECD)

	$k = 3$		$k = 4$	
C	Group ECS	Group ECD	Group ECS	Group ECD
0	2	6	3	2
1	4	5	8	3
2	2	0	2	3
3	5	4	1	3
4	1	0	0	1
5	0	0	1	0
6	0	0	0	3
7	1	0	0	0
Mean	3.266	1.133	1.333	2.666
SD	1.159	0.995	0.888	1.644

In summary, the analysis of graphs suggests that these were not constructed randomly. Rather, biases very similar to the ones observed in the preceding two chapters operated in the early part of the task, and certain pairs of emotion names, e.g., LOVE-JOY, SADNESS-GRIEF, FEAR-WORRY, and CONTEMPT-DISGUST were more popular with the majority of subjects in Groups ET, ECS, and ECD than others. The relationships between graph and cluster analyses suggest that clusters will be formed around these pairs. We will test this conjecture in the following section.

Cluster Analysis

The Connectedness and Diameter methods were applied to the mean proximity matrix of each group, and to five individual proximity matrices selected randomly from each group. Similar HCSs were yielded by the two clustering methods for the mean proximity matrices, with more terms forming significant clusters under the Diameter method than under the Connectedness method. The number of significant clusters for the mean data was either one or two, and the significant clusters obtained by the Connectedness method were always subclusters of the significant clusters obtained by the Diameter method when applied to the same data. Neither of the two clustering methods yielded any significant cluster for nine out of the 20 individual proximity matrices analyzed. For the remaining 11 cases, the HCSs of the subjects in Groups ECS, ECD, and ER typically corresponded to the HCS of the mean data, while this was not the case for Group ET. It seems, then, that the HCS for the mean proximity matrix of Group ET may not adequately represent the individual HCSs in this group.

Figures 6-4, 6-5, 6-6, and 6-7 portray the HCSs, obtained by the Diameter method, of the mean proximity matrices of Groups ET, ECS, ECD, and ER, respectively. As in previous chapters, significant clusters are denoted by lines connecting the corresponding "x's", while the numbers in the right-hand column of each figure are the α measures of the clusterings. The major finding is that the HCSs of Groups ECS, ECD, and ER are essentially the same. Two significant clusters, which consist of all 15 terms, emerge in each of the three groups, yielding zero distances among the MAXC clusterings. The first significant cluster, consisting of PRIDE, LOVE, JOY, SURPRISE, and ANTICIPATION, may be interpreted, though somewhat hesitantly, as a Pleasantness cluster (note, however, that *surprises* are not always pleasant and *anticipations* may be quite frustrating). The second significant cluster, formed by the remaining ten terms, is a sort of Unpleasantness cluster. The cluster analysis results for Groups ECS, ECD, and ER are consistent with the cluster analysis of Block's data which yielded two significant clusters, i.e., a Pleasantness cluster consisting of LOVE, PRIDE, ANTICIPATION, SYMPATHY, CONTENTMENT, and ELATION, and an Unpleasantness cluster including the terms ANGER, ENVY, FEAR, HUMILI-ATION, NOSTALGIA, BOREDOM, GRIEF, WORRY, and GUILT. The ten terms out of 15, which appeared in both lists, were clustered in precisely the same way.

The close similarity of Figs. 6-5, 6-6, and 6-7 may be better noticed when other features of the HCS, in addition to the significance of clusters, are carefully examined. Inspection of these three figures shows that the pairs LOVE-JOY and SADNESS-SORROW are among the first to be clustered, as conjectured in the preceding section; CONTEMPT-DISGUST-HUMILIATION is

```
                                                                          Z
                           Z                                              O
                           O                                             H
                          H                                              H
                         H                                              A
                   T     A                          S           S       P
                   P     I                          S           S       I
                   M     L                          E           I       C
                   E  T  I              E       E   N       S   R       I
                   T  S  M           R  V    D  D   D       E   P       T
                   N  U  U  R     E  R  Y  L  I  R  A  J    S   R       N
             L     O  G  H  E  Y  V  O  O  R  E  O  D  O    I   I       A
             e     C  S  A  G  N  O  R  V  P  O  E  N  L    R   S        |
             v     O  I  N  N  E  R  P  E  I  W  F  E  I    G   U        |
             e     C  D  G  A  V  P  W  F  G  W  G  S  G  J  O  S  ...   α
             l     N  I  U  N  N  R  O  E  U  O  U  A  R  O  Y  R        |
                   T  S  M  G  Y  I  R  A  I  R  I  D  I  Y     P        |
                      T  I  E     D  R  R  L  R  L  N  E     E           |
                         L  R     E  Y        T  Y  E  F     R

    1    ·  ·        ·  ·  ·  ·        XXXX        ·  ·  ·  ·    ·   ·         3.3
    2    ·  ·        ·  ·  ·  ·        XXXX     ·  XXXX         ·      ·      ·     4.4
    3    XXXX  ·     ·  ·  ·  ·        XXXX     ·  XXXX         ·      ·      ·    11.3
    4    XXXX  ·     ·  ·  ·  ·        XXXX     ·  XXXX    XXXX       ·•           12.4
    5    XXXXXXX     ·  ·  ·  ·        XXXX     ·  XXXX    XXXX            ·       14.1
    6    XXXXXXX  ·  XXXX  ·           XXXX     ·  XXXX    XXXX            ·       15.2
    7    XXXXXXX  ·  XXXX  ·       XXXXXXX  XXXX  XXXX                     ·       19.1
    8    XXXXXXX  ·  XXXX  ·       XXXXXXX  XXXX  XXXXXXX                          21.3
    9    XXXXXXX  ·  XXXX  ·     XXXXXXXXXXXXX    XXXXXXX                          21.7
   10    XXXXXXX  ·  XXXXXXX     XXXXXXXXXXXXX    XXXXXXX                          27.4
   11    XXXXXXX     XXXXXXXXXX  XXXXXXXXXXXXX    XXXXXXX                          31.6
   12    XXXXXXX     XXXXXXXXXX  XXXXXXXXXXXXXXXXXXXXXXXX                          36.7
   13    XXXXXXX     XXXXXXXXXXXXXXXXXXXXXXXXXXXXXXXXXXXXXXX                       41.7
   14    XXXXXXXXXXXXXXXXXXXXXXXXXXXXXXXXXXXXXXXXXXXXXXXX                          54.1
```

Fig. 6-4. HCS for Group ET (Diameter method).

```
                                                            Z
                           Z                                O
                           O                               H
                          H                                H
                         H                                A            E
                   T     A                          S     P           S
                   P     I                          S     I           I
                   M     L                          E     C           R
                   E  T  I           E              N  R  I           P
                   T  S  M           V        D     D  E  T        N  R
                   N  U  U  R     F  Y  L  S  R  A  A  G  N  E  L  O  U
             L     O  G  H  W  E  E  L  O  U  I  N  D  N  A  V  O  I  S
             e     C  S  A  O  A  A  I  V  I  E  G  N  A  T  N  V  T  E
             v     O  I  N  R  R  R  G  E  L  F  E  E  T  I  Y  E  A   |
             e     C  D  G  R     (…)                 S  I  C            |
             l     N  I  U  Y                         S  P  A  ...       α
                   T  S  M                              R  A             |

    1    ·  ·  ·        ·     ·     ·        ·     ·     ·      XXXX   ·   ·      95.7
    2    ·  ·  ·     ·  XXXX        ·     ·     ·     ·        XXXX    ·   ·      92.9
    3    ·  ·  ·     ·  XXXX  XXXX        ·  ·     ·        XXXX       ·   ·      90.2
    4    ·  ·  ·     XXXXXXX  XXXX        ·  ·     ·        XXXX       ·   ·      84.9
    5    XXXX  ·     XXXXXXX  XXXX        ·  ·     ·        XXXX       ·   ·      79.7
    6    XXXX  ·     XXXXXXX  XXXX  XXXX        ·        XXXX          ·   ·      74.6
    7    XXXX  ·     XXXXXXX  XXXX  XXXX        ·        XXXXXXX           ·      73.1
    8    XXXXXXX     XXXXXXX  XXXX  XXXX        ·        XXXXXXX           ·      68.9
    9    XXXXXXX     XXXXXXXXXXXXX  XXXX        ·        XXXXXXX           ·      67.4
   10    XXXXXXX     XXXXXXXXXXXXX  XXXX        ·     XXXXXXXXX                   57.4
   11    XXXXXXX     XXXXXXXXXXXXXXXXXXXX       ·     XXXXXXXXX                   50.9
   12    XXXXXXX     XXXXXXXXXXXXXXXXXXXXXXX       XXXXXXXXXXXX                   39.2
   13    XXXXXXXXXXXXXXXXXXXXXXXXXXXXXXXXXXXX       XXXXXXXXXXXX                  38.5
   14    XXXXXXXXXXXXXXXXXXXXXXXXXXXXXXXXXXXXXXXXXXXXXXXX                          5.1
```

Fig. 6-5. HCS for Group ECS (Diameter method).

Level	CONTEMPT	DISGUST	HUMILIATION	WORRY	FEAR	GUILT	SADNESS	GRIEF	ANGER	ENVY	PRIDE	LOVE	JOY	SURPRISE	ANTICIPATION	α
1	·	·	·	·	·	·	·	·	·	·	·	X	X	·	·	9.1
2	·	·	·	X	X	·	·	·	·	·	·	X	X	·	·	15.3
3	·	·	·	X	X	·	X	X	·	·	·	X	X	·	·	18.1
4	X	X	·	X	X	·	X	X	·	·	·	X	X	·	·	19.8
5	X	X	X	X	X	·	X	X	·	·	·	X	X	·	·	27.9
6	X	X	X	X	X	X	X	X	·	·	·	X	X	·	·	29.7
7	X	X	X	X	X	X	X	X	X	X	·	X	X	·	·	31.3
8	X	X	X	X	X	X	X	X	X	X	·	X	X	X	·	32.5
9	X	X	X	X	X	X	X	X	X	X	·	X	X	X	X	37.3
10	X	X	X	X	X	X	X	X	X	X	·	X	X	X	X	53.8
11	X	X	X	X	X	X	X	X	X	X	·	X	X	X	X	56.3
12	X	X	X	X	X	X	X	X	X	X	X	X	X	X	X	61.3
13	X	X	X	X	X	X	X	X	X	X	X	X	X	X	X	64.9
14	X	X	X	X	X	X	X	X	X	X	X	X	X	X	X	95.7

Fig. 6-6. HCS for Group ECD (Diameter method).

Level	DISGUST	CONTEMPT	HUMILIATION	WORRY	FEAR	GUILT	SADNESS	GRIEF	ANGER	ENVY	PRIDE	LOVE	JOY	SURPRISE	ANTICIPATION	α
1	·	·	·	X	X	·	·	·	·	·	·	·	·	·	·	2.6
2	·	·	·	X	X	·	X	X	·	·	·	·	·	·	·	3.6
3	·	·	·	X	X	X	X	X	·	·	·	·	·	·	·	3.9
4	·	·	·	X	X	X	X	X	·	·	·	X	X	·	·	5.7
5	·	X	X	X	X	X	X	X	·	·	·	X	X	·	·	5.8
6	·	X	X	X	X	X	X	X	·	·	·	X	X	X	X	5.9
7	·	X	X	X	X	X	X	X	X	X	·	X	X	X	X	7.7
8	·	X	X	X	X	X	X	X	X	X	X	X	X	X	X	8.5
9	X	X	X	X	X	X	X	X	X	X	X	X	X	X	X	9.3
10	X	X	X	X	X	X	X	X	X	X	X	X	X	X	X	9.9
11	X	X	X	X	X	X	X	X	X	X	X	X	X	X	X	12.3
12	X	X	X	X	X	X	X	X	X	X	X	X	X	X	X	14.1
13	X	X	X	X	X	X	X	X	X	X	X	X	X	X	X	15.3
14	X	X	X	X	X	X	X	X	X	X	X	X	X	X	X	17.5

Fig. 6-7. HCS for Group ER (Diameter method).

a cluster formed early merged with the cluster WORRY-FEAR-GUILT-SADNESS-GRIEF-ANGER-ENVY only on level 13; the latter cluster consists of three (nonsignificant) distinct clusters, i.e., WORRY-FEAR-GUILT, SADNESS-GRIEF, and ANGER-ENVY, which are merged together on level 11; and PRIDE is either the last (Groups ECS and ECD) or the one before the last (Group ER) term to be clustered. Moreover, with only two minor interchanges of adjacent terms (ANTICIPATION and SURPRISE in Fig. 6-5, and DISGUST and CONTEMPT in Fig. 6-7) the 15 terms are arranged in the top row of each figure in exactly the same order. The α measures for Group ECD and the $105-\alpha$ measures for Group ECS are also quite close for all levels of clustering, showing that similar clusterings in these two groups were formed at approximately the same stage of the ranking process.

The HCS for Group ET (Fig. 6-4) not only does not seem to represent the individual results in Group ET, but also seems to have little in common with the other three HCSs (Figs. 6-5, 6-6, and 6-7). For one thing, it consists of two significant clusters which do not include all the 15 terms. These clusters vary considerably from the two significant clusters obtained for Groups ECS, ECD, and ER, they do not exhibit the Pleasantness-Unpleasantness contrast, and they defy interpretation. A closer look at Fig. 6-4, however, shows that the four HCSs for the mean proximity data share some other features. In particular, if the two clusters (which are kept distinct up to level 11): ANGER-ENVY-LOVE-PRIDE, and WORRY-FEAR-GUILT-SADNESS-GRIEF were interchanged in Fig. 6-4, the arrangement of the 15 terms in all four groups would be approximately the same. Note, also, that the four clusters WORRY-FEAR, SADNESS-GRIEF, CONTEMPT-DISGUST, and JOY-SURPRISE in Fig. 6-4 are among the first to be formed, as in the other three groups, that the cluster CONTEMPT-DISGUST-HUMILIATION is kept distinct until the last level of clustering, and that PRIDE is the one before the last term to be clustered. The MDS analysis of the mean data may better show how close Group ET is to the other three groups.

Multidimensional Scaling Analysis

We applied the Young-Torgerson nonmetric MDS to the proximity matrices of the 20 randomly selected subjects, five from each group, and to the four mean proximity matrices. One-, two-, and three-dimensional representations were obtained for both the Euclidean and City Block metrics, with the former metric yielding smaller stress values in almost all cases. The stress values for the Euclidean representations for one, two, and three dimensions are presented in Table 6-6. The table shows that the stress values of Groups ECS, ECD, and ER are very close to one another, but that the stress values of Group ET for three and two dimensions are considerably smaller. Similar, though somewhat smaller discrepancies between the stress values of the four tree construction groups and

TABLE 6-6 Stress Values for Euclidean Representations

Dimensions	No. 4	No. 5	Group ET No. 9	No. 11	No. 13	Mean
3	0.022	0.017	0.090	0.014	0.021	0.034
2	0.030	0.038	0.107	0.015	0.028	0.072
1	0.104	0.103	0.210	0.104	0.295	0.283
Dimensions	No. 2	No. 4	Group ECS No. 8	No. 9	No. 14	Mean
3	0.143	0.144	0.128	0.132	0.121	0.098
2	0.239	0.194	0.212	0.212	0.176	0.164
1	0.397	0.386	0.360	0.322	0.265	0.279
Dimensions	No. 4	No. 6	Group ECD No. 7	No. 8	No. 12	Mean
3	0.153	0.168	0.117	0.017	0.146	0.084
2	0.247	0.246	0.215	0.023	0.229	0.153
1	0.442	0.393	0.342	0.041	0.427	0.268
Dimensions	No. 1	No. 4	Group ER No. 9	No. 10	No. 15	Mean
3	0.117	0.137	0.156	0.168	0.151	0.089
2	0.188	0.208	0.214	0.241	0.217	0.153
1	0.377	0.389	0.319	0.418	0.347	0.287

the group constructing complete undirected graphs, were reported in Chapter 4 (Table 4-9). A comparison of the kinship study with the present study shows that, for three and two dimensions, the stress values of the tree construction groups in both studies are about the same, but that the stress values of Group KC are smaller than the ones for Groups ECS and ECD. Moreover, the stress values for individual subjects constructing complete graphs (with the exception of subject No. 8 in Group ECD) are larger in both studies than the stress values for the mean data, whereas the stress values for individual and mean data in the tree construction groups are about the same.

A comparison of the stress values of the mean proximity data with the critical cut-off values presented in Chapter 2 shows the former to be considerably smaller for $m = 2$. The break in the stress values between $m = 1$ and $m = 2$, as well as the attainment of two-dimensional representations in other studies of emotion names, presented in the introductory section of this chapter, suggests an adequate representability of our data in a two-dimensional Euclidean space. Figures 6-8 to 6-11 portray these representations for the mean proximity data of the four groups. Significant clusters discovered by the Diameter method (see Figs. 6-4 to 6-7) are circled in each figure. If the clusters plotted on the representations are ignored, all four figures seem to be remarkably similar to one

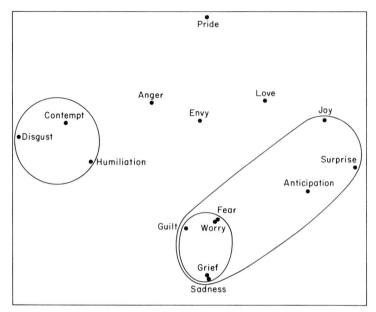

Fig. 6-8.   Two-dimensional Euclidean representation for Group ET.

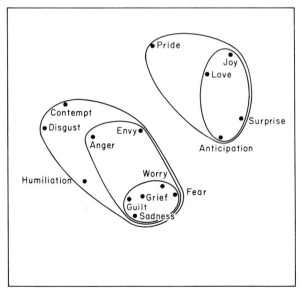

Fig. 6-9.   Two-dimensional Euclidean representation for Group ECS.

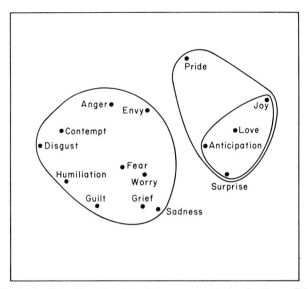

Fig. 6-10. Two-dimensional Euclidean representation for Group ECD.

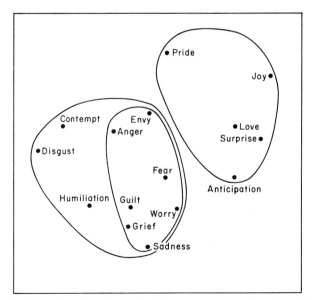

Fig. 6-11. Two-dimensional Euclidean representation for Group ER.

another. To get a better measure of similarity than is possible by simple inspection of the figures, the distances between all the points and the origin were computed for each group, and then intercorrelated. All six product-moment correlations were highly significant ($p < 0.01$), ranging between 0.76 and 0.89. In particular, the correlation between the distances of Group ET and those of Groups ECS, ECD, and ER, were 0.81, 0.76, and 0.86, respectively, indicating that Group ET is as highly similar to the other three groups as they are to one another.

The remarkable degree of similarity among the four two-dimensional representations implies that as far as the mean proximity data are concerned there were no significant differences among the four data collection methods. One must be careful, though, in any attempts at substantive interpretation of the resulting representations, since discrepancies between representations for individual subjects and mean data in all four groups are larger than the ones obtained in the preceding chapters. Attempts to interpret individual representations or to classify subjects according to their representations were, by and large, fruitless. Some of the individual representations were quite similar to the ones portrayed in Figs. 6-8 to 6-11, but most of them were dissimilar, with the same clusters arranged in all sorts of patterns in the two-dimensional representations.

DISCUSSION

We shall begin with some methodological comments with regard to the yield of different methods of obtaining data and the conjoint use of cluster and MDS procedures in the analysis of data, and shall then turn to some observations on the substantive outcomes of the present study.

The results provide a clear answer to our question regarding the relations among the four techniques for collection of data—the four two-dimensional representations are essentially the same; three out of the four HCSs are just about identical and while the fourth, that for Group ET obtained by use of the tree building technique, differs in some ways from others it also has some important features in common with them. Thus these procedures, all of which are unconstrained in that they do not prespecify the bases for judgment but only require the assessment of similarities among items in various ways, yield largely similar mean or average results.

In principle, the concurrent use of MDS and clustering procedures should provide a systematic technique for evaluating the appropriateness of typal and dimensional models, a problem dealt with in an informal and intuitive way by Osgood (1966a) and more formally by Degerman (1968). However, in the present case, the results leave this question quite open. While the fit of the MDS scaling solution is adequate in two dimensions, no coherent interpretation of the configurations obtained seems possible (beyond noticing the ever-present Pleasantness-Unpleasantness contrast) and examination of the plots for the three-dimensional solutions does not clarify matters. Further, inspection of the clusters embedded in the MDS solution indicates that these are by no means compact. All of the above suggests that a spatial model may not be an appropriate one in this instance. However, the clustering results are very gross indeed; the two significant clusters obtained, which again involve a Pleasantness-Unpleasantness contrast, hardly provide strong justification for a typal or hierarchical model. While the present clustering results agree with those of Block with regard to the presence of a Pleasantness-Unpleasantness contrast (which in a sense may also be found in Ekman's data if one recalls Dietze's reanalysis and considers the ACCEPTANCE super-cluster versus the REJEC-TION and DISTURBANCE super-clusters), the configurations obtained by MDS analysis in the present study by no means resemble the circular configuration obtained for Block's data, and the ten terms common to both lists are rather differently distributed in the corresponding representations. Discrepancies in results between the present study and that of Block may be due to differences with regard to any one or more of the following: (1) in methods of data collection—Block had his subjects rate the terms using a set of Semantic Differential scales while we required less constrained similarity judgments; (2) in proximity measures used—Block used correlation coefficients, while we used graph distances or ratings; and (3) in emotion terms presented for evaluation—there was only partial overlap between the lists, which in Block's case were composed of English terms, and in our case of Hebrew ones. In either case one might wonder as to the likelihood of providing an adequate or comprehensive sampling of the vast array of emotion names by use of only 15 terms.

Why were there no clear-cut and interpretable substantive findings? The fact that the different methods of data collection yielded rather similar results upon MDS analysis and fairly similar results upon clustering analysis, as well as the graph results which indicate systematic departures from randomness, argue that there really is something orderly in the data; the difficulty lies in identifying the basis for this order. One possibility is that, for the case of emotion names, the mean data may be relatively unrepresentative and, therefore, not particularly revealing. As was noted earlier, discrepancies between representations for individual subjects and for the mean data were larger than those obtained in the previous chapters. Perhaps it is not that people fail to distinguish among emotion names, but rather that the bases for such discriminations are more likely to be idiosyncratic, once some very gross contrasts such as that of Pleasantness-Unpleasantness are out of the way. The reason for such greater idiosyncratic differences in the judgment of emotion terms may reside in the fact that insofar as they name internal experiential states, their referents cannot be externalized; it is therefore very difficult to get precise consensual validation in their use, and there may arise systematic individual differences with regard to their organization, and with regard to the basis governing discrimination among such terms. Clearly such speculations can only be checked by means of intensive, comparative consideration of individual data, a matter to which we did not address ourselves in the present study. One might hazard the guess that while such an enterprise would reveal significant inter-individual differences in the organization of the semantic domain of emotion terms, the bases for such different organizations might still be very difficult to determine. Consider by way of example the MDS scaling results for Subject 8 in Group ECD, who rank ordered all 105 pairs of emotion names in terms of a dissimilarity criterion. The stress values for this subject were particularly low (see Table 6-6), and inspection of his two-dimensional representation showed the terms to be nicely arranged on the circumference of a half-circle in the following order: LOVE, JOY, PRIDE, SURPRISE, ANTICIPATION, SADNESS, GRIEF, FEAR, WORRY, ANGER, ENVY, GUILT, CONTEMPT, HUMILIATION, and DISGUST. There is something sensible about the arrangement of the terms in that most of them seem to be appropriately bracketed or surrounded by other terms; nevertheless, we have not been able to formulate any intelligible principle to account for the half circle swept out by them.

By way of summary, it must be obvious that while our results permit some methodological observations, they do not provide much warrant for any positive substantive conclusions. Rather, the present results as well as the outcomes of our reanalysis of some earlier work might be regarded as constituting fairly impressive evidence against the adequacy of the various sorts of theoretical conceptualizations that have been offered for the realm of emotions or emotion names. Our results, which are largely invariant over different methods of data collection, appear to be inconsistent with these accounts. While the principal substantive burden of the results is thus negative, the finding of pervasive individual differences in the use of emotion terms, which may make averaged data unrevealing, suggests that what may be required is not one theory for the domain of emotions, but perhaps a set of characterizations whose members may differ systematically in important ways.

Chapter 7   *PREPOSITIONS*

While syntactic considerations often govern the choice of prepositions, some prepositions have independent semantic content. As Fillmore puts it (1969b, p. 367) "In locative phrases, though in some cases the preposition may be automatically determined, generally the choice is optional: *over, under, in, on, beside,* etc., these are the prepositions that bring with them semantic information." Prepositions which appear to involve some sort of spatial reference, whether of location or direction, constitute a relatively small, closed set of terms, and are often critical for accurate description. While distinctions between prepositions may often be fine ones, they are important in capturing significant differences in meaning. Children have considerable and persistent difficulty in acquiring control of prepositions (see, e.g., the work of Feovanov and that of Sokhin as cited in Slobin, 1966), and so do adults trying to cope with a foreign language (in a recent advertising supplement to the *New York Times* sponsored by the West German government there was prominently displayed a drawing said to be of "a German student in Harvard)." These problems may stem both from difficulties in identifying the primitive semantic elements or markers which are constitutive of the meaning of the prepositions, and difficulties in discovering the "minimal combination of markers which differentiates one preposition from another within a given language (Cooper, 1968)." Such problems may be exacerbated by the fact that many of the prepositions are polysemous, see, e.g., Sastri (1968), who describes the various senses in which some ten prepositions are used in a small sampling taken from *Chemical Abstracts*, or see West (1953), based on a much larger sample.

While there have been various linguistic analyses of English prepositions (see, e.g., Bennett, 1968), and some psycholinguistic work (see comments in Riegel,

1970), by way of background we shall focus on one linguistic analysis of locative prepositions, that of Cooper (1968), and what is perhaps the most directly pertinent and extensive experimental study available, that of Clark (1968). Cooper has attempted to characterize English locative prepositions in terms of a set of properties of visual space, in terms of perceptual properties of objects that the various prepositions make salient. Locative prepositions are considered as specifying relation-concepts with two or more arguments:

> A reading for a preposition consists of a complex semantic marker which itself consists of a relation marker and function markers operating as objects. The markers themselves are concepts relating to the perceptual space viewed and occupied by speakers of a language . . . the meaning of the preposition can be analyzed first with function concepts which pick out the relevant characteristics to be related and second with the relation concept describing the special relation between the values of the functions (pp. 1, 4).

Using as primitive semantic markers such notions as Space, Location, Contiguity-Separation, Boundary-Surface, Side, and Distal-Proximal, Cooper sought to specify the senses of the various prepositions in terms of complex relation markers defined in terms of these primitives or functions of them. Thus, to take an example, ABOVE in "X above Y" is defined as "X and Y are separate. X is located internal to the space Z, a bottom boundary of which is contiguous with the top of Y," and BELOW is defined identically except that the last part of the second condition now reads ". . . bottom of Y."

Cooper's procedure permits the identification of synonyms and near synonyms, e.g., BELOW, UNDER, UNDERNEATH, BENEATH, and of antonyms, where the contrast between terms is with regard to the value on just one marker, e.g., ABOVE versus BELOW, IN FRONT OF versus IN BACK OF. It also permits the specification of some other local relations or distinctions as e.g., that between ON TOP OF and ABOVE in terms of a contrast between contiguity and separation. However, the nature of the general system governing the organization of the whole domain is nowhere indicated by Cooper, and is by no means clear. The system is clearly not a paradigmatic one in any strong sense since all items do not have values on all markers. Besides, selection restrictions, indicating properties which limit the domain of some of the relations, are introduced in a (perhaps necessarily) unsystematic fashion. The fact that an attempt is being made to characterize these prepositions in terms of properties of visual space of itself obviously does not entail any simple dimensional or spatial representation. The fact that the analysis reveals the nature of some local relations between pairs or small subsets of terms as well as some further general organization, since the primitives sometimes recur, does not unambiguously indicate the overall properties of the system assumed to govern these relations.

There are other more general problems. While Cooper has quite properly restricted herself to a characterization of the locative senses of the prepositions she dealt with, many, if not most, of these terms have other nonspatial senses. Moreover, for quite a few of the terms, such senses may indeed be the more common or even predominant senses (seven of the ten prepositions whose polysemy Sastri documented are on Cooper's list and many of their uses, as indicated by the examples given, are nonspatial). In our study, however, the setting in which the terms were given to the subjects was one which probably made a spatial characterization salient, since they were presented *en masse*, without context, and some sort of spatial reference was one property all had in common. Thus, our data, insofar as there is overlap in about two-thirds of the terms between our list and that of Cooper, may be directly pertinent to her account. However, this in no way copes with the general problem, for if interest is in specifying the semantic structure underlying the relations among a set of prepositions, many of which have both spatial and nonspatial senses, then any procedure which at best only provides information with regard to spatial senses, which sometimes may not even be the dominant ones, will necessarily yield a partial account. Such a limitation in scope has its virtues, however, since in their other senses the use of these prepositions may be conditioned in complex ways by syntactic considerations, and be so constrained that any semantic analysis of the sort attempted here becomes impossible or yields results that are largely irrelevant. While recognizing this restriction on the scope of any findings, one can nevertheless examine the results of a study such as the present one to determine to what extent expectations regarding local structure are verified, and attempt to provide some general characterization of the overall structure obtaining for the entire set of prepositions, considered principally as spatial terms.

As the title of Clark's 1968 paper indicates ("On the use and meaning of prepositions"), he was particularly concerned with the relation between meaning and use, in characterizing the relations between the cognitive units involved in the processing of sentences built around prepositions and those involved in free association to these prepositions and in direct judgments of the similarities among them, and in demonstrating that, in a sense, the same cognitive units were always involved. Thus he attempted to indicate how a subject's implicit knowledge of syntax and semantics was involved in all three tasks (sentence composition, free association, and direct grouping), showing, for example, how free associations rather directly reflected a phrase-structure analysis of the prepositional phrases. To some extent Clark was less concerned with providing an account of the particular semantic structure actually governing the organization of the prepositions. Of the five measures he obtained and analyzed, the one most specifically relevant to that concern, which is our principal concern here, is the one based on a grouping task in which he had his subjects group the 33 prepositions he used according to their meanings. Similarity indices based on these groupings were subjected to MDS and clustering analyses, and "tight" and "loose" clusters were embedded in the two-dimensional solution. An inspection of this plot, Clark's Figure 1e, reveals that more or less synonymous and antonymous terms were characteristically clustered closely together (the latter, if anything more closely than the former), that "at a grosser level each cluster seems to neighbor on other clusters similar to it (p. 425)," and that in a very rough way some sort of dimensional interpretation might be imposed on the data in "that the largest differences in meaning among prepositions can be attributed to what might be called a movement-implied dimension—at the top are prepositions implying much movement (*up, down, above, across, over, off,* etc.), but at the bottom are prepositions devoid of movement connotations (p. 425)."

It should be stressed that this is a very rough account, for while in some measure the clusters seem to abut on each other in a sensible way it is difficult to specify what is involved in this. The dimensional interpretation noted above is a very rough one indeed, for it is not at all obvious that ABOVE and OVER, which fall at the "movement" end of this axis, involve more of a directional or motion component than TO and FROM, which fall toward the static end, and certainly the terms most extreme at that end, viz. AFTER, DURING, OF, and FOR, are devoid of movement but not so much because they are static as because they are not spatial terms at all. Clark does not attempt any interpretation of the other axis in the two-dimensional solution; at least some of the clusters in it are not compact, and nothing is said of the stress or adequacy of the two-dimensional solution except that "the true configuration is of many more dimensions (p. 424)." It seems fair to observe that no overall characterization of the nature of the underlying structural organization has been provided, and there is very little indication, even, as to whether a dimensional or a clustering representation is likely to be more appropriate.

There are some problems with the grouping data arising both from the way in which they were collected and the manner in which they were scored. Clark specified that the prepositions were to be sorted initially into from two to six groups, and each of these major groups was then to be divided into as many subgroups as the subject felt necessary. For each subject any pair of prepositions falling into the same subgroup was then given a score of 1, pairs falling in different subgroups of the same main group were given a score of 0.5, and pairs falling into different main groups were given a score of 0. The final values serving as input for the MDS and clustering analyses were the mean grouping scores over subjects for every pair of prepositions. It is not at all clear what biases may have been introduced by the original requirement limiting the number of main groups to be used (Clark does not indicate the average number actually formed) taken together with the arbitrary scoring that weights membership in the same subgroup twice as heavily as membership in the same main group. If, in fact, many subjects used only very few main groups with temporal and manner terms falling into separate groups and most of the remaining spatial terms into one or two other main groups, then the scoring system which gives heavy weight to differences in main group location might have unduly compacted the spatial terms. Given the averaging effects of individual differences, the scoring system may have made it more difficult to discern any clear structure in the data. The point is not so much that the preceding suggestion is necessarily correct, as that one cannot tell what constraints may have been imposed on the data by the procedures used. Parenthetically, it might be noted that while there are similarities between the solution yielded for the grouping data and those yielded for the other variables, these similarities are only moderate. Considering the rank-order correlations of the 528 similarity measures across the four most related variables, out of five, one obtains an average correlation of only 0.41 (the average correlation between the remaining variable—"words modified"—and the other variables is 0.10).

In the present study, working on the supposition that "the total pattern of similarity gives a comprehensive picture of the semantic relations . . . [that one needs] to treat prepositions and their meanings as a system of relations (Clark, 1968, p. 422)," we shall examine the similarity relations that obtain among some 29 English prepositions. Actually, two terms, AWAY and TOGETHER, are more properly to be considered as adverbs. They were included here since they both frequently occur in adverb-preposition clusters such as *away from* and *together with*. Each of the 29 terms has some spatial sense, although of course many of them also have other senses as well. As noted earlier, the experimental setting was such as to make the spatial senses of the terms salient for the subjects. In obtaining the data we used both a tree construction method and an unconstrained direct grouping method where, as usual, the similarity between any pair of terms is indexed by the frequency with which they are classified together. These data were analyzed by means of graph, MDS, and clustering procedures. We shall be interested in determining (1) whether the results are more or less invariant over different methods of data collection, (2) how the results compare with those of Clark, (3) whether, as indicated earlier, at least expectations with regard to local structure are borne out, and (4) whether a dimensional or a clustering representation is more appropriate for the data.

METHOD

Two groups of subjects participated in this experiment. Group PT consisted of 20 male and female undergraduates, enrolled at the University of North Carolina, who were requested to construct labeled trees using the standard instructions for this method (see Chapter 2). Group PDG consisted of 41 male and female subjects, sampled from the same population, who received the instructions for the Direct Grouping task. The subjects in Group PT were given the list of prepositions arranged alphabetically; they were run together in a large room and took about an hour to complete the task. The subjects in Group PDG were run in small groups of five to ten each. Each subject was given a large envelope containing four separate decks of IBM cards (the decks consisted of prepositions, HAVE, GOOD, and BAD words; the latter three sets of words will be discussed in the following chapters). Each card had a word printed on it, the cards in each deck being arranged alphabetically. The deck of prepositions always came either second or third in the series. Most subjects took between 10–15 minutes to sort the prepositions into as many separate piles as they wished.

The list of 29 prepositions presented to both groups is given in Table 7-1.

TABLE 7-1   Mean Node Degree and Mean Number of Terms Clustered with Each Preposition (Groups PT and PDG)

Term	Mean node degree	Mean number of terms clustered with each preposition
+ *ABOVE	2.40	2.76
+ *ACROSS	1.90	1.73
*ALONG	1.70	2.49
+ *AMONG	3.00	3.27
+ *AROUND	1.50	2.20
+ *AT	1.65	2.44
AWAY	2.15	2.44
+ BEHIND	1.75	1.00
+ BELOW	2.05	2.29
+ BESIDE	2.95	2.56
+ *BETWEEN	1.65	2.51
+ BEYOND	2.45	2.41
+ *BY	2.25	2.51
+ *DOWN	1.40	2.42
+ *FROM	2.45	2.05
+ *IN	2.15	2.80
*INTO	1.85	2.15
*OF	1.20	1.73
+ *ON	1.30	2.15
OUT	1.40	2.39
+ *OVER	2.45	2.71
*THROUGH	1.65	2.12
+ *TO	1.65	1.90
TOGETHER	1.55	3.02
*TOWARD	1.85	1.76
+ *UNDER	1.75	2.44
+ *UP	1.20	2.78
*WITH	2.55	3.24
+ *WITHIN	2.20	2.71

+ = terms discussed by Cooper; * = terms employed by Clark.

Appearing on the list are 20 of the prepositions discussed by Cooper (the + terms in Table 7-1), and 22 out of the 33 prepositions employed by Clark (the starred terms in Table 7-1). As mentioned above, with OF as a possible exception, our list included only locative and directional prepositions. We have not employed prepositions, many of which appear on Clark's list, which are devoid of spatial meaning.

RESULTS

Graph Analysis

Following the same order as in the preceding chapters, we begin the analysis by examining several statistical properties of the proximity data for the two groups. Starting with Group PT, the first property to be examined is the number of subtrees constructed by the subjects. Tracing over labeled links in each tree, counting the number of separate subtrees that were formed, and then averaging over subjects in Group PT resulted in a mean number of subtrees of 7.50 and a standard deviation of 2.53. With no exception, the subjects in Group PT used all three options in constructing trees, first building a relatively large number of subtrees and then merging these in the final stages of the task.

Table 7-2 shows the predicted and observed frequency distributions of node degree. The fit of the Poisson distribution is seen to be excellent, suggesting either that trees were constructed randomly, or, more likely, that the distribution of node degree cannot differentiate between randomly and nonrandomly constructed trees, and hence that other statistics ought to be examined.

TABLE 7-2 Observed and Predicted Frequency Distributions of Node Degree (Group PT)

Degree	Predicted	Observed
1	221	221
2	213	222
3	103	104
4	33	26
5	8	5
6+	2	2

Table 7-3 presents the observed and predicted distributions of pairs of adjacent nodes selected by y subjects, $y = 0, 1, \ldots, 20$. The values of the parameters of the predicted (negative binomial) distribution, estimated by the method of moments, are given in the lower part of the table. The difference between the observed and predicted distributions, tested by the one-sample Kolmogorov-Smirnov test, is nonsignificant ($p > 0.20$), as in all previous studies.

TABLE 7-3   Observed and Predicted Frequency Distributions of Pairs of Adjacent Nodes (Group PT)[a]

y	Predicted	Observed
0	263	274
1	50	47
2	26	21
3	17	12
4	11	8
5	9	9
6	6	6
7	5	6
8	4	5
9	3	2
10	2	6
11	2	0
12+	8	10

[a]Parameters:

p	s
0.137	0.219

The discrepancies between predicted and observed frequencies, though small and nonsignificant, are consistent with the ones observed in Chapters 3 and 4, i.e., the predicted frequency is smaller than the observed frequency for $y = 0$, but larger for $y = 1, 2, 3, 4$, thus casting doubt on the validity of the assumption of gamma distributed popularity of pairs of prepositions.

Inspection of Table 7-3 reveals that more than 67% of all pairs of prepositions were not linked (chosen) by even one subject, that ten pairs were selected by more than half of the subjects, and that relative to previously reported values of s, the present value ($s = 0.219$) is quite low, indicating a stronger "popularity bias." The most "popular" pairs of (adjacent) nodes, selected by at least 14 out of the 20 subjects, were (in decreasing order): BELOW-UNDER (20), ABOVE-OVER (19), TO-TOWARD (18), BESIDE-BY (17), IN-WITHIN (16), TOGETHER-WITH (16), AMONG-BETWEEN (14), AWAY-FROM (14), ACROSS-OVER (14), and ABOVE-UP (14).

More evidence disconfirming the hypothesis of a random construction of trees is obtained by an analysis of preposition degree. Counting for each subject the number of links affixed to each preposition (the preposition degree) and then analyzing these degrees by one-way ANOVA with repeated measures, yielded a highly significant label effect, $F(28, 332) = 6.56, p < 0.001$. The distribution of preposition mean degree, presented in Table 7-1, shows that AMONG, BESIDE, and WITH, all three of which are locative prepositions, have the highest mean degrees, whereas OF, UP, ON, OUT, and DOWN, most of which are directional prepositions, have the lowest. Interpreting the mean degree of a labeled node as a measure of its "centrality" or "relatedness in meaning" suggests that directional prepositions have more specific meanings than locative prepositions. Exceptions to this "rule" may be noted, however, e.g., FROM and BETWEEN, suggesting that this interpretation may not hold when the set of terms includes subsets (subtrees) of synonymous or quasi-synonymous terms, since the mean degree of a term in such a subset will be primarily determined by the size of its subset. When subtrees are "tight" it seems more appropriate to interpret the mean degree of a labeled node as a measure of "centrality" or "relatedness in meaning" relative to its subtree. With this interpretation in mind, consider the mean node degree of IN, WITHIN, BETWEEN, and AMONG, all of which fall in one cluster in both Clark's study and the cluster results to be reported in the following section. Table 7-1 shows that AMONG has the largest mean degree, followed by IN and WITHIN, which have approximately the same degree, and by BETWEEN with the smallest mean degree. As another example, consider the cluster (identified as such by Clark's as well as by our cluster results) OVER-ABOVE-UP-ACROSS, in which OVER and ABOVE have the largest mean degree, followed by ACROSS with a mean degree of 1.90, and by UP with a mean degree of 1.20. The interpretation suggested for the mean preposition degree seems intuitively reasonable for both examples.

We next examine the results of Group PDG, whose subjects were permitted to form as many distinct groups as they wished. The number of groups actually formed reflects the ability of the subject to detect subtle semantic differences between prepositions, and, perhaps more important, an individual response bias determined by the subject's understanding and interpretation of the instructions. The mean number of groups formed was 12.34 which, with 29 prepositions, shows a high degree of sensitivity to differences in meaning between prepositions. The standard deviation was 4.12, and the range 5–23, indicating considerable individual differences.

The right-hand column of Table 7-1 presents the mean number of terms grouped together with each preposition. Thus, ABOVE was grouped together with 2.76 other terms on the average, ACROSS was clustered with 1.73 other terms on the average, and so on. Since the number of groups formed was large relative to the number of terms, one should not expect marked discrepancies among the means. Indeed, the means are similar, although a few terms stand out, e.g., BEHIND was clustered with only one preposition, and OF, TOWARD, ACROSS, and TO were clustered with less than two other terms. Since terms with a low mean degree are likely to be placed in small clusters, a positive correlation between the mean preposition degree (Group PT) and the mean number of terms clustered with each preposition (Group PDG) is expected. The correlation should not be expected to be high, however, since the mean number of subtrees and the mean number of groups in this study are quite different. A product moment correlation between the two columns of Table 7-1 yielded a value of 0.40 ($p < 0.01$).

Instead of looking at the mean cluster size for individual prepositions, one may examine the frequencies of pairs (and triples, quadruples, etc.) of prepositions clustered together. Table 7-4 presents the observed frequency distribution of pairs of prepositions sorted together. The table shows that 161 pairs out of the 406 possible pairs of prepositions were sorted together by none of the subjects, 69 pairs were clustered together by only one subject, and so on.

TABLE 7-4   Observed Frequency Distribution of Pairs of Prepositions Sorted Together (Group PDG)

y	Frequency	y	Frequency	y	Frequency
0	161	7	10	14	2
1	69	8	6	15	1
2	42	9	9	16	1
3	31	10	11	17	2
4	17	11	5	18	0
5	10	12	1	19	3
6	5	13	6	20+	14

Comparison of Tables 7-3 and 7-4 shows the two observed distributions to be quite similar, with subjects in Group PT showing more agreement among themselves. The similarity between the two groups with respect to the distribution of pairs of prepositions selected (Group PT) or sorted together (Group PDG) is further evident when the pairs sorted together by the majority of the subjects are examined. Table 7-4 shows that 14 pairs of prepositions were sorted together by 20 or more subjects. These were: BELOW-UNDER (39), ABOVE-UP (38), DOWN-UNDER (37), BELOW-DOWN (37), TO-TOWARD (33), ABOVE-OVER (33), OVER-UP (30), TOGETHER-WITH (29), IN-WITHIN (29), AWAY-OUT (27), BESIDE-BY (23), AMONG-TOGETHER (21), FROM-OUT (20), and AMONG-BETWEEN (20). Eight out of the ten most "popular" pairs of (adjacent) nodes selected by the majority of subjects in Group PT are included in this list.

To summarize, the analysis performed in this section shows that proximity measures were not generated randomly, that the results for the two groups were similar, and that both groups showed a high degree of sensitivity to differences in meaning among prepositions. The large mean number of subtrees, the large mean number of distinct groups of prepositions, the strong popularity bias, and the highly skewed distribution of pairs of prepositions sorted together strongly suggest that a cluster analysis of the data is appropriate, and further predict a relatively large number of distinct clusters centered around the pairs of prepositions selected (Group PT) or sorted together (Group PDG) by the majority of subjects in both groups.

Cluster Analysis

The two clustering methods were applied to the mean proximity matrices of the two groups as well as to the individual proximity matrices of five subjects randomly selected from Group PT. To test the ultrametric inequality (see Chapter 3), the distance between the MAXC clusterings yielded by the two clustering methods was computed for each group. The distances were 0.18 and 0.15 for Groups PT and PDG, respectively, indicating good agreement between the methods. The agreement between the two methods applied to Group PT is actually much better than it seems to be since, as may be easily demonstrated, the distance measure is highly affected by differences between two clusterings, C_h and $C_h{}'$, say, which merely result from the merging of two clusters in C_h into one cluster in $C_h{}'$. The two MAXC clusterings for Group PT are exactly the same with only the exception that the two largest clusters yielded by the Diameter method (clusters 3 and 4 below) are combined by the Connectedness method. Matters are somewhat more obscure in Group PDG, where the two clustering methods yield the same number of significant clusters, but only about one-half of the terms are clustered in exactly the same way by both methods.

Figures 7-1 and 7-2 portray the HCSs obtained by the Diameter method for

```
                                                                           T
                                                              B            H
           B                           O                      E            R
           E           B               V                      T            O
           H   D       E       F       E               T      W            U
           I   O   B   U   A   R   B   R   A       A   O       E   W        G
           N   W   E   N   W   O   E   O   C   O   B   G   B   E       I    H   T
           D   N   L   D   A   U   M   Y   R   V   A   R   E   S   T   N   T    R   O
               O   O   E   Y   T   O   O   O   E   B   O   T   I   O   I   H    O   W
               W   W   R       .   M   N   S   R   O   U   W   D   G   T   I    U   A
Level                                        S       V   N   E   E   E   H   N  G   R   D   α
  1    . . XXX . . . . . . . . . . . . . . . . . . . . . . . . . .                   4.65
  2    . . XXX . . . . . . XXX . . . . . . . . . . . . . . . . . \ .                  6.75
  3    . . XXX . . . . . . XXX . . . . . . . . . . . . . XXX . . . .                  9.90
  4    . . XXX . . . . . . XXX . . . . . . . . . . . . . XXX . . XXX                 10.40
  5    . . XXX . . . . . . XXX . . . . . . . . XXX . . XXX . . XXX                   19.75
  6    . . XXX . . . . . . XXX . . . . . . XXX XXX . . XXX . . XXX                   19.85
  7    . . XXX . . . . . . XXX . . . . . XXX XXX XXX XXX . . XXX                     20.60
  8    . . XXX XXX . . . . . XXX . . . . . XXX XXX XXX XXX . . XXX                   26.15
  9    . . . XXX XXX . . . . . XXX . . . . . XXX XXX XXX XXXXX . XXX                 26.80
 10    . . . XXX XXX . . . . XXXXX . . . . . XXX XXX XXX XXXXX . XXX                 27.00
 11    . XXXXX XXX . . . . . XXXXX . . . . XXX XXX XXX XXXXX . XXX                   33.30
 12    . XXXXX XXX . . . . . XXXXX . . . . XXXXXX XXX XXXXX . XXX                    36.80
 13    . XXXXX XXXXX . . . . XXXXX . . . . XXXXXX XXX XXXXX . XXX                    36.95
 14    . XXXXX XXXXXX . . . XXXXX . . . . XXXXXXX XXX XXXXX . XXX                    43.60
 15    . XXXXX XXXXXX . . . XXXXXXX . . . XXXXXXX XXX XXXXX . XXX                    46.20
 16    . XXXXX XXXXXX . . . XXXXXXX . . . XXXXXXXXXXX XXXXX . XXX                    50.40
 17    . XXXXX XXXXXX . . . XXXXXXX . . . XXXXXXXXXXX XXXXXXX XXX                    54.25
 18    . XXXXX XXXXXXX . XXXXXXXXX . . . XXXXXXXXXXX XXXXXXX XXX                     55.00
 19    . XXXXX XXXXXXX . XXXXXXXXX . XXX XXXXXXXXXXX XXXXXXX XXX                     55.40
 20    . XXXXX XXXXXXX . XXXXXXXXX XXXXX XXXXXXXXXXX XXXXXXX XXX                     64.10
 21    . XXXXX XXXXXXX . XXXXXXXXX XXXXXXXXXXXXXXXXX XXXXXXX XXX                     69.70
 22    XXXXXXX XXXXXXX . XXXXXXXXX XXXXXXXXXXXXXXXXX XXXXXXX XXX                     70.05
 23    XXXXXXX XXXXXXX . XXXXXXXXX XXXXXXXXXXXXXXXXX XXXXXXXXXX                      71.65
 24    XXXXXXX XXXXXXX . XXXXXXXXX XXXXXXXXXXXXXXXXXXXXXXXXXXXX                      92.70
 25    XXXXXXX XXXXXXXX XXXXXXXX XXXXXXXXXXXXXXXXXXXXXXXXXXXXX                      100.40
 26    XXXXXXXXXXXXXXX XXXXXXXX XXXXXXXXXXXXXXXXXXXXXXXXXXXXX                      119.45
 27    XXXXXXXXXXXXXXXXX XXXXXXXXXXXXXXXXXXXXXXXXXXXXXXXXXXXX                      120.15
 28    XXXXXXXXXXXXXXXXXXXXXXXXXXXXXXXXXXXXXXXXXXXXXXXXXXXXXXXXXXX                  147.50
```

Fig. 7-1. HSC for Group PT (Diameter method).

```
                                                              TOGETHER
           BEHIND                           BEYOND                                  BETWEEN      THROUGH
           DOWN                   ACROSS     OVER       AROUND                WITHIN            INTO
           BELOW      AWAY   FROM             ABOVE        ALONG    BY   WITH          AMONG         TOWARD
           UNDER      OUT                      UP    ON  AT   BESIDE    IN                  OF        TO
Level

  1    . . XXX . . . . . . . . . . . . . . . . . . . . . . . . . .          39
  2    . . XXX . . . . . . XXX . . . . . . . . . . . . . . . . . .          38
  3    . XXXXX . . . . . . XXX . . . . . . . . . . . . . . . . . .          37
  4    . XXXXX . . . . . . XXX . . . . . . . . . . . . . . . . XXX          33
  5    . XXXXX . . . . . XXXXX . . . . . . . . . . . . . . . . XXX          30
  6    . XXXXX . . . . . XXXXX . . . . . . XXX XXX . . . . . . XXX          29
  7    . XXXXX XXX . . . XXXXX . . . . . . . XXX XXX . . . . . XXX          27
  8    . XXXXX XXX . . . XXXXX . . . . XXX XXX XXX . . . . . XXX          23
  9    . XXXXX XXX . . . XXXXX . . . . XXX XXX XXX XXX . . XXX          20
 10    . XXXXX XXXXX . . XXXXX . . . . XXX XXX XXX XXX . . . XXX          19
 11    . XXXXX XXXXX . . XXXXX . . . . XXX XXX XXX XXX . XXX XXX       17
 12    . XXXXX XXXXX . XXXXXXX . . . XXXX XXX XXX XXX . XXX XXX       13
 13    . XXXXX XXXXX . XXXXXXX XXX . XXXXX XXX XXX XXX . XXX XXX    11
 14    . XXXXX XXXXX . XXXXXXX XXX XXXXXXX XXX XXX XXX . XXX XXX   10
 15    . . XXXXX XXXXX . XXXXXXX XXX XXXXXXX XXX XXXXXXX . XXX XXX    9
 16    XXXXXXX XXXXX . XXXXXXX XXX XXXXXXX XXX XXXXXXX . XXX XXX    7
 17    XXXXXXX XXXXX . XXXXXXX XXX XXXXXXXXXXX XXXXXXX . XXX XXX    6
 18    XXXXXXX XXXXX . XXXXXXX XXX XXXXXXXXXXX XXXXXXXX XXX XXX    5
 19    XXXXXXX XXXXX XXXXXXXXX XXXXXXXXXXXXXX XXXXXXXX XXXXXXX    3
 20    XXXXXXX XXXXXXXXXXXXXXX XXXXXXXXXXXXXXXXXXXXXX XXXXXXX    1
 21    XXXXXXXXXXXXXXXXXXXXXXXXXXXXXXXXXXXXXXXXXXXXXXXXXXXXXXXX  0
```

Fig. 7-2. HCS for Group PDG (Diameter method).

the mean proximity matrices of Groups PT and PDG, respectively. On inspecting the figures, one may note about seven to ten distinct and rather small clusters, which are merged into larger clusters only very late in the clustering process. Relative to the cluster analysis results reported in the preceding three chapters, more clusters are formed and kept separate for more levels, and significant clusters with only few terms emerge early in the clustering process, thus indicating the existence of highly compact clusters. Moreover, inspection of the z values of significant clusters at various levels of the HCS shows them to be much larger than 4, and to drop, but still remain above the critical z value, when terms such as BEHIND, ACROSS, OF, and AT, all of which were frequently kept separate by subjects in Group PDG, are added to the already formed compact clusters.

The MAXC clustering for Group PT consists of five (significant) clusters:

1. An UNDER cluster [UNDER, BELOW, DOWN, BEHIND].
2. An OVER cluster [OVER, ABOVE, UP, ON, ACROSS].
3. A SPATIAL CONTIGUITY cluster [BESIDE, BY, ALONG, AROUND, WITH, TOGETHER, AMONG, BETWEEN, AT].
4. An INWARD cluster [TO, TOWARD, THROUGH, IN, INTO, WITHIN].
5. An OUTWARD cluster [OUT, FROM, AWAY, BEYOND, OF].

Since significant subclusters were formed quite early in the HCS, interpretation of the clusters will be affected both by the actual terms falling in a significant cluster and the level at which they were clustered. The first three clusters, as suggested by their labels, consist mainly of locative prepositions describing positional relations between objects or events. The first two clusters are well-defined, with the exception of BEHIND in the first and ACROSS in the second. Figure 7-1 shows, however, that these two terms were the last to be added to their respective clusters; BEHIND was clustered on level 22, and ACROSS on level 18. The third cluster is also composed of locative prepositions, with the exception of AT, which has both locative and directional (and also temporal) meanings, and, as shown in Fig. 7-1, was the last term to be added to Cluster 3. The remaining eight terms in Cluster 3 may be divided into three subclusters in terms of the "spatial contiguity" of the objects or events which they relate. AROUND and ALONG are the farthest off; BETWEEN and AMONG relate a given object to one or more objects surrounding it; and BESIDE, BY, TOGETHER, and WITH indicate the closest contiguity. Clusters 4 and 5 include locative and directional prepositions, as well as terms possessing both locative and directional meanings. IN and WITHIN, the former being typically employed as a locative preposition, should have been clustered together with AMONG and BETWEEN in Cluster 3. The remaining four terms in Cluster 4 are directional prepositions referring to a movement directed from the outside. Cluster 5 also includes two kinds of terms—BEHIND is a locative preposition, AWAY and OUT possess locative and directional meanings, whereas FROM has mainly a directional meaning. OF does not seem to "belong" to any cluster and, indeed, Fig. 7-1 shows that it was the last preposition to be clustered. It may be noted that the ten most popular pairs of adjacent nodes, selected by at least 14 out of the 20 subjects of Group PT, are kept together in the MAXC clustering and serve as foci of the five significant clusters.

Figure 7-2 presents the HCS for Group PDG with six (significant) clusters:
1. An UNDER cluster [UNDER, BELOW, DOWN, BEHIND].
2. An OVER cluster [ABOVE, ACROSS, OVER, UP, BEYOND].
3. A SPATIAL CONTIGUITY cluster [BESIDE, BY, ALONG, AROUND, TOGETHER, WITH, AT, ON].
4. An IN cluster [IN, WITHIN, AMONG, BETWEEN, OF].
5. A TO cluster [TO, TOWARD].
6. An OUTWARD cluster [OUT, FROM, AWAY].

INTO and THROUGH are not included in the MAXC clustering.

A comparison of Figs. 7-1 and 7-2 shows them to be very similar. With only few interchanges involving terms such as ON, OF, and BEYOND, all of which possess several meanings, the terms in both figures are arranged in the same way, are clustered at about the same level (taking into consideration that Fig. 7-2 has fewer levels), and, despite the different number of significant clusters in the two MAXC clusterings, the distance between them is only 0.14. Clusters 1, 2, and 3 clearly correspond to the first three clusters in Group PT. The only exceptions are BEYOND, included in Cluster 5 of Group PT and in Cluster 2 of Group PDG, ON which is clustered together with the SPATIAL CONTIGUITY rather than the OVER terms, and AMONG and BETWEEN, which rather than being included in Cluster 3 are clustered together with IN and WITHIN—another two locative prepositions—to form Cluster 4. Cluster 5 consists of only two directional prepositions—TO and TOWARD, and Cluster 6 includes three out of the five terms in Cluster 5 of Group PT, i.e., OUT, FROM, and AWAY. The z value of the (nonsignificant) cluster TO-TOWARD-INTO-THROUGH is 3.82, only slightly smaller than the critical value $z = 4$, suggesting, perhaps, that INTO and THROUGH should also be included in Cluster 5. The three prepositions AT, ON, and OF, which seem to be misplaced, are among the last terms to be clustered. Since the z values of the clusters in which these three terms fell dropped markedly at the level on which these terms were clustered, they should probably not have been clustered at all.

The hierarchical cluster analysis of the five subjects randomly selected from Group PT yielded three clusters in the MAXC clustering of each subject. Since the number of clusters is smaller than the one observed in the group MAXC clustering, and since, as was said before, a difference between the number of clusters increases the distance between two clusterings regardless of the way the terms are clustered, the distances between the individual and group MAXC clusterings were not computed. Rather, an inspection of the six HCSs shows that, with only minor interchanges, the 29 prepositions were arranged in the same order in each case, and that most of the prepositions were clustered in the same way in the individual and group MAXC clusterings.

Since the analysis of only a small subset of subjects cannot reveal any consistent and systematic differences between individuals in terms of their preferences, response habits, or semantic judgments, we approached the analysis of individual subjects in Group PDG in an entirely different manner. It may be recalled from our discussion in Chapter 2 that the "point of view" method of Tucker and Messick (1963) attempts to identify points of view by computing intercorrelations between subjects, based on the experimentally obtained proximity measures, factor analyzing the correlation matrix to produce a subject space, and then identifying clusters of subjects in this space and defining "idealized" subjects corresponding to these clusters. Proceeding in the spirit of the "point of view" method, but rejecting its metric assumptions, we computed a 41 x 41 matrix of distances between the subjects in Group PDG, based on the clusterings that they had yielded, and subjected it to the hierarchical clustering methods of Johnson. Both methods yielded essentially the same HCS—a triangular structure to which one or at the most two points (subjects) were added on each level. The MAXC clustering yielded by the Diameter method had only one cluster including 39 out of the 41 subjects.

To account for the highly regular triangular shape of the HCS and the lack of any clusters, we correlated the number of groups formed by each subject with the level at which he was clustered. The resulting correlation was negative and highly significant, $\rho = -0.85$ ($p < 0.001$), clearly showing that the number of groups formed by the subjects rather than the way in which the prepositions were clustered was primarily responsible for the clustering results.

Multidimensional Scaling Analysis

The Young-Torgerson MDS program yielded one-, two-, and three-dimensional solutions for the five subjects randomly selected from Group PT and for the two mean proximity matrices. Table 7-5 presents the stress values for the Euclidean representations, which, in all cases, were smaller than the corresponding City Block values. Table 7-5 shows that a two-dimensional representation adequately describes both the individual and mean proximity matrices of Group PT, but is inadequate for Group PDG. Indeed, the three-dimensional solution for Group PDG yields almost the same stress value as the two-dimensional solution for Group PT.

TABLE 7-5   Stress Values for Euclidean Representations

| Dimensions | Group PT | | | | | | Group PDG |
	No. 2	No. 6	No. 10	No. 14	No. 18	Mean	Mean
3	0.054	0.025	0.050	0.038	0.037	0.065	0.119
2	0.089	0.035	0.088	0.075	0.063	0.121	0.230
1	0.306	0.078	0.216	0.147	0.141	0.282	0.456

A comparison of the cluster and MDS results for Group PT (see Fig. 7-3) shows only a moderate amount of correspondence between the two. The UNDER cluster, with the exception of BEHIND, the OVER cluster, with the exception of ACROSS, and three out of the five terms forming the OUTWARD cluster, i.e., AWAY, FROM, and OUT, appear as compact clusters in the two-dimensional representation. The remaining two clusters intersect each other. However, with the exception of AT, LONG, and AROUND, the remaining six terms of Cluster 3, i.e., BETWEEN, TOGETHER, WITH, BESIDE, BY, and AMONG, and the six terms of Cluster 4, i.e., TO, TOWARD, IN, WITHIN, INTO, and THROUGH, appear as tight clusters in the representation. Even if the results are interpreted as supporting, or at least not rejecting, a dimensional model, there seems to be no way to interpret the dimensions. The "movement-implied" dimension, suggested by Clark in interpreting his data, is clearly not supported by our results. Terms such as ABOVE, DOWN, OUT,

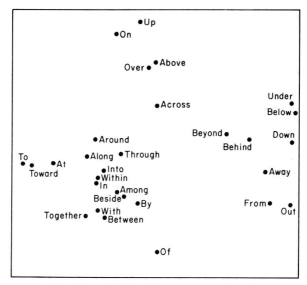

Fig. 7-3. Two-dimensional Euclidean representation for Group PT.

AWAY, TO, and TOWARD, which fall toward the "movement" end of the axis proposed by Clark, can be seen to be scattered unsystematically over the entire representation.

Additional evidence incongruent with a dimensional model is yielded by the two-dimensional representation for Group PDG, depicted in Fig. 7-4, which is not amenable to a dimensional interpretaion. A close examination of the

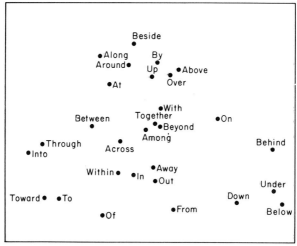

Fig. 7-4. Two-dimensional Euclidean representation for Group PDG.

three-dimensional representation for Group PDG results in the same conclusion. Moreover, a comparison of the clustering and MDS results for Group PDG shows an even poorer correspondence between the two than the one obtained for Group PT. The clusters BELOW-UNDER-DOWN, ABOVE-OVER-UP, TO-TOWARD (Cluster 5), and OUT-FROM-AWAY (Cluster 6) appear as tight clusters in the two-dimensional representation, but the eight terms of the SPATIAL CONTIGUITY cluster are mixed with the four terms of the OVER cluster, and even the terms of the relatively homogeneous IN cluster fall far apart.

DISCUSSION

Cluster analysis of the data obtained by the tree construction method and the Direct Grouping procedure yielded quite similar results. This is not the case if one considers the outcomes of the multidimensional scaling analyses. While a two-dimensional representation provided an adequate depiction of the results for Group PT, such a representation was not satisfactory for Group PDG. Further, when the cluster results are embedded in the MDS representations for each group the clusters characteristically are not compact, and, perhaps more important, it is impossible to provide any sensible, coherent interpretation of the putative dimensions involved. On the other hand the similar cluster results yielded by the two different data gathering procedures constitute intelligible, sensible groupings. All the above argues for use of a cluster or typal model rather than a dimensional model to represent the structure obtaining among the set of prepositions examined in the present study.

Before attempting to compare these results with those obtained by Clark (1968), something should be said concerning the outcome of the individual difference analysis which examined the distances among the 41 subjects in Group PDG. It will be recalled that this analysis yielded essentially a single cluster, and that there was a very highly significant correlation, $\rho = -0.85$, between the number of groups formed by each subject and the level at which he clustered with the others, indicating that the distance between any pair of subjects was primarily determined by differences in the number of groupings formed by each, rather than by differences in the ways in which items were grouped together. An examination of the cluster analysis results for five randomly selected subjects from Group PT indicated that, with minor exceptions, the 29 prepositions were arranged in the same way. Further, it will be recalled that both methods of obtaining data yielded a number of (similar) tight clusters of pairs of prepositions. What all this suggests is that generally the clusters formed by a subject using relatively few groupings were the unions of the greater number of clusters formed by a subject using relatively many groupings, with items which went together in the small groupings characteristically going together, without rearrangement, with other items to form the larger groupings. Since differences in the number of groups formed may be due either to differences in response biases or differences in the ability to discriminate relatively subtle differences in meaning in a specific domain, or both, no simple interpretation of these results appears possible. Some light may be thrown on this matter in the following chapters where the number of groups formed for different sets of terms will be correlated for the subjects serving under direct grouping instructions. To the extent that the correlations obtained are low, this may be taken as evidence against a general response bias interpretation; substantial positive correlations, however, would provide little basis for distinguishing between the two possibilities noted above. Perhaps the main point to stress here is that, with respect to the set of prepositions employed, differences between subjects do not appear to stem from differences in ways in which items are categorized so much as from differences in the fineness or coarseness with which commonly held criteria are applied. This result is intelligible for otherwise it is difficult to understand how adequate communication would be possible, given the often critical differentiating role of these prepositions in discourse.

As might be expected in terms of what has just been said, there was considerable variability in the number of groupings formed by subjects in Group PDG, with range from 5-23. Given this substantial variability, and particularly the large mean value (12.34), Clark's procedure of constraining his subjects to use initially only 2-6 main groups seems a particularly unfortunate one, and may have introduced some biases in his results; we shall recur to this point later. It may be instructive to compare the results of Group PDG with those of Miller (1969), who used similar direct grouping instructions in a task where subjects, 50 Harvard and Radcliffe students, were asked to sort 48 common nouns into as many piles as they wished "on the basis of similarity of meaning." Unlike the present study, the nouns were unrelated and were assumed to be "conceptually distinct to a native speaker." Despite the larger number of terms, and the presumably larger differences of meaning among the terms, the number of categories used to sort the nouns in Miller's study was only slightly larger than that obtained in the present study with a mean of 14.3, standard deviation of 5, and a range of 6-26. The similarity between these values and those obtained in the present study may reflect some sort of a response bias, suggesting an empirical upper limit on the number of categories used or usable in a task of this sort. Given the license to successively subclassify the initial set of categories, a procedure which minimizes cognitive load by externalizing the problem of record keeping and converts the task into a series of sequential subtasks, these limits may be considerably expanded. To return to the comparison of our results with those of Miller, an analysis of pairs of terms sorted together, rather than of the number of categories used, shows differences between the studies consistent with differences in the nature of the items constituting each set of terms. Table 1 of Miller's paper shows that 55% of the pairs of nouns were not grouped together by more than a single subject and that 5.6% of the nouns were grouped together by more than half of the subjects, compared to values of 40% and 3.4% in the present study.

We turn now to a comparison of the present results with those obtained by Clark (1968). Attention will be focused on the findings for the 22 prepositions common to both studies. These fall into seven "loose" clusters, if one considers the data yielded under direct grouping instructions in Clark's experiment, and into six significant clusters for Group PDG, with two of the prepositions, INTO and THROUGH, not falling into a significant cluster (although these terms together with TO and TOWARD, which do cluster together significantly, form an almost significant single larger cluster). These results are presented in Table 7-6.

TABLE 7-6   Clusterings Involving Only the 22 Terms Common to Clark's Study and Group PDG

Clark's study	Group PDG
[IN, WITHIN, BETWEEN, AMONG]	[IN, WITHIN, BETWEEN, AMONG, OF]
[UNDER, DOWN, UP, ABOVE, OVER, ON]	[UNDER, DOWN], [UP, ABOVE, OVER, ACROSS]
[AROUND, ALONG], [AT, BY], [WITH, OF]	[AROUND, ALONG, AT, BY, WITH, ON]
[TOWARD, TO, FROM]	[TOWARD, TO], [FROM]
[ACROSS, INTO, THROUGH]	[INTO], [THROUGH]

It may be seen by inspection of this table that there is considerable similarity in these two sets of cluster results, for example the first cluster [IN, WITHIN, BETWEEN, AMONG] is the same in both studies except that OF, which is added very late, also falls into this cluster for Group PDG. However, there are also some differences. Items falling into separate clusters in Clark's results may form one larger cluster in our results, e.g., what we have been calling the SPATIAL CONTIGUITY cluster composed of AROUND, ALONG, AT, BY, WITH, and ON decomposes essentially into three clusters in Clark's results, and, conversely, our distinct OVER and UNDER clusters collapse into a single cluster in Clark's results. Perhaps the principal difference is that antonymous terms, which always fall into separate clusters in our results, characteristically cluster together in Clark's results, e.g., as just noted, the OVER and UNDER terms fall together, and in another cluster there are to be found TOWARD, TO, and FROM. The tendency for antonyms to group together in Clark's results may be a consequence of the greater heterogeneity of his sample of prepositions (these included temporal and manner terms as well as locative and directional terms) taken together with his instructions to form 2–6 main "groups that seem most natural to you" and the weighting system he employed in scoring main group and subgroup differences. In the circumstances of his study it is almost inevitable that antonyms be sorted into the same main groups, and, given the lesser weighting of subgroup differences, it seems plausible that antonyms fall relatively close together, or cluster together. With regard to the 22 common terms, if one plots the cluster results yielded by the present study on Clark's two-dimensional MDS representation, the resulting clusters are quite compact (with OF producing the principal exception); however, if one does the converse, plotting Clark's clusters on our two-dimensional representation for Group PDG, the clusters are certainly not compact. One of the principal reasons for this is that antonyms which are distinct both in our MDS and cluster results fall close together both in cluster terms and in the spatial representation in Clark's results. In any case, it is difficult, if not impossible, to provide any plausible interpretation of the spatial representation obtained in either study, while it is possible to make some sense of the cluster results which have some definite similarities in the two studies.

Given that the clustering model seems to provide a more appropriate representation than the MDS model, and that the cluster results for Groups PT and PDG are very similar, what can be said as to the properties or features that appear to govern these results? With regard to locative prepositions, the principal groups or clusters that appear do indeed seem to be defined in terms of relative spatial position. Thus there is an UNDER cluster and an OVER cluster and, as concerns SPATIAL CONTIGUITY, the prepositions appear to segregate more or less into an IN cluster and a SURROUNDING or ADJACENCY cluster (this last result is clearer for Group PDG than for PT). While there are some inconsistencies in the findings, these usually result from the fact that the focal terms in a cluster are so tightly compact that adding a more distant term still leaves the resulting cluster significant, although the z value may drop noticeably, e.g., when terms such as BEHIND, ACROSS, and OF are added to their respective clusters. The term OF is the one perhaps least related to any of the other prepositions, a result which is sensible enough given its polysemy, syntactic conditioning, and difficulties in locating it unambiguously in terms of any spatial scheme.

For both groups BEHIND was clustered, at a relatively late level, with the UNDER terms. One might speculate that if there had been additional terms in our sample such as IN BACK OF, AFTER, IN FRONT, BEFORE, etc., then there might well have emerged two additional polar clusters defining these relative spatial locations. It may be of some interest that BEHIND, the only preposition of this sort in our sample, clustered with the UNDER terms, for if one regards UP (or HIGH) and IN FRONT (or FORWARD) as unmarked terms, respectively, when contrasted with their marked polar opposites DOWN (or LOW) and BEHIND, then this suggests that marked terms may go together. (Presumably unmarked terms would also go together in turn, i.e., if IN FRONT had occurred in our sample in place of BEHIND we expect that it would have clustered with the OVER terms.) The directional terms appear to fall into two clusters, one a sort of TOWARD (direction to) cluster, the other an AWAY (direction from) cluster, with some tendency, particularly for Group PT, for the TOWARD cluster to merge with the IN cluster, a finding which becomes intelligible if we note that many of the terms involved have both locative and directional senses.

Among the 15 prepositions included by Jones and Fillenbaum (1964) in a study of grammatically classified word association, there are 13 terms which overlap with those of the present study. Examining the intersection coefficients for associations to these prepositions, Deese (1965) comments that the words are highly related that "there seem to be two basic patterns combined there. One pattern is defined by the strong polar-opposite pairs *out-in* and *up-down*. The remaining words are related but no simple pattern emerges (except possibly for the weak polar pair, *to-from*) (p. 116)." It is obvious that these results based on an analysis of overlaps in associative responses are quite consistent with those reported in the present study using quite different, more direct, methods to assess similarities among the terms. A factor analysis of the association data by Deese did "not yield any readily characterizable structure," a result consistent with our finding that the MDS analysis did not yield any satisfactory spatial or dimensional representation, but one that hardly requires Deese's conclusion "that we are left with the strong possibility that the class of prepositions is not well organized conceptually (p. 116)."

A consideration of the significant clusters obtained, while it reveals no obvious inconsistency with the scheme proposed by Cooper (1968), may appear to be rather disappointing insofar as our results only capture some of the grossest distinctions with regard to spatial location. Note, however, that the present results permit a weighting of the cognitive significance of some of the semantic markers involved. For example, we noted that in terms of Cooper's account, ABOVE and BELOW differed in only a single feature or condition. Now we can assert that differences with regard to this feature make a very substantial cognitive difference whereas differences with regard, say, to the features that distinguish BELOW and DOWN are not particularly consequential. The latter terms are significantly clustered at the very start in Group PDG, and somewhat later, but still relatively early, are also significantly clustered in Group PT. Similarly, one can show that terms that are synonyms or near synonyms in Cooper's scheme, e.g., UNDER and BELOW or OVER and ABOVE, are always clustered together early, i.e., some of the local similarities or relations specified by Cooper's analysis can readily be verified.

Further, consider that we are not restricted simply to an inspection of the significant clusters formed, but that we may also examine the successive stages through which the clusters are constituted and note when, at what level, particular items accrete to a cluster. Previously this logic led us to the suggestion that items added at a very late stage to relatively tight clusters, and whose addition noticeably loosens such clusters, may, in fact, be misgrouped. This suggestion allowed us to account for some otherwise rather anomalous findings, e.g., with regard to the grouping of BEHIND, or particularly OF. Now we may look at matters from the other end. By a consideration of the items that form the foci of the clusters, as revealed by tight pairings in the graph analysis, and of the order of accretion of further items to these clusters, we may perhaps be able to make some comments on the significance or lack of significance of differentiating features. The earlier an item joins a cluster, or that clusters merge into a larger cluster, the less important or salient the features that differentiate that item from the other members of the cluster, or that differentiate between the clusters involved. Thus, as was noted earlier, there were 14 pairs of terms which were sorted together by 20 or more of the 41 subjects in Group PDG, and eight of the ten most "popular" pairs selected by the majority of subjects in Group PT, viz. BELOW-UNDER, ABOVE-OVER, TO-TOWARD, BESIDE-BY, IN-WITHIN, TOGETHER-WITH, AMONG-BETWEEN, and ABOVE-UP are also included in this list. It seems reasonable to argue that whatever features differentiate these terms they are of relatively low salience or cognitive significance. The use of one rather than another member of these pairs may often be syntactically determined, or controlled by the sorts of subsidiary semantic considerations that govern the use of BETWEEN as a preposition, when two items are involved, and AMONG, when more than two items are involved.

As to the order in which items are added to a cluster, or the level at which clusters merge, consider as an example the nine items constituting the SPATIAL CONTIGUITY cluster for Group PT, viz., BESIDE, BY, ALONG, AROUND, WITH, TOGETHER, AMONG, BETWEEN, and AT. First at about the same level 1 [BESIDE, BY], 2 [TOGETHER, WITH] and 3 [AMONG, BETWEEN] form small tight clusters; a while later 1 and 2 are merged, and somewhat later still this larger cluster merges with 3; finally this larger cluster is joined by 4 [AROUND, ALONG and AT], immediately after these latter terms have been grouped together. As suggested earlier, the property that controls these sequential amalgamations seems to be one referring to closeness in space. Thus items in 2 represent actual contiguity, items in 1 adjacency, 1 and 2 are closer to each other than to 3, which indexes surroundedness, and 1, 2 and 3 are closer to each other than to 4, which refers to some neighboring or regional property. The only item misclassified in this scheme is AT, which was in fact the last item to join the cluster and also functions in other ways, e.g., as a temporal term.

While it seems clear that a cluster representation is more appropriate to the data for locative prepositions than is a spatial or dimensional model, and while something can be said as to the nature of the properties defining the principal clusters in terms, say, of an UNDER/OVER contrast and an IN/ADJACENT contrast, it is difficult to make any general statements as to the kinds of properties governing intra-cluster relations. Indeed, it is not at all obvious that such organization is really generally hierarchical. Thus, in the example of the SPATIAL CONTIGUITY cluster immediately above, it would appear that differences in regard to proximity determined the order of clustering of items. There was a sort of a spatial dimension embedded within the SPATIAL CONTIGUITY cluster, while for the UNDER and OVER clusters, at least for Group PT, a principal determinant of order of clustering seems to have been the contrast between relative and absolute location, with BELOW and UNDER and ABOVE and OVER clustering very early, joined only distinctly later by DOWN and UP, respectively. In short, it appears to be the case not only that intra-cluster organization may not be properly hierarchical, but further that different sorts of properties may control the organization of the various clusters that were formed.

Chapter 8   *CONJUNCTIONS*

Terms which serve as propositional operators, sentence connectors, or truth functional constants, play a basic, critical function in logical analysis, particularly with regard to the truth or falsity of propositions and their combinations. It is clear, however, that there is only a partial overlap between the meaning or interpretation of each of these operators and that of the expressions of ordinary speech with which it is, more or less informally, identified, and that, therefore, an analysis of these operators can only provide a partial account of the meaning of such expressions. To illustrate, the connective "." controls a commutative relation such that "p.q" is logically equivalent to "q.p", yet it is obvious that "and" with which "." is characteristically identified often does not function in this fashion, but may indicate temporal or causal sequence such that "He fell and broke his neck" is a very different proposition from "He broke his neck and fell."

Logicians, of course, are quite aware of problems of this sort, and, in introductory texts, caution the student about the dangers involved in identifying logical operators with the not-so-corresponding expressions of the vernacular. They have been less concerned, however, with providing an analysis of these expressions, of the use of these "ordinary words." Some hints are to be found in Reichenbach (1947), especially in a section titled "Logical terms in a semantical capacity," and more richly in Strawson (1952), particularly in a section on "Truth-functional constants and ordinary words." There has been considerable work on entailment by logicians (see, e.g., Bennett, 1969) which does bear on the ways in which "if ... then" expressions are understood, and also work by psychologists such as Wason and Johnson-Laird on "How implication is understood," to cite the title of a recent paper (1969) by Johnson-Laird and

Tagart, in which relevant references to the psychological literature may also be found.

However, there is very little work either by philosophers or by psychologists on conjunctions as used in ordinary speech. With regard to perhaps the most common of all conjunctions, namely "and," we have already noted that it often serves not only a combinatorial function but also indicates temporal or causal sequence. Further, as Strawson has pointed out, it "can be used to couple nouns or adjectives or adverbs . . . to form plural subjects or compound predicates," functions which have no counterpart in the case of ".", which "can be used only to couple expressions which could appear as separate sentences (pp. 79, 80)." In addition, it must be obvious that many connectives such as "but," "although," "however," etc., while typically assumed to be truth functionally equivalent to "and" differ from it in some significant respects. The above is not meant as an attack on the propositional calculus for its inadequacies in providing an analysis of the vernacular; that is not the job it is supposed to do. Rather it is meant to indicate that there are problems here and that the task of specifying the senses and relations among the various conjunctions as used in ordinary speech lies largely ahead.

While it may be that some of the differences among conjunctions are syntactically conditioned, it would appear that often semantic or pragmatic distinctions are involved. As Strawson has suggested, "the words 'but,' 'although,' 'nevertheless' are not mere stylistic variants on 'and.' Their use implies at least that there is some element of contrast between the conjoined statements or attributes; and, sometimes, that the conjunction is unusual or surprising (1952, p. 48)." Reichenbach, in a similar vein, argues that " 'but' means 'and' with the indication 'the following statement seems to contradict the preceding one without doing so' (1947, p. 329)." Bendix (1966) notes that "*but R*" in "*P but R*" contradicts "a connotation of *P,* i.e., a usual semantic accompaniment of *P* that is not, however, one of its criterial semantic components (p. 23)," and then proceeds to use this property to construct a test for the criteriality of putative semantic components. Indeed, to cite a psychologist, contrastive conjunctions of which *but* is the most frequently used provide a linguistic coding for cognitively dissonant relations (Brown, 1965 p. 598).

In addition to the gross distinction between contrastive and simply combinatorial conjunctions mentioned above, one may wonder about possible differences in the extremity of the contrast, as does Weinreich when he glosses "but" as "and, surprisingly" and "yet" as "and, very surprisingly (1963, p. 127)." Also one may surmise that, with regard to differences among conjunctions, there may be involved differences in *emphasis*—" 'although' means the same as 'but' but is added to the other of the two connected sentences, so that 'a but b' means the same as 'although a, b' or 'b although a.' The sentence 'b' carries the emphasis in this usage, both for the 'but' and the 'although' (Reichenbach, 1947, p. 329)."

Surmises of the sort mentioned above may be regarded as hypotheses concerning semantic or pragmatic properties that distinguish the various conjunctions from each other. So far there is the suggestion that use of a particular conjunction may indicate (1) whether or not there is something contrastive or surprising about one proposition given the other (and perhaps something as to the strength of the surprise), and (2) which, if either, of the two conjoined sentences is to be given greater emphasis. One may wonder about other aspects of the relation between the to-be-conjoined sentences which might systematically affect choice of a conjunction. Thus two sentences may be *correlative* in the sense that either might equally well come first or second, and that any implicational relations between them are bidirectional as in (a) "He loves his mother" and (b) "He loves his father." Or they may be *implicational* in the sense that tacit implicational relations are more unidirectional, such that one sentence has more obvious implications for the other than conversely, as, e.g., in (a) "He is very old" and (b) "He is very strong," where given (a) it would appear that (b) is unexpected, but where given (b) a relation to (a) is not as obvious. This leads us to ask (3) whether the difference between *correlative* and *implicational* sentence pairs might have any consequences regarding choice of conjunction.

We constructed a sentence completion task where for each sentence pair the subject was required to select that conjunction, out of the 18 provided, which best satisfied a set of conditions based on the hypotheses presented above. We were interested in seeing whether, indeed, there would be a systematic effect of these conditions on the choice of conjunction, and, if so, what conjunction(s) would be chosen to satisfy each condition or combination of conditions, and how the conjunctions would cluster in satisfying the conditions (as saying something about the similarities among them and the relative importance of the putative features involved). Also, as usual, we obtained similarity judgments on the conjunctions by use of the method of labeled trees and subjected these data to MDS and clustering analyses in an attempt to determine the nature of the system governing the relations among the conjunctions, and the sorts of features involved in the distinctions among them. We were interested in these data for their own sake, with regard to their relation to the data yielded by the sentence completion task, and, particularly, in seeing whether the sorts of underlying distinguishing properties that have been suggested above would emerge from an analysis of such direct similarity judgments.

In the tree building task one group of subjects (actually two groups who yielded very similar data and were therefore combined) dealt with the complete set of 18 conjunctions while another group judged only the 14 conjunctions which, on a preliminary scrutiny, all appeared to some extent or other to share some contrastive properties. We followed this procedure since we suspected that the distinction between simply combinatorial and contrastive terms might be by far the most significant one, and that consequently given the relatively great "distance" between terms differing in this respect other possible differences might be washed out or masked in any spatial or clustering solution. Thus, examination of results for the group dealing with the complete set should reveal something as to the importance of the *contrastive* feature. An examination of the results for the subset in conjunction with this might also permit us to assess possible quantitative variations in this feature and the role of other determinants, and might provide some methodologically relevant information concerning the extent to which differences in some features may or may not be masked, given differences with regard to some particularly gross or salient property.

METHOD

Three groups of subjects participated in this experiment—Group CSC, performing a sentence completion task, Group CTA, which constructed labeled trees using the complete list of 18 conjunctions given in Table 8-1, and Group CTB, which also built trees using the 14 starred conjunctions in Table 8-1.

TABLE 8-1   Number of Times that Each Conjunction was Selected (Group CSC)

	Correlative pair	Implicational pair	Total
AND	66	67	133
*BUT	47	50	97
*NEVERTHELESS	40	44	84
*EVEN THOUGH	48	34	82
*ALTHOUGH	32	41	73
*DESPITE	34	39	73
ALSO	27	37	64
AS WELL AS	29	32	61
*YET	24	36	60
*IN SPITE OF	33	27	60
*WHILE	35	16	51
*HOWEVER	20	22	42
*STILL	21	19	40
*ON THE OTHER HAND	23	13	36
*NOTWITHSTANDING	15	19	34
*WHEREAS	19	14	33
*FOR ALL THAT	17	15	32
TOO	10	15	25

Group CSC consisted of 30 male and female undergraduate students enrolled at the University of North Carolina. They were provided with two statements, which we denote by A and B, and were asked to join them together "into a single meaningful statement by means of an appropriate conjunction" selected from the list of Table 8-1. In each instance the subjects were given additional specifications and were asked "to choose that conjunction which best satisfies these specifications." These additional specifications were of three types, involving emphasis (on A, on B, or on both equally), preliminary assumptions (either A or B is known to be true), and expectation (given one of the two statements, the other is either expected, contrary to expectation, or very much contrary to expectation), thus generating a $3 \times 2 \times 3$ matrix such as the one presented in Table 8-2. Subjects were further told that "any particular conjunction may be used as often or rarely as you please," that the interest of the study was in their "sensitivity to nuances and shades of meaning," and that they should not "be concerned about the grammatical elegance of the sentence as long as it most accurately conveys the desired shade of meaning."

TABLE 8-2   Design of the Sentence Completion Task and an Example

	Emphasis		
	On A	On B	On both
Given A:			
B is expected			
B is contrary to expectation			
B is very contrary to expectation			
Given B:			
A is expected			
A is contrary to expectation			
A is very contrary to expectation			

An Example

(A) He loves his father   (B) He hates his mother
Emphasis on (B)
Given (B), (A) is contrary to expectation
                  (A) _____(B)

Two pairs of sentences were used in the experiment, a "correlative" pair:
A. He loves his father
B. He hates his mother
and an "implicational" pair:
A. He is old
B. He is very strong
in the sense discussed in the previous section. The Cartesian product of the two

pairs of sentences, the two conditions (either A or B is given), the three levels of emphasis, and the three levels of expectation yielded 36 "derived" pairs of sentences—one of which is presented in Table 8-2. These pairs were typed on 36 separate sheets, which were presented to the subjects in a random order.

Group CTA consisted of 20 undergraduate and 20 graduate male and female students enrolled at the University of North Carolina, who were requested to construct labeled trees, using the complete list of conjunctions and the standard instructions for the tree construction method. There were 21 male and female subjects in Group CTB, who were provided with the shorter list of 14 contrastive conjunctions and with a slightly modified version of the standard instructions for the tree construction method. After completing the construction of a tree, the subjects in Group CTB were asked to rate each link on a nine-point rating scale in terms of the similarity in meaning between its two endpoints. These ratings rather than the ranks of the links were taken as measures of proximity, whereas the latter served to determine for each subject the number of separate subtrees that he constructed.

RESULTS

Sentence Completion Task

Each subject in Group CSC was free to choose any of the 18 conjunctions for each of the 36 "derived" pairs of sentences. A comparison of the frequencies of choice for the original two pairs of sentences showed them to yield similar results. Columns 2 and 3 of Table 8-1 present the frequencies of choice of each conjunction for the correlative and implicational pairs, respectively; the correlation between these is high ($\rho = 0.84$) and significant ($p < 0.01$). Since none of the remaining analyses of the data of Group CSC showed any significant differences between the original two pairs, suggesting that the type of semantic implication between statements examined in the present study has only minor, if any effects at all, on the frequency of choice of conjunctions, results were combined over the two pairs. The last column of Table 8-1 shows the frequency distribution of the conjunctions summed over the original two pairs. The distribution is skewed, with AND chosen less than four times on the average by each of the 30 subjects, BUT chosen less than three times, and each of the last four terms in the list—NOTWITHSTANDING, WHEREAS, FOR ALL THAT, and TOO—chosen less than once on the average by each subject.

All three factors—expectation, condition (either A or B is given), and emphasis—affected to some degree the frequencies of choice of the conjunctions. The last factor had a significant effect ($p < 0.01$, by a chi-square one-sample test) on only six out of the 18 conjunctions, independently of the effects of the remaining two factors. The frequency of choice of AND and ON THE OTHER

HAND increased as emphasis shifted from (1) A to (2) B to (3) both A and B equally (the respective frequencies were 20, 40, and 67 for AND, and 7, 10, and 19 for ON THE OTHER HAND), while the frequency of choice of ALSO and DESPITE exhibited the opposite tendency (the respective frequencies were 33, 22, and 9 for ALSO, and 31, 24, and 18 for DESPITE). NEVERTHELESS was chosen most frequently (47 out of 84) when emphasis was placed on B, and least frequently (17 out of 84) when emphasis was placed on A, whereas BUT reached its highest frequency (47 out of 97) when emphasis was placed on both A and B equally and its lowest frequency (21 out of 97) when emphasis was placed on B alone.

The effects of the other two factors—condition and expectation—were considerably stronger. Since most of the subjects did not seem to differentiate between "contrary to expectation" and "very contrary to expectation," distributing the conjunctions more or less evenly over these two categories, these two categories were combined. Table 8-3 shows the effects of condition and expectation on each of the 18 conjunctions, where the frequencies of choice are summed over all subjects, the two pairs of sentences, and the three levels of emphasis. Inspection of Table 8-3 suggests that both condition and expectation affected the frequency of choice of most of the conjunctions. This hypothesis is not strictly testable by the chi-square test; since different subjects contributed different frequencies to the 2 x 2 frequency tables in Table 8-3, samples are not independent. Since differences between subjects were small, and most subjects selected almost all the conjunctions at least once, we tested the null hypothesis, nevertheless, which specifies the following table of proportions for each conjunction:

	Given A	Given B
Expected	1/6	1/6
Not expected	2/6	2/6

(The 2/6 in the last row results from combining "contrary to expectation" and "very contrary to expectation" into one category, i.e., "not expected.") The null hypothesis was tested by a chi-square test ($df = 3$) for each conjunction separately, employing the observed frequencies in Table 8-3. It was strongly rejected ($p < 0.001$) in 15 out of 18 cases, the exceptions being FOR ALL THAT ($\chi^2 = 10.5$), STILL ($\chi^2 = 6.0$), and WHEREAS ($\chi^2 = 1.7$).

A further inspection of Table 8-3 shows that expectation had a stronger effect on the frequency of choice than the given condition (either A or B), and suggests no interaction between these two factors. The hypothesis of no interaction could not be rejected ($p > 0.20$) in 14 out of the 18 cases, applying the usual chi-square test for independence (with $df = 1$). The four exceptions were: AS WELL AS ($\chi^2 = 6.3$, $0.01 < p < 0.05$), NEVERTHELESS ($\chi^2 = 4.6$,

TABLE 8-3   Frequency of Choice of Each Conjunction by Condition and Expectation

	AND			EVEN THOUGH			NOTWITHSTANDING	
	given A	given B		given A	given B		given A	given B
Exp.	71	55	Exp.	3	5	Exp.	0	0
−Exp.	4	3	−Exp.	19	55	−Exp.	16	18
	ALSO			HOWEVER			FOR ALL THAT	
	given A	given B		given A	given B		given A	given B
Exp.	31	18	Exp.	3	2	Exp.	1	2
−Exp.	11	4	−Exp.	28	9	−Exp.	18	11
	AS WELL AS			YET			ON THE OTHER HAND	
	given A	given B		given A	given B		given A	given B
Exp.	22	26	Exp.	2	1	Exp.	4	2
−Exp.	1	12	−Exp.	50	7	−Exp.	22	8
	WHILE			DESPITE			STILL	
	given A	given B		given A	given B		given A	given B
Exp.	10	26	Exp.	1	8	Exp.	7	1
−Exp.	3	12	−Exp.	15	49	−Exp.	16	16
	ALTHOUGH			IN SPITE OF			TOO	
	given A	given B		given A	given B		given A	given B
Exp.	3	7	Exp.	1	4	Exp.	10	8
−Exp.	14	49	−Exp.	12	43	−Exp.	3	4
	BUT			NEVERTHELESS			WHEREAS	
	given A	given B		given A	given B		given A	given B
Exp.	3	4	Exp.	2	4	Exp.	6	7
−Exp.	62	28	−Exp.	58	20	−Exp.	8	12

$0.01 < p < 0.05$), STILL ($\chi^2 = 3.7$, $0.05 < p < 0.10$), and BUT ($\chi^2 = 2.0$, $0.10 < p < 0.20$).

The results of the two tests thus suggest a 2×2 classification of the conjunctions used in the experiment. The four classes are:

Class I. *Given A, B is expected.* The two terms falling in this class are AND and ALSO.

Class II. *Given B, A is expected.* This class also includes two terms—WHILE and AS WELL AS.

Class III. *Given A, B is not expected.* The members of this class are BUT, HOWEVER, YET, ON THE OTHER HAND, NEVERTHELESS, FOR ALL THAT, and STILL.

Class IV. *Given B, A is not expected*. This class includes ALTHOUGH, EVEN
THOUGH, DESPITE, and IN SPITE OF.

The major difference between the conjunctions is due to expectation, i.e.,
between the simply combinatorial terms (Classes I and II) and the contrastive
terms (Classes III and IV). Three terms do not seem to be classified uniquely in
terms of the 2 x 2 classificatory scheme: TOO, which is a combinatorial term
falling in either Class I or II, NOTWITHSTANDING, a contrastive term falling in
either Class III or IV, and WHEREAS, which seems to have been chosen
randomly.

One may look at the results from a slightly different vantage point by
determining directly what proportion of total usage is contributed by each
conjunction for each of the four combinations of expectation and condition.
These results are presented in Table 8-4. Inspection of this table reveals that
AND, ALSO, AS WELL AS, TOO, and WHILE account for 0.800 of the entries
for Class I and 0.737 of the entries for Class II (and in each case are the five
most popular conjunctions), that BUT, HOWEVER, NEVERTHELESS, YET,
ON THE OTHER HAND, FOR ALL THAT, and STILL account for 0.705 of

TABLE 8-4   Use of Various Conjunctions for Each Combination of Expectation and
Condition

	Given A, B is exp.		Given A, B is not exp.		Given B, A is exp.		Given B, A is not exp.	
	p	*f*	*p*	*f*	*p*	*f*	*p*	*f*
AND	0.394	71	0.011	4	0.305	55	0.008	3
ALSO	0.172	31	0.031	11	0.100	18	0.011	4
ALTHOUGH	0.017	3	0.039	14	0.039	7	0.136	49
AS WELL AS	0.122	22	0.003	1	0.144	26	0.033	12
BUT	0.017	3	0.172	62	0.022	4	0.078	28
DESPITE	0.006	1	0.042	15	0.044	8	0.136	49
EVEN THOUGH	0.017	3	0.053	19	0.028	5	0.153	55
FOR ALL THAT	0.006	1	0.050	18	0.011	2	0.031	11
HOWEVER	0.017	3	0.078	28	0.011	2	0.025	9
IN SPITE OF	0.006	1	0.033	12	0.022	4	0.119	43
NEVERTHELESS	0.011	2	0.161	58	0.022	4	0.056	20
NOTWITHSTANDING	0.000	0	0.044	16	0.000	0	0.050	18
ON THE OTHER HAND	0.022	4	0.061	22	0.011	2	0.022	8
STILL	0.039	7	0.044	16	0.006	1	0.044	16
TOO	0.056	10	0.008	3	0.044	8	0.011	4
WHILE	0.056	10	0.008	3	0.144	26	0.033	12
WHEREAS	0.033	6	0.022	8	0.039	7	0.033	12
YET	0.011	2	0.139	50	0.006	1	0.019	7
		180		360		180		360

the entries for Class III (constituting six of the seven most popular conjunctions), and that ALTHOUGH, EVEN THOUGH, DESPITE and IN SPITE OF account for 0.544 of the entries for Class IV (and are the four most popular conjunctions in this class). Thus, 16 of the 18 conjunctions fall rather clearly into three distinct groups, with only two terms, WHEREAS and NOTWITHSTANDING, left unclassified. It will be seen later that these groups correspond rather well to the results yielded by a cluster analysis of the data from the tree construction task.

The analysis of the sentence completion data shows that of the four independent variables manipulated in this experiment, expectation was the most influential in determing the frequency of choice of the conjunctions, differentiating AND, ALSO, AS WELL AS, TOO, and WHILE, from the remaining terms. Subjects were also affected, though to a smaller extent, by the specification of which of the yet to-be-conjoined statements was known to be true. This knowledge seemed to play a somewhat stronger role when the "unconditional" statement was not expected than when it was expected, i.e., the differences between Classes III and IV were larger than the ones between Classes I and II. The emphasis placed on either of the two statements (or on both equally) affected the frequency of choice of only a few conjunctions, all of which, with the exception of DESPITE, were used when the antecedent statement (A) was known to hold. The type of semantic relations between the two statements (whether primarily a directional or bidirectional implication) seemed to have no effect at all on the choice of conjunctions, this result being obviously limited to the particular two pairs of sentences employed in the present experiment.

Tree Construction Task (Complete Set)

As mentioned in the introduction to this chapter, we had two main purposes in obtaining similarity judgments on the conjunctions. First, we were interested in the data for their own sake, and, second, we wished to see whether the underlying distinguishing features discovered above—expectation, condition, and, to a lesser extent, emphasis—would emerge from a cluster or an MDS analysis of the directly obtained proximity measures. In reporting the results, Groups CTA and CTB will be kept separate, and the presentation will follow the same order as that of previous chapters, i.e., graph, cluster, and MDS analyses will be presented in that order.

The mean and standard deviation of the number of separate subtrees constructed by the subjects in Group CTA were 5.25 and 1.593, respectively. Compared with previously reported results, the standard deviation is particularly small. All 40 subjects used all three options in constructing the trees, first building subtrees and then merging them together, and none of the subjects built less than three subtrees. Many of the trees were highly similar; indeed, the following three subtrees, which, with one exception, correspond to Classes I + II, Class IV, and Class III above, were constructed by most of the subjects:

> AND-ALSO-AS WELL AS-TOO,
> ALTHOUGH-EVEN THOUGH-DESPITE-IN SPITE OF,
> and BUT-HOWEVER-YET-STILL-ON THE OTHER HAND-
> FOR ALL THAT-NEVERTHELESS.

Presented on the left-hand side of Table 8-5 are the predicted and observed distributions of node degree for Group CTA. The difference between the two distributions is significant ($p < 0.05$ by the one-sample Kolmogorov-Smirnov test), suggesting that trees were not constructed randomly. The discrepancies between predicted and observed frequencies are of the same kind as those observed in Chapters 3, 4, 5, and 6, i.e., there are fewer nodes with degree 1 and more nodes with degree 2 than predicted by chance alone.

TABLE 8-5   Observed and Predicted Frequency Distributions of Node Degree
(Groups CTA and CTB)

	Group CTA		Group CTB	
Degree	Predicted	Observed	Predicted	Observed
1	280	241	116	120
2	265	349	108	109
3	125	103	50	53
4	39	23	16	11
5+	11	4	4	1

The left-hand side of Table 8-6 shows the predicted and observed distributions of the number of pairs of adjacent nodes chosen by y subjects, $y = 0, 1, \ldots, 40$. The parameters of the predicted distribution, p and s, are presented below the table. The fit of the negative binomial distribution is good, as in all previous studies ($p > 0.20$, by the one-sample Kolmogorov-Smirnov test), and the discrepancies between observed and predicted frequencies provide additional evidence against the hypothesis of a random construction of trees. The value of s is of about the same order of magnitude as that reported in Chapters 5 and 6, indicating a "moderate" popularity bias. The most "popular" pairs of (adjacent) nodes, selected by more than half of the subjects, were (in decreasing order): ALSO-TOO (40), DESPITE-IN SPITE OF (34), ALTHOUGH-EVEN THOUGH (32), WHILE-WHEREAS (30), AND-AS WELL AS (29), STILL-YET (26), AND-ALSO (24), BUT-HOWEVER (21), HOWEVER-

TABLE 8-6   Observed and Predicted Frequency Distributions of Selected Pairs of Adjacent Nodes (Groups CTA and CTB)[a]

y	Group CTA		y	Group CTB	
	Predicted	Observed		Predicted	Observed
0	55	48	0	21	21
1	21	29	1	17	16
2	14	17	2	13	15
3	10	11	3	10	15
4	8	5	4	8	3
5	6	10	5	6	5
6	5	3	6	4	2
7	4	3	7	3	5
8	4	3	8	2	1
9	3	1	9	2	3
10	3	2	10	1	1
11	2	3	11	1	1
12	2	1	12+	3	3
13	2	2			
14	2	1			
15	1	2			
16	1	2			
17+	10	10			

[a]Parameters:

	p	s
Group CTA	0.085	0.273
Group CTB	0.413	1.127

NEVERTHELESS (21). All of these pairs, with the exception of WHILE-WHEREAS, are included in the three subtrees specified in the immediately preceding sections and may be expected to form the nuclei of the clusters obtained by the Connectedness and Diameter methods.

The two clustering methods were applied to the mean proximity matrix and to ten individual proximity matrices selected randomly from Group CTA. A comparison of the two MAXC clusterings for the mean proximity matrix obtained by the Connectedness and Diameter methods showed them to be very close to each other. The two MAXC clusterings are exactly the same with only the exception that the two largest clusters yielded by the Diameter method, Clusters 2 and 3 below, are combined into one cluster by the Connectedness method.

Figure 8-1 portrays the HCS obtained by the Diameter method for the mean proximity matrix of Group CTA. There are three significant clusters:

Cluster 1 [AND, ALSO, AS WELL AS, TOO].

Cluster 2 [ALTHOUGH, EVEN THOUGH, DESPITE, IN SPITE OF, NOTWITHSTANDING, WHILE, WHEREAS].

Cluster 3 [BUT, HOWEVER, FOR ALL THAT, ON THE OTHER HAND, NEVERTHELESS, STILL, YET].

These clusters clearly correspond to the results obtained for Group CSC, and to the graph analysis of Group CTA. Specifically, Cluster 1 consists of the

```
                                                                    ON THE OTHER HAND
                                                       NOTWITHSTANDING
                                                  EVEN THOUGH  FOR ALL THAT
                                                     IN SPITE OF
                                  AS WELL AS     ALTHOUGH  DESPITE       HOWEVER   NEVERTHELESS
                              AND   ALSO  WHILE  WHEREAS          BUT            STILL  YET
            Level             |  |  |  |  |  |  |  |  |  |  |  |  |  |  |  |  |  |    α
             1                . . XXX . . . . . . . . . . . . . . .              3.50
             2                . . XXX . . . . XXX . . . . . . . . .              5.50
             3                . . XXX . . XXX XXX . . . . . . . . .             11.50
             4                XXX XXX . . XXX XXX . . . . . . . . .             13.50
             5                XXX XXX . . XXX XXX . . XXX . . . .               18.00
             6                XXXXXXX . . XXX XXX . . XXX . . . .               20.25
             7                XXXXXXX . . XXX XXX . . XXX . XXX .               20.50
             8                XXXXXXX . . XXX XXXXX . XXX . XXX .               20.75
             9                XXXXXXX XXX XXX XXXXX . XXX . XXX .               23.00
            10                XXXXXXX XXX XXX XXXXX . XXX . XXXXX               23.75
            11                XXXXXXX XXX XXX XXXXX . XXXXX XXXXX               28.00
            12                XXXXXXX XXX XXX XXXXX . XXXXXXXXXX                30.50
            13                XXXXXXX XXX XXXXXXXX . XXXXXXXXXX                 31.25
            14                XXXXXXX XXX XXXXXXXXX XXXXXXXXXXX                 40.00
            15                XXXXXXX XXXXXXXXXXXX XXXXXXXXXXX                  47.25
            16                XXXXXXX XXXXXXXXXXXXXXXXXXXXXXXXX                 51.75
            17                XXXXXXXXXXXXXXXXXXXXXXXXXXXXXXXXXXXX               66.50
```

Fig. 8-1. HCS for Group CTA (Diameter method).

combinatorial terms in Classes I and II, chosen when the "unconditional" statement is expected. The only exception is WHILE. Cluster 2 corresponds to Class IV, with the exception of WHILE and WHEREAS, which are included in the former but not in the latter. Inspection of Fig. 8-1 shows that these two terms were clustered together on stage 9, and were the last terms to be merged with Cluster 2. Finally, Cluster 3 includes the same terms which constitute Class III. The correspondence between the graph analysis and the cluster analysis of Group CTA is very good; the three distinct subtrees, which were identified in most of the individual trees and account for 15 out of the 18 conjunctions, correspond, with the exception of NOTWITHSTANDING, WHILE, and WHEREAS, to Clusters 1, 2, and 3.

Figure 8-1 further shows that the most important variable in determining the clustering results is expectation. Cluster 1 appears to be very compact; it was formed rather early (stage 6) and was merged with the remaining terms only at the very last stage. The distinction in terms of whether the first (A) or the second (B) statement is given is not reflected in the construction of this cluster, i.e., the distinction between AND and ALSO on one hand and AS WELL AS (and possibly TOO) on the other hand is not maintained. The former distinction, however, is clearly reflected in the remaining terms; when the "unconditional" statement is not expected, knowledge of which of the two statements is the "conditional" one seems to affect similarity judgments. Similar conclusions may be drawn when Fig. 8-2, portraying the two-dimensional Euclidean representation for the mean proximity data of Group CTA, is inspected.

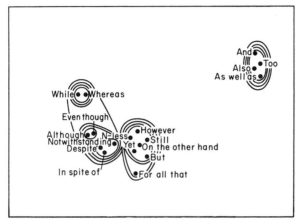

Fig. 8-2. Two-dimensional Euclidean representation for Group CTA.

Following the method used in Chapters 4 and 5, we plotted the results of stages 12 through 16 of the HCS obtained by the Diameter method (Fig. 8-1) on the MDS representation. Clusters 1, 2, and 3 appear to be very compact and the MDS results are similar to the clustering results in most of their details. In particular, the main distinction is seen to be that between Cluster 1 and the remaining two clusters, and the terms WHILE and WHEREAS are farther away from the remaining terms of Cluster 2 than the latter are from the terms constituting Cluster 3. The distinction between ALTHOUGH and EVEN THOUGH on one hand, and DESPITE and IN SPITE OF on the other hand, which was observed in Fig. 8-1, can also be observed in Fig. 8-2, and the term FOR ALL THAT, the last to be added to Cluster 3, is seen to be farther away from the center of its cluster than any other term of this cluster. While the nature of the distinction between coordinating and subordinating conjunctions is perhaps not entirely clear in English, if one follows the criterion suggested by Gleitman (1965), viz. that subordinating conjunctions permit pronominalization to precede their antecedent noun, then it would appear that Cluster 2 [ALTHOUGH, EVEN THOUGH, DESPITE, IN SPITE OF, NOTWITH-

STANDING, WHILE, WHEREAS] is largely or entirely comprised of subordinating conjunctions.

In addition to being applied to the mean proximity matrix, the Young-Torgerson MDS program was also applied to the individual proximity matrices of ten randomly selected subjects from Group CTA. Following the same procedure as in the previous chapters, we obtained solutions in one, two, and three dimensions, with the Euclidean metric yielding smaller stress values

TABLE 8-7   Stress Values for Euclidean Representations

| Dimensions | Group CTA | | | | |
	No. 4	No. 8	No. 12	No. 16	No. 20
3	0.034	0.021	0.068	0.071	0.034
2	0.056	0.043	0.099	0.094	0.075
1	0.179	0.280	0.192	0.168	0.115

Dimensions	No. 101	No. 105	No. 109	No. 114	No. 117	Mean
3	0.075	0.043	0.080	0.031	0.004	0.037
2	0.120	0.080	0.107	0.061	0.083	0.081
1	0.300	0.178	0.194	0.240	0.240	0.103

than the City Block metric in almost all cases. Table 8-7 presents the stress values for the Euclidean representations. A comparison between the stress values of the individual and mean proximity matrices shows them to be about equal for $m = 3, 2$. The break in the stress values between $m = 1$ and $m = 2$, especially noticeable for individual subjects, and a comparison between the stress values in Table 8-6 and the critical values reported in Chapter 2, showing the former to be considerably smaller than the latter for $m = 2, 3$, suggests an adequate representability of individual and mean data in a two-dimensional Euclidean space. Inspection of the individual representations does not add much to the picture portrayed in Fig. 8-2. The distinction between simply combinatorial and contrastive terms appears in almost all the individual representations, although it is not as sharp as the one shown in Fig. 8-2, and the significant clusters (from one to three clusters for each subject) are considerably less compact. Attempts to classify subjects according to their HCSs were unsuccessful.

Tree Construction Task (Reduced Set)

Both the cluster and MDS analyses of Group CTA confirmed our earlier suspicion that when proximity measures obtained by the tree construction method are used, the difference between simply combinatorial and contrastive terms would be large and might thus mask other possible differences among the conjunctions. To assess possible variations as a function of other variables, such as those considered in the sentence completion task, we ran a second group of subjects–Group CTB–using essentially the same method and a reduced set of conjunctions composed of the contrastive terms only.

The graph analysis of Group CTB yielded results which were hardly interpretable, and quite different from the results obtained in the previous study, which employed the same method. The mean number of subtrees was 3.05 with standard deviation equal to 1.40. Four of the 21 subjects constructed only one tree and none built more than five subtrees. The observed distribution of node degree presented on the right-hand side of Table 8-5, did not differ significantly from the predicted Poisson distribution, which is derived from the assumption of randomly generated data. A one-way ANOVA with repeated measures performed on the degrees of the labeled nodes showed no significant differences among the means. Furthermore, the observed frequency distribution of selected pairs of adjacent nodes, which was fitted rather well by the predicted negative binomial distribution ($p > 0.20$ by the one-sample Kolmogorov-Smirnov test), resulted in an unusually large value of s. All the values of s reported in previous chapters ranged between 0.2 and 0.6, while the value for Group CTB was 1.127. It may be recalled that the larger the value of s, the weaker the popularity bias, and that as the popularity bias decreases, the negative binomial distribution approaches the Poisson distribution with parameter $\lambda = bY$. In the present case $\lambda = 3.0$ for Group CTB, and the observed distribution of selected pairs of adjacent nodes, presented in the right-hand side of Table 8-6, is, in fact, significantly different from the Poisson distribution. However, in view of the unusually low popularity bias, lack of significant difference between the observed and predicted distributions of node degree, and the results of the ANOVA, one may doubt that the cluster and MDS results for Group CTB warrant presentation or would permit interpretation. These results will not be considered here; however, some comment will be made on them in the discussion that follows below.

DISCUSSION

We shall begin with some methodological observations regarding the results for Group CTB, the most appropriate representation of the results for Group CTA, and the relation between these results and those yielded by the sentence completion task; we shall then consider the substantive outcome of the present study.

Subjects were run on the reduced set of contrastive conjunctions only (Group CTB) to minimize the danger that differences among these conjunctions might be washed out as a function of the grosser and more salient differences between these conjunctions and the simply combinatorial ones. However, while not completely random, the graph results for Group CTB were closer to randomness than the results of any other study to be reported in the present work. If the various contrastive conjunctions are indeed quite close in meaning, then individual differences in the way in which they are interpreted may be sufficiently large to mask any systematic differences among them, i.e., our tree construction technique may not be powerful enough to capture any such differences. Given these graph findings, there may not be much justification for a further consideration of the cluster analysis and MDS results; however, it may be worth while to indicate the main tenor of these findings. If in the cluster results one examines only pairs or triads of items clustered together, then there is a fair agreement between the results for Groups CTA and CTB, with pairs such as ALTHOUGH-EVEN THOUGH, DESPITE-IN SPITE OF, STILL-YET, and triads such as BUT-HOWEVER-ON THE OTHER HAND falling together in very similar ways. However, the only significant cluster for Group CTB, which includes eight of the 14 items, viz. ALTHOUGH, EVEN-THOUGH, DESPITE, IN SPITE OF, NEVERTHELESS, BUT, HOWEVER, ON THE OTHER HAND, merges items from two distinct significant clusters obtained for Group CTA. Also, STILL, YET, WHILE, and WHEREAS fall into one significant cluster in CTB, whereas in CTA the first two terms fall into one, larger significant cluster, and the latter two terms into another, larger significant cluster. While the stress value of the two-dimensional Euclidean solution for the mean proximity matrix of Group CTB is somewhat larger than that for Group CTA (0.114 versus 0.081) the fit is still acceptable, given the criteria indicated in Chapter 2. However, an inspection of the two-dimensional MDS plot does not permit any intuitively plausible interpretation of the findings, nor can the outcomes of either the cluster analysis or of the MDS analysis for Group CTB be juxtaposed with the results of the sentence completion task in any manner that appears to be at all revealing. In short, the results for Group CTB are puzzling: a manipulation designed to focus attention on relatively subtler differences among items, by limiting the set to contrastive conjunctions only, appears to have resulted rather in less intelligible and more random findings.

The two-dimensional Euclidean representation for Group CTA provides a relatively good fit, and the three significant clusters embedded in it are relatively compact. Nevertheless, no dimensional interpretation of these results appears possible. The observation that the two clusters of contrastive conjunctions fall much closer to each other than to the cluster of simply combinatorial terms should not be regarded as implying that the combinatorial-contrastive distinction involves some sort of a graded continuum (the results of the sentence completion task also argue against any such implication), nor is there any obvious interpretation of the fact that some conjunctions falling into the same significant cluster are farther removed from each other in the spatial solution than are other conjunctions which fall into distinct, significant clusters. A hierarchic or cross-classificatory representation would seem to be a more appropriate one for these findings, with a principal distinction between contrastive and simply combinatorial terms, and a further differentiation between classes of contrastive terms. This suggestion is supported by the considerable degree of agreement or consistency between the results based on a direct similarity scaling and the results yielded by the sentence completion task, an agreement not only with regard to the gross distinction between contrastive and simply combinatorial conjunctions, but with regard to other properties of the results as well.

What of the substantive yield of this work with regard to properties important in specifying the meanings of the various conjunctions, and in differentiating among them? The results of the sentence completion task indicated no differences as a function of sentence type and, of course, the direct similarity data have nothing to say on this score since the propositions to-be-conjoined are not specified in the tree construction task. While one-third of the conjunctions were significantly affected as a function of which of the conjoined propositions was emphasized, there is no indication that this factor has any noticeable effect on the direct similarity judgments, thus, e.g., AND and ALSO fall very close together in the graph, cluster, and MDS results, even though they show exactly opposite trends as a function of what is to be emphasized (note however that in other regards these two terms are responded to in a very similar fashion on the sentence completion task).

The two factors that made the major difference in the sentence completion task were *condition* and *expectation*, the latter having considerably more weight. An inspection of these results led to a cross-classification of the conjunctions in terms of these two factors which unambiguously located 15 of the 18 terms. Of the remaining three terms one (TOO) fell equally well into either of the first two classes (combinatorials), one (NOTWITHSTANDING) could be placed equally well in either of the latter two classes (contrastives), and only one (WHEREAS) could not be unambiguously located at all. The principal result of graph, cluster, and MDS analyses of the direct similarity data yielded by the tree construction task was the identification of three groupings of items, the first composed of combinatorial terms corresponding closely to Classes I and II of the sentence construction task, the other two groupings corresponding to Classes III and IV, with only minor and qualified exceptions in regard to the identity of the items falling into the groupings and those falling into the classes. The finding that the contrast with regard to expectation serves to differentiate all the items, while that with regard to condition only serves to distinguish the contrastive terms, and that the two groups of contrastive terms are much closer to each other than either is to the group of combinatorial terms in the spatial MDS solution, corroborates the findings of the sentence completion task.

While the results of the sentence completion task and of the tree construction task are in agreement in identifying both expectation and condition factors as relevant in characterizing and differentiating among the meanings of the various conjunctions, and in assigning greater weight to the former factor, they differ in that the results of the sentence completion task suggest a cross-classification with regard to these factors as the most appropriate structural representation of the data, while the results of the direct similarity procedure suggest rather some sort of hierarchic representation with a first principal distinction between combinatorial and contrastive terms, and then a subsequent differentiation of the latter as a function of condition, i.e., in terms of which the two to-be-conjoined propositions is given. While there are no compelling reasons in support of either alternative, we tend to prefer the former on the grounds that the sentence completion procedure imposes a more specific task on the subject and, given a general consistency between the results of such a procedure and those of a less constrained procedure, the former may be able to elicit information and distinctions not accessible by the latter.

To return to the data, can one argue that conjunctions falling into the same cluster and contiguously located in the spatial solution are really synonymous or semantically equivalent? The negative answer to this question is implicit in what has been said above. While items falling in different clusters clearly are not equivalent, items falling into the same cluster may be, but certainly need not be, equivalent. For it is quite possible, indeed likely, that application of further tests or procedures would permit one to distinguish or differentiate among at least some such items. We have already seen that items falling into Cluster 1 in the direct similarity data appear to fall into two distinct classes when the results of the sentence completion task are considered, and, further, that items falling into Class I, viz. AND, ALSO, and perhaps TOO, can be differentiated in terms of differences in what is to be emphasized. Thus, while not denying the possibility that some conjunctions may indeed be semantically equivalent, no such assertion can be made with any confidence until they have been shown to behave in similar fashion under a variety of specific, locally pertinent tests. Further, it would appear quite likely that even if some conjunctions are functionally synonymous, differences in their use may be syntactically conditioned. Thus BUT and HOWEVER may be very similar semantically, yet the latter term can be used as the initial word in a sentence while the former would not characteristically be so used, except in dialogue; further, BUT requires a sentence in which the contrasted propositions both appear, whereas HOWEVER requires only one of them although, of course, it permits both. Rather similar comments may be made about combinatorial terms such as AND and ALSO. As to grammatical constructions in which the conjunctions enter, terms such as EVEN THOUGH and IN SPITE OF, even if semantically equivalent, may differ in that the latter is almost constrained to take a gerund while the former is perhaps more likely to enter in some different construction, e.g., compare "EVEN THOUGH he loved her . . ." and "IN SPITE OF loving her . . . ." The only point in mentioning such obvious examples is to remind the reader that all differences among conjunctions are not semantically or pragmatically determined. Perhaps one additional cautionary comment may be appropriate here. The fact that the language user might be able to draw consistent distinctions of many sorts under some variety of close questioning surely does not imply or require that he characteristically makes such distinctions under normal conditions of usage. Thus, bearing in mind a proviso with regard to syntactic conditioning of conjunction choice, the three gross clusters emerging from the analyses of direct similarity data may indeed provide a fairly adequate representation of the semantic distinctions normally governing selection of a particular conjunction.

We shall make one final observation on the results. The great weight or salience of the distinction between combinatorial and contrastive terms should not be surprising if one considers that in most instances the choice of a combinatorial or contrastive conjunction is completely determined (and therefore categorically redundant), given the senses of the two propositions to be conjoined. Thus given P_1 = "He is a Republican" and P_2 = "He always votes for the Democratic candidate" there would be something paradoxical in using anything other than a contrastive conjunction to connect the two propositions, even though there would be freedom with regard to which particular contrastive term to use as a function of which is taken as the logically prior proposition, which is to be emphasized, etc. Although the above is generally true, there are cases when there may be no clear implicational or correlative relation between the propositions to be conjoined, and where the choice of combinatorial or contrastive conjunction indicates, for that particular case, whether or not the second proposition was to have been expected given the first: Thus given P_1 = "He ran for Congress" and P_2 = "He lost the election" either AND or BUT may be used to conjoin P_1 and P_2, and the particular term chosen says something as to the speaker's expectations. Note further that if P_2 had been "He won the election" then, unless the speaker intended to convey a very extraordinary suggestion indeed, he would have been constrained to use AND, and avoid BUT. These last examples touch on the possible uses of conjunctions as probes to get at putative semantic components in verbs (see the use that Bendix, 1966, makes of the BUT test), and on possible temporal and causal components of conjunctions which are realized in certain contexts; these are matters beyond the scope of the present discussion.

Chapter 9   *HAVE VERBS*

The term "semantic field" has been used by various theorists, who argue that a language may be subdivided into different conceptual spheres,

> that the vocabulary of a language divides into classes of items, each marking off an integrated conceptual domain within which the conceptual space is differentiated into elementary regions whose boundaries delimit and are delimited by the boundaries of others. These elementary regions, either individually or taken together in groups, are labeled by words in a vocabulary, the elementary region or compound region labeled by a word being regarded as its meaning (Katz, in press).

A general survey of this work with extensive documentation and bibliography may be found in Ullman (1962, pp. 243-253), who emphasizes the value of a field theory approach particularly in "introducing a truly structural method . . . what matters is the structure of a semantic field as a whole (p. 250)," but who also comments that

> the neatness with which words delimit each other and build up a kind of mosaic, without any gaps or overlaps, has been greatly exaggerated. This is true only of specialized and rigidly defined systems such as army ranks; in ordinary language, vagueness, synonymy, ambiguity, and similar factors will produce a much less tidy picture (p. 249).

Up to this point we have been concerned primarily with the analysis of terms coming from relatively well-defined or delimited domains. Actually, one may note some sort of continuity in this regard from chapter to chapter. We have two well-defined domains where there are no sampling problems at all, since the domains or subdomains can be exhaustively specified (kinship, pronouns), two domains which are well-defined but where there are some problems in the sampling of terms (color names, emotion terms), and two perhaps somewhat less well-defined domains, where a relatively exhaustive listing of the principally used terms is possible, but where again there are some problems in the sampling of these terms (prepositions, conjunctions). Domains of this sort "are essentially natural subsets and are not representative of the more loosely structured general lexicon (Bendix, 1966, p. 3)." Insofar as our techniques have yielded sensible or plausible results when applied to the study of relatively restricted, structured domains, perhaps this may be taken as a partial validation of these techniques, and a challenge to apply them to cases where the class of terms is open, with ill-defined and indefinite boundaries, but where, nevertheless, all the terms involved appear to have some important meaning component(s) in common.

We shall now attempt to apply our techniques toward the study of two or three such semantic fields, in each case "selecting a set of words that is only part of a larger system of mutual oppositions which, unlike a kinship terminology, for example, is not clearly delimitable (Bendix, 1966, p. 3)." In applying techniques of the sort used in the present study to the investigation of semantic fields whose boundaries are fuzzy and whose structures may be complex and fragmented, we intend them to serve in part as discovery procedures, and in part as routines for the investigation of some partial, gross hypotheses as to factors relevant to the organization of these semantic fields. It must be clear that in the study of ill-defined domains there arise a number of critical problems which are not encountered when some closed, well-defined domain or subdomain is under investigation. Just because a domain is ill-defined, it is impossible to exhaustively specify or identify all of its members, it is unclear how to sample from an extensive list of putative members, it is unclear what the effect may be of having a relative concentration of items (many quasi-synonymous and perhaps relatively infrequent) in some region of the conceptual space, or of omitting items that appear to be scattered widely over other regions of the space, and it is unclear where one domain merges or overlaps with some other domain. Decisions with regard to any or all of these sorts of considerations may significantly affect the nature of the underlying properties that emerge, and their apparent structural organization. While arbitrary decisions will have to be made in selecting the items which are to constitute some semantic field or domain, it should be recognized that the problems or difficulties encountered here are not peculiar to the work of the psychologist, but equally affect the work of the linguist who is attempting to define a domain for semantic analysis. To the extent that he makes use of some sort of *Sprachgefühl* or linguistic intuition in making his decisions, and that these are not regarded as completely arbitrary and simply responsive to the whim of the investigator, so a similar license ought to be given to the psychologist engaged on a similar endeavor. In any case, the above points to the need for some sorts of explicit criteria for decision procedures in identifying the possible members of relatively ill-defined semantic domains.

In the present chapter we shall be concerned with verbs of the HAVE family (including such verbs as FIND, GAIN, GIVE, HOLD, TAKE, etc.) because of the intrinsic importance and generality of use of these verbs, and because a structural analysis has recently been offered for a restricted subset by Bendix (1966). In the next chapter we shall examine a set of interpersonal verbs of praising and blaming, or more generally JUDGING (including such terms as ACCUSE, APPROVE, BLAME, CHARGE, PRAISE, etc.), some of which have been discussed previously by Fillmore (1969a). Finally, in Chapter 11, we shall consider two sets of quite heterogeneous terms related only in that all terms in the one set are GOOD adjectives, and all terms in the other set BAD adjectives (i.e., two sets which are polar with respect to an evaluation dimension), and in that for each item in each set, one or two of its most obvious antonyms may be found in the other set.

As the title of his monograph indicates *(Componential Analysis of General Vocabulary: The Semantic Structure of a Set of Verbs in English, Hindi and Japanese),* Bendix carried out a cross-linguistic study of a subset of HAVE verbs requiring subjects, among other things, to respond to a number of semantic tests including matching and interpretation tasks. Making use of concepts such as " 'inherence,' 'negation,' 'relation,' 'cause,' 'activity,' 'state,' and 'change' (p. 119)," Bendix attempted to define this subset of HAVE verbs in paradigmatic fashion in terms of marked shared features such as possession/nonpossession at given time, status before and after that time, causal locus or chance determination, and ownership (see his fourth chapter titled "Minimal definitions for a selected set of English verbs"); for an appreciation and critique of this enterprise see Fillmore's review (1968).

A number of important differences between Bendix's procedure and that followed in the present study should be noted. Since he believes "that the basic unit of semantic description is not the word, but a function in the form of a schematic kernel sentence containing a given item of vocabulary (p. 119)," Bendix always works with lexical terms embedded in sentence frames; we have dealt with them as isolated items. In seeking "minimal definition by componential analysis," Bendix had his informants make judgments on two or three sentence frames at a time (with terms selected from the ten verbs at interest); we required our subjects to consider, as a group, all the 29 verbs in our larger sampling from the HAVE domain. Obviously, any procedure that considers only two or three items at a time becomes almost impossibly cumbersome as the number of items of interest increases to any even moderate size. Bendix employed various tests of interpretation, ranking and matching, with particular emphasis on the open ended interpretation of sentences in which two forms are contrasted to get at components that distinguish meaning. He found a ranking procedure using the conjunction BUT particularly useful "to construct tests for components and for the criteriality of components (p. 23)."

Proceeding in a much grosser way, we tried to get our subjects to provide information about the strengths of the similarity relations obtaining among the 29 items, considered as a set. Finally, while Bendix did use his procedures as formal tests in the case of Hindi and Japanese informants (and rejected those tests that did not yield clear results), in the case of English, "although a small number of informants was considered (p. 61)," basically the tests are presented only as possible procedures to be followed; as he says "In the Chapter on English we only illustrate this procedure, and it is left to the reader to check the tests against his intuitions as a speaker of the language (p. 9)." We, of course, shall be reporting in full the data actually yielded by our subjects.

Wexler has very recently (1970a, b) reexamined nine of the ten HAVE verbs studied by Bendix and, in place of the paradigmatic model suggested by Bendix, has developed a model in terms of "embedding structures," where an "embedding structure" is defined as a "hierarchy with cross-classification possible at each level or node," i.e., as a mixed organization involving both hierarchic and cross-classificatory components. Using a triad test both on words and sentences, and also examining choice latencies for the case of word triads, Wexler has shown that his model fits the data much more adequately than does the componential model more informally developed by Bendix. We shall see that, insofar as comparison is possible, the results of the present study are in good agreement with those obtained by Wexler.

While Bendix has attempted to provide an explicit account for a subset of ten HAVE verbs, treating these more or less as an isolated example of how one might proceed in a particular semantic analysis, Katz has tried to show how one may mesh a semantic theory with a transformational theory of grammar and then go on to an analysis of semantic fields (Katz, in press). Katz indicates how one might provide an account of the converse terms "buy" and "sell," and of the relation between them, and then generalizes his analysis, or at least hints as to how it might be generalized

> to provide an account of the conceptual domain that is covered in English by the class of words including, besides "sell" and "buy," the words "trade," "exchange," "swap," "give," "receive," "lend," "borrow," "inherit," "lease," "hire," "rent," and so forth.

Considering such concepts as *possession* and *transfer of possession* as basic to the domain involved, Katz assumes "that each of these words that label regions in this domain can be defined by lexical readings that vary in formal structure in ways that leave the basic structure of the domain invariant." Systematically changing the number of conjuncts in the reading, the conditions specified by state semantic markers, and the selection restrictions on categorized variables, Katz illustrates how one may go from one word to another word in the domain. Thus if the second process semantic marker in "buy" and "sell" which indexes an *exchange* component is eliminated, we get to "receive" and "give;" if one changes "the semantic markers that specify the condition in the state semantic markers representing the initial and terminal states of the process" and marks these for time as temporary, we can get to "hire" or "let" (or more generally "rent"); making both sorts of changes simultaneously one gets "borrow" and "lend," etc. Essentially, Katz is trying to provide a general schema for the analysis of semantic fields, and is here illustrating such a schema by reference to some of the components or markers relevant to the domain of HAVE verbs.

METHOD

The subjects were 58 male and female undergraduate students enrolled at the University of North Carolina. There were two groups of subjects—Group HTM, consisting of 17 male subjects who constructed labeled trees following the standard instructions (see Chapter 2), and Group HDG, consisting of 41 male and female subjects, who sorted the terms into clusters, employing the instructions for the Direct Grouping task (see Chapter 2). The subjects in Group HDG are the same as those in Group PDG (Chapter 7), who sorted prepositions into clusters. In the present study, the deck of HAVE words always came either second or third in the series of four decks (prepositions, HAVE words, GOOD words, and BAD words; the latter two sets of terms will be discussed in Chapter 11), and most subjects in Group HDG took between 10 and 15 minutes to sort the words in this deck into as many separate piles as they wished.

The list of 29 HAVE words employed in this study and presented to both groups is shown in Table 9-1. Included in the list are nine out of the ten words used by Bendix (1966), plus 20 more words which we regarded as falling into the same semantic field. As indicated in the previous section, the semantic field of HAVE words is ill-defined, the 29 terms, though highly representative, do not exhaust the domain, and the decision as to whether or not to include terms such as USE, LACK, or WANT, etc., is, to a large extent, an arbitrary one.

RESULTS

Graph Analysis

Counting the number of distinct subtrees that were formed and then averaging over the 17 subjects in Group HTM resulted in a mean number of 6.00 subtrees, with a standard deviation of 2.93. All three options were used by the subjects in constructing the trees. The labeling of the links shows that, as in all previous studies, nodes were first grouped into clusters that were merged into larger clusters and then into a tree at the final stages of the construction.

TABLE 9-1   Mean Node Degree and Mean Number of Terms Clustered with Each Verb
(Groups HTM and HDG)

Term	Mean node degree	Mean number of terms clustered with each verb
ACCEPT	1.53	3.00
BEG	1.76	1.90
BELONG	1.24	3.05
*BORROW	1.88	2.59
BRING	1.24	0.90
BUY	1.59	2.44
EARN	2.00	2.95
*FIND	1.06	2.24
GAIN	2.53	3.32
*GET	3.71	3.54
*GET RID OF	2.59	2.51
*GIVE	2.76	3.00
HAVE	2.41	3.39
HOLD	1.82	3.27
*KEEP	2.06	3.07
LACK	1.82	2.05
*LEND	1.47	2.71
*LOSE	1.65	1.98
NEED	2.35	2.15
OFFER	1.76	2.61
OWN	2.29	3.39
RECEIVE	2.18	3.15
RETURN	1.65	1.76
SAVE	1.59	2.98
SELL	1.53	2.44
STEAL	1.24	2.51
*TAKE	3.24	3.07
USE	1.29	1.56
WANT	1.76	2.39

*Terms analyzed by Bendix.

Table 9-2 shows the observed and predicted frequency distributions of node degree. The difference between the observed and predicted distributions is nonsignificant, suggesting, as in Chapter 7, either that trees were constructed randomly, or that the distribution of node degree is not sensitive to the judgmental processes operating in the task. To decide between these two alternatives a number of further statistics were examined.

Presented in Table 9-3 are the observed and predicted distributions of pairs of adjacent nodes selected by y subjects, $y = 0, 1, \ldots, 17$. Consistent with all studies reported in earlier chapters, the difference between the two distributions

TABLE 9-2   Observed and Predicted Frequency Distributions of Node Degree (Group HTM)

Degree	Predicted	Observed
1	187	193
2	181	189
3	87	79
4	28	23
5	7	5
6+	3	4

TABLE 9-3   Observed and Predicted Frequency Distributions of Pairs of Adjacent Nodes (Group HTM)[a]

y	Predicted	Observed
0	272	274
1	49	62
2	25	21
3	16	8
4	11	7
5	8	3
6	6	4
7	4	4
8	3	3
9	2	6
10	2	2
11	2	1
12+	6	11

[a]Parameters: p s
                0.154   0.214

is nonsignificant ($p > 0.20$ by the one-sample Kolmogorov-Smirnov test). The discrepancies between observed and predicted frequencies, although nonsignificant, are of the same kind reported in Chapters 3, 4, and 7, i.e., the predicted frequency is smaller than the observed frequency for $y = 0$, and larger for $y = 2, 3, \ldots, 6$. This finding reinforces our previously stated suspicion that the hypothesis of gamma-distributed "popularity bias" might not prove tenable if a considerably larger amount of data were collected.

The parameters of the predicted negative binomial distribution, p and s, are given in the lower part of Table 9-3. They assume values very close to the ones observed in Group PT (Chapter 7); the value of s is 0.214, compared with $s = 0.219$ in Chapter 7. Indeed, a comparison of Table 7-3 in Chapter 7 with Table 9-3 in this chapter shows the two observed distributions to be remarkably similar; the small difference between them is mainly due to the difference in the number of subjects (17 in Group HTM compared with 20 in Group PT). The low value of s indicates a relatively strong popularity bias. Table 9-3 shows that 11 pairs of nodes were selected by at least 12 out of the 17 subjects. These are (in decreasing order): STEAL-TAKE (16), ACCEPT-RECEIVE (14), BELONG-OWN (13), GET RID OF-LOSE (13), GET RID OF-SELL (13), HOLD-KEEP (13), KEEP-SAVE (13), LACK-NEED (13), GIVE-OFFER (12), HAVE-OWN (12), and NEED-WANT (12). These 11 pairs include 18 out of the 29 terms employed in the study. In particular, the 11 pairs include all the terms describing a condition of "having and holding" (BELONG, HAVE, OWN, HOLD, KEEP, and SAVE), and all the terms referring to a condition of "not having or lacking" (LACK, NEED, WANT).

More evidence rejecting the hypothesis of randomly generated proximity data was provided by one-way ANOVA with repeated measures performed on the degrees of the labeled nodes. The analysis yielded a highly significant label effect ($p < 0.001$). The distribution of the mean degree of the verbs, presented in Table 9-1, is even more skewed than the one obtained with Group PT in Chapter 7. It reveals that GET, TAKE, and GIVE have the highest mean degree, whereas FIND, STEAL, BRING, and BELONG have the lowest.

We next examined the results of Group HDG where the HAVE words were sorted into distinct groups. It may be recalled that in interpreting the results of Group PDG in Chapter 7, we could not determine whether the number of distinct groups formed by these subjects reflected individual differences in response bias or individual differences in the ability to discriminate relatively subtle variations in meaning in a particular semantic domain, or both. Because of the high similarity in the graph results of Groups PT and HTM and, more important, because the same subjects participated in Groups PDG and HDG, one might expect similar results for the latter two groups. Indeed, the mean number of groups formed and the standard deviation, 12.59 and 4.25, respectively, are only slightly larger than the values of these statistics in Group PDG, viz. 12.34 and 4.12. The number of groups formed by the subjects ranged from 3 to 22, indicating considerable individual differences.

The right-hand column of Table 9-1 shows the mean number of terms sorted together with each verb. Thus, GET was sorted together with 3.54 terms on the average, whereas BRING, on the average, was sorted with less than one term. As was argued in Chapter 7, a positive corrrelation is to be expected between columns 2 and 3 in Table 9-1, since terms with a low mean degree are likely to be placed in groups with a relatively large number of members, and vice versa. Since the mean number of subtrees is considerably smaller than the mean number of groups for Group HDG, the correlation should be moderate or low. Computing this correlation, we obtained $\rho = 0.55$ ($p < 0.01$).

Another interesting statistic is the frequency distribution of pairs of terms sorted together by y subjects, $y = 0, 1, \ldots, 41$. This frequency distribution is presented in Table 9-4, showing that 166 pairs out of the 406 possible pairs of terms were sorted together by none of the subjects, 80 pairs were sorted together by one subject only, and 19 pairs were sorted together by at least one-half of the subjects. A direct comparison between Tables 9-3 and 9-4 is not possible since each table is based on a different number of subjects. The similarity between Groups HTM and HDG in terms of pairs of terms chosen (Group HTM) or sorted together (Group HDG) is more convincingly demonstrated when the nine pairs that were sorted together by more than 70% of the subjects in Groups HDG are examined. These are (in decreasing order): BELONG-OWN (36), NEED-WANT (35), HOLD-KEEP (32), HAVE-OWN (32), ACCEPT-RECEIVE (32), KEEP-SAVE (31), GIVE-OFFER (30), HOLD-SAVE (29), and BELONG-HAVE (29). Seven out of the 11 pairs of nodes selected by at least 70% of the subjects in Group HTM are included among these pairs.

TABLE 9-4   Observed Frequency Distribution of Pairs of HAVE Words Sorted Together in the Same Cluster (Group HDG)

y	Frequency	y	Frequency
0	166	11	4
1	80	12	6
2	28	13	6
3	16	14	4
4	14	15	3
5	16	16	5
6	7	17	1
7	11	18	1
8	7	19	0
9	7	20	0
10	5	21+	19

To sum up, the graph analysis performed on the data of Group HTM shows that the proximity measures were not generated randomly. Rather, a strong popularity bias governed the construction of the trees and a large mean number of subtrees was discovered; this suggests the appropriateness of a cluster analysis of the proximity data. The performance of Groups HTM and HDG was highly similar, as reflected by the relatively large number of subtrees and clusters and by the selection of more or less the same pairs of terms by the majority of the subjects in both groups. The remarkable similarity between Groups HTM and HDG on one hand, and Groups PT and PDG on the other hand, reflected in all the statistics that we have computed, strongly suggests that the results reported in the following sections will resemble the ones obtained in Chapter 7.

Cluster Analysis

Both the Connectedness and the Diameter method were applied to the mean proximity matrix of Group HTM and to the proximity matrix of Group PDG (a 29×29 symmetric matrix, where any entry (i, j) gives the frequency with which subjects sort terms i and j into the same group). The distances between the two MAXC clusterings obtained for each group by the two clustering methods were small compared to the ones obtained in the preceding chapters; they were 0.096 and 0.062 for Groups HTM and HDG, respectively. Figures 9-1 and 9-2 portray the HCSs, yielded by the Diameter method, for the proximity matrices of Groups HTM and HDG. The MAXC clusterings consist of four and six clusters for Groups HTM and HDG, respectively, each of these accounting for 28 out of the 29 terms. USE is the only term not accounted for in either of the two HCSs. The distance between the two MAXC clusterings is 0.192, and primarily reflects the difference between the two groups in the number of clusters. With only minor exceptions, the MAXC clusters of Group HDG are included in the MAXC clusters of Group HTM. The two clusters, BELONG-OWN-HAVE, and HOLD-KEEP-SAVE, in Fig. 9-2 are merged into one cluster in Fig. 9-1, and the nine terms RECEIVE, ACCEPT, GET, GAIN, EARN, BUY, TAKE, STEAL, and FIND, which are grouped into two clusters in Fig. 9-2, are grouped into one cluster (together with BRING, BEG, and BORROW) in Fig. 9-1.

As we have already noted, significance of the clusters should not serve as the sole criterion in determining the number of clusters to be interpreted, nor need it be assumed, necessarily, in order to compute a distance between two clusterings. Any two clusterings, i.e., two partitions of the same set of N words may be used. Indeed, since the significance of clusters depends to some extent on the method used for gathering the proximity data and on the number of subjects, the MAXC criterion may yield a clustering with more clusters for one group than for another, and the distance between the two clusterings will then be artificially high. But if the MAXC criterion is rejected in this case, what other criterion might substitute for it in selecting a clustering? Clearly, picking two rows (clusterings) at random, one from each HCS, and computing the distance between them, will not do, since the distance will depend on the selected clusterings, and if weak or strong clusterings are selected, will equal zero. Another alternative, which we have already employed in Chapter 4, is to fix the number of clusters at k, say, select two clusterings of k clusters each, interpret them, and compute the distance between them.

Since subjects in Group HTM constructed, on the average, six subtrees, since the MAXC clustering for Group HDG consisted of six clusters, and since six

Level	BELONG	OWN	HAVE	HOLD	KEEP	SAVE	RECEIVE	GET	GAIN	EARN	FIND	ACCEPT	BUY	BEG	BORROW	TAKE	STEAL	BRING	LEND	GIVE	OFFER	RETURN	GET RID OF	SELL	USE	LOSE	LACK	NEED	WANT	α
1																														11.53
2																														13.59
3																														14.88
4																														15.12
5																														18.00
6																														19.88
7																														23.59
8																														25.35
9																														25.88
10																														27.24
11																														27.71
12																														28.94
13																														39.29
14																														45.65
15																														46.12
16																														47.18
17																														48.18
18																														55.41
19																														60.88
20																														64.12
21																														65.53
22																														65.76
23																														76.71
24																														87.35
25																														99.53
26																														105.06
27																														117.12
28																														131.47

Fig. 9-1. HCS for Group HTM (Diameter method).

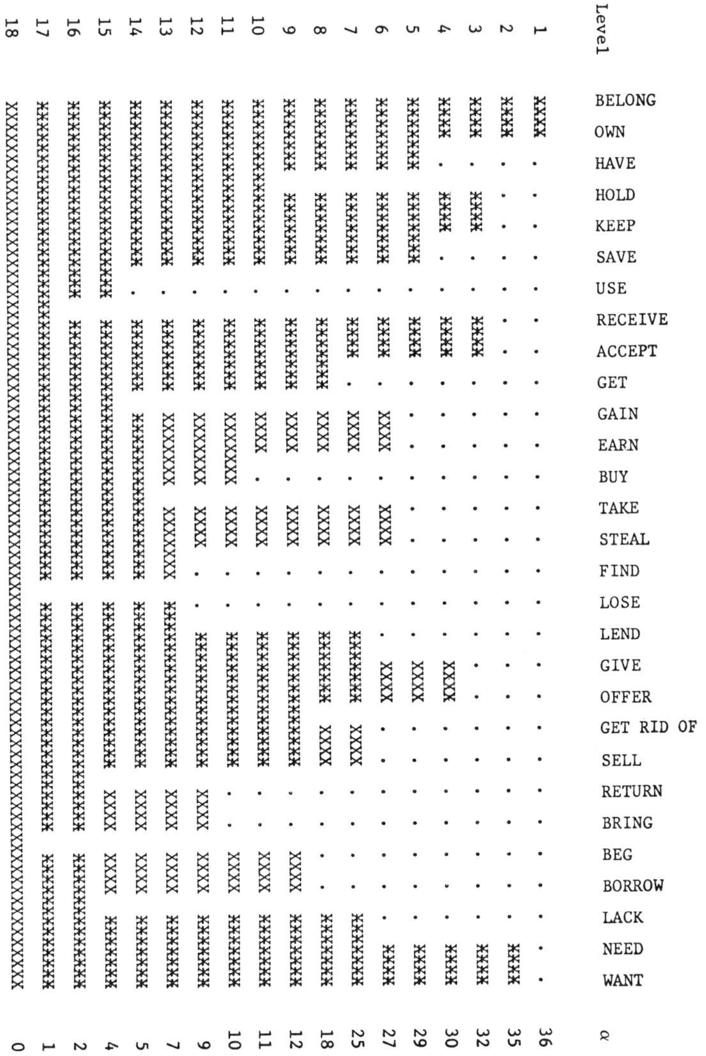

Level

| 1 | 2 | 3 | 4 | 5 | 6 | 7 | 8 | 9 | 10 | 11 | 12 | 13 | 14 | 15 | 16 | 17 | 18 | | α |

BELONG
OWN
HAVE
HOLD
KEEP
SAVE
USE
RECEIVE
ACCEPT
GET
GAIN
EARN
BUY
TAKE
STEAL
FIND
LOSE
LEND
GIVE
OFFER
GET RID OF
SELL
RETURN
BRING
BEG
BORROW
LACK
NEED
WANT

α: 36, 35, 32, 30, 29, 27, 25, 18, 12, 11, 10, 9, 7, 5, 4, 2, 1, 0

Fig. 9-2. HCS for Group HDG (Diameter method).

clusters captured at least 26 out of the 29 terms in each group, we fixed $k = 6$ and obtained two clusterings—C_{20} and C_{15} in the HCSs of Groups HTM and HDG, respectively. The six clusters in Group HTM C_{20} are:

1. HAVING [BELONG, OWN, HAVE, HOLD, KEEP, SAVE].
2. ACQUIRING [RECEIVE, GET, GAIN, EARN, FIND, ACCEPT, BUY].
3. BORROWING [BEG, BORROW].
4. TAKING [TAKE, STEAL].
5. DISPOSING [LEND, GIVE, OFFER, RETURN, GET RID OF, SELL].
6. LACKING [LACK, NEED, WANT].

BRING, LOSE, and USE are not included in any cluster in C_{20}.

The six clusters for Group HDG C_{15} are:

1. HAVING [BELONG, OWN, HAVE, HOLD, KEEP, SAVE, USE].
2. ACQUIRING [RECEIVE, ACCEPT, GET, GAIN, EARN, BUY, FIND, TAKE, STEAL].
3. DISPOSING [LOSE, LEND, GIVE, OFFER, GET RID OF, SELL].
4. BRINGING BACK [RETURN, BRING].
5. BORROWING [BEG, BORROW].
6. LACKING [LACK, NEED, WANT].

Neither LOSE nor USE seem to belong to their respective clusters and should probably be excluded. It can be seen that they were the last terms to be clustered in Group HDG C_{15} and they are also excluded from Group HTM C_{20}.

Group HTM C_{20} and Group HDG C_{15} are very closely related. The HAVING (and holding) cluster (with the exception of USE in Group HDG), the LACKING cluster, the BORROWING cluster, and the DISPOSING cluster (with the exceptions of RETURN in Group HTM and LOSE in Group HDG) are exactly the same in both groups. Clusters 2 and 4 in Group HTM, the ACQUIRING and TAKING clusters, are merged into one cluster in Group HDG, and Cluster 4 in Group HDG which includes two terms only, RETURN and BRING (the latter term is not included in Group HTM C_{20}) is the last cluster, of the six, to be formed. The distance between the two clusterings, each with six clusters, is 0.076. Inspection of Figs. 9-1 and 9-2 reveals additional similarities between the two HCSs. It is noted that the last terms to be clustered in Fig. 9-1 (going from the bottom of the figure up) are USE, LOSE, BRING, BUY, RETURN, ACCEPT, BEG, and BORROW and that seven of these eight terms are also the last to be clustered in Fig. 9-2, maintaining almost exactly the same order.

The Diameter method was also applied to the proximity matrices of five subjects randomly selected from Group HTM. The individual HCSs obtained by the cluster analysis were very similar to the HCS of the mean proximity matrix, but, as in previous chapters, the number of MAXC clusters was smaller than four, and the proportion of terms included in the MAXC clusters was smaller than the one in the MAXC clusters for the group data. Therefore, instead of computing distances between MAXC clusterings, we computed the distances between individual clusterings, each including six clusters, and Group HTM C_{23} (which also consists of six clusters with USE making a distinct cluster). The distances between the five individual clusterings and Group HTM C_{23} were 0.259, 0.187, 0.108, 0.202, and 0.153.

Analysis of individual subjects in Group HDG was carried out in the same way as the analysis of Group PDG in Chapter 7—we computed a 41 x 41 matrix of distances between the subjects in terms of the way each of them sorted the 29 HAVE words and subjected it to analysis by the Diameter method. The resulting MAXC clustering had only one significant cluster including 40 out of the 41 subjects. The results obtained in Chapter 7 with the same group of subjects suggest that the clustering results reflect primarily the number of groups of terms formed by each subject. Indeed, the correlation between the level on which each subject was clustered and the number of groups formed by each subject was negative and highly significant, $\rho = -0.79$, ($p < 0.001$).

Multidimensional Scaling Analysis

The nonmetric MDS program yielded solutions to the individual and mean proximity data in one, two, and three dimensions, for both Euclidean and City Block metrics. Table 9-5 shows the stress values for the Euclidean solutions,

TABLE 9-5   Stress Values for Euclidean Representations

Dimensions	Group HTM						Group HDG
	No. 3	No. 7	No. 11	No. 15	No. 14	Mean	Mean
3	0.084	0.083	0.062	0.039	0.043	0.068	0.110
2	0.120	0.117	0.092	0.063	0.057	0.095	0.152
1	0.201	0.218	0.152	0.150	0.222	0.231	0.369

which, with the exception of two cases, were always smaller than the corresponding stress values for the City Block solutions. The stress values for the mean proximity matrices are fairly close to the ones obtained with the preposition data—0.068, 0.095, and 0.231 in Group HTM versus 0.065, 0.121, and 0.182 in Group PT, and 0.110, 0.152, and 0.369 in Group HDG versus 0.119, 0.230 and 0.456 in Group PDG. The break in the stress values between one and two dimensions and the significant departures of the stress values from the critical cut-off points (see Chapter 2) argue for a two-dimensional Euclidean representation.

Figure 9-3 portrays the two-dimensional representation for the mean proximity data of Group HTM. The six clusters obtained by the Diameter method (C_{20} in Fig. 9-1) are circled in the two-dimensional plot. The two dimensions are difficult to interpret and, as the tight clusters appearing on the plot suggest, any attempt at a dimensional representation imposes structure on the data which is not there, and "can easily lead one to overlook special features of the configuration; features which, if noticed, would lead to a vastly different

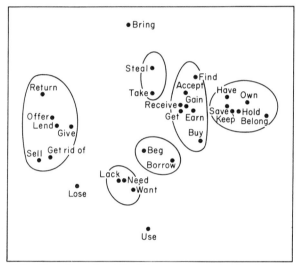

Fig. 9-3.   Two-dimensional Euclidean representation for Group HTM.

interpretation of the underlying structure (Torgerson, 1968, pp. 215–216)." Attempts at interpreting the three-dimensional Euclidean solution yielded similar results—the dimensions seemed to be uninterpretable and, more important, the same six clusters identified by the Diameter method appeared as more or less tight clusters on each of the three two-dimensional plots.

Inspection of the two-dimensional representations for the five subjects, randomly selected from Group HTM, tells a similar story—the dimensions seem uninterpretable in almost all cases and the significant clusters identified by the Diameter method appear as tight clusters in the two-dimensional plots. This result for individual subjects is to be expected since subjects used all three options and constructed several subtrees, later connected into a tree, and by doing so simply built an HCSC.

Figure 9-4 portrays the two-dimensional representation for the proximity data of Group HDG. The two dimensions are somewhat easier to interpret in this case. The horizontal axis is a sort of an OFFER-RECEIVE dimension. On the left-hand side of the axis are words such as GIVE, GET RID OF, SELL (but not LOSE), all of which indicate a purposeful activity. On the right-hand side of the axis are words such as RECEIVE, GET, ACCEPT, indicating a passive reception, but also words such as TAKE, BUY, and EARN, which clearly are not "passive." The vertical axis is a HAVE-LACK dimension, which, however, is less clearly defined because of words such as WANT and NEED, on the one hand, and SAVE and KEEP, on the other hand, which are clearly not simply opposites of each other. The six clusters of C_{15} (Fig. 9-2), which are circled in the

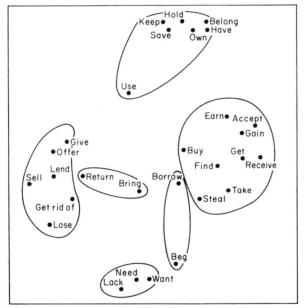

Fig. 9-4.   Two-dimensional Euclidean representation for Group HDG.

two-dimensional plot, suggest again that without carrying out additional analyses, a dimensional representation may conceal or misrepresent the underlying structure.

DISCUSSION

The high skewness of the distribution of words sorted into the same cluster by different subjects (Table 9-4), the finding of a popularity bias for pairs of words, the significant departure of the stress values from the critical cut-off points, and, finally, the intuitive plausibility of the clusterings all argue that the proximity data were not generated randomly and thus justify a further examination of the results.

The first thing to note is that the tree construction method and the direct grouping method yield essentially the same results. In each case there is an OWN or HAVE cluster, a NEED or LACK cluster, a GIVE or DISPOSE OF cluster, and an ACQUIRE cluster (which breaks down into a passive RECEIVE and more active TAKE cluster for Group HTM), and finally a small BEG-BORROW cluster. In addition, there is a small BRING cluster for Group HDG, and the word USE is not really clustered in either group.

Examination of Fig. 9-4 suggests some of the bases for the contrasts. There are two clusters on the horizontal axis—a DISPOSE OF cluster on one side and an ACQUIRE cluster on the other side, which appear to index the difference between (1) presently having and, in one way or another, being in the process of disposing of, and (2) presently not having and, in one way or another, being in the process of acquiring. The vertical axis defined by an OWN or HAVE cluster toward one end and a NEED or LACK cluster toward the other end appears to index the difference between (3) having and holding, and (4) not having or lacking. Given this characterization, it makes some sense that BEG falls near the LACK terms and BORROW near the ACQUIRE terms, that RETURN falls near the DISPOSE OF cluster, that BRING falls between the ACQUIRE and DISPOSE OF clusters, and that USE is the most remotely located term since it does not closely share the properties that define the various clusters. The above comments should not be construed as arguments for a dimensional representation since the clusters of Group HTM (Fig. 9-3) cannot be accounted for by the same two dimensions, and since the words certainly do not fall in any sensibly graded fashion on the dimensions. These comments should only indicate the heuristic value of such a representation in helping to suggest what may govern the obtained clusterings.

The nine verbs from Bendix (1966) which were included in our larger set are: BORROW, FIND, GET, GET RID OF, GIVE, KEEP, LEND, LOSE, and TAKE. As we have noted, Bendix defined these in paradigmatic fashion in terms of marked shared features such as possession/nonpossession at given time, status before that time, causal locus or chance determination, and ownership. With respect to our clustering results, GET, FIND, and TAKE fall together in what we have been calling the ACQUIRE cluster, GIVE, LEND, and GET RID OF fall into the DISPOSE OF cluster, with LOSE near but somewhat set off from this cluster, KEEP falls into the OWN cluster, and BORROW falls into the BEG-BORROW grouping. Clearly some of the differentiating features, such as possession/nonpossession at given time, serve to define the clusters while others appear to be rather less important with differences in them making relatively little difference in the location or clustering of the terms. So, in a sense, our procedure provides a weighting of the importance of the various putative features. It should not be surprising that with more terms added, a neat paradigmatic structure no longer obtains, but rather that now oppositions with regard to some of the features serve as foci for the clustering of the terms, others being much less significant in differentiating them. The structure governing the larger expanded set of terms is likely to be much looser and more complex, perhaps a largely taxonomic structure, some segments of which may have componential or paradigmatic properties.

In fact, if one considers the analyses and results provided by Wexler (1970a, b) it does not appear as though a paradigmatic structure characterizes even the small set of terms considered by Bendix. Wexler has suggested that an "embedding structure" model with a componential component or components embedded in a taxonomic structure may provide a more appropriate representation even for this subset of HAVE verbs. In this model the first distinction, (1), is that between having an object *after* time t and not having it; then (2), the terms in the former class are subclassified in terms of possession or nonpossession *before* time t. This yields:

[[HAVE, KEEP] [GET, TAKE, FIND, BORROW]] , [GIVE, LEND, LOSE].

Thus far the analysis is a hierarchic one. Now the terms in each of these three classes are further distinguished in terms of a componential analysis, which is exemplified by a consideration of the structure obtaining for the terms GET, TAKE, FIND, and BORROW. Thus, GET and FIND are discriminated terms of the presence or absence of an "accidental" component, GET and BORROW in terms of a component indexing the presence or absence of an "obligation" to return the object, and GET and TAKE in terms of the absence or presence of an "active" component in the acquisition of the object. Wexler develops a "process" model to operate on this sort of a structure. The hierarchical process model "works down from the root." It begins by looking at the first level of features. If the words differ at this level, a decision is made, if not, it goes down to the next level where the procedure is repeated, etc. Thus the model seeks the first difference and makes a decision as soon as it is found, ignoring anything deeper or later in the tree. This process model together with some probability assumptions permits Wexler to predict the relative frequency with which pairs of items drawn from a triad will be classified together. When these theoretical values were correlated with the values found for judgments on verb triads, a value of 0.98 was obtained. The correlation between the obtained values and theoretical values generated by stepping off on a componential grid in the most adequate version of a model based upon Bendix' paradigmatic analysis was only 0.68. Basically similar results were obtained when judgments were made on triads of sentences rather than on triads of their main verbs, as above.

If, indeed, the hierarchical model proposed has direct implications for real time processing, then one might expect that triads that have to be processed less deeply should take a shorter time to process. Thus it should be easier and faster to discover the most different item in the triad HAVE, KEEP, LOSE, where the last term differs from the others with regard to the most dominant distinction of possession/nonpossession *after* time t, than for the triad GIVE, LEND, LOSE, where the terms are all the same at the second level in the hierarchy and differ only in terms of their positions in the embedded componential structure. Wexler carried out a choice reaction time study and found, indeed, that triads at level 1 were responded to more rapidly than those at level 2, and that these, in turn, were responded to more rapidly than those at level 3 (where the level number indicates the level in the structure at which the first difference among the members of the triad appears).

The results obtained in the present study may be assessed in a general way with reference to the analysis suggested by Wexler, and also, more specifically, results may be compared for the verbs which were identical in the two studies. So far as general comparisons go it will be recalled that we found four principal clusters, viz. ACQUIRE, DISPOSE OF, HAVE, and NEED. For Group HDG, the ACQUIRE cluster includes GET, TAKE, and FIND, the DISPOSE OF cluster includes GIVE, LEND, and possibly LOSE, and the HAVE cluster includes HAVE and KEEP. Thus, with the exception of BORROW, which forms its own little cluster with BEG, three of the four principal clusters obtained in the present study correspond very closely to those to be expected on Wexler's model; and results with regard to the fourth cluster are irrelevant insofar as Wexler did not consider any of the terms that comprise the NEED cluster. The question does arise, however, whether Wexler's analysis would still hold in the form in which it was presented if terms from this cluster had been included. Such terms, as, e.g., LACK, would presumably be characterized in terms of nonpossession both *before* and *after* time t, and it now becomes an open question whether this should be represented by a redundant hierarchic structure which first makes a distinction regarding possession or nonpossession *after* time t, and then for each set of terms provides the same subclassification with regard to possession or nonpossession *before* time t, or whether a cross-classification with regard to possession/nonpossession *before* and *after* time t, which is formally more economical, is also cognitively more appropriate.

As to more specific comparisons with regard to the nine verbs common to the two studies, one may correlate mean frequencies with which verb pairs were classed together on the triad test in Wexler's study with (1) the frequencies with which these verb pairs were grouped together by our subjects in Group HDG, and with (2) the distances between these verb pairs obtained from the mean proximity matrix for subjects in Group HTM. When one does this one obtains correlations of 0.815 and −0.863, respectively (the last value should be negative, as found, since the more similar two terms are the less distance there is between them). If one correlates the theoretical relative frequencies from Wexler with (1) and (2) one obtains correlations of 0.775 and −0.846, respectively. These values indicate a very considerable consistency between the present results and those obtained by Wexler, a consistency that is perhaps even more impressive if one remembers that there were 29 different terms in our study, that we have singled out for examination only nine of these, that our results are subject to whatever "noise" is generated by the presence of the other 20 items, and that Wexler's process model was developed for the triad task, not tasks of the sort employed in the present study.

How can judgments of similarity be made for terms like the HAVE verbs? If the judge knows the language, he must know how to use these verbs appropriately in a differentiating fashion, assuming that they are conceptually distinct (that there are no full synonyms in the set). In order to sort the terms into different groups or to build a similarity tree, he must ignore some of their distinguishing features. The fewer the features distinguishing two terms or the less important these features the more likely that the terms will be assigned to the same group, or that they will be closely adjacent on a similarity tree. The issue then becomes one of trying "to discover which conceptual features have been ignored and, thus, by indirection, what the features are (Miller, 1969, p. 170)" and, further, of trying to determine the organization of these features—whether the structure is paradigmatic, with complete cross-classification, taxonomic, with hierarchic properties and dominance relations holding between features, mixed, or whatever.

With regard to the present data, it seems clear that a dimensional representation is not really appropriate, for the axes of these solutions cannot readily be interpreted and the terms are not distributed in an appropriately graded and intuitively sensible way in the space. On the other hand, the cluster analysis does yield intuitively sensible groupings and one can say something, as was done earlier, both about what seems to govern assignment to a particular cluster and what seems to differentiate between clusters. Essentially, what we seem to have is a sort of taxonomic structure characterized by inclusion relations of the sort that Bendix describes as "B is a kind of A . . . for example 'lending,' 'granting,' 'conferring,' 'imparting,' etc. could all be considered as kinds of 'giving' (1966, p. 6)," or what Miller (1969) describes in terms of the common presuppositional structure of words where, e.g., both DOCTOR and COOK presuppose PERSON, but with different qualifications, i.e., each is a special kind of person. Thus, in our data, the terms falling into the ACQUIRE cluster all have this as a common meaning core, and represent different ways in which one may acquire, e.g., FIND, where there is the additional feature of chance distinguished by Bendix, TAKE, where there is some active causal attribution as contrasted to the passive attribution of RECEIVE, STEAL, with the additional feature of illegitimacy as contrasted with BUY which specifies legitimacy and indicates its basis, etc. Analogous analyses could obviously be performed for the items constituting the other clusters; thus to SELL disposes of something in a way different from to LEND, which in turn differs from to GET RID OF, etc. Thus, what we seem to have obtained is a kind of a meaning organization in which local, componential, or paradigmatic properties are embedded in an overall cluster structure.

Here we shall make only two observations: (1) While some of the components differentiating items in one cluster may also differentiate items falling in another cluster, e.g., the chance component in LOSE and FIND, or the exchange component in BUY and SELL, there is no reason to expect that these components will recur in all clusters. As Weinreich puts it (1963, p. 149) "whereas in the highly patterned or 'terminologized' domains of vocabulary such as kinship or color, distinguishing components recur in numerous sets of signs, the bulk of the vocabulary is of course more loosely structured and is full of components unique to single pairs, or small numbers of pairs" of signs, thus precluding any paradigmatic system with complete cross-classification. (2) Suppose that similarities among items which constitute the input to a cluster analytic routine are a function of the identity of the items comprising the total set, and that differences with regard to some features, as say ACQUIRE versus DISPOSE OF, have much greater weight or importance than differences in other features. Then it follows that items differing in regard to the former features will be assigned to different clusters and that items with these features in common but differing in other features will fall close together, i.e., in the same cluster, and that paradigmatic, componential distinctions among these items, which might be revealed if one were dealing with limited subsets, may be masked. However, a detailed examination of the way in which minimal clusters are merged into larger and then larger clusters should allow one to extract relevant information on the finer details of structure, although this information may sometimes be difficult to interpret if, e.g., there is a local paradigmatic structure embedded in a larger taxonomic one. Be that as it may, one of the major virtues of a hierarchical clustering procedure is that in addition to yielding clusters it also reveals how these are successively merged into larger and larger clusters, and in so doing provides information about the weighting or importance of the features involved, the later the merging with regard to some property the more significant that property as a differentiating factor.

We may end with a cautionary observation. A semantic field may involve some core concept or concepts, as say *possession* and *transfer of possession* in the case of the domain of HAVE verbs, and there may be some systematic contrasts for limited subsets of terms in the domain, as with regard to BUY-SELL, RECEIVE-GIVE, BORROW-LEND in the present case. Yet different subsets may be structurally organized on the basis of different underlying features governed by different relations, and some terms may legitimately fall within the domain and yet be related to other terms only in the loosest and most indirect ways, with the result that the domain as a whole (given substantial sampling of items from it) may be organized in a very complex, fragmented fashion. Techniques of the sort that we have employed, which attempt to assess the structure of the domain as a whole, may blur or distort the structural relations that obtain among relatively coherent, close subsets of items. Thus any overall analysis should probably be followed up with some further analyses that probe more directly with regard to the relations among closely situated or relatively tightly clustered terms.

Chapter 10   VERBS OF JUDGING

Verbs which refer to interpersonal actions, intentions, and evaluations obviously cover a very large amount of significant ground when it comes to human communication and interaction. Among these, the more restricted but yet still large and perhaps inchoate set of terms which involves judgments of worth and responsibility is of particular importance and interest, in that matters of attribution and evaluation are central to the "naive psychology" of interpersonal relations (see Heider, 1958). As in the case of HAVE verbs, discussed in the preceding chapter, the domain covered by verbs of JUDGING is extensive, with boundaries which are very hard to delimit, so that the inclusion or exclusion of any particular term will necessarily involve quite arbitrary decisions.

There is work by Osgood, directed to the analysis of a large set of interpersonal verbs, which includes a substantial number of verbs of JUDGING among the approximately 200 verbs considered (see Osgood, 1966b, 1968a; Osgood and Ayer, 1968). Osgood attempted to provide an analysis of these verbs in terms of a set, finally, of ten *a priori* semantic features which were intended to capture the most important meaningful properties of these verbs, and to maximally discriminate among them. The features used were: Moral/Immoral; Potent/Impotent; Active/Passive; Associative/Dissociative; Initiating/Reacting; Ego/Alter; Supraordinate/Subordinate; Terminal/Interminal; Future/Past; and Deliberate/Impulsive. Osgood found ". . . that subjects can use the *a priori* features to discriminate semantically among interpersonal verbs and do so with almost total agreement with prior feature ratings made for each verb . . . (Abstract, Osgood and Ayer, 1968)," and that when a variety of empirical tests were made of the way in which these verbs were understood and used (with particular emphasis on a *semantic interaction technique*, where inferences as to underlying semantic features are made in terms of judgments of whether some syntactic combination of words—here an adverb-verb combination—is apposite, anomalous, or simply permissible) something corresponding roughly to five or six of these *a priori* features characteristically emerged. While promising, this sort of an analysis still leaves us with some considerable problems. For example, in terms of the set of ten *a priori* features, the words ACCUSE, BLAME, and CONDEMN are equivalent, and, as a group, differ from CRITICIZE only in that the latter is marked "+" on the Active/Passive feature and on the Deliberate/Impulsive feature, while the other three terms are marked "0" on these features (where "+" or "−" indicates that a particular verb has the given feature in its positive or negative form respectively, and "0" indicates that the verb is not differentiated by that feature). While one might agree that the first three verbs mentioned are very similar in many respects, one would surely boggle nevertheless at treating them as equivalent. And one may certainly wonder whether CRITICIZE really differs from the aforementioned verbs in being marked "+" with regard to an Active/Passive feature and a Deliberate/Impulsive feature, while they are unmarked in these respects. Even if one were to grant this, one might have severe doubts as to whether these are the most significant respects in which CRITICIZE differs from ACCUSE, BLAME, and CONDEMN. In short, there is a very real problem with regard to the adequacy or sufficiency of the set of *a priori* features in marking important differences in meaning. Further, it is not at all clear how these features are supposed to be organized, and the data obtained by the various empirical procedures do not permit any very clear or coherent account of this, perhaps in part because of the enormous "territory" covered by the 198 terms involved (or even by a heterogeneous subset of 40 of them studied in greater detail).

A very different approach to the problem, in the context of a close examination of some 10 or 11 verbs of "praising and blaming," may be found in Fillmore (1969).[1] He distinguishes between the explicit "illocutionary force" of an utterance, the explicit assertion involved or the range of things one can accomplish by that utterance, and its implicit presuppositions, and approaches the lexical description of a subset of verbs of JUDGING in these terms, with particular attention to presuppositional aspects, "conditions which must be satisfied in order for a particular illocutionary act to be effectively performed in saying particular sentences (p. 97)." In carrying out such an analysis, in attempting to describe the "role structure" of these verbs, Fillmore makes use of concepts such as *Situation,* the *Affected* (by the situation), *Defendant*

---

[1] We are grateful to Dr. Kenneth Wexler, University of California, Irvine, for drawing our attention to Fillmore's work, and showing us some of his own preliminary MDS results.

(responsible for the situation), *Judge* (who makes or states some moral evaluation regarding the situation or the defendant's responsibility for it), and the *Addressee* of such a statement.

Perhaps some idea as to Fillmore's approach may be obtained by considering his characterization of ACCUSE, BLAME, and CRITICIZE, or, more particularly, of some ways in which these verbs differ. All three verbs require, at least, a *Judge, Defendant,* and *Situation.* ACCUSE and CRITICIZE require that the Judge says something to someone, while BLAME, for which at least three different senses may be distinguished, characteristically refers to "opinions, or thoughts, or internal judgments." ACCUSE and CRITICIZE differ particularly in that "what is presupposed by use of one of these verbs is part of the linguistic act referred to by the other," and vice versa. Thus

> a speaker of English uses the word *accuse* when talking about a situation which is unquestionably bad and (when) he wishes to report the claim that a certain person is responsible for that situation; he would use the word *criticize* when talking about a situation in which there is no question about who is responsible for it and (when) he wants to report the claim that the situation was blameworthy (p. 105).

In addition, CRITICIZE presupposes the factuality of the *Situation,* but ACCUSE does not, since I can accuse someone of doing something that in fact he never did, but I can hardly criticize him for something that never occurred. Further, ACCUSE may be used performatively (in Austin's sense where a statement with this verb in the first person present tense may itself constitute the named act; think of Zola's "J'accuse") while CRITICIZE is not a performative verb. Fillmore points out that BLAME may be understood in senses that correspond to ACCUSE and CRITICIZE, respectively, with the principal difference (mentioned above) that nothing is being said overtly, or may be used in still a third sense which is like ACCUSE and does involve the *Judge* in saying something to somebody, but where it is presupposed that the *Defendant* is not responsible for the situation, "is not the *Addressee* of the *Judge's* statement, and (that) the *Judge* is not the *Defendant.*" In a similar vein, Fillmore attempts an analysis of some other verbs involving judgments of worth and responsibility. It must be obvious that an approach of this sort, as exemplified above, does capture some important meaning properties that are not readily accessible given Osgood's analysis, and does clarify and index some significant differences between verbs which are ignored on the latter analysis.

In the present study we shall obtain similarity judgments for a fairly extensive set of some 30 verbs of JUDGING, including all the verbs considered by Fillmore, and 11 included in Osgood's large set of interpersonal verbs. As usual, we shall subject these proximity data to graph, cluster, and MDS analyses in an attempt to discover something as to the underlying features and properties involved, and the nature of their organization. We shall also be interested to see to what extent the present results are compatible with Osgood's analysis, and to what extent they can capture some of the subtle and very important distinctions suggested by Fillmore; in particular we shall try to see whether they will reveal anything relevant to the distinction between the explicit illocutionary force or assertions of a given verb, and the implicit presuppositions of that verb. Miller (1969) has argued "that an adult speaker of English must have this lexical information stored in such a manner that he can distinguish the presupposition from the assertion (p. 184)" of a term, and that subjects will exploit their knowledge of presuppositional structure in sorting terms. It will be very important to find out whether, in the present situation, subjects indeed largely make their decisions "on the basis of what the items presuppose, rather than what they assert (Miller, 1969, p. 185)," or whether indeed any such distinction between presuppositions and assertions can be viably maintained on the basis of analyses of the results of similarity data of the present sort. Of course, if such a distinction cannot be maintained, this may say more about the inadequacies of our data than about the inappropriateness of the distinction.

METHOD

Twenty-six male and female undergraduates, enrolled at the University of North Carolina, participated in the experiment; they will be referred to as Group JT. The subjects were requested to construct labeled trees following the standard instructions for this method (see Chapter 2). After completing the task they were asked to go over the trees and to rate each of the 29 links on a nine-point rating scale, assigning the number "1" to pairs of verbs which were very similar to each other relative to the other pairs, and the number "9" to pairs of verbs which were most dissimilar. No further restrictions were imposed, and the subjects were not required to use all nine categories. The weights assigned directly to the links of the tree were employed as measures of proximity in the MDS analysis of individual and group results, rather than the rank orderings of the links. The subjects were run in small groups of five to ten each. They were given a list of 30 JUDGING verbs, arranged alphabetically, and ample time to complete the task. Most subjects took between one and one-and-a-half-hours to build the tree.

The list of JUDGING verbs presented to the subjects is given in Table 10-1. The starred terms correspond to the ones analyzed by Fillmore (1969), the terms marked "+" are those discussed by Osgood. The remaining terms were selected from a longer list consisting of more than 50 terms, which we judged to be familiar to the subjects and to provide a wide coverage of the somewhat ill-defined semantic field of verbs which involve judgments of worth.

TABLE 10-1   Verbs of JUDGING and Their Mean Node Degrees (Group JT)

ACCLAIM	1.846	CONDONE	1.538
+ *ACCUSE	2.500	+ *CONFESS	2.077
ACKNOWLEDGE	1.962	CONVICT	1.462
ACQUIT	1.923	*CREDIT	2.192
ADMIT	1.923	+ *CRITICIZE	2.000
+ *APOLOGIZE	1.692	DENOUNCE	2.231
APPROVE	2.462	DISAPPROVE	2.231
ATTRIBUTE	1.885	+ *EXCUSE	1.923
+ *BLAME	2.116	+ *FORGIVE	1.654
CENSURE	1.577	IMPUTE	1.077
CHARGE	2.231	*JUSTIFY	1.500
CHIDE	1.731	+PARDON	2.654
CLEAR	1.808	*PRAISE	2.000
COMMEND	1.885	REPROACH	1.846
+CONDEMN	2.538	+ *SCOLD	1.538

+ Terms analyzed by Osgood; * Terms analyzed by Fillmore.

RESULTS

Graph Analysis

The first property of trees to be examined is the number of subtrees constructed by the subjects of Group JT. Tracing over labeled links in each individual tree, counting the number of subtrees that were formed, and then averaging over the 26 subjects, resulted in a mean of 5.31 and standard deviation of 3.27. The three options were used by the majority of the subjects; there were three subjects who used option 1 only. The mean number of subtrees is smaller than the corresponding means for Groups PT and HTM (7.50 and 6.00, respectively). This suggests that it is somewhat easier to judge similarity among HAVE verbs and among prepositions than among the present set of verbs of JUDGING.

Table 10-2 presents the predicted and observed frequency distributions of node degree. The fit of the Poisson distribution is not very good, and is worse

TABLE 10-2   Observed and Predicted Frequency Distributions of Node Degree (Group JT)

Degree	Predicted	Observed
1	296	272
2	287	346
3	139	131
4	45	27
5+	13	4

than the one observed in most of our previous studies. The difference between the two distributions, tested by the one-sample Kolmogorov-Smirnov test, almost reaches significance ($0.05 < p < 0.10$).

Presented in Table 10-3 are the predicted and observed distributions of pairs of adjacent nodes selected by y subjects, $y = 0, 1, \ldots, 26$. Consistent with the results in the previous chapters, the difference between the observed frequency distribution and the predicted negative binomial distribution is nonsignificant ($p > 0.20$, by the one-sample Kolmogorov-Smirnov test). It may be noted that the discrepancies between the observed and predicted frequencies, though small and nonsignificant, are opposite to the ones observed in Chapters 3, 4, 7, and 9, thus strengthening the tenability of the negative binomial assumption. The predicted frequency is slightly larger than the observed frequency for $y = 0$, but smaller for $y = 1, 2, \ldots, 5$. On the other hand, the small discrepancy in the tail of the distribution is of the same type as observed in previous studies—the number of labeled nodes paired together by the majority of the subjects is larger than the predicted frequency. As was indicated before, the negative binomial distribution is highly insensitive to small but consistent discrepancies in the tail of the distribution.

Table 10-3 shows that more than 59% of all possible pairs of JUDGING verbs were not linked together by even one subject, that about 15% were linked together by only one out of the 26 subjects, and that 16 out of the 435 pairs were selected by more than half of the subjects. The values of the parameters of

TABLE 10-3   Observed and Predicted Frequency Distributions of Pairs of Adjacent Nodes (Group JT)[a]

Y	Predicted	Observed
0	267	258
1	54	63
2	29	30
3	19	21
4	14	18
5	10	11
6	8	4
7	6	5
8	5	4
9	4	2
10	3	1
11	3	0
12	2	1
13	2	1
14+	9	16

[a] Parameters

p	s
0.116	0.227

the predicted negative binomial distribution are very close to the ones observed in Groups PT and HTM, where each tree consisted of 29 labeled nodes. The value of s is 0.227 in this study, compared to 0.219 in Group PT, and 0.214 in Group HTM. If the assumption of the negative binomial distribution were accepted, at least as a first approximation only, the similarity in s would suggest a similar distribution of popularity bias in the semantic fields of prepositions, HAVE verbs, and JUDGING verbs. The most popular pairs of (adjacent) nodes, selected by at least 14 out of the 26 subjects, were (in decreasing order): ADMIT-CONFESS (24),   COMMEND-PRAISE (24),   EXCUSE-PARDON (24), ACCUSE-BLAME (20),   ACQUIT-CLEAR (20),   ACCUSE-CHARGE (19), CONDEMN-DENOUNCE (19),   ATTRIBUTE-CREDIT (18),   ACCLAIM-PRAISE (17),   APPROVE-CONDONE (17),   CONDEMN-CONVICT (17), FORGIVE-PARDON (17),   APOLOGIZE-CONFESS (16),   APPROVE-COMMEND (15),   CHIDE-SCOLD (15),   and   CRITICIZE-DISAPPROVE (15). The 16 most popular pairs include 25 out of the 30 verbs; the five terms that are excluded are ACKNOWLEDGE, CENSURE, IMPUTE, JUSTIFY, and REPROACH.

A one-way ANOVA with repeated measures, performed on the degrees of the labeled nodes, yielded a significant label effect ($p < 0.01$); this further rejects the hypothesis of a random construction of trees. The distribution of mean degree, presented in Table 10-1, shows that PARDON, CONDEMN, ACCUSE, and APPROVE have the highest mean degrees. Interpreting the mean degree of a labeled node as a measure of relative "centrality" or relative "relatedness in meaning" (see Chapter 7), one may expect to find clusters of terms centered around these terms. This conjecture will be examined in the next section. Following the same line of interpretation, it is expected that the terms IMPUTE, CONVICT, JUSTIFY, SCOLD, and CONDONE, all of which have relatively low mean degree, will be located on the periphery of their respective clusters.

Cluster Analysis

The Connectedness and Diameter methods were applied to the mean proximity matrix and to the individual proximity matrices of five subjects randomly selected from Group JT. The two methods yielded the same MAXC clustering for the mean proximity data, with three significant clusters. The resulting HCS is portrayed in Fig. 10-1. The figure shows six to eight clusters, combined into the three MAXC clusters. These are:

1. An ADMIT-FORGIVE cluster [APOLOGIZE, ADMIT, CONFESS, JUSTIFY, ACQUIT, CLEAR, FORGIVE, EXCUSE, PARDON].
2. An ATTRIBUTE-PRAISE cluster [CONDONE, ACKNOWLEDGE, ATTRIBUTE, CREDIT, APPROVE, ACCLAIM, COMMEND, PRAISE].

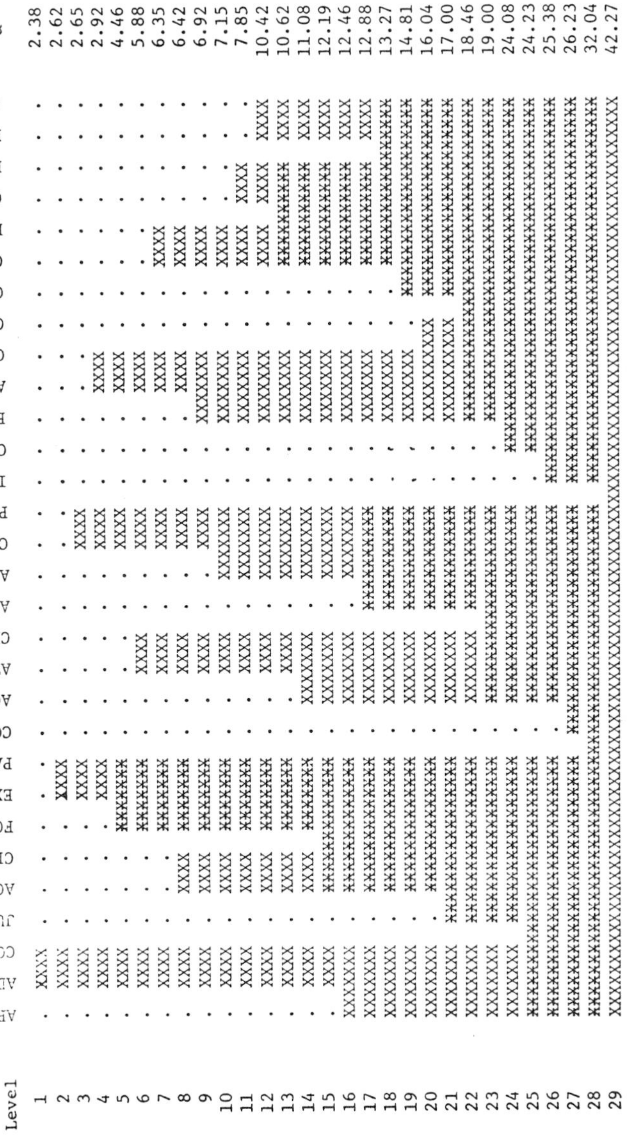

Fig. 10-1. HCS for Group JT (Diameter method).

3. An ACCUSE-CONDEMN cluster [IMPUTE, CHIDE, BLAME, ACCUSE, CHARGE, CONVICT, CENSURE, CONDEMN, DENOUNCE, CRITI-CIZE, DISAPPROVE, REPROACH, SCOLD].

Figure 10-1 shows that the terms CONDONE, IMPUTE, CHIDE, JUSTIFY, CONVICT, and CENSURE are the last ones to be clustered, and should probably be left as individual clusters. This suggestion is consistent with the graph analysis results reported in the immediately preceding section; Table 10-1 shows that four out of these six terms have the lowest mean degrees, and that the remaining two terms have degrees smaller than 1.8, indicating that all six terms are relatively unrelated in meaning to the remaining 24 terms.

Inspection of Fig. 10-1 suggests that each of the MAXC clusters may be further divided into at least two subclusters; Cluster 1 has one subcluster consisting of APOLOGIZE, ADMIT, and CONFESS, and a second subcluster composed of ACQUIT, CLEAR, FORGIVE, EXCUSE, and PARDON, where the terms of the first set involve an owning to something bad or undesirable (plus a request for forgiveness in the case of APOLOGIZE) while the terms in the second set involve some sort of exoneration (ACQUIT, CLEAR) or absolution (FORGIVE, EXCUSE, PARDON) for some such bad act. In Cluster 2 the first subcluster is composed of ATTRIBUTE, CREDIT, ACKNOWLEDGE, and the second of PRAISE, COMMEND, ACCLAIM, and APPROVE, with the terms in the first set ascribing some act to another or to self (ACKNOWLEDGE) without any explicit evaluation of that act (except perhaps for CREDIT which characteristically has a positive evaluation), whereas the terms in the second set all explicitly involve an assertion of the positive value of the act or person referred to. Cluster 3 again has two subclusters: BLAME-ACCUSE-CHARGE, and CONDEMN-DENOUNCE-CRITICIZE-DISAPPROVE-REPROACH-SCOLD. The terms in the first set all presuppose some bad act which is being attributed to a given person. The terms in the second set are rather more mixed; CRITICIZE, SCOLD, and DISAPPROVE involve an assertion as to the negative value of some act ascribed to a particular person, while CONDEMN, DENOUNCE, and REPROACH all presuppose that the act was bad and involve additional properties (e.g., REPROACH indicates a direct confrontation with the doer of the evil act, who is taken to task for that act). While CHIDE would appear to be very similar to SCOLD, in fact it joins Cluster 3 only at a very late stage, and is removed from SCOLD within the cluster and in the MDS solution. CONVICT and CENSURE also fall into this cluster very late, and the results for these terms are hard to interpret since, e.g., CONVICT, which falls in the BLAME subcluster on a hierarchic analysis, is considerably removed from the terms constituting that grouping in the MDS solution.

The cluster analyses of individual results were carried out as in the previous chapters and yielded similar results. The individual HCSs obtained for five randomly selected subjects were close to the HCS of the mean proximity matrix. For each of the five subjects the MAXC clustering included all the 30 terms and the number of significant clusters varied from three to four. The individual differences were mainly reflected in the clustering of terms with a low mean degree. Because of the relatively large size of the MAXC clusters, the individual differences resulted in large distances between individual and mean HCSs, ranging from 0.180–0.385.

Multidimensional Scaling Analysis

The MDS yielded solutions in one, two, and three dimensions for the individual and mean proximity matrices. As in all previous chapters, the Euclidean model provides a better fit to the results than the City Block model. The stress values for the Euclidean model for individual and mean proximity data are presented in Table 10-4 for $m = 1, 2, 3$. (The right-hand column of the table will be discussed subsequently.) Compared to the stress values reported in previous chapters, and in Chapters 7 and 9 in particular, the fit provided by the Euclidean model to the mean proximity data is very good. The stress values for $m = 1, 2, 3$ are about half of the corresponding values for Groups HTM and PT, for which $N = 29$. Table 10-4 shows only small differences in the stress values between individual and mean results. The break in the stress values between $m = 2$ and $m = 1$ suggests that a two-dimensional representation can adequately describe the individual and group results.

TABLE 10-4   Stress Values for Euclidean Representations

Dimensions	Group JT					Weighted mean	Unweighted mean
	No. 6	No. 12	No. 18	No. 20	No. 25		
3	0.051	0.049	0.026	0.038	0.032	0.055	0.052
2	0.090	0.080	0.034	0.054	0.056	0.078	0.082
1	0.226	0.221	0.084	0.107	0.196	0.176	0.189

Figure 10-2 portrays the two-dimensional Euclidean representation for the mean proximity data. To compare the cluster and MDS results, levels 20 through 25 of the HCS depicted in Fig. 10-1 are plotted on the two-dimensional representation. There seems to be a very close correspondence between the MDS and the cluster results. The three MAXC clusters are compact and nicely separated from one another. Moreover, with the exception of APOLOGIZE, which falls closer to the FORGIVE-CLEAR-EXCUSE-PARDON subcluster than to the ADMIT-CONFESS subcluster, the two subclusters of each of the three MAXC clusters are clearly distinguishable in the representation.

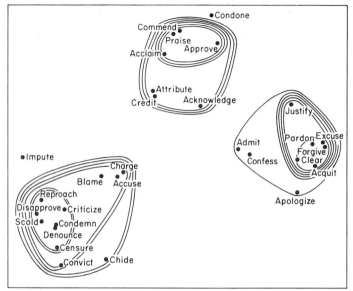

Fig. 10-2.   Two-dimensional Euclidean representation for Group JT.

Further similarities between the MDS and the cluster analyses may be noted. Pairs of terms which are clustered on low levels in Fig. 10-1, such as ADMIT-CONFESS, EXCUSE-PARDON, COMMEND-PRAISE, ACCUSE-CHARGE, and ATTRIBUTE-CREDIT, fall within a short distance from each other in the two-dimensional plot. And, conversely, terms which are clustered very late, such as CONDONE, IMPUTE, CHIDE, and JUSTIFY, fall at a relatively large distance from the centers of their respective clusters. Moreover, even within subclusters, the level at which a particular term is clustered determines to some extent its distance from the remaining terms in its respective subcluster. This can be noticed in the case of APOLOGIZE, APPROVE, ACKNOWLEDGE, and, to a lesser extent, in the case of BLAME and ACCLAIM.

The low stress values and the close similarity between the dimensionality-free cluster analysis and the MDS solution might appear to favor a multidimensional model as a representation for these data. However, given our inability to impose any plausible or sensible substantive interpretation on the dimensions that might be involved, the usefulness of a dimensional interpretation is presently doubtful.

In analyzing the mean proximity matrices, we have been making the restrictive assumption that the proximity measures, whether defined in terms of the rank-ordering of the links in the construction of the tree, or, as in this study, in terms of direct rating responses, are additive within and between trees. This assumption may be weakened by redefining the proximity between two nodes on the same tree as the sum of unweighted links connecting them. One might suspect that, when averaging over individual proximity matrices, the weights assigned to the links by individual subjects will have only a negligible effect on the mean proximity between nodes, and that regardless of how the proximity between two nodes is defined, either as the sum of weighted links or as the sum of unweighted links, the results of both the cluster and MDS analyses will hardly be affected.

Defining the number of links connecting each pair of nodes as a measure of their proximity, individual proximity matrices were computed and then averaged over subjects to yield a mean (unweighted) proximity matrix. As expected, a cluster analysis of this matrix resulted in an HCS which is almost identical to Fig. 10-1. Similarly, the two-dimensional representation yielded by the MDS analysis is practically identical to Fig. 10-2. The two-dimensional plot is presented in Fig. 10-3, and the stress values for $m = 1, 2, 3$ are shown in the last

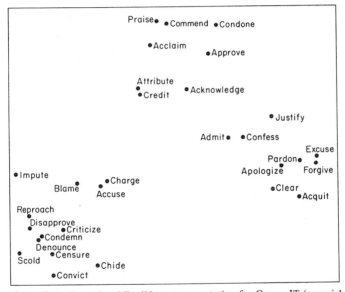

Fig. 10-3. Two-dimensional Euclidean representation for Group JT (unweighted).

column of Table 10-4. A comparison of Figs. 10-2 and 10-3 shows that the two definitions of the proximity measure yield essentially the same dimensional solution. There are only minor differences in the location of a few terms in the FORGIVE-ACQUIT cluster which have no effect on the interpretation of the results.

DISCUSSION

The substantive results obtained are revealed most clearly if we consider the yield of the cluster analysis. It will be recalled that there were three MAXC clusters, each of which was comprised of roughly two subclusters. Cluster 1 (ADMIT-FORGIVE) consisted of an ADMIT subcluster and a FORGIVE and ACQUIT subcluster or subclusters, with all the terms in this cluster involving some negatively evaluated act which was conceded in the terms of the first subcluster, and with regard to which the individual was either absolved or exonerated in the terms of the other subcluster or subclusters. Cluster 2 (ATTRIBUTE-PRAISE) consisted of an ATTRIBUTE subcluster and of a PRAISE subcluster, with all the terms in this cluster involving the ascription of some action either without explicit evaluation (ATTRIBUTE subcluster) or with a definite positive evaluation of that action (PRAISE subcluster). Cluster 3 (ACCUSE-CONDEMN) was comprised of an ACCUSE subcluster and a CONDEMN and REPROACH subcluster or subclusters, with all the terms in the cluster involving something which was presupposed to be bad or asserted to be bad, and generally some further evaluation or attribution on that basis. Thus the principal properties differentiating between the three clusters were (1) the worth of the action referred to, which was either neutral or positive in Cluster 2 and negative in Clusters 1 and 3, and (2) the association or dissociation of the action with its doer. The latter relation is associative in Cluster 3 (and in Cluster 2) and dissociative in Cluster 1, certainly with regard to the FORGIVE and ACQUIT terms, and perhaps also with regard to the ADMIT terms insofar as confession is the first step to purging oneself of sin.

Of the 30 terms studied, 24 fall rather readily into these three clusters, three more (CHIDE, CONVICT, CENSURE) join the ACCUSE-CONDEMN cluster rather late (the first two terms joining the ACCUSE subcluster, and the last term reasonably enough the CONDEMN subcluster), one (JUSTIFY) joins the ACQUIT subcluster of Cluster 1 quite late, and two (IMPUTE and CONDONE) appear to cluster only because of the exigencies of the clustering routine. As was noted previously, both these terms have very low mean degrees, indicating that they are relatively unrelated in meaning to the other terms, a result confirmed by the MDS solution which reveals them to be the most peripheral terms of their respective clusters. All this is perhaps the case because our judges are not really sure or clear as to meaning of these terms—certainly by reference to any dictionary definition IMPUTE should fall close to ATTRIBUTE, and CONDONE near to PARDON, which happens neither with regard to the clustering nor the MDS results.

While the MDS solution in two dimensions appears to be an adequate one with low stress, and while there is a close correspondence between the MDS results and the clustering results in that the three MAXC clusters are compact and well segregated from each other in the two-dimensional representation, the two dimensions of that representation defy interpretation. One might perhaps argue for a bipolar Good-Bad dimension lying along the main diagonal, with terms such as DISAPPROVE, CRITICIZE, CONDEMN, and DENOUNCE, all of which involve a bad *Situation*, falling toward one end, and the terms

COMMEND, PRAISE, ACCLAIM, and APPROVE, all of which involve a good *Situation*, defining the other end, and the somewhat more neutral terms such as ATTRIBUTE, CREDIT, and ACKNOWLEDGE falling in between. This does not appear particularly convincing for it seems implausible, e.g., to argue that SCOLD is worse than ACCUSE, and in any case the second dimension appears to be quite uninterpretable. Because of the uninterpretability of these dimensions, and particularly because of the fact that a plausible interpretation could be imposed on the clustering results not only with regard to the clusters themselves but also with regard to their subclusters and the merging of these into the larger clusters, we prefer an account of these data phrased in the latter terms.

To what extent are the present results compatible with Osgood's model? We shall consider this question specifically with regard to 10 of the 11 terms from Osgood's set which are included among our 30 terms, and more generally with regard to Osgood's analysis as a cross-classification in feature terms. In particular, let us consider those terms which are very similar on Osgood's analysis and see if they fall close together in the present data. FORGIVE, EXCUSE, and PARDON have a very similar description in terms of Osgood's feature set and indeed fall very close together in the FORGIVE subcluster of Cluster 1. ACCUSE, BLAME, CONDEMN, CRITICIZE, and SCOLD are quite similar in Osgood's scheme—indeed the first three are identical in his characterization. In fact all these terms do fall into Cluster 3; however ACCUSE and BLAME fall into one subcluster while the other three terms fall into the other subcluster, i.e., terms described identically are somewhat differently situated, and terms differing in some of Osgood's features, e.g., CONDEMN and CRITICIZE, are quite close. APOLOGIZE and CONFESS, which differ in quite a number of features in Osgood's analysis, fall into the same ADMIT subcluster of Cluster 1 in the present data. Thus, for many cases, terms which are very similar in Osgood's analysis do indeed fall very close together in the present results, while for some cases this does not hold fully, or one finds terms rather set apart on Osgood's analysis falling quite close together.

While it seems intuitively clear how to make these sorts of comparisons for terms that are supposed to be very similar to each other, it is more difficult to know how to proceed for terms differing in many features. Any scheme that simply counts feature differences between pairs of terms does not appear to be particularly plausible, and we have no idea as to the weighting to give differences with regard to the various features. More important, we do not know what the relation is supposed to be among the features. Osgood clearly does not intend the system to be a simply paradigmatic one with cross-classification on independent features, but argues rather that the features are to various degrees dependent or correlated and that the

semantic system for interpersonal verbs (1) is not nested, (2) is partially replicated (features applying to all terms only when zero codings are allowed), (3) is partially ordered (but in terms of psychological salience rather than logical inclusion), and (4) is partially dependent with features correlated in usage to various degrees (Osgood, 1968a, p. 131).

Given that sort of general characterization, it becomes obvious that even if one were sure of the appropriateness of the features suggested, it would still be very difficult to know what sorts of relations to expect among the terms, given the complexity and obscurity of the underlying structural system This suggests that, in general, it will be very difficult to assess the appropriateness of such a model. About all that one can do is to focus on terms that are supposed to be identical or close together, and note whether or not there appear to be important meaning differences among them. In addition, one may note whether or not such differences appear to be appropriately captured by the feature differences indicated (see, e.g., our comments on ACCUSE, BLAME, CONDEMN, and CRITICIZE in the introduction to the present chapter), and look at similarity data of the present sort, and see whether or not such presumably close terms indeed fall together. It should be obvious that such tests are weak, and that even if Osgood's model were to pass such tests (and we have noted some contrary cases earlier), matters would still be left largely indeterminate since one would still not know what to expect as to the structure of relations among items which are described as differing in various features, and which are not supposed to be very close in meaning.

One final observation: insofar as Osgood believes that the system governing interpersonal verbs (and presumably verbs of JUDGING as a subset of these) is not nested, where nesting requires both hierarchical ordering and independence of features, his analysis is incompatible with the taxonomic approach involved in a cluster analysis procedure of the sort used in the present study. Osgood justly observes that "not only is a particular empirical discovery procedure appropriate to a semantic domain of a particular type, but when it is applied to a domain of a *different* type it will tend to force the data toward correspondence with the system for which it is appropriate (1968b, p. 131)." Just because of such considerations we have always applied a variety of different analytic procedures to our data. We shall recur to this problem in Chapter 12.

Next let us consider (1) whether, or to what extent, our data are compatible with the sort of analysis suggested by Fillmore (1969a), (2) whether they reveal anything as to the distinction between the presuppositions of a verb and its explicit assertions, and (3) whether they support Miller's suggestion (1969) that subjects are likely to make their decisions as to similarity among items largely on the former basis. Let us review again the clustering results obtained, looking at these from the perspective provided by Fillmore. In Cluster 1 the items comprising the ADMIT subcluster (APOLOGIZE*, ADMIT, CONFESS*) all presuppose a bad *Situation*, with APOLOGIZE also presupposing responsibility

---

* Asterisks indicate the first mention of one of the terms analyzed by Fillmore.

for it (and asking for forgiveness), while the latter terms explicitly assert the responsibility of the speaker who is the *Defendant*. The FORGIVE and ACQUIT subcluster (or subclusters) of Cluster 1 includes FORGIVE*, EXCUSE*, PARDON, ACQUIT, and CLEAR. All these terms presuppose a *Defendant* responsible for a bad *Situation* and an active *Judge*, who either explicitly denies the responsibility of the *Defendant* for the bad *Situation* (ACQUIT, CLEAR, and perhaps EXCUSE) or absolves him of its consequences (FORGIVE, PARDON). Note the intimate relation between APOLOGIZE and FORGIVE (the former essentially constituting a request for the latter), which fall into two subclusters of Cluster 1. The term JUSTIFY* which falls, marginally, into the same subcluster as EXCUSE differs from it principally in that the former term involves a denial of the badness of a *Situation* for which the *Defendant* is responsible, whereas the latter term involves a denial of responsibility for a *Situation* which is undoubtedly bad.

The second cluster has an ATTRIBUTE subcluster (ATTRIBUTE, ACKNOWLEDGE, and CREDIT*) and a PRAISE subcluster (PRAISE*, COMMEND, ACCLAIM, and APPROVE). All the items in the first subcluster involve an assertion as to the responsibility of the *Defendant* for the *Situation*, with CREDIT, in addition, perhaps presupposing the goodness of that *Situation*, and ATTRIBUTE and ACKNOWLEDGE differing principally in whether the *Situation* is ascribed to an other or to self. The terms in the PRAISE subcluster all presuppose the responsibility of the *Defendant* for the *Situation*, and all express the *Judge's* positive evaluation of that *Situation*. Note how PRAISE and CREDIT, which fall into the two subclusters of Cluster 2, differ principally in that what is the presupposition of the first (responsibility) is the assertion of the second, and what is the presupposition of the second (goodness of the *Situation*) is the assertion of the first.

The third cluster consists of an ACCUSE subcluster (BLAME*, ACCUSE, CHARGE) and a CONDEMN and REPROACH subcluster (or subclusters) comprised of CONDEMN, DENOUNCE, CRITICIZE*, DISAPPROVE, REPROACH, and SCOLD*. The terms in the first subcluster all presuppose a bad *Situation* for which the *Judge* is asserting the responsibility of the *Defendant*. In the second subcluster, CRITICIZE and DISAPPROVE presuppose the responsibility of the *Defendant* for the *Situation* and express the *Judge's* negative evaluation of that *Situation*. SCOLD is like CRITICIZE, except that the *Defendant* and the *Addressee* must be one and the same person; CONDEMN, DENOUNCE, and REPROACH all presuppose the responsibility of the *Defendant* for a bad *Situation* and involve additional conditions or assertions as well, e.g., REPROACH is analogous to SCOLD in that the *Defendant* and *Addressee* are identical, while DENOUNCE would seem to require that the *Defendant* and *Addressee* be different persons. And, of course there are great differences in the extremity of the terms or of the seriousness of the *Situation* presupposed; one would hardly *scold* someone else for committing a murder or *denounce* him for his impoliteness.

It might be noted that terms differing only in the permutation of presuppositions and assertions often fall into different subclusters of the same cluster, see, e.g., PRAISE and CREDIT noted above, or ACCUSE and CRITICIZE. On the other hand, terms differing principally in the evaluation of the *Situation* as CREDIT and BLAME, or PRAISE and CRITICIZE, fall into distinct clusters, well separated and segregated in terms of the MDS solution, arguing for the great importance of the nature or sign of the evaluation with regard to the semantics of interpersonal judgment. On the whole (consistent with Miller's suggestion), it does seem as though terms with shared presuppositions, especially with regard to a positive or negative evaluation of the *Situation*, are regarded as similar by our respondents and generally do cluster rather closely together. Dissociation from a negatively evaluated *Situation* (Cluster 1: ADMIT-FORGIVE) is seen as very different from association with a negatively evaluated *Situation* (Cluster 3: ACCUSE-CONDEMN), and both of these sets of terms are regarded as quite different from terms which are either evaluatively neutral or involve association with a positively evaluated *Situation* (Cluster 2: ATTRIBUTE-PRAISE). It may be of some interest, parenthetically, to note a certain parallel between the present results and some of the analyses advanced by Heider (1958), in *The Psychology of Interpersonal Relations,* in terms of *Unit* relationships (including belonging and responsibility) and *Sentiment* relationships (including positive and negative evaluations).

In some measure the present results would appear to be consistent with Fillmore's analysis, although one could hardly claim that they reveal in any clear way the subtleties exhibited by that analysis. That, of course, is hardly surprising given the necessarily coarse and crude means subjects had to indicate their understanding of the similarities in meaning among the 30 terms judged, and also given that Fillmore's account, while perhaps only revealing the obvious (at the end and after the fact), constituted a rather deep analysis of this semantic field, something probably not within the power of our subjects. In any case, in a certain sense, our subjects were required to do something above and beyond that attempted by Fillmore, namely, understanding the meanings of the various verbs in whatever ways available to them, they were required to weight and combine such criteria as best they saw fit, in making their similarity judgments.[2] It may be mildly paradoxical that, given a principal interest in meaning criteria used and their organization, there is no direct way to extract such information from

---

[2] It would surely have been interesting to see, on the one hand, how Fillmore's data would have looked had he been a subject in our experiment, and, on the other hand, whether or not our subjects would have been willing to assent to the appropriateness of the sorts of distinctions made by Fillmore in his analysis, had they been explicitly confronted with them.

subjects, but one may only make inferences with regard to this by examining their performance on a task which, *in addition*, requires them to make very complex decisions as to the relative importance of these criteria and how they should be combined.

A word might be said by way of comparison of Osgood's approach with that of Fillmore. In some respects Osgood's analysis is both simpler, in that it involves merely a classification or cross-classification on some ten features, and more ambitious, in that it seeks to comprehend a very large set of interpersonal verbs, whereas Fillmore's analysis is directed to a very much smaller set of verbs of praising and blaming. To some extent, the greater simplicity of Osgood's model is only an apparent one, since his system is not meant to be a paradigmatic one with cross-classification on independent features but, as noted earlier, assumes complex and largely unspecified relations among these features. This last observation touches on perhaps the most important difference between Osgood's analysis and that of Fillmore. The latter analysis explicitly identifies a set of concepts in terms of which the "role structure" of these verbs involving judgments of worth and responsibility is articulated, and attempts to exhibit the structural relations among these for each individual case, with particular emphasis on the distinction between the implicit presuppositions and explicit assertions or illocutionary aspects of each term. Thus the principal difference between these accounts resides in the greater explicitness with which Fillmore specifies the richer complex structural apparatus used in his analysis. It is interesting to note that recently Osgood (1970) has become very much concerned with an analysis of the presuppositional components of meaning, arguing that these are not necessarily linguistic at all, but may involve nonlinguistic cognitive presuppositions as a function of perceptual-situational context. On this point there need not be any conflict between Osgood and Fillmore, since the latter has explicitly indicated that the sorts of characterizations he has provided for the various verbs of praising and blaming do not encompass the "full roster of lexical information" about these words, and that such characterizations in fact require very complex information—"just about anything imaginable."

While our data are tolerably consistent with the sort of structural analysis advanced by Fillmore, and while they suggest the importance of common presuppositions as governing similarity judgments, it is obvious, as has already been noted, that they provide very coarse information, at best. What sorts of additional procedures might be of value in revealing something as to the presuppositions involved in various verbs? If it is the case that the basis for separating presuppositions from the rest of the meaning of a word is that presuppositions obtain even when a sentence is negated or interrogated, then one might perhaps make use of this condition as a potential discovery procedure, presenting subjects with sentences and their corresponding negations or interrogations, and asking them to indicate what still remains true even under such circumstances. As to possible implications of differences in presuppositions, it might be of some value to make use of a subjective inference technique developed by Abelson (see, e.g., Abelson and Kanouse, 1966), who has shown that when it comes to making inductive or deductive inferences from evidence, the particular verb involved is the most important determinant of the conclusions reached. Abelson has not been able to provide any very convincing account as to the basis for these findings, in large part because of the unavailability of any semantic analysis for the verbs he employed. It would be very interesting if it should turn out to be the case that some aspects of the presuppositions of the verbs were important in governing these differential effects.

In conclusion, we should voice some cautions similar to those noted in our discussion of the results for HAVE verbs. The domain of verbs of JUDGING is very loosely structured and ill-defined, and it is difficult to draw any boundaries circumscribing that domain or to specify explicit criteria for sampling terms from the domain. Consequently one cannot be sure to what extent any results obtained are a function of the particular verbs selected, and of their distribution over the domain or semantic field. What is most needed, perhaps, is both an attempt to sample as extensively as possible over the domain, and an attempt to examine as intensively as possible terms that fall relatively close to each other within it, in order to discover some of the general properties characterizing the domain as well as properties that differentiate closely related terms. It is very possible that the overall organization of the domain may be quite differently structured from the organization of particular (as it were) locally compact regions.

Chapter 11   GOOD-BAD TERMS

Matters of evaluation, whether of humans and their actions or, more generally, of all sorts of objects, artifacts, and ideas, clearly represent some very pervasive and significant uses of language; the continual presence of a strong Evaluative factor in work using the semantic differential technique is only one not-so-mute testimony to this. It is immediately clear, however, that there are different ways or respects in which something may be good or bad, and that various modes of evaluation may be appropriate for different frames of reference or with respect to different objects of judgment. For example, Osgood, Suci, and Tannenbaum (1957), examining some of their semantic differential data, speak of goodness as "meek" or "dynamic" or "dependable" or "hedonistic," and distinguish between morally, aesthetically, socially, and emotionally evaluative terms (although in general their treatment does not maintain or stress such distinctions). Miller (1967), using a classification technique on some of the antonymous adjectives studied by Osgood and his associates, found that terms seemed to cluster in such ways as to require a distinction between moral, intellectual, and aesthetic evaluation.

Our logic and purpose in the present study of evaluative adjectives is essentially the same as that governing the examination of HAVE verbs and of verbs of JUDGING, namely to provide some account of the semantic structure of a very broad and ill-defined domain. One might note two differences between this study and those of the two preceding chapters. The first is that the domain of evaluative terms is more extensive and even worse defined than these other domains in that, in principle, there are an indefinitely large number of criteria with regard to each of which a positive or negative evaluation might be made. In fact, matters may not be quite so impossible, since the general bases of evaluation which are specifically communicated by terms explicitly indexing positive and negative evaluations in those regards are certainly far more limited. Nevertheless, it is probably a fair guess that the domain of evaluative adjectives is a particularly extensive one, that the structural relations obtaining among the terms in this domain may be quite various, and that the domain may be quite fragmented. A second difference between the present study and the two others is that in each of the latter cases there was available some analysis or model of the domain or part of the domain, while this is not true in the present case (except for the sorts of hints noted in the opening paragraph). For this reason we decided to attempt a sort of internal matching analysis. Instead of choosing a more or less random set of evaluative terms, we deliberately selected two sets of terms which might reasonably be supposed to be polar with respect to an Evaluation factor, with the constraint that for any term in the one set there should always appear in the other set one or two of its most obvious antonyms. Thus we were interested in seeing what structure might emerge in each set, and whether or not the two structures could be mapped reasonably well into each other, thus providing some internal check on and warrant for the analysis.

We chose terms believed to be extreme with regard to evaluation, i.e., GOOD and BAD terms, in an attempt to eliminate the Evaluation factor *per se,* so as to minimize the likelihood that adjectives would be grouped in terms of degree of favorable or unfavorable evaluation. Thus by studying only (variously) very good and very bad terms we hoped to accomplish by item selection the same sort of goal as Kuusinen (1969) sought to bring about by statistical analysis, when, in studying the "denotative" structure of personality ratings, he partialled out the correlations of E-P-A relevant scales from the correlations of the other personality scales, and then factored (or refactored) the residual correlation matrix. We attempted to constitute antonymous sets of terms, since for any pair of antonyms all semantic markers or features may be considered to be the same except for one feature, or more accurately, the opposing values taken on that one feature. Thus BEAUTIFUL and UGLY presumably represent parallel characterizations with regard to the aesthetic value of some object, except that the first term is marked positive, while the second is marked negative. On this logic, insofar as one can constitute roughly antonymous sets of terms differing only in their positive or negative evaluative marking, with all terms in each set respectively positive or negative, similar structural relations may be expected to emerge upon an analysis of each set. This is so since the antonymous sets are much alike, and positive or negative marking cannot discriminate among the items in the sets, as all items in the one or the other set share either the positive or negative marking.

A number of important qualifications must be noted with regard to the preceding comments. First, there is no guarantee that, in fact, we have been able to select antonymous sets of terms. Indeed it is almost necessarily the case that we must fail in this, to some extent, because of individual differences in the understanding of shades of meaning of terms, many of which are very similar. We had subjects match terms from the two lists, i.e., indicate the best antonym from the one list for each term in the other list, but while this information should prove valuable (e.g., in revealing agreement among subjects) there are still serious problems, in that a subject could not select a term outside the other set as the most appropriate antonym for a given term, nor could he choose a given term as the best antonym more than once. Second, note that polar or antonymous adjectives may differ in that one term may be unmarked and the other marked, where the unmarked term may label both the category or scale involved and one member of that category, while the marked term can serve only in the latter role. For example, consider the terms GOOD and BAD, where the scale is one of goodness, and a question about whether or not something is good, or as to how good it is, may be answered with an evaluation anywhere on the scale, while a question of how bad it is presupposes its badness in some degree (on the unmarked-marked distinction see Greenberg, 1966; and Clark, 1969). The marked term will always be more complex in meaning than the unmarked one, by at least that feature marking, and if it should be the case, as it appears to be, that GOOD terms are more likely to be unmarked and BAD terms more likely to be marked, then it is possible that this difference may make a difference in regard to the structure characterizing two such sets of terms. Third, and perhaps related to the above, there is some evidence (reviewed in Boucher and Osgood, 1969) that evaluatively positive words differ from evaluatively negative words in a number of respects, e.g., the former are used more frequently and more diversely. This last finding of greater diversity of usage of positively evaluated terms, i.e., their use in modifying a wider range of different nouns, may well have consequences such that the structure emerging from the analysis of a set of positively evaluative terms may differ in some ways from that emerging from an analysis of their correlative negative terms. All the above argues for the possibility that, indeed, there might be some, perhaps systematic, differences between the structural organization of GOOD and BAD terms.

METHOD

Fifty-five male and female students, enrolled at the University of North Carolina, participated in the GOOD-BAD study. Some subjects constructed labeled trees, and some sorted the GOOD or the BAD terms into clusters. Whatever the method employed for obtaining proximity measures, similarity judgments were made for the GOOD and the BAD terms separately, to allow a comparison between the two semantic domains. There were 14 subjects who were requested to construct labeled trees using the standard instructions for this method. They will be referred to as Group GT or Group BT, depending whether their similarity judgments of the GOOD or the BAD terms, respectively, are considered. When no distinction is to be made between the two sets of terms, the subjects who constructed trees will be referred to as Group GBT.

Group GBDG consisted of 41 subjects who sorted terms into clusters, using the standard instructions for the Direct Grouping method. They are the same as the people who sorted prepositions and HAVE verbs into clusters, and whose proximity data were analyzed in Chapters 7 and 9, respectively. When a distinction is to be made betwen the direct clustering of GOOD or BAD terms, the subjects in Group GBDG will be referred to as Group GDG or BDG, respectively.

The 14 subjects in Group GBT participated in two sessions, about two weeks apart. In the first session about half of them constructed labeled trees using a set of 20 GOOD terms, whereas the remaining subjects performed the same task using a set of 20 BAD words. The two sets are presented in Table 11-1. In the second session the two sets of words were reversed At the end of the second

TABLE 11-1   Mean Node Degree and Mean Number of Terms Clustered with Each Word
(Groups GT, GDG, BT, BDG)

Term	Mean node degree	Mean number in the same cluster	Term	Mean node degree	Mean number in the same cluster
ATTRACTIVE	1.857	1.780	BAD	3.000	3.383
BEAUTIFUL	1.714	1.732	BLAMEWORTHY	1.786	3.302
BENEFICIAL	1.786	2.317	BRUTAL	1.214	3.503
FAVORABLE	1.929	2.537	DISHONEST	2.357	3.402
GENEROUS	1.571	2.878	GUILTY	1.643	3.041
GOOD	2.714	4.366	HARMFUL	1.929	3.490
HONEST	1.857	3.951	IMMORAL	1.643	3.484
INNOCENT	1.286	1.732	LAWLESS	1.714	3.577
JUST	2.500	4.171	MEAN	2.429	3.367
KIND	2.643	3.293	NASTY	1.857	3.034
LAUDABLE	1.500	2.805	REPULSIVE	1.929	3.002
LAWFUL	1.643	3.537	UGLY	1.643	3.085
MORAL	1.929	3.951	UNFAIR	1.286	3.499
NICE	2.357	3.341	UNFAVORABLE	1.714	3.084
NOBLE	1.429	3.585	UNPLEASANT	1.929	3.072
PLEASANT	2.143	2.854	USELESS	1.571	2.904
PRECIOUS	1.214	1.073	VILE	1.929	3.148
RIGHT	1.786	3.732	WICKED	2.500	3.280
USEFUL	1.571	2.146	WORTHLESS	1.429	2.904
VIRTUOUS	2.571	3.683	WRONG	2.500	3.409

session each subject was given the two lists of GOOD and BAD terms and the following instructions, requiring him to match opposites:

> Now, as a final task, you have to match up opposites. Look over the lists on the left and right sides of the page and pick two words, one from each list, which are the most natural pair of opposites. Write these down on the far right and cross these terms off the list. Then scan the lists again choosing another pair of opposites. Write them down, and then cross these terms off the lists. Continue like this until all the words have been used.

Clearly, the resulting matched pairs for a given subject should not be regarded as strict antonyms, since a subject could not refer to the same word, whether a GOOD or a BAD word, twice, nor could he provide new words which did not appear on the two lists.

The subjects in Group GBDG were run in small groups of five to ten each. It may be recalled from Chapters 7 and 9 that they were required to sort four decks of cards, consisting of prepositions, HAVE, GOOD, and BAD words. For about half of the subjects, the deck of GOOD words appeared first in the series, and the deck of BAD words was the last. The other subjects in Group GBDG dealt with the same two decks in the reverse order.

RESULTS

Graph Analysis

To allow a comparison between the structural properties of the semantic spaces of GOOD and BAD terms, Groups GT and BT were kept separate. Following the same order of analysis as in the preceding chapters, the first statistical property of trees to be examined is the number of subtrees constructed by the subjects. With only three exceptions, the subjects in both groups used all three options in constructing the trees. Tracing over labeled links in each individual tree, counting the number of distinct subtrees that were formed, and then averaging over subjects resulted in a mean number of subtrees of 4.14 and a standard deviation of 4.22 for Group GT. The respective values for Group BT were 4.07 and 3.04; the difference between the two groups, tested by a correlated t test, is not significant at the 0.05 level.

The next statistical property of trees to be examined is the distribution of node degree. The observed and predicted frequency distributions are presented in Table 11-2 for the GOOD and the BAD terms, separately. A comparison of the two distributions shows them to be significantly different for Group BT ($p < 0.05$ by the one-sample Kolmogorov-Smirnov test) but not for Group GT. The discrepancy between the two distributions in the former group is very much like the one observed in Chapters 6 and 10, namely, the Poisson distribution overestimates the observed frequencies for $d = 1$, 3, 4, and 5+, and

TABLE 11-2   Observed and Predicted Frquency Distributions of Node Degree
(Groups GT and BT)

Degree	Group GT		Group BT	
	Predicted	Observed	Predicted	Observed
1	108	106	108	92
2	103	114	103	133
3	49	44	49	47
4	15	15	15	7
5+	5	1	5	1

underestimates them for $d = 2$. Comparing the observed frequencies between the two groups suggests that the GOOD trees, in general, are slightly more compact than the BAD trees, since they have a larger number of nodes with degrees 4 and 1, and a smaller frequency of nodes with degree 2. However, the difference between the two observed frequency distributions of node degree is not significant at the 0.05 level.

Presented in Table 11-3 are the predicted and observed frequency distributions of pairs of adjacent nodes selected by y subjects, where $y = 0$, 1, . . ., 14 for each group. The fit provided by the negative binomial distribution is excellent in each case ($p > 0.20$ by the one-sample Kolmogorov-Smirnov test). Moreover, the small but consistent discrepancies between the two distributions,

TABLE 11-3   Observed and Predicted Frequency Distributions of Pairs of Adjacent Nodes
(Groups GT and BT)[a]

y	Group GT		Group BT	
	Predicted	Observed	Predicted	Observed
0	102	109	98	99
1	34	26	36	37
2	18	14	20	22
3	11	14	12	6
4	8	11	8	6
5	5	4	5	6
6	3	2	3	3
7	2	3	2	5
8	2	1	2	0
9	1	2	1	3
10	1	0	1	1
11+	3	4	2	2

[a]Parameters:

	p	s
GT	0.237	0.434
BT	0.261	0.492

observed in several of the preceding chapters, do not appear in Groups GT and BT. The parameters of the predicted negative binomial distributions, presented in the lower part of Table 11-3, assume very similar values for the two groups. The small difference between the two s values (0.434 and 0.492) is consistent with Table 11-2 in showing a slightly stronger popularity bias for the GOOD than for the BAD terms. The two s values are larger than the s values reported in Chapters 7, 8, 9, and 10, but are of the same order of magnitude as the s values of Group ET in Chapter 6, and the two kinship groups, KTM and KTF, in Chapter 4. The popularity bias seems to assume a similar strength in the sets of kinship terms, emotion names, and GOOD- BAD adjectives.

The most popular pairs of (adjacent) nodes, selected by at least 11 out of the 14 subjects in Group GT, were (in decreasing order of frequency): ATTRACTIVE-BEAUTIFUL (14), BENEFICIAL-USEFUL (11), GENEROUS-KIND (11), and NICE-PLEASANT (11). There were only two pairs of labeled nodes selected by at least 11 subjects in Group BT; these are USELESS-WORTHLESS (12), and BLAMEWORTHY-GUILTY (11). One should expect these pairs to be clustered in the upper levels of the HCS yielded by the clustering methods, and to fall very close to each other in the MDS representations.

Analyses of variance performed on the degrees of the labeled nodes yielded a highly significant label effect ($p < 0.001$) for each group. The distributions of mean node degree, presented in Table 11-1, reveal that GOOD, KIND, VIRTUOUS, and JUST have the highest mean degree in Group GT, whereas PRECIOUS, INNOCENT, and NOBLE have the lowest. In Group BT, the words BAD, WICKED, WRONG, and MEAN have the highest mean degree, and BRUTAL, UNFAIR, and WORTHLESS have the lowest. As before, it is expected that the terms with a high mean degree will be found in the centers of their respective clusters. And, conversely, terms with a low mean degree are expected to be located on the periphery of their respective clusters.

The analysis is continued by examining the results of Groups GDG and BDG and, when possible, comparing these results with the results for Groups GT and BT. The first statistic to be examined is the number of groups of words formed by each subject, which may reflect a response bias or the ability of the subject to discriminate relatively subtle variations in meaning in a particular semantic domain. The subjects in Group GDG formed, on the average, 7.95 groups with a standard deviation of 3.06. The results for Group BDG are highly similar, with values of 7.93 and 2.45, respectively. It may be recalled that the same 41 subjects in Groups GDG and BDG also sorted the prepositions and the HAVE terms into distinct clusters, forming, on the average, 12.34 and 12.59 clusters, respectively. Since there were 29 terms in each of the latter two sets, the difference in the mean number of clusters is not surprising. Indeed, dividing the number of terms in each of the four sets by the mean number of clusters yields the following mean number of terms in each cluster: 2.35, 2.30, 2.52, and 2.53 for the prepositions, HAVE verbs, GOOD terms, and BAD terms, respectively.

The mean number of terms sorted together with each of the 20 words is presented in Table 11-1 for the GOOD and BAD words separately. The table shows a marked difference between the two groups in terms of the distributions of means. The distribution of the means of the GOOD terms is moderately skewed, with terms such as GOOD and JUST sorted together with more than four terms on the average, and terms such as PRECIOUS, BEAUTIFUL, INNOCENT, and ATTRACTIVE sorted with less than two terms. On the other hand, the distribution of means of the BAD terms is more or less uniform. The difference between the two distributions is consistent with the graph analysis results reported in the preceding section, which showed a slightly stronger "popularity bias" for GOOD than for BAD terms.

In addition to looking at the mean cluster size and mean number of terms clustered with each word, one may also examine the frequencies of pairs of terms clustered together by a given number of subjects. Presented in Table 11-4 are the observed frequency distributions of pairs of GOOD or BAD terms sorted together. The table shows that 20 out of the 190 pairs of GOOD words were sorted together by none of the 41 subjects, 22 pairs by one subject only, and 13

TABLE 11-4   Observed Frequency Distributions of Pairs of Words Sorted Together (Groups GDG, BDG)

y	Group GDG	Group BDG
0	20	0
1	22	42
2	30	21
3	23	25
4	15	18
5	7	16
6	7	10
7	7	8
8	8	2
9	7	7
10	3	5
11	4	3
12	10	5
13	2	3
14	3	3
15	3	2
16	1	1
17	2	6
18	1	2
19	2	2
20+	13	9

pairs by 20 or more subjects. The results for the BAD pairs are different; each of the 190 pairs was sorted together by at least one subject, 42 pairs were sorted together by exactly one subject, 21 pairs by two subjects, and 9 pairs by at least 20 subjects. A comparison of the results in Table 11-4 with the corresponding results for Groups PDG and HDG in Chapters 7 and 9, respectively, shows a considerably larger amount of agreement among the subjects in sorting prepositions and HAVE words than in sorting the GOOD and BAD words. This is as expected, since, as we noted at the beginning of this chapter, the domain of evaluative terms is more extensive and worse defined than the domains of prepositions and HAVE words. Whereas approximately 60% of the pairs of prepositions and HAVE words were sorted together by no more than one subject, the values for Groups GDG and BDG are less than 25%.

There were seven pairs of words that were sorted together by at least two thirds of the subjects in Group GDG. These are (in decreasing order of frequency): BENEFICIAL-USEFUL (34), ATTRACTIVE-BEAUTIFUL (33), JUST-LAWFUL (30), NICE-PLEASANT (28), HONEST-JUST (27), and JUST-RIGHT (27). They include the four most "popular" pairs of (adjacent) nodes, selected by at least 11 out of the 14 subjects in Group GT, suggesting a high degree of similarity between Groups GT and GDG. Only three pairs were sorted together by the same percentage of subjects in Group BDG, namely, USELESS-WORTHLESS (37), REPULSIVE-UGLY (33), and BLAMEWORTHY-GUILTY (28); they also include the two most "popular" pairs in Group BT, indicating a high degree of similarity between the latter two groups.

In summary, several results reported in this section seem to point in the same direction. The relatively large values of the parameters of the negative binomial distributions presented in Table 11-3, the approximately uniform distribution of the mean node degree shown in Table 11-1, and the observed frequency distributions given in Table 11-4, all seem to suggest that relative to most of the previously discussed sets of terms, and to the prepositions and HAVE words in particular, the GOOD and BAD words are much more homogeneous in terms of the similarity relations among them. The results suggest that, whether or not a dimensional model can describe the proximity data adequately, the clusters in the dimensional representation will be less compact and the terms will be more uniformly distributed than they were in the preceding chapters. Findings pertaining to these expectations will be presented in the following sections.

Cluster Analysis

To test the ultrametric inequality, both the Connectedness and the Diameter methods were applied to the mean proximity matrices of Groups GT and BT, and to the proximity matrices of Groups GDG and BDG, where the entry (i,j) in each of the latter two matrices, $i \neq j$, $i,j = 1, \ldots, 20$, gives the number of subjects, out of 41, who sorted terms i and j into the same group. The distance between the two MAXC clusterings yielded by the two methods was computed for each of the four groups. For three out of four groups the distance was larger than 0.20, thus indicating only a fair amount of agreement between the two clustering methods. A more detailed comparison of the two methods, which took into account not only the distance between the two MAXC clusterings but also the number of significant clusters in each MAXC clustering and the number of terms accounted for by these clusters, indicated a better agreement between the two methods for Groups BT and BDG than for Groups GT and GDG, thus providing a somewhat greater justification for applying hierarchical clustering techniques to the results of the former than to those of the latter two groups.

Figures 11-1 and 11-2 display the two HCSs, obtained by the Diameter method, for the mean proximity matrices of Group GT and BT, respectively. The MAXC clustering for Group GT includes only one significant cluster with nine terms. These are:

MORAL EVALUATION [INNOCENT, MORAL, HONEST, JUST, LAWFUL, GOOD, RIGHT, NOBLE, VIRTUOUS].

Level	INNOCENT	MORAL	HONEST	JUST	LAWFUL	GOOD	RIGHT	NOBLE	VIRTUOUS	ATTRACTIVE	BEAUTIFUL	PRECIOUS	LAUDABLE	FAVORABLE	KIND	GENEROUS	PLEASANT	NICE	USEFUL	BENEFICIAL	α
1	.	.	.	.	.	.	.	.	.	XXXX	.	.	.	.	.	.	.	.	.	.	1.39
2	.	.	.	.	.	.	.	.	.	XXXX	.	.	.	.	.	.	XXXX	.	.	.	1.65
3	.	.	.	.	.	.	.	.	.	XXXX	.	.	.	.	.	XXXX	XXXX	.	.	.	1.72
4	.	.	XXXX	.	.	.	.	.	.	XXXX	.	.	.	.	.	XXXX	XXXX	.	.	.	2.09
5	.	.	XXXX	.	.	.	.	.	.	XXXX	.	.	.	.	.	XXXX	XXXX	XXXX	.	.	2.65
6	.	.	XXXX	.	.	.	.	XXXX	.	XXXX	.	.	.	.	.	XXXX	XXXX	XXXX	.	.	2.85
7	.	.	XXXX	XXXX	.	.	.	XXXX	.	XXXX	.	.	.	.	.	XXXX	XXXX	XXXX	.	.	2.91
8	.	.	XXXX	XXXX	XXXX	.	.	XXXX	.	XXXX	.	.	.	.	.	XXXX	XXXX	XXXX	.	.	2.98
9	XXXX	.	XXXX	XXXX	XXXX	.	.	XXXX	.	XXXX	.	.	.	.	.	XXXX	XXXX	XXXX	.	.	3.74
10	XXXX	XXXX	XXXX	XXXX	XXXX	.	.	XXXX	.	XXXX	.	.	.	.	.	XXXX	XXXX	XXXX	.	.	3.93
11	XXXX	XXXX	XXXX	XXXX	XXXX	XXXX	XXXX	XXXX	.	XXXX	.	.	.	.	.	XXXX	XXXX	XXXX	.	.	4.46
12	XXXX	XXXX	XXXX	XXXX	XXXX	XXXX	XXXX	XXXX	XXXX	XXXX	XXXX	.	XXXX	.	.	XXXX	XXXX	XXXX	.	.	4.84
13	XXXX	XXXX	XXXX	XXXX	XXXX	XXXX	XXXX	XXXX	XXXX	XXXX	XXXX	.	XXXX	.	.	XXXX	XXXX	XXXX	XXXX	XXXX	4.97
14	XXXX	XXXX	XXXX	XXXX	XXXX	XXXX	XXXX	XXXX	XXXX	XXXX	.	.	XXXX	.	XXXX	XXXX	XXXX	XXXX	XXXX	XXXX	4.99
15	XXXX	XXXX	XXXX	XXXX	XXXX	XXXX	XXXX	XXXX	XXXX	XXXX	.	.	XXXX	.	XXXX	XXXX	XXXX	XXXX	XXXX	XXXX	6.30
16	XXXX	XXXX	XXXX	XXXX	XXXX	XXXX	XXXX	XXXX	XXXX	XXXX	XXXX	.	XXXX	.	XXXX	XXXX	XXXX	XXXX	XXXX	XXXX	6.35
17	XXXX	XXXX	XXXX	XXXX	XXXX	XXXX	XXXX	XXXX	XXXX	XXXX	XXXX	.	XXXX	XXXX	XXXX	XXXX	XXXX	XXXX	XXXX	XXXX	7.17
18	XXXX	XXXX	XXXX	XXXX	XXXX	XXXX	XXXX	XXXX	XXXX	XXXX	XXXX	XXXX	XXXX	XXXX	XXXX	XXXX	XXXX	XXXX	XXXX	XXXX	9.08
19	XXXX	XXXX	XXXX	XXXX	XXXX	XXXX	XXXX	XXXX	XXXX	XXXX	XXXX	XXXX	XXXX	XXXX	XXXX	XXXX	XXXX	XXXX	XXXX	XXXX	10.27

Fig. 11-1.   HCS for Group GT (Diameter method).

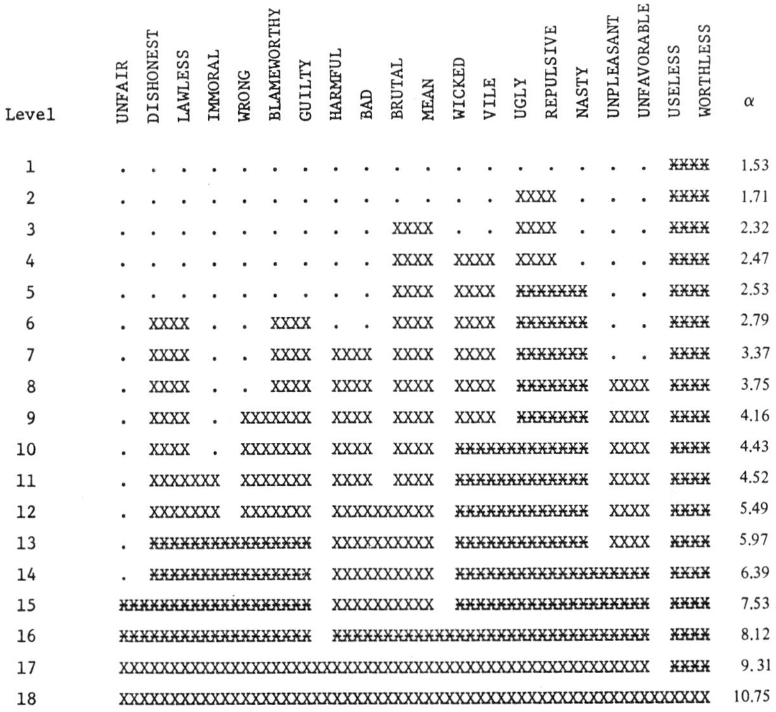

```
Column key (left→right):
UF=UNFAIR  DI=DISHONEST  LA=LAWLESS  IM=IMMORAL  WR=WRONG  BL=BLAMEWORTHY
GU=GUILTY  HA=HARMFUL  BA=BAD  BR=BRUTAL  ME=MEAN  WI=WICKED  VI=VILE
UG=UGLY  RE=REPULSIVE  NA=NASTY  UP=UNPLEASANT  UV=UNFAVORABLE
US=USELESS  WO=WORTHLESS

       UF DI LA IM WR BL GU HA BA BR ME WI VI UG RE NA UP UV US WO      α

 1     .. .. .. .. .. .. .. .. .. .. .. .. .. .. .. .. .. .. XXXXX     1.53
 2     .. .. .. .. .. .. .. .. .. .. .. .. .. XXXXX .. .. .. XXXXX     1.71
 3     .. .. .. .. .. .. .. .. .. XXXXX .. .. XXXXX .. .. .. XXXXX     2.32
 4     .. .. .. .. .. .. .. .. .. XXXXX XXXXX XXXXX .. .. .. XXXXX     2.47
 5     .. .. .. .. .. .. .. .. .. XXXXX XXXXX XXXXXXXX .. .. XXXXX     2.53
 6     .. XXXXX .. .. XXXXX .. .. XXXXX XXXXX XXXXXXXX .. .. XXXXX     2.79
 7     .. XXXXX .. .. XXXXX XXXXX XXXXX XXXXX XXXXXXXX .. .. XXXXX     3.37
 8     .. XXXXX .. .. XXXXX XXXXX XXXXX XXXXX XXXXXXXX XXXXX XXXXX     3.75
 9     .. XXXXX .. XXXXXXXX XXXXX XXXXX XXXXX XXXXXXXX XXXXX XXXXX     4.16
10     .. XXXXX .. XXXXXXXX XXXXX XXXXX XXXXXXXXXXXXXX XXXXX XXXXX     4.43
11     .. XXXXXXXX XXXXXXXX XXXXX XXXXX XXXXXXXXXXXXXX XXXXX XXXXX     4.52
12     .. XXXXXXXX XXXXXXXX XXXXXXXXXXX XXXXXXXXXXXXXX XXXXX XXXXX     5.49
13     .. XXXXXXXXXXXXXXXXX XXXXXXXXXXX XXXXXXXXXXXXXX XXXXX XXXXX     5.97
14     .. XXXXXXXXXXXXXXXXX XXXXXXXXXXX XXXXXXXXXXXXXXXXXXXX XXXXX     6.39
15     XXXXXXXXXXXXXXXXXXXX XXXXXXXXXXX XXXXXXXXXXXXXXXXXXXX XXXXX     7.53
16     XXXXXXXXXXXXXXXXXXXX XXXXXXXXXXXXXXXXXXXXXXXXXXXXXXXX XXXXX     8.12
17     XXXXXXXXXXXXXXXXXXXXXXXXXXXXXXXXXXXXXXXXXXXXXXXXXXXXXXX XXXXX   9.31
18     XXXXXXXXXXXXXXXXXXXXXXXXXXXXXXXXXXXXXXXXXXXXXXXXXXXXXXXXXXXXX  10.75
```

Fig. 11-2.   HCS for Group BT (Diameter method).

With the possible exception of NOBLE and VIRTUOUS which, as Fig. 11-1 shows, were the last two terms to be clustered, the terms falling in this cluster are typically employed for moral evaluation. None of the remaining 11 terms shares this property.

There are three significant clusters in the MAXC clustering of Group BT, accounting for all the 20 BAD terms:

MORAL EVALUATION [UNFAIR, DISHONEST, LAWLESS, IMMORAL, WRONG, BLAMEWORTHY, GUILTY].

SOCIAL–EMOTIONAL–AESTHETIC EVALUATION [HARMFUL, BAD, BRUTAL, MEAN, WICKED, VILE, UGLY, REPULSIVE, NASTY, UN-PLEASANT, UNFAVOURABLE].

PRACTICAL EVALUATION [USELESS, WORTHLESS].

With the possible exception of UNFAIR, which, as Fig. 11-2 shows, was the last term to be clustered, the six terms falling into the MORAL EVALUATION cluster clearly justify its name. The second cluster consists of socially, emotionally, and aesthetically evaluative terms. The two terms in the third cluster, USELESS and WORTHLESS, are typically employed for PRACTICAL or INTELLECTUAL evaluation.

A comparison of the clustering results of Groups GT and BT suggests that, relative to the small set of terms employed in the present study, morally evaluative terms, whether positive or negative, are more easily distinguishable than other terms, and constitute tighter clusters. We hesitate in drawing any similar conclusion regarding practically evaluative terms since only two of them were included in each of the two sets. Emotionally, socially, and, to a lesser extent, aesthetically evaluative terms are more difficult to distinguish from one another since many of them, such as NASTY, NICE, PLEASANT, and their antonyms, may be used to express emotions, aesthetic evaluation, and social judgments at the same time.

```
Terms (left to right):
INNOCENT HONEST JUST LAWFUL RIGHT GOOD MORAL VIRTUOUS NOBLE LAUDABLE KIND
GENEROUS PRECIOUS ATTRACTIVE BEAUTIFUL PLEASANT NICE FAVORABLE USEFUL BENEFICIAL

Level                                                                        α
 1    .  .  .   .   .  .  .   .   .   .   .   .   .   .   .   .   .    .   XXXX      34
 2    .  .  .   .   .  .  .   .   .   .   .   .   .  XXXX  .   .   .   XXXX      33
 3    .  .  XXXX  .  .  .   .   .   .   .   .   .  XXXX  .   .   .   XXXX       30
 4    .  .  XXXX  .  .  .   .   .   .   .   .   .  XXXX XXXX  .   XXXX          28
 5    .  .  XXXX  .  .  .   .   .  XXXX  .  XXXX XXXX  .   XXXX                 27
 6    .  .  XXXXXXX  .  .  .   .  XXXX  .  XXXX XXXX  .   XXXX                  26
 7    .  .  XXXXXXX  .  XXXX  .  .  XXXX  .  XXXX XXXX  .   XXXX                24
 8    .  .  XXXXXXX  .  XXXX  .  .  XXXX  .  XXXX XXXX XXXXXXX                  20
 9    .  XXXXXXXXXX   .  XXXX  .  .  XXXX  .  XXXX XXXX XXXXXXX                 17
10    .  XXXXXXXXXX  XXXXXXX   .  .  XXXX  .  XXXX XXXX XXXXXXX                 15
11    .  XXXXXXXXXX  XXXXXXX  XXXX XXXX  .  XXXX XXXX XXXXXXX                   14
12    .  XXXXXXXXXXXXXXXXXX   XXXX XXXX  .  XXXX XXXX XXXXXXX                    9
13    .  XXXXXXXXXXXXXXXXXX   XXXXXXXXXX  .  XXXX XXXX XXXXXXX                   7
14    .  XXXXXXXXXXXXXXXXXX   XXXXXXXXXX  .  XXXXXXXXX  XXXXXXX                  6
15    XXXXXXXXXXXXXXXXXXXX   XXXXXXXXXX  .  XXXXXXXXX  XXXXXXX                   3
16    XXXXXXXXXXXXXXXXXXXXXXXXXXXXXX   XXXXXXXXXXXX  XXXXXXX                     2
17    XXXXXXXXXXXXXXXXXXXXXXXXXXXXXXXXXXXXXXXXXXXXXXXXXX                        0
```

Fig. 11-3. HCS for Group GDG (Diameter method).

Figure 11-3 shows the HCS of Group GDG, obtained by the Diameter method. There are three significant clusters in the MAXC clustering, accounting for 19 out of 20 GOOD terms.

MORAL AND SOCIAL EVALUATION [INNOCENT, HONEST, JUST, LAWFUL, RIGHT, GOOD, MORAL, VIRTUOUS, NOBLE, LAUDABLE, KIND, GENEROUS].

AESTHETIC EVALUATION [ATTRACTIVE, BEAUTIFUL, PLEASANT, NICE].
PRACTICAL EVALUATION [FAVORABLE, USEFUL, BENEFICIAL].

The first eight terms are morally evaluative; they are included among the nine terms in the only significant cluster in Group GT. The remaining four terms, NOBLE, LAUDABLE, KIND, and GENEROUS, were added to the latter eight terms quite late in the clustering process; characteristically they lack presuppositions of moral or legal responsibility and may best be classified as socially evaluative terms. There are four terms in the second cluster, two of which, ATTRACTIVE and BEAUTIFUL, are typically used for aesthetic evaluation, whereas the other two terms, PLEASANT and NICE, are less specific in meaning and are used more frequently to assess emotional and social desirability. The three terms in the third cluster are commonly used for practical or social evaluation.

A comparison of Figs. 11-1 and 11-3 shows several similarities between them. The terms in the two HCSs are ordered in almost the same way. The morally evaluative terms, with the exception of NOBLE, and the practically-socially evaluative terms, with the exception of FAVORABLE, are identically ordered in both HCSs and constitute relatively tight clusters. It may also be noted that PRECIOUS is the last term to be clustered in both HCSs, and that in each case it is clustered with the aesthetically evaluative terms ATTRACTIVE and BEAUTIFUL. The difference in the number of significant clusters between the two HCSs may be attributed, as in Chapters 7 and 9 in which comparisons between tree construction and direct grouping were carried out, to the difference between the two data generating methods, and, more important, to the difference in the number of subjects in Groups GT and GDG. Since Fig. 11-1 had only one significant cluster, the distance between the two MAXC clusterings was not computed.

The HCS of Group BDG, portrayed in Fig. 11-4, is almost identical to the one for Group BT shown in Fig. 11-2. With very few exceptions the terms in the two HCSs are ordered in the same way. There are four significant clusters in the MAXC clustering for Group BDG, accounting for 19 out of the 20 terms. The first cluster is identical to the MORAL EVALUATION cluster of Group BT, the second and the third significant clusters, with the exception of WICKED and UNFAVORABLE, correspond to the first and second subclusters, respectively, of the second cluster of Group BT, and the fourth cluster is formed by the same two terms constituting the PRACTICAL EVALUATION cluster of Group BT. Comparing Figs. 11-1 and 11-3 on one hand and Figs. 11-2 and 11-4 on the other hand, the agreement between the clustering results yielded by the tree construction and the Direct Grouping methods is observed to be considerably better for the BAD than for the GOOD terms.

Level	UNFAIR	DISHONEST	LAWLESS	IMMORAL	WRONG	BLAMEWORTHY	GUILTY	HARMFUL	BRUTAL	MEAN	BAD	WICKED	VILE	NASTY	REPULSIVE	UGLY	UNPLEASANT	UNFAVORABLE	USELESS	WORTHLESS	α
1	.	.	.	.	.	.	.	.	.	.	.	.	.	.	.	.	.	.	X	X	37
2	.	.	.	.	.	.	.	.	.	.	.	.	.	.	X	X	.	.	X	X	33
3	.	.	.	.	.	X	X	.	.	.	.	.	.	.	X	X	.	.	X	X	28
4	.	X	X	.	.	X	X	.	X	X	X	X	.	.	X	X	.	.	X	X	22
5	.	X	X	.	.	X	X	.	X	X	X	X	.	.	X	X	X	.	X	X	19
6	.	X	X	.	.	X	X	.	X	X	X	X	X	X	X	X	X	.	X	X	17
7	.	X	X	X	X	X	X	.	X	X	X	X	X	X	X	X	X	.	X	X	16
8	.	X	X	X	X	X	X	.	X	X	X	X	X	X	X	X	X	.	X	X	13
9	.	X	X	X	X	X	X	X	X	X	X	X	X	X	X	X	X	.	X	X	12
10	.	X	X	X	X	X	X	X	X	X	X	X	X	X	X	X	X	.	X	X	9
11	.	X	X	X	X	X	X	X	X	X	X	X	X	X	X	X	X	X	X	X	6
12	X	X	X	X	X	X	X	X	X	X	X	X	X	X	X	X	X	X	X	X	5
13	X	X	X	X	X	X	X	X	X	X	X	X	X	X	X	X	X	X	X	X	4
14	X	X	X	X	X	X	X	X	X	X	X	X	X	X	X	X	X	X	X	X	2
15	X	X	X	X	X	X	X	X	X	X	X	X	X	X	X	X	X	X	X	X	0

Fig. 11-4.   HCS for Group BDG (Diameter method).

The analysis of individual subjects in Group GBDG followed exactly the same procedure applied to Groups PDG and HDG in Chapters 7 and 9, respectively. A 41 x 41 matrix of intersubject distances was computed separately for the GOOD and the BAD terms and then subjected to cluster analysis by the Diameter method. Each of the resulting two MAXC clusterings resembled a triangle and had only one significant cluster, including 38 subjects in Group GDG and 40 subjects in Group BDG. As in Chapters 7 and 9, in which the preposition and the HAVE data of the same 41 subjects were analyzed, the clustering results of the GOOD and BAD terms reflected primarily the number of groups (clusters) of terms formed by each subject. The rank-order correlation between the number of groups of GOOD and BAD terms formed by the 41 subjects assumed a moderate value of 0.58 ($p < 0.01$).

Multidimensional Scaling Analysis

The nonmetric MDS program, applied to individual and mean proximity matrices of the four groups, yielded solutions in one, two, and three dimensions. Both the Euclidean and City Block metrics were used as before, the former yielding slightly smaller stress values for most of the cases. Table 11-5 shows the Euclidean stress values for the mean proximity matrices of the four groups of subjects as well as the stress values for five subjects selected randomly from

TABLE 11-5   Stress Values for Euclidean Representations

Dimensions	Group GT						Group GDG
	No. 2	No. 5	No. 8	No. 11	No. 14	Mean	Mean
3	0.049	0.066	0.049	0.046	0.109	0.081	0.087
2	0.094	0.084	0.080	0.083	0.168	0.132	0.171
1	0.280	0.154	0.147	0.335	0.365	0.233	0.416
Dimensions	Group BT						Group BDG
	No. 2	No. 5	No. 8	No. 11	No. 14	Mean	Mean
3	0.017	0.017	0.094	0.069	0.033	0.078	0.093
2	0.051	0.037	0.158	0.116	0.064	0.112	0.165
1	0.141	0.100	0.336	0.242	0.122	0.389	0.356

Group GBT. Relative to the results reported in the preceding chapters, the stress values for the mean proximity data of Groups GT and BT are high, suggesting that the nonmetric MDS analysis may be less adequate for the present data. The stress values for Groups GT and BT are considerably higher, for example, than the ones reported in Chapters 9 and 10, in which the number of terms involved were 29 and 30, respectively, compared to only 20 terms in the former two groups. The stress values of Groups GDG and BDG are of the same order of magnitude as those reported for Group HDG in Chapter 9. The break in the stress values between $m = 1$ and $m = 2$, the unsatisfactory fit in one dimension for all four groups, and the fact that the three-dimensional solutions did not provide any clearer insight into the data than the two-dimensional solutions, provide some justification for the decision to continue confining attention to the two-dimensional representations.

Consider first the two-dimensional representation for the mean proximity matrix of Group GT, displayed in Fig. 11-5. Even a cursory inspection of the figure shows that the terms are distributed more or less uniformly over the two-dimensional surface with no clear indication of tight clusters. This approximately uniform distribution is consistent with the conclusions drawn from the graph analysis of the same data. Figure 11-5 shows that the nine morally evaluative terms, which form the only significant cluster (see Fig. 11-1), fall relatively close to each other, thus constituting a compact, though not particularly tight cluster, but that the remaining terms are scattered all over the representation, and that even terms very close in the cluster representation and intuitively very similar, such as KIND and GENEROUS, or USEFUL and BENEFICIAL, fall quite apart from each other. Attempts to interpret the two dimensions of Fig. 11-5 failed completely.

Figure 11-6 depicts the two-dimensional representation of the mean proximity data of Group BT. To compare the cluster analysis and the nonmetric

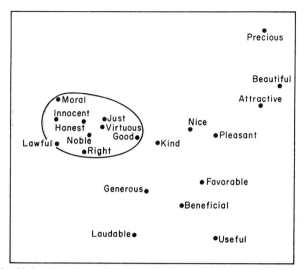

Fig. 11-5.   Two-dimensional Euclidean representation for Group GT.

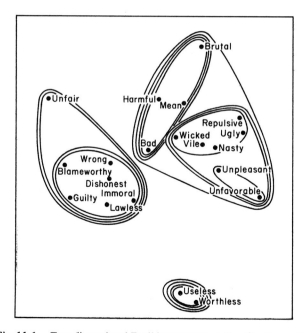

Fig. 11-6.   Two-dimensional Euclidean representation for Group BT.

MDS results, levels 13 through 16 of the HCS in Fig. 11-2 are plotted on the two-dimensional representation. The three significant clusters as well as their subclusters are identifiable as such in the representation; they form compact, though not very tight, clusters with no overlap among them. The agreement between the graph and the MDS results is quite good—the terms are more uniformly distributed in the two-dimensional plot than in previous chapters, as predicted above, and terms such as BRUTAL and UNFAIR, which have the lowest mean degree, are indeed located on the periphery of their respective clusters. The correspondence between the cluster analysis and the MDS results is not entirely satisfactory, however, because of the relatively large distance between certain pairs of terms falling in the same cluster, e.g., BAD-BRUTAL, VILE-UGLY, LAWLESS-BLAMEWORTHY, and, more seriously, because of the relatively small distances between certain terms which belong to different clusters, e.g., BAD-WRONG, BAD-DISHONEST, and WICKED-DISHONEST. Because the two dimensions are uninterpretable, and because of the relatively high stress values reported above, the MDS analysis can add very little to the conclusions drawn from the clustering analysis of the data.

It may be recalled, from the introductory remarks to this chapter, that we attempted to constitute roughly antonymous sets of terms, differing only in their positive or negative markings, so that isomorphic structural relations might emerge upon the MDS analysis of each set. Since success in this task can hardly be guaranteed *a priori,* the subjects in Group GBT were asked at the end of the experiment to match opposite terms from the two lists, i.e., to select the best antonym from one list for each term in the other list, subject to the constraint that a subject could not choose a given term more than once, nor select a term outside the other set as the most appropriate antonym for a given term. A comparison of the structural relations between the two sets was first performed on the group results. To characterize a pair of terms as antonyms we required that at least 13 out of the 14 subjects select that pair. Nine pairs of terms satisfied this very stringent criterion; they are given below with the number of subjects selecting them written in parentheses: USEFUL-USELESS (14), RIGHT-WRONG (14), INNOCENT-GUILTY (14), PLEASANT-UNPLEASANT (14), FAVORABLE-UNFAVORABLE (14), HONEST-DISHONEST (14), MORAL-IMMORAL (13), LAWFUL-LAWLESS (13), and GOOD-BAD (13). The agreement among the subjects is actually better than it seems to be if the requirement for a one-to-one match is relaxed. Thus, all 14 subjects selected either UGLY or REPULSIVE as an antonym to either BEAUTIFUL or ATTRACTIVE. The latter four terms will also be included in the comparison of structural relations between the subsets of antonymous terms.

As pointed out in Chapter 2, the results of the MDS program are determined up to an arbitrary rigid motion and change of scale. Consequently, before attempting a comparison between the two representations, with respect to the structural relations between the 11 antonymous pairs of terms, "it is first necessary to bring them into a good mutual fit by means of an appropriate similarity transformation (including a rigid rotation as well, possibly, as a translation, reflection, and uniform expansion or contraction) (Shepard and Chipman, 1970, p. 11)." Unlike Shepard and Chipman's study, the similarity transformation was here performed subjectively—the two-dimensional solution obtained for Group GT (Fig. 11-5) was taken as fixed while the solution obtained for Group BT (Fig. 11-6) was rotated (but not stretched) so as to minimize the sum of the distances between the 11 antonymous pairs. Better mutual fit might possibly have been obtained by adapting Cliff's (1966) least squared method for "orthogonal rotation to congruence."

The final representations are presented, as thus superimposed, in Fig. 11-7. Each of the nine antonymous pairs is represented by an arrow positioned in such a way that the head end coincides with its "good" member, and the tail end coincides with its "bad" member. The terms BEAUTIFUL and ATTRACTIVE and their antonyms REPULSIVE and UGLY are connected by four arrows. Roughly speaking, the arrows indicate how much the relative positions of the 11 GOOD words implied by the judgments of similarity are displaced from the relative positions of their antonyms. This statement, of course, is not entirely accurate, since the relative positions of each of the 11 GOOD or 11 BAD terms

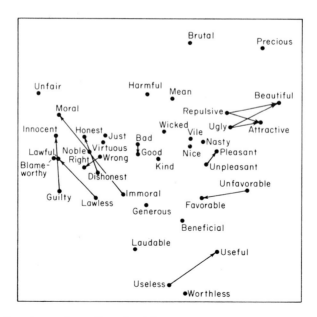

Fig. 11-7.   Superimposed two-dimensional Euclidean representations for Group GT (heads of arrows) and Group BT (tails of arrows) based upon mean proximity data.

is determined by the MDS analysis of the entire 20 x 20 symmetric proximity matrix rather than that of the 11 x 11 submatrix.

Inspection of Fig. 11-7 shows that the positions of a few of the GOOD terms (in particular MORAL, and to a lesser extent USEFUL and LAWFUL) are displaced to a noticeable extent. The relations among the majority of the antonymous terms remained, however, about the same. At present, there is no satisfactory quantitative measure of agreement between two subsets of the representations. Compared to the relations displayed in Fig. 1 of Shepard and Chipman (1970), which were judged to remain "remarkably the same (p. 11)," the structural isomorphism between sets of antonymous terms in the present study seems to appear quite satisfactory.

Table 11-5 shows that the stress values for the five subjects selected randomly from Group GBT, though lower than the critical values for $N = 20$ established in Chapter 2, are, nevertheless, equal or larger than the stress values for individual subjects (for $N > 20$) presented in the preceding chapters. Inspection of the individual two-dimensional plots showed that several of them had peculiar patterns such as incomplete circles or forks, possibly reflecting the biases imposed on the individual proximity matrices by the tree construction method. Attempts to interpret the ten two-dimensional representations obtained from the five subjects were, by and large, unsuccessful.

Following the work of Shepard and Chipman, who introduced the notion of "second order" isomorphism and demonstrated a methodology for investigating the resemblance between the structural relations holding among different internal representations (see also Chapter 3), we attempted to determine for each subject whether his two representations ($m = 2$) for the GOOD and for the BAD terms could be superimposed on each other, by an appropriate similarity transformation, relative to his matching of the 20 pairs of antonyms. This attempt was also unsuccessful for each of the five subjects.

Figure 11-8 displays the two-dimensional representation of Group GDG. Heavy lines surround the three significant clusters, presented in Fig. 11-3, which account for 19 terms. The clusters are compact, though not very tight and not well separated from one another. The agreement between the clustering and the MDS results is not very satisfactory, though it is slightly better than for Group GT. On the one hand, pairs and triples of terms which were clustered together fairly early in Fig. 11-3, such as ATTRACTIVE-BEAUTIFUL, PLEASANT-NICE, KIND-GENEROUS, JUST-LAWFUL-RIGHT (but not GOOD-MORAL-VIRTUOUS), and FAVORABLE-USEFUL-BENEFICIAL, form very tight clusters in Fig. 11-8. But on the other hand, the distances between members of certain pairs of terms which fall in different clusters, such as GOOD and PLEASANT, KIND and NICE, and GOOD and NICE, are smaller than the ones between certain terms falling within the same cluster, such as INNOCENT and RIGHT, LAUDABLE and VIRTUOUS, or BEAUTIFUL and PLEASANT. As in Group GT, the two dimensions appear uninterpretable.

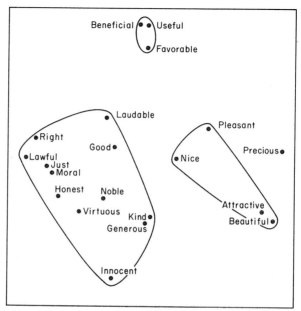

Fig. 11-8.   Two-dimensional Euclidean representation for Group GDG.

Next we present in Fig. 11-9 the two-dimensional representation for Group BDG. Since a somewhat better agreement was obtained between the clustering and the MDS results for the BAD (Group BT) than the GOOD terms, we plotted levels 10 through 14 on the two-dimensional representation. Note that with the exception of UNFAVORABLE, which was not included in the MAXC clustering, the four outer lines in Fig. 11-9 circle the four significant clusters yielded by the Diameter method. As in Group GDG, the agreement between the clustering and the MDS results is not very satisfactory—the clusters are compact but not tight, and very poorly separated from one another, and there are relatively small distances between terms such as BAD and IMMORAL, WICKED and VILE, and BAD and VILE, which belong to different clusters. As in all previous cases, the two dimensions are uninterpretable.

To compare the two representations for Group GBDG, i.e., Figs. 11-8 and 11-9, with respect to the structural relations between antonymous pairs of terms, we followed the same procedure as in Fig. 11-7. The solution for Group GDG was taken as fixed while the solution for Group BDG was rotated and reflected by eye (but not stretched), so as to minimize the sum of distances between the 11 antonymous pairs. The final representations, as thus superimposed, are displayed in Fig. 11-10. As in Fig. 11-7, the head end of each arrow coincides with the "good" member and the tail end coincides with the "bad" member of each pair of antonyms. Figure 11-10 shows that the positions

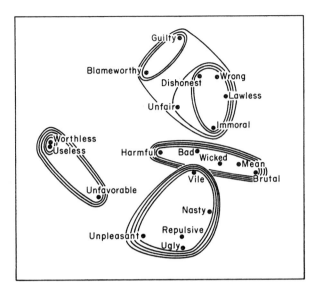

Fig. 11-9. Two-dimensional Euclidean representation for Group BDG.

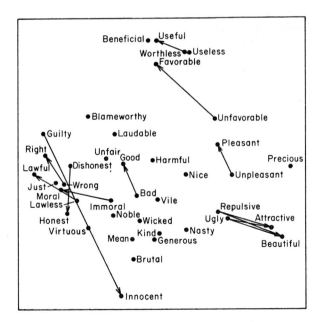

Fig. 11-10. Superimposed two-dimensional Euclidean representations for Group GDG (heads of arrows) and Group BDG (tails of arrows).

of only two GOOD terms, INNOCENT and FAVORABLE, are displaced to a noticeable extent. The relations among the remaining pairs of antonyms stayed about the same (and might further be improved by "stretching" the representation for Group BDG), showing a quite satisfactory structural isomorphism between antonymous terms.

DISCUSSION

Given the uninterpretability of the results in the MDS representations, it seems fair to conclude that a spatial or dimensional representation is not appropriate for the present data. While the results of the cluster analyses are somewhat more coherent and intelligible, particularly for the case of BAD terms, there would still appear to be little warrant for considering the terms to be truly hierarchically structured or related in general. It may be more realistic to consider the clusters, at most, as relatively separate, discrete nominal classes.

With regard to the GOOD terms, something like a *moral evaluation* grouping emerges both when the tree construction and the direct grouping procedures are used, although in the latter case this grouping also includes terms such as KIND and GENEROUS, which might more properly be characterized as referring to some sort of *social evaluation.* There are no other significant clusters in the data for Group GT, but in the case of Group GDG there is also a clustering of *aesthetically* evaluative terms, and a cluster of three terms, FAVORABLE, USEFUL, and BENEFICIAL, which seem to index some kind of *practical* or *instrumental* evaluation. In general, see Figs. 11-1 and 11-3, the terms in the HCSs obtained by the two methods are ordered in roughly the same way. The BAD terms appear to be somewhat more clearly organized. By either method of obtaining the data there emerges the same cluster of *morally* evaluative terms and of *practically* or *instrumentally* evaluative terms, and the large significant cluster of *social-emotional-aesthetic* terms, found by use of the tree method, breaks essentially into two significant clusters when the direct grouping procedure is employed. The terms in the HCSs obtained by the two methods are very similarly arranged, see Figs. 11-2 and 11-4, the agreement in results between the two methods being distinctly better for the BAD than for the GOOD terms. While the substantive yield of all this is hardly startling or especially revealing, these findings are intuitively sensible and roughly consistent with those of Osgood and those of Miller in identifying *morally* evaluative terms, as well as suggesting that *aesthetically* and *practically* evaluative terms, respectively, may fall together.

In addition, the results reveal some consistent differences between GOOD and BAD terms, in that the latter seem to be more clearly organized and segregated into relatively distinct groupings. We noted earlier that GOOD terms are more likely to be unmarked than their BAD antonyms. Insofar as an unmarked term serves to label both a category or scale and one member of that category or pole of the scale, while a marked term can serve only the latter function, the usage of GOOD terms must characteristically be more frequent and varied than that of BAD terms. Further, and to the same general point, Boucher and Osgood (1969) have presented considerable evidence to indicate that positively evaluative terms are used more diversely, i.e., that GOOD terms are used as qualifiers to modify a wider range of different nouns than their BAD opposites. To take an example, consider the term BEAUTIFUL in its recent usage, where it has become very much equivalent to GOOD or, better, VERY GOOD, generally without any necessary aesthetic evaluation, while there is no corresponding use of something like UGLY as a generalized term to express the judgment VERY BAD. This greater applicability or diversity of GOOD terms is consistent with and may provide some explanation for the greater homogeneity of similarity relations among GOOD terms than among BAD terms obtained in the present study. To the extent that the use of the latter terms is more specific, it seems reasonable that any groupings obtained should be clearer and more distinct.

We turn next to the problem of mapping sets of GOOD and BAD terms into each other. In the absence of any useable theoretical model for the domain of evaluative terms we sought to provide some sort of internal check on any results obtained by selecting terms so that they might constitute antonym sets differing only in their marking on the evaluative dimension, and then determining whether the structures emerging in each set could be more or less adequately matched or mapped into each other. Any *a priori* selection of supposedly antonymous terms needs some external, independent validation or check, and, as we have indicated earlier, only about half of the pairs chosen survived such a test. Thus any matching analysis must be restricted to these terms only. Before considering the outcome of this analysis we should note at least two facts, each of which imposes constraints on any results that might be obtained. First, as discussed above, there seem to be some over-all systematic differences between the structures obtained for GOOD and BAD terms, with the latter more clearly, distinctly organized. Second, in making comparisons between structures, we attempted to align the two dimensional MDS solutions based on an analysis of the total proximity matrices involving all 20 terms in each case, rather than determining relative positions on the basis of the two 11 x 11 proximity submatrices.[1] Insofar as the remaining nine terms in each set do not have comparable "partner" terms in the other set, this will inevitably introduce noise into the results, distorting and fuzzing, in unknown and unknowable ways, the

[1] Note that in making comparisons in terms of the MDS solutions we imply no substantive interpretation of them, but use these representations only as a device to depict the relations among terms in each set and to assess, in a rough way, the similarity between the two sets of relations.

relative positions of the critical 11 terms in each set. Both of these considerations militate against any close match in structures.

In light of these constraints, and whatever additional artifacts may be introduced by forcing data into a two-dimensional solution, the outcomes of the matching analysis reveal a very considerable structural isomorphism, whether we consider the results using the tree construction task (Fig. 11-7), or the direct grouping results (Fig. 11-10). In each instance, only two or three of the 11 terms are displaced to any noticeable extent when the two subsets of terms are mapped into each other. It must be observed, of course, that both the aligning of solutions and judgments as to the degree of the resemblance between them were carried out in a subjective manner in the present study. However, this is not an absolutely unavoidable drawback since there are objective techniques, such as that of Cliff (1966), for rotation to congruence, and for assessing the agreement between the coordinates of the points in the transformed and target configurations (see Shepard and Chipman, 1970, for an illustration of the use of such techniques). In general, procedures which seek to map sets of relations into each other and to assess the similarity between two or more sets of relations would appear to constitute absolutely necessary tools for the investigation of internal representations and, therefore, of semantic domains. One may consider the case where a well-specified theoretical model is already available as that special case, where a target set of relations against which an empirically obtained set is to be assessed can be directly, theoretically generated.

While the present results are clearly nonrandom, reasonably plausible, and consistent with earlier work in identifying terms which are morally evaluative, as well as terms evaluative in some other respects, it would appear presumptuous, in the extreme, to claim that they are in any substantive way particularly revealing with regard to the structure of the domain of evaluative terms. What explanation might there be for this, and for the fact that earlier work, too, has only yielded the coarsest of characterizations, especially granted the sovereign importance of evaluation in so many matters of human interaction, intercourse with the environment, and intercourse with the artifacts in it? We shall argue that, in principle, there may not exist any coherent, definable domain of evaluative terms, and that, again, in principle, the only property shared by all evaluative terms is their positive or negative marking with regard to evaluation. We shall also argue that objects, persons, actions, etc., may be evaluated against a vast variety of standard as well as *ad hoc* criteria, and that when the evaluative component is partialled out, by selecting only very positive or very negative terms, the meaning properties that remain may be very heterogeneous indeed. Essentially we are arguing, in the spirit of Katz (1964), that the meaning of "good" (and equally of "bad") is *syncategorematic*, cannot stand alone, and is not an independent attribute. Rather, it is a function that operates on other meanings and plays its role in combination with "the conceptual content of other words and expressions." The latter may be quite heterogeneous, so that when the evaluative component of the meanings of particular GOOD or BAD terms has been factored out the residual meaning components may be quite various, and need not constitute any coherent semantic field or domain. Even if the above argument is correct, leading to the expectation that, in principle, there should be no orderly structural relations whatsoever among evaluative terms, in fact one should anticipate some communalities among subsets of commonly used evaluative terms since there are presumably a relatively limited set of general respects in regard to which evaluations are characteristically made, such as use, function, purpose, etc., and since single terms having sufficient currency to index a specific sort of evaluation are likely to fall into one or the other of these broad and rather ill-defined classes. In these circumstances it should not be surprising that some broad, gross groupings may emerge, such as *morally* evaluative, *socially* evaluative, *practically* evaluative terms, etc. However, it should also not be surprising that there are no clear relations among these groupings (given qualitatively distinct grounds of evaluation) or even, perhaps, any well-defined structural relations within each grouping (although this last point warrants further investigation using an extensive set of terms drawn from those relevant to a particular kind of evaluation).

In the case of evaluative terms, more than in any other case considered in this work, the problem of item selection or sampling comes to be absolutely critical. Any findings will be very much contingent on the particular terms chosen for study. There is less basis for confidence here than in any of the other instances that the terms selected can really comprise a properly broad, diverse, and, thus, sufficiently adequate sampling even from the set of commonly used evaluative terms (leaving aside the completely intractable problem of terms used for evaluation for idiosyncratic and special *ad hoc* purposes).

Considering its substantive yield, the present study may be regarded as signaling a failure in method, and the problem thus becomes that of identifying the grounds for such a failure in order to draw from the failure some instructive methodological moral or lesson. The studies previously reported in this work span the gamut from well-defined domains, whose members could be exhaustively specified, to rather ill-defined domains which, nevertheless, have some coherence in that their members are characterizable in terms of some common meaning properties or conditions. In the case of GOOD-BAD terms, discussed in present chapter, we may have an instance where the terms do not constitute any coherent or definable domain except for the single property which they share of all being evaluative terms. When this property is partialled out, as was done here, we may be left with a set of essentially heterogeneous terms, and any structural analysis, whether using graph techniques, dimensional scaling techniques, dimension free clustering techniques, or any other techniques whatsoever, may simply be inappropriate in that it can hardly reveal structure which is not there in the first place. That some structure did emerge in the present case reflects the fact that many commonly used evaluative terms can be subsumed under some broad, rather ill-specified general criteria. The implication of all this must be obvious: unless a domain or semantic field is coherent in some measure, subjecting it to a structural analysis is a pointless and futile exercise. Sometimes it may not be possible to make such a determination in advance, and in such cases the outcomes of the structural analysis will presumably provide information either as to the incoherence of the domain, or as to its structure, if it is in some degree coherent.

Chapter 12   ASSESSMENT

The present work sought to examine a variety of semantic domains running the gamut from delimited well-specified domains to extensive, open, and ill-specified ones, in order to determine how people "reckon" in assessing the relations among terms in a given domain. Basic data, obtained in a number of different ways, characteristically consisted of similarity judgments for terms in a domain, these judgments being unconstrained, in that criteria for judgment were not imposed or specified in advance. These data were subjected concurrently to a number of different structural analyses in an attempt to reveal underlying meaning properties, and the nature of their organization. Our interest was both methodological, with regard to problems encountered in any enterprise of this sort, seeking to determine underlying semantic structures or to evaluate the fit between data and some independently specified model, and substantive, with regard to the actual yield of the various studies. We shall comment first on some principally methodological issues, and then pass on to more substantive matters. Mainly, we shall be in the position of noting problems without being able to offer anything definitive toward their solution.

METHODOLOGICAL ISSUES

While one can find relations and similarities among almost any set of terms, even if randomly chosen, our interest was not in the uses of the creative imagination but in the discovery of semantic properties on which there is substantial consensual agreement in the service of communication. We therefore tried to select terms so that in each case they might constitute a more or less coherent semantic domain by sharing some meaning properties, or having some class reference in common. Such an endeavor is straightforward enough if one is dealing with a delimited well-specified domain, such as that of kinship terms, where the simplex terms of the domain, or some part of it, may be exhaustively listed. Matters become much more difficult when, as is more commonly the case, one must deal with a domain, as that of HAVE verbs, which, although appearing intuitively to involve some core concepts, such as POSSESSION and TRANSFER OF POSSESSION, plus various conditions, nevertheless, has no clear boundaries and therefore provides no firm criteria for specifying the universe of relevant terms. Thus, in advance, one cannot know whether a set of terms of this sort can really be considered as coherent, but this, of itself, is not fatal since (as indicated earlier) the results of a structural analysis will reveal in some measure whether or not it is coherent.

There is a more serious problem of item sampling or selection, given that it is impossible to study all the items in a putative domain. How is one to sample if one cannot properly specify the universe from which to sample, and what sorts of rules should one follow in sampling? The problem becomes particularly awkward if one considers (1) that it is quite possible that the underlying structure that does emerge may be conditioned in important ways by the particular item set examined; (2) that results might be quite different if most of the terms are relatively compactly located in the unknown conceptual or semantic space as against being more widely or evenly distributed over it or falling in tight but set-apart clusters; (3) that a few relatively distant terms may unduly compact judgment, masking differences among relatively closely located terms, etc., etc. And note that the apparent coherence or incoherence of the domain may itself depend on the particular items chosen for study. In fact, matters may not be quite as bleak as the above might suggest. For just about any domain that one might wish to study there will be some terms that will be so central and constitutive of the domain that there can be little quarrel about their selection, e.g., consider terms such as GIVE, TAKE, BUY, SELL, GET, LOSE, if one is interested in the family of HAVE verbs. Beyond this it would seem reasonable to study a domain both extensively and intensively, first selecting items so as to provide as diverse a coverage as possible for the domain, and then selecting items so as to obtain a more detailed account of local structure or structures, if there are regions which are densely "populated." It would also seem reasonable to use some obvious central or core items as "marker" items, and carry out an analysis of these items, first together with one set of less central items, then the "marker" items together with another set of less central items, in order to determine whether more or less the same structure emerges in each case, and whether the "marker" items maintain their relative locations. While none of this provides any recipe or guarantee for success, it should at least provide some safeguards against gross distortion of results.

Once one has obtained similarity judgments for terms believed to be drawn from some more or less coherent domain or semantic field, one must decide on procedures for structural analysis which may provide the most appropriate representation for the set of similarity or proximity measures. Two rather different possibilities obtain, although it may be more appropriate to consider them as defining the opposite ends of a continuum: (1) in the absence of any prior knowledge about the domain one may be looking for some sort of discovery procedure, or (2) given an independent theoretical analysis or model, or strong constraints from previous findings, one may wish to test or evaluate some particular structural hypothesis. Clearly the second alternative constitutes a more tractable problem, for the particular structural hypothesis to be tested will govern or strongly determine the choice of analytic technique. If one believes that the underlying organization is paradigmatic, then one should follow the sort of rule of thumb suggested by Miller (1969), using MDS techniques aimed at a dimensional representation. If one believes that a taxonomic class-inclusion structure obtains, then one should employ some hierarchic clustering technique. Thus, if, as in the present work, one is dealing with color terms a geometric representation would appear to be a natural one, and if one is dealing with kinship terms for which there are strong grounds for expecting an underlying paradigmatic structure, one should again attempt to provide a dimensional representation. On the other hand, if one is dealing with a set of names for body parts, as was done by Miller in one of his studies (Miller, 1968) then a taxonomic class-inclusion organization would appear to be the natural one, and one ought to use some variety of hierarchical clustering procedure to analyze and represent the data.

What if one has no prior structural hypotheses, but rather is seeking a discovery procedure for exploring a completely unknown domain? If nothing whatsoever is known about a domain, then it is probably impossible to use the sorts of techniques discussed in this work as discovery procedures. But, characteristically, something, in fact, will be known about a particular domain, for if this were not the case then it would have been impossible to select a set of terms supposed to be related, chosen from a domain supposed to be more or less coherent. To say that something of this sort is true is not to say that, ahead of time, there is or need be any articulated account for the domain, only that some minimum knowledge, suggesting that the terms chosen for study are related and drawn from a more or less coherent domain, is a precondition for the interpretability of any results obtained by use of such structural analyses. With reference to the domains examined in the present work, it must be apparent that they are distributed over a continuum ranging from "pure" hypothesis testing to "pure" discovery procedure, with more of them falling toward the latter pole (indeed the very ordering of chapters reflects this in a rough way). Thus, the study of color names and that of kinship terms constitute instances where, in each case, there are relatively well articulated models and considerable prior evidence against which present results may be evaluated. This prior work suggests, indeed, the form in which our results should be represented, and, thus, the techniques most appropriate for their analysis. On the other hand, when it comes, say, to the study of HAVE verbs, while there were grounds for believing that they do form a coherent set, and there was available a semantic analysis for a subset of the terms, courtesy of Bendix (1966), there was little basis for specifying in advance the nature of the structural organization governing this domain. This problem is perhaps sharpest when we consider the GOOD-BAD words or evaluative terms. In this case, no independent model of any sort was available and we sought to buttress our analysis by matching the results for GOOD terms with those for their antonyms from the set of BAD terms.

For our purposes here, there is one principal difference between studies directed toward the testing of some structural hypothesis and those more innocent of prior knowledge, operating rather in the spirit of discovery procedures. Studies of the former sort may determine, or at least present some strong guidance as to the most appropriate procedures for structural analysis and representation of results, whereas such guidance is lacking in the latter case. It might be noted that for the foreseeable future, in the absence of well developed semantic accounts, most studies will be of the latter sort. Further, one might observe that even if there is available some well specified semantic model for a given domain, if the similarity data as appropriately analyzed depart in some significant or important respects from expectation, as will surely often be the case, then, in searching for a new way of more adequately accounting for the structure that obtains, we shall always have to consider the possibility that a different sort of representation might be more appropriate, thus again finding ourselves in circumstances characteristic of the use of discovery procedures.

Why all this fuss about choice of procedures for the structural analysis of similarity data? The reason must be obvious, namely, that particular procedures for analysis of data (and for obtaining data) *may force or impose a structure on the data.* We take this to be one of the central methodological problems in this area. After a word on some possible artifacts, consequent upon use of particular procedures for gathering data, we shall comment on this issue with regard to "empirical discovery procedures" as embodied in different sorts of techniques for the structural analysis of similarity data.

One of the principal techniques we employed to gather data was the tree construction method, which does not permit cycles, since, among other things, the presence of cycles would make it impossible to specify uniquely the distance between every pair of nodes. As we have already pointed out, this makes it impossible to obtain closed and therefore circular representations for individual subjects, and thus, for the case of color terms, almost certainly serves to distort the data. Again, for the case of the tree construction method, a subject may have constructed a number of distinct subtrees or similarity shrubs with considerable subjective confidence about his judgments, and feel that it is very much an arbitrary matter how these are connected to each other, finally, to form a single tree. Yet the particular linkages he makes can substantially affect the distances between some items, and thus aspects of the structure that can emerge from an analysis of the similarity matrix. Note, finally, that if data are obtained by a grouping method, then no information about structures for individuals can ever become available, other than the set of nominal classes revealed by particular groupings.

We take the position, which is perhaps philosophically naive, that the job of analysis is to discover whatever structure is in some sense immanent or latent in the data, and that one must avoid forcing or distorting the data by use of techniques with Procrustean properties. In some degree, all techniques for structural analysis have such properties, and therefore it is essential that, in any particular case, we have some information about the extent of the distortion imposed, and the residual misfit. It must be obvious that if we use some sort of MDS technique we shall end up with a dimensional or spatial representation. Inevitably the fit to data will not be perfect, and there will be some question as to whether the discrepancies found are large or small, random or systematic. Similarly, if we use a hierarchic clustering technique we will end up with a taxonomic structure, even if the data really fall into distinct nominal classes. With the exception of some suggestions by Degerman (1968), which involve difficulties of their own (some of which were noted in Chapter 2), we do not even have techniques available for analyzing mixed structures, involving both typal and dimensional properties.

In principle, the kinds of structures that may characterize a semantic domain can be quite various, and it must be obvious that the sorts of examples mentioned in this report, viz. linear, cross-classificatory or paradigmatic structures, nominal class structures, and taxonomic structures do not, even in combination, exhaust all the possibilities (for a mention of some others of these, see Deese, 1969; and Osgood, 1968a). If this is the case, then techniques which can only pick up or impose dimensional structure or taxonomic structure on the data will often, to an unknown greater or lesser extent, misrepresent the actual underlying meaning configurations. The sort of solution offered by Osgood: *"restrict the semantic domain under study to a pure type of system and then apply the appropriate discovery procedure* (1968a, p. 132)" would appear to be largely impossible, and probably undesirable even if it were possible. It is largely impossible precisely because, generally, we do not know in advance the sort of structural organization characterizing a particular semantic domain (this is what the discovery technique is to accomplish) and because, generally, a domain will not constitute a pure system. The solution would appear undesirable since, insofar as many domains are not pure systems, such a maxim would restrict our investigation to a subset of "neat" cases, and rule out of consideration many important complexly structured domains. Insofar as Osgood is suggesting that any complexly structured domain be decomposed into more homogeneous subdomains, and that each of these then be studied by techniques appropriate to it, the advice is excellent, subject only to the great difficulty, noted immediately above, of discovering ahead of time the kind of structure obtaining for each of these subdomains.

There are, of course, safeguards which can give us some indications as to whether or not a representation is adequate to the data. Of these, some are internal to each procedure, and others depend on the *concurrent* use of a number of different techniques for obtaining and analyzing data. Assume that different data gathering procedures yield roughly the same similarity data. One may then determine whether any of the graph results depart significantly from chance, note whether the stress values of the MDS solution are less than the critical cut-offs and where there is an elbow in the stress function, see whether significant clusterings are obtained, etc. Further, one may demand some significant graph results as a precondition for the application of MDS and cluster procedures. Given some MDS representation of low dimensionality, following the advice of Shepard (1969), one may embed a cluster solution in it to guard against undue dimensional compression by showing that the MDS representation is consistent with the clustering results in that the contours drawn around the latter are compact and simple. Beyond this and perhaps more important, one may consider the intelligibility of results yielded respectively by concurrent use of dimensional and dimension free techniques, preferring that representation which yields the more interpretable results. While various techniques may have Procrustean properties, there may be a saving "recalcitrance" of data, resulting in unintelligible or absurd findings, when much forcing or distortion has taken place, thus signaling to the investigator, as a knowledgeable user of the language, that something has gone awry (on this point see Osgood, 1968a, p. 131). In the last analysis, accordingly, there must, perhaps, be recourse to some unspecified and, perhaps, unspecifiable criterion of appropriateness or interpretability. Recall how again and again it was on the basis of interpretability that we selected one kind of representation rather than another, e.g., regardless of the fact that a MDS solution might provide an acceptable fit to the data, we sometimes preferred a hierarchic representation if the latter, but not the former, permitted an intuitively sensible interpretation of the findings. Goodness of fit is clearly a necessary but not sufficient condition in determining choice of representation. The principal advantage of the use of a number of techniques for data analysis, involving basically different structural assumptions, is that instead of being faced with some absolute judgment of interpretability, as would be the case if only one technique had been used, one may, rather, make a comparative judgment under more informative circumstances.

One further point: the stated aim of this work has been (1) the discovery of meaning relevant properties, and (2) a characterization of the nature of their structural organization. These two questions are obviously very intimately related, in that results will always simultaneously yield information about both, and in that any answer to the latter question presupposes an answer to the former. Yet it seems at least possible that even if there are doubts about aspects of the organization revealed by a structural analysis, because of some Procrustean properties of a given technique, nevertheless, if the results appear to be intelligible one might still have considerable confidence that the sorts of meaning properties that seem to be involved have been correctly identified. Thus, even on the most conservative view, something of value will have been revealed, and some possibilities and directions for further work established.

Tacitly, throughout this monograph we have been taking what might be called a "realist" or "essentialist" position, assuming that there is a unique, correct structural solution for the relations obtaining among a set of lexical items constituting or drawn from a particular semantic domain (certainly for a given individual subject). We have been writing as though, in some sense, this structure "existed in mind," and have argued that our job was to reveal such structure without distorting it by the techniques used to make it manifest. Obviously this is not the only possible position or perspective. One might take a "conventionalist" view, arguing that the structure obtained in a given case merely constitutes an efficient device for representing a set of relations, without making any claims as to the cognitive reality of that structure. It seems to us that, in principle, there is no possible basis for choosing between such a "conventionalist" position and the position we have taken, that a choice in this regard is perhaps more revealing of philosophical-epistemological commitments than of anything else, and that nothing empirical hinges on that choice.

There is another empirically interesting possibility, however; one might argue that the particular structural mapping of a set of lexical items may be task specific, and that quite different results might be obtained with different task instructions. Changes in the instructions might make other properties or attributes of the terms salient for the subject, and thus might lead him to conceive of the relations among the terms in different ways. This obviously is an empirical issue, and we do have some data which are pertinent and which suggest that at least some task changes may make little difference to the results. Thus, e.g., for the case of color names, it made little difference whether subjects employed a "similarity" or "dissimilarity" criterion in making their judgments, and, in the case of kinship terms, we obtained very similar results whether a "family relation" or "mutual affection" criterion was used. However, these data are quite limited and it is very possible that different tasks and contexts might elicit data organized in rather different ways. For some suggestions and comments on this see Deese (1970, p. 96). One should at least raise the question of whether some task may be particularly appropriate for eliciting underlying meaning relations, whether some task or tasks should be assigned a sort of canonical status so that data thus obtained could be considered particularly basic or revealing. If one takes the view that meaning is to be defined in terms of meaning relations holding among the items in a particular semantic domain, then perhaps at least a *prima facie* case might be made for tasks, of the sort employed in the present work, which directly require judgments of similarity for a set of related terms, for such judgments can presumably only be made on the basis of the meaning relations obtaining among the terms.

But, granted that this last assertion is true, why require judgments of "similarity in meaning" rather than judgments of "relatedness in meaning?" if one seeks to study meaning relations then, as suggested by H. Clark (personal communication), a criterion of "relatedness" of meaning would appear to be the more appropriate one, and to get more directly at the matter of principal concern. Furthermore, the notion of "relatedness" would appear to be the more basic and generic one, with "similarity" as a special, if particularly common and salient form of "relatedness." In particular, considering antonymous terms, subjects might regard these as rather dissimilar just because they are "opposite" in meaning, even though they would surely recognize that antonyms are, in fact, intimately related. Thus it is quite possible that, had a criterion of "relatedness" rather than one of "similarity" been employed, terms, especially antonymous ones, might have been clustered rather differently, and the semantic structures obtained might have been rather different Note, for example, that in his study of prepositions Clark (1968) employed a "relatedness" criterion, and that, in that study, antonymous terms characteristically fell rather close together, while this was nowhere near as much the case in the present study which employed a "similarity" criterion. The issue is an empirical one, clearly worthy of study, in that one must determine the nature and magnitude of differences in the semantic space(s) as a function of differences in the judgmental criterion specified for the subjects.

There is also a methodological issue here. We suspect that there would be great difficulty in instructing subjects to employ a "relatedness" criterion rather than a "similarity" criterion, that many or most subjects would end up taking "relatedness" to mean "similarity." Thus we should expect greater individual differences in results if a "relatedness" criterion were specified, possibly obtaining different clusters of subjects or "points of view," depending on how this criterion was understood. It seems quite possible that such understanding would vary with the particular semantic domain under consideration, that in some cases "relatedness" could only be understood as "similarity," while in other cases it might be understood as "similarity" or taken differently and more generally, by at least some subjects. *A priori,* it would seem plausible that differences in the judgmental criterion employed might be most consequential, or, perhaps, might only be consequential for those domains which in fact include a few pairs of natural "opposites" or antonyms. In the present study the domain of prepositions, that of HAVE verbs, and, to some extent, the domain of verbs of JUDGING would seem to be of this sort. The domain of GOOD-BAD words also qualifies, of course, but in that instance there is no problem since the GOOD words and the BAD words were judged separately. Finally, we wish to note that even "similarity" as an otherwise unspecified relation or criterion sets the subject a rather unclear and difficult task, since we do not wish to specify the sorts of similarities that he is to consider, and that all these problems would necessarily be exacerbated for the subject if the still broader, more vague criterion of "relatedness" were used. All this notwithstanding, it would obviously be of interest and importance to employ a "relatedness" criterion as well as a "similarity" criterion, and to see what differences this makes in the results.

SUBSTANTIVE ISSUES

We turn now to a few observations on the substantive outcomes of this work. The first observation to be made is at once substantive and methodological in its implications. The studies presented in the early chapters (color names, kinship terms, pronouns) yielded what appear to be very plausible, sensible results, consistent with some prior models or structural hypotheses. Even if one were to consider these outcomes as trivial, truistic demonstrations of the obvious, nevertheless they would be methodologically important in validating our investigative techniques in clear cases, and thus justifying their applications to other domains, where matters are very far from clear. Further, as has already been argued, it would seem unrealistic to consider these results as demonstrations of the obvious. For the case of both kinship terms and that of pronouns, the findings support a very particular model, where other possibilities have been suggested. Thus, in the former case the results strongly support Romney and D'Andrade's (1964) "reciprocity" model over the "absolute generation" model advanced by Wallace and Atkins (1960). In the latter case, the results indicate that the feature "person" may be hierarchically organized with an initial distinction between "first" person and "other," and a subsequent differentiation of the latter into "second" and "third" persons (in the spirit of Lyons, 1968), rather than in terms of a direct three-valued uni-level differentiation of this feature, as the more common view might have it. Also, in each case the results indicate something about the cognitive weighting or salience of the features involved. Thus, for kinship terms they indicate that differences in "sex" always have less consequence than differences in otherwise matched direct and collateral terms, and, for pronouns, that differences in "case" are always cognitively less important than differences in "person" or "number." With regard to the results for color names, these provide evidence for a higher order isomorphism between representations (colors and color terms) of the sort considered by Shepard and Chipman (1970). In so doing the results reveal something of the structural organization of a set of terms differing only in their "distinguishers," to use the terminology of Katz and Fodor (1963). The results indicate that in this case the features that distinguish the idiosyncratic meanings of these color terms are themselves very clearly organized, in a way that appears to be modeled directly on a salient property of the color space or colors to which they refer. Since color terms have constituted one of the principal examples used to argue for the necessity of "distinguishers" as idiosyncratic, unsystematic meaning relevant properties, results of the present kind at least call for a reexamination of any notion of this sort, and again raise questions as to how a distinction between semantic "markers" and "distinguishers" is to be drawn, or whether it can be drawn at all (on this see, e.g., Bolinger, 1965).

In looking back at the results of the various studies, it must be obvious that in some instances findings are quite clear both with regard to the meaning properties involved and the nature of their structural organization (see some of the studies mentioned above). In other instances there is valuable information about the sorts of meaning properties involved, but obviously there is still a considerable way to go in exactly specifying their interrelations (see prepositions, conjunctions, HAVE verbs, and verbs of JUDGING). And in at least two cases, Emotion names and Evaluative terms, the substantive yield is somewhat disappointing, possibly because of pervasive individual differences in the use of Emotion names and possibly because GOOD-BAD terms really do not constitute any coherent domain, having in common only the property of evaluation.

As to the structural organization of the various domains studied, there are clearly cases requiring a dimensional or spatial solution, either in full form, e.g., color names, or in some degenerate form, as might be expected if the underlying system is a cross-classificatory one. There are cases requiring a typal solution, see e.g., HAVE verbs and verbs of JUDGING, although it is not always clear whether the underlying structure is really hierarchical or whether it would be more appropriate to consider the classes as nominal classes (see, e.g., the results for GOOD-BAD terms, insofar as any structure at all obtains there). And there are cases, for example that of pronouns, which appear to represent a mixed structure with a taxonomic component embedded in a cross-classificatory system. Further, to consider the case of prepositions, not only is there some doubt that the clustering is generally hierarchical, but it appears that different sorts of principles may govern the organization of the various clusters formed, with some kind of proximity dimension embedded in the SPATIAL CON-TIGUITY cluster, and some sort of contrast between absolute and relative location determining clustering in the UNDER and OVER clusters. The general lesson of this is that different domains may be organized in terms of different structural principles, and, indeed, that it is very likely that any particular domain which is not very circumscribed and well defined is likely to be characterized by some complex mixture of structures, and that simple structures, of various sorts, are to be anticipated only in local subregions of the domain. This result, which is hardly startling, would appear to be all the more compelling if one recalls that the techniques used in the present study, and, for that matter, any others currently available, tend to impose uniform structure of a given kind on the similarity data.

One of the criteria controlling choice of domains for study was the availability of some prior independent analysis or theoretical model, however tentative or partial (the only domain constituting an exception being that of Evaluative terms, where an internal matching analysis was attempted). In some cases these models were sufficiently clear and well articulated that our data could be used to evaluate a particular account or to choose between competing accounts. But even in cases where this was not true, even in cases where further examination revealed unclarities or indeterminacies as to the overall properties of a model, as, say, in the case of Cooper's analyses of spatial prepositions, or Osgood's analysis of verbs of JUDGING, these models were nevertheless of value in providing some orientation to our scrutiny of the results, at the very least with regard to local properties or subregions in a domain. Thus, even if the logic of a particular study is that of discovery rather than hypothesis testing, the availability of some independent theoretical account is of heuristic value in providing a perspective or perspectives from which to consider the data. For example, it appears clear that some aspects of the results for verbs of JUDGING would not have been brought into relief had there not been available to us Fillmore's analysis in terms of presuppositions and assertions. Distinctions of this type also guided Miller (1969) in the analysis of grouping data obtained for a set of terms much more heterogeneous than any employed in the present work.

A word might be said about the use of techniques other than those requiring global similarity or dissimilarity judgments to provide data for structural analysis. The two cases of interest in the present study involve (1) a task where the subject was asked to complete a sentence by choosing a conjunction best satisfying certain specified meaning conditions, and (2) a task where the subject learned pronouns as the response members in a paired associate task. An important difference between the tree construction method employed to obtain direct similarity data and the sentence completion technique is that while the former technique can be used to test specific structural hypotheses as, e.g., in our study of kinship terms, it may also be employed without any *a priori* hypotheses as to the nature of underlying properties involved. A technique of the latter sort can only be used insofar as one does have some *a priori* basis for specifying relevant conditions. Clearly, if successful, the latter sort of procedure is a more powerful one to the extent that it explicitly indicates some of the bases of similarity among the items. On the other hand, any such techniques may yield misleading results by focusing on irrelevant properties or relatively peripheral ones, and failing to specify crucial or criterial properties. To the extent that these two kinds of techniques give convergent results, with patterns of similarity obtained by the less constraining routine generally consistent with those yielded by the other, we may perhaps have some confidence that at least some relevant or significant features underlying the data have been captured, that there exists some basis for the interpretation of these features and their organization, and some justification for preferring the possibly more specific or articulated findings yielded by the more constraining technique. Indeed, for the case of conjunctions, the results from the tree construction task and the sentence completion task were in large agreement as to the identification of underlying meaning properties and their weighting, but differed in that the former results suggested some sort of hierarchic structure, and the latter some sort of cross-classification as the most appropriate representation for the data. Given a general consistency between the results from the less and more constrained procedures, we opted, without overwhelming conviction, for the structural representation most appropriate to the latter results, on the grounds that the more specific and analytic technique might be able more directly to reveal properties of organization or structure that could have been masked by the requirements of the more global judgment task.

It may well be the case that indirect data of the sort represented by errors on a memorial task or confusions during learning may not be directly useful or revealing when it comes to the determination of the underlying system governing the relations among a set of lexical terms. This is so since, in the best of circumstances, such data provide information simultaneously about underlying structures and memorial and retrieval processes, and generally it will not be possible to factor this information into its components. Further, the sort of processing required for single items in a memory task may differ from that involved in full understanding when a whole set of items is being examined (on these matters more generally, in the context of studies of underlying syntactic structures, see Fillenbaum, 1970). The basic point involved is obvious: if one is interested in how people learn or recall items coming from a structurally coherent domain, then one has to study learning and recall. If one is primarily interested in discovering underlying structures, then more direct tests of understanding (which minimize processing and memorial constraints) are more appropriate. To the extent that these two sorts of investigations yield similar or compatible results, one may infer that items really are held in mind in terms of the underlying structural features, and also draw some relatively straightforward conclusions as to possible processing mechanisms. To the extent that results diverge, problems of interpretation with regard to the nature of the processing strategies involved become far more complex. In any case one point must be absolutely clear: any research which seeks to investigate the perception or learning or recall of lexical items will need first to specify them as objects of perception, learning, or recall, and any such specification will require, as one of its essential parts, a characterization of the similarity relations obtaining among them, which in turn is dependent upon the underlying structure of meaning relations. In a sense, the determination of such structure thus represents a very early, basic, and completely necessary step, preliminary and prior to almost any work whatsoever.

In comparing the present work with other recent efforts by psychologists directed toward the discovery of underlying semantic structures, one should note that, so far as choice of terms for analysis, it occupies some sort of middle ground. On the one hand Miller (1969) examined a heterogeneous set of 48 nouns, and Osgood (1968a) studied some 200 or so interpersonal verbs; on the other hand Steinberg (1970) carefully selected 13 lexical items "in order to yield a variety of similarities and contrasts with respect to postulated underlying semantic dimensions (p. 39)." It appears to us that a strategy which focuses attention on relatively limited sets of lexical terms, where there are independent grounds for believing the sets to be more or less coherent, has advantages over both the other kinds of approaches mentioned above. On the one hand, it guards against the possibility that one is dealing with a set of items many of which are not really related to each other, or a case where the domain is so extensive and diffuse that no overall structure could possibly emerge. On the other hand, it avoids the problems that result when one cunningly selects terms so as to tailor make a neat *ad hoc* domain. When this happens, what is found is, and can only be, at best, precisely what was built in by judicious item selection in the first place, and, consequently, any inferences to more naturally constituted domains are blocked, or, if possible, very perilous. Our procedure in choosing items or domains for study is rather in the spirit of the linguist exploring some more or less demarcated semantic field, or of the anthropologist seeking to provide a componential analysis for some restricted domain. It differs from the work of such investigators in that we are directly concerned with matters of "cognitive reality," whereas the practitioner of componential analysis may often be primarily concerned with developing an economical and powerful theoretical representation, without seeking to establish "God's truth," or its psychological validity.

So far as procedures for obtaining and analyzing data, the work of Miller (1969) is more restricted than ours in that only one technique (grouping) is used to gather data, and only one technique (hierarchic clustering) is employed to analyze data. Osgood (1968a), quite to the contrary, uses a great variety of techniques, both to obtain and to analyze data, with special interest in procedures which examine words in a combination rather than in isolation, with particular emphasis on a "semantic interaction technique." In this regard, Osgood's work is considerably richer than ours. While these studies appear promising in revealing some of the important features involved in the subjective lexicon, they do not go very far in characterizing the structural organization of such features. Thus, in the case of Osgood, we have already pointed out (Chapter 10) that his analysis of interpersonal verbs does not involve a cross-classificatory system, as at first might seem to be the case, but rather a very much more complicated system whose properties are largely unspecified. Similarly, while Miller has stressed the importance of common presuppositions in determining similarity judgments, he has not exhibited any clear overall structural properties, except for the special case of a study of body parts (Miller 1968).

One further respect in which the present work differs from that of Miller and most of the work of Osgood is that, given a procedure such as the tree building technique for obtaining data, we can determine similarity structures for individual subjects, as well as for grouped or pooled data. While we have presented structural analyses for the data from individual subjects, often noting general consistencies between such analyses and the results based on averaged data, we have not really been able to capitalize on this property of our data gathering procedures. One reason for emphasizing group rather than individual results was that careful inspection of about 25% of all the individual data obtained by the tree-construction method failed to reveal any consistent differences between subjects or to indicate any clearly defined subgroups of subjects. Also, the stress values for individual subjects yielded by the Euclidean model were almost uniformly lower than the ones yielded by the City Block model, indicating, contrary to Hyman and Well's suggestion (1967), that when a dimensional representation of the group data was found adequate, the particular value of r (for $r = 1.0$ or $r = 2.0$) did not reflect individual differences with respect to the subjects' ability to extract information from the component dimensions. Moreover, the cluster analysis of individual subjects on the direct grouping data (Chapters 7, 9, and 11) did not provide any evidence for distinguishably different frames of reference or clearly defined "points of view." To the extent that individual differences were detectable, they were mainly related to the number of clusters formed by each subject, which might reflect the subject's ability to notice the more subtle semantic differences between lexical items, or simply a response bias determined by the subject's interpretation of the instructions.

A second reason for emphasizing group rather than individual results was that in many of the studies, particularly where the semantic spaces were less well defined, we were not willing to trust too much the individual data, which seemed to us to be too weak or noisy to support MDS analyses. In this respect we were unfortunate not to know of, or to have access to Carroll and Chang's (1970) method, briefly described in Chapter 2, which takes advantage of communalities among subjects. Clearly, with the further development of truly nonmetric MDS methods designed to account for individual differences by differentially weighting the individual dimensions, taking advantage of communalities among subjects, and allowing for nonlinear as well as linear relationships between individual subject spaces and the corresponding "common" space, considerably more attention can and should be given to the question of individual differences in semantic space.

If one is interested not only in describing properties of the adult subjective lexicon, but also in saying something about the ways in which semantic structures develop, it would seem essential to have techniques available that can yield similarity structures for individual subjects, and which can feasibly be employed with young children. Data obtained by such techniques might reveal something as to the nature of early semantic structures and the ways in which they change to approximate adult structures. They might tell us something as to what sorts of structures are ontogenetically early and which come in late or later, and how new meaning distinctions enter into the subjective lexicon. Data on such matters would be of extraordinary importance, for at present except perhaps for some rather complex inferences based on changes in the nature of associative responses (see, e.g., McNeill, 1970), we have very little information about the manner in which semantic knowledge develops. As far as adults are concerned, our suspicion is that, given the constraints of adequate communication, in general semantic structures for different individuals should be rather similar with principal differences only in the "fine grain" of the structures (representing relatively subtle distinctions), rather than in major properties or overall organization.

What do the present results have to say as to the nature of mind or, more modestly and appropriately, as to the organization of the subjective lexicon? Recall, first, that our investigations dealt with a number of distinct, more or less well demarcated domains. While it seems plausible, for example, to suppose that cabbages and kings are not entirely unrelated, both after all can be characterized as *concrete* rather than *abstract,* and *animate* rather than *inanimate,* etc., nevertheless, it is very difficult to conceive of the properties of the complex network in which both "cabbages" and "kings" can find their proper place. We know very little about the general organizational properties in terms of which restricted lexical domains are tied together or connected in the subjective lexicon. (For some broad speculations on "Semantic Information Processing" see, e.g., Minsky, 1968, particularly the paper by Quillian on "Semantic Meaning" where there are some suggestions as to how a path might be traced connecting any lexical item with any other lexical item; for pertinent experimental findings see Collins and Quillian, 1969.) It does seem "unrealistic to claim that the entire vocabulary is covered by fields in the same organic way in which the fields themselves, or at least some of them are built up (Ullman, 1962, p. 249)." In any case, in terms of our data, we have nothing to contribute on this issue.

With reference to the items constituting or drawn from some particular domain of the subjective lexicon, we have directed attention to the network of relations defining their meanings as nodes in the structure, and pointed out some of the principles in terms of which such networks appear to be organized. Obviously this raises general questions as to limits on the number of features with regard to which a particular lexical item may be cross-classified, the depth of the hierarchic tree in which it may be located, the possibilities of embedding a taxonomic structure in a cross-classificatory one or vice versa, etc., and more generally, with regard to which of the conceivable structural possibilities are ever actually realized. On this score again there is little we can say except to make the obvious point that various sorts of structures are to be found in our results, suggesting very strongly that "semantic interpretations depend on not one but a variety of cognitive structures" as Deese (1969) has argued. This has some general implications for the organization of semantic theory. While there is no reason why the definitional schemes of any such theory should directly mirror properties of the subjective lexicon, nevertheless, if models of semantic competence and performance are to be readily compatible, then a semantic theory must characterize lexical items in ways consistent with the organization of the subjective lexicon. At least the formalisms employed should not be so restrictive that they cannot accomodate the quite various structures that are to be found in the subjective lexicon. Indeed, one might perhaps argue that a rich knowledge of properties of the subjective lexicon, yielded in part by techniques of the sort explored in the present work, is absolutely essential for any linguistic theory, insofar as such information constitutes the data with which any such theory must cope.

We have no firm basis for believing that certain structures are particularly difficult for the adult to master, although there are some speculations by Deese (1969) to the effect that people will have inordinate difficulties with extensive taxonomic structures, even though they can readily make use of relationships of subordination and superordination. Note that many structural complexities that may actually characterize the subjective lexicon will never appear in data of the sort we have obtained. Given that terms were always chosen so as to constitute relatively coherent domains, then a principle of relativity of judgment entails that any properties common to all terms in a set will never be revealed since, of necessity, similarity judgments can only reflect the ways in which subjects evaluate the (residual) differences among terms. To discover properties that all terms in some set have in common, and the nature of their organization, would require techniques where subjects must simultaneously consider distinct and diverse sets of terms, i.e., studies directed to an analysis of the relationships that hold among semantic domains.

It has been suggested, see, e.g., Lyons (1963, 1968) that meaning should be treated as a function of meaning relations, that the notion of semantic structure be defined "in terms of certain relations that hold between the items of a particular lexical sub-system." The research which has been reported in the present work may be regarded as an attempt at the experimental exploration of meaning from this perspective.

REFERENCES

Abelson, R. P., and Kanouse, D. E. Subjective acceptance of verbal generalizations. In S. Feldman (Ed.), *Cognitive consistency.* New York: Academic Press, 1966.

Abelson, R. P., and Sermat, V. Multidimensional scaling of facial expressions. *Journal of Experimental Psychology,* 1962, **63,** 546–554.

Allport, F. H. *Social psychology.* Cambridge, Mass.: Houghton-Mifflin, 1924.

Anisfeld, M., and Knapp, M. Association, synonymity, and directionality in false recognition. *Journal of Experimental Psychology,* 1968, **77,** 171–179.

Attneave, F. Dimensions of similarity. *American Journal of Psychology,* 1950, **63,** 516–556.

Attneave, F. Perception and related areas. In S. Koch (Ed.), *Psychology: A study of a science.* Vol. 4. New York: McGraw-Hill, 1962, 619–659.

Beals, R., Krantz, D. H., and Tversky, A. Foundations of multidimensional scaling. *Psychological Review,* 1968, **75,** 127–142.

Bendix, E. H. Componential analysis of general vocabulary: The semantic structure of a set of verbs in English, Hindi and Japanese. Part II. *International Journal of American Linguistics,* 1966, **32,** No. 2.

Bennett, D. C. English prepositions: A stratificational approach. *Journal of Linguistics,* 1968, **4,** 153–172.

Bennett, J. Entailment. *Philosophical Review,* 1969, **78,** 197–236.

Block, J. Studies in the phenomenology of the emotions. *Journal of Abnormal and Social Psychology,* 1957, **54,** 358–363.

Bolinger, D. The atomization of meaning. *Language,* 1965, **41,** 555–573.

Boucher, J., and Osgood, C. E. The Pollyanna hypothesis. *Journal of Verbal Learning and Verbal Behavior,* 1969, **8,** 1–8.

Brown, R. *Social psychology.* New York: Free Press, 1965.

Busacker, R. G., and Saaty, T. L. *Finite graphs and networks: An introduction with applications.* New York: McGraw-Hill, 1965.

Carroll, J. D. Individual differences and multidimensional scaling. Bell Telephone Laboratories, Murray Hill, N.J., 1969 (mimeographed).

Carroll, J. D., and Chang, J. J. Analysis of individual differences in multidimensional scaling via an *N*-way generalization of "Eckart-Young" decomposition. *Psychometrika,* 1970, **35,** 283–319.

Chapanis, A. Color names for color space. *American Scientist,* 1965, **53,** 327–346.

Clark, H. H. On the use and meaning of prepositions. *Journal of Verbal Learning and Verbal Behavior,* 1968, **7,** 421–431.

Clark, H. H. Linguistic processes in deductive reasoning. *Psychological Review,* 1969, **76,** 387–404.

Cliff, N. Orthogonal rotation to congruence. *Psychometrika,* 1966, **31,** 33–42.

Cliff, N. The "idealized individual" interpretation of individual differences in multidimensional scaling. *Psychometrika*, 1968, **33**, 225–232.

Cliff, N., and Young, F. W. On the relation between unidimensional judgments and multidimensional scaling. *Organizational Behavior and Human Performance*, 1968, **3**, 269–285.

Collins, A. M., and Quillian, M. R. Retrieval time from semantic memory. *Journal of Verbal Learning and Verbal Behavior*, 1969, **8**, 240–247.

Constantinescu, P. The classification of a set of elements with respect to a set of properties. *Computer Journal*, 1966, **8**, 352–357.

Constantinescu, P. A method of cluster analysis. *British Journal of Mathematical and Statistical Psychology*, 1967, **20**, 93–106.

Coombs, C. H. *A theory of data*. New York: Wiley, 1964.

Coombs, C. H., and Kao, R. C. On a connection between factor analysis and multidimensional unfolding. *Psychometrika*, 1960, **25**, 219–231.

Cooper, G. S. A semantic analysis of English locative prepositions. AFCRL-68-0056, USAF, Bedford, Mass. Report No. 1587, Bolt, Beranek and Newman, Inc., 1968.

D'Andrade, R. G. Trait psychology and componential analysis. In E. A. Hammel (Ed.), *Formal semantic analysis. American Anthropologist*, 1965, **67**, No. 5, Part 2 (Special Publication).

Deese, J. *The structure of associations in language and thought*. Baltimore: Johns Hopkins Press, 1965.

Deese, J. Conceptual categories in the study of content. In G. Gerbner, (Ed.), *Communication and content*. New York: Wiley, 1969.

Deese, J. *Psycholinguistics*. Boston: Allyn and Bacon, 1970.

Degerman, R. Multidimensional analysis of complex structures: Mixtures of class and quantitative variation. Unpublished doctoral dissertation, Johns Hopkins University, 1968.

Dietze, A. G. Types of emotions or dimensions of emotions? A comparison of typal analysis with factor analysis. *Journal of Psychology*, 1963, **56**, 143–159.

Ekman, G. Dimensions of color vision. *Journal of Psychology*, 1954, **38**, 467–474.

Ekman, G. Dimensions of emotion. *Acta Psychologica*, 1955, **7**, 103–112.

Engen, T., Levy, N., and Schlosberg, H. A new series of facial expressions. *American Psychologist*, 1957, **12**, 264–266.

Engen, T., Levy, N., and Schlosberg, H. The dimensional analysis of a new series of facial expressions. *Journal of Experimental Psychology*, 1958, **55**, 454–458.

Erdös, P., and Rényi, A. On random graphs I. *Publicationes Mathematicae (Debrecen)*, 1959, **6**, 290–297.

Erdös, P., and Rényi, A. On the evolution of random graphs. *Publications of the Mathematical Institute of the Hungarian Academy of Sciences*, 1960, **5**, 17–61.

Fillenbaum, S. Words as feature complexes: False recognition of antonyms and synonyms. *Journal of Experimental Psychology*, 1969, **82**, 400–402.

Fillenbaum, S. On the use of memorial techniques to assess syntactic structures. *Psychological Bulletin*, 1970, **73**, 231–237.

Fillenbaum, S., and Jones, L. V. Grammatical contingencies in word association. *Journal of Verbal Learning and Verbal Behavior*, 1965, **4**, 248–255.

Fillmore, C. J. Review of E. H. Bendix, "Componential analysis of general vocabulary: The semantic structure of a set of verbs in English, Hindi and Japanese." In C. J. Fillmore, and I. Lehiste (Eds.), *CISRC Working Papers in Linguistics No. 2*, Ohio State University, 1968.

Fillmore, C. J. Verbs of judging: An exercise in semantic description. *Papers in Linguistics*, 1969a, **1**, 91–117.

Fillmore, C. J. Toward a modern theory of case. In D. A. Reibel, and S. A. Schane (Eds.), *Modern studies in English: Readings in transformational grammar.* Englewood Cliffs, N.J.: Prentice Hall, 1969b.

Gleitman, L. R. Coordinating conjunctions in English. *Language,* 1965, **41**, 260–293.

Green, P. E., and Morris, T. W. Individual difference models in multidimensional scaling: An empirical comparison. Unpublished manuscript, 1969.

Greenberg, J. H. Language universals. In T. A. Sebeok (Ed.), *Current trends in linguistics: Vol. III,* The Hague: Mouton, 1966.

Guttman, L. A general nonmetric technique for finding the smallest coordinate space for a configuration of points. *Psychometrika,* 1968, **33**, 469–506.

Hammel, E. A. (Ed.), *Formal semantic analysis. American Anthropologist,* 1965, **67**, No. 5, Part 2 (Special Publication).

Heider, F. *The psychology of interpersonal relations.* New York: Wiley, 1958.

Helm, C. E., and Tucker, L. R. Individual differences in the structure of color-perception. *American Journal of Psychology,* 1962, **75**, 437–444.

Henley, N. M. A psychological study of the semantics of animal terms. *Journal of Verbal Learning and Verbal Behavior,* 1969, **8**, 176–184.

Henley, N. M., Noyes, H. L., and Deese, J. Semantic structure in short-term memory. *Journal of Experimental Psychology,* 1968, **77**, 587–592.

Horan, C. B. Multidimensional scaling: Combining observations when individuals have different perceptual structures. *Psychometrika,* 1969, **34**, 139–165.

Hyman, R., and Well, A. Judgments of similarity and spatial models. *Perception and Psychophysics,* 1967, **2**, 233–248.

Isaac, P. D. Dissimilarity judgments and multidimensional scaling configurations as indices of perceptual structure: A study of intra-individual consistencies. Ann Arbor, Michigan: *Michigan Mathematical Psychology Program,* 68–3, 1968.

Johnson, S. C. Hierarchical clustering schemes. *Psychometrika,* 1967, **32**, 241–254.

Johnson, S. C. A simple cluster statistic. Unpublished manuscript (a).

Johnson, S. C. Metric clustering. Unpublished manuscript (b).

Johnson-Laird, P. N., and Tagart, J. How implication is understood. *American Journal of Psychology,* 1969, **82**, 367–373.

Jones, L. V., and Fillenbaum, S. Grammatically classified word-associations. Chapel Hill, N.C.: Psychometric Laboratory, Research Memorandum No. 15, 1964.

Katz, J. J. Semantic theory and the meaning of "good". *Journal of Philosophy,* 1964, **61**, 739–766.

Katz, J. J. *Semantic Theory.* In press.

Katz, J. J., and Fodor, J. A. The structure of a semantic theory. *Language,* 1963, **39**, 170–210.

Katz, J. J., and Postal, P. M. *An integrated theory of linguistic descriptions.* Cambridge, Mass.: M.I.T. Press, 1964.

Kintsch, W. Models for free recall and recognition. In D. A. Norman (Ed.), *Models of human memory.* New York: Academic Press, 1970.

Klahr, D. A Monte-Carlo investigation of the statistical significance of Kruskal's nonmetric scaling procedure. *Psychometrika,* 1969, **34**, 319–330.

Kruskal, J. B. Multidimensional scaling by optimizing goodness of fit to a nonmetric hypothesis. *Psychometrika,* 1964a, **29**, 1–28.

Kruskal, J. B. Nonmetric multidimensional scaling: A numerical method. *Psychometrika,* 1964b, **29**, 115–130.

Kruskal, J. B. How to use MDSCAL, a program to do multidimensional scaling and multidimensional unfolding. Bell Telephone Laboratories, Murray Hill, N.J., 1968 (mimeographed).

Kuusinen, J. Affective and denotative structures of personality ratings. *Journal of Personality and Social Psychology*, 1969,12, 181–188.

Lingoes, J. C. An IBM-7090 program for Guttman-Lingoes smallest space analysis–I. *Behavioral Science*, 1965, 10, 183–184.

Lyons, J. *Structural semantics: Analysis of part of the vocabulary of Plato*. Oxford: Blackwell, 1963.

Lyons, J. *Introduction to theoretical linguistics*. Cambridge: Cambridge University Press, 1968.

McGee, V. E. The multidimensional analysis of "elastic" distances. *The British Journal of Mathematical and Statistical Psychology*, 1966, 19, 181–196.

McGee, V. E. Multidimensional scaling of *N* sets of similarity measures: A nonmetric individual differences approach. *Multivariate Behavioral Research*, 1968, 3, 233–248.

McNeill, D. *The acquisition of language*. New York: Harper and Row, 1970.

McQuitty, L. L. Elementary linkage analysis for isolating orthogonal and oblique types and typal relevancies. *Educational and Psychological Measurement*, 1957, 17, 207–229.

McQuitty, L. L. Hierarchical linkage analysis for the isolation of types. *Educational and Psychological Measurement*, 1960, 20, 293–304.

McQuitty, L. L. Capabilities and improvements of linkage analysis as a clustering method. *Educational and Psychological Measurement*, 1964, 24, 441–456.

Miller, G. A Psycholinguistic approaches to the study of communication. In D. L. Arm (Ed.), *Journeys in science: Small steps–great strides* Albuquerque: The University of New Mexico Press, 1967.

Miller, G. A. Algebraic models in psycholinguistics. In C. A. J. Vlek (Ed.), *Algebraic models in psychology*. Proceedings of the NUFFIC International Summer Session at "Het Oude Hof," The Hague, 1968.

Miller, G. A. A psychological method to investigate verbal concepts. *Journal of Mathematical Psychology*, 1969, 6, 169–191.

Minsky, M. (Ed.), *Semantic information processing*. Cambridge, Mass.: M.I.T. Press, 1968.

Norman, W. T. Toward an adequate taxonomy of personality attributes: Replicated factor structure in peer nomination personality ratings. *Journal of Abnormal and Social Psychology*, 1963, 67, 574–583.

Nummenmaa, T. *The language of the face*. Jyväskylä Studies in Education, Psychology and Social Research. Jyväskylä: Yyväskylän Yliopsistoyhdistys, 1964.

Osgood, C. E. Dimensionality of the semantic space for communication via facial expressions. *Scandinavian Journal of Psychology*, 1966a, 7, 1–30.

Osgood, C. E. Speculations on the structure of interpersonal intentions. Technical Report No. 39, Institute of Communications Research, Urbana, University of Illinois, 1966b.

Osgood, C. E. Interpersonal verbs and interpersonal behavior. Technical Report No. 64, Institute of Communications Research, Urbana, University of Illinois, 1968a.

Osgood, C. E. Toward a wedding of insufficiencies. In T. R. Dixon, and D. L. Horton (Eds.), *Verbal behavior and general behavior theory*. Englewood Cliffs, N.J.: Prentice Hall, 1968b.

Osgood, C. E. Where do sentences come from? In D. D. Steinberg, and L. A. Jakobovits (Eds.), *Semantics: An interdisciplinary reader in philosophy, linguistics and psychology*. Cambridge: Cambridge University Press, 1970.

Osgood, C. E., and Ayer, J. G. Further validation and methodological extension of ten *a priori* semantic features for interpersonal verbs and adverbs. Technical Report No. 66, Institute of Communications Research, Urbana, University of Illinois, 1968.

Osgood, C. E., Suci, G. J., and Tannenbaum, P. H. *The measurement of meaning*. Urbana, Ill.: University of Illinois Press, 1957.

Peay, E. R., Jr. An iterative clique detection procedure. Ann Arbor, Michigan: *Michigan Mathematical Psychology Program*, 70-4, 1970.

Plutchik, R. *The emotions: Facts, theories and a new model.* New York: Random House, 1962.

Quillian, M. R. Semantic memory. In M. Minsky (Ed.), *Semantic information processing.* Cambridge, Mass.: M.I.T. Press, 1968.

Rapoport, A. A comparison of two tree-construction methods for obtaining proximity measures among words. *Journal of Verbal Learning and Verbal Behavior.* 1967, **6**, 884–890.

Rapoport, A., Rapoport, A., Livant, W. P., and Boyd, J. A study of lexical graphs. *Foundations of Language,* 1966, **2**, 338–376.

Reichenbach, H. *Elements of symbolic logic.* New York: Macmillan, 1947.

Rényi, A. Some remarks on the theory of trees. *Publications of the Mathematical Institute of the Hungarian Academy of Sciences,* 1959, **4**, 73–85.

Riegel, K. F. The language acquisition process: A reinterpretation of selected research findings. In L. R. Goulet, and P. B. Baltes (Eds.), *Theory and research in life-span developmental psychology.* New York: Academic Press, 1970.

Romney, A. K., and D'Andrade, R. G. Cognitive aspects of English kin terms. In A. K. Romney, and R. G. Andrade (Eds.), *Transcultural studies in cognition. American Anthropologist,* 1964, **66**, No. 3, Part 2 (Special Publication).

Roskam, E. E. A comparison of principles for algorithm construction in nonmetric scaling. Ann Arbor, Michigan: *Michigan Mathematical Psychology Program*, 69-2, 1969.

Ross, J. A remark on Tucker and Messick "Points of View" analysis. *Psychometrika,* 1966, **31**, 27–31.

Sanday, P. R. The "psychological reality" of American-English kinship terms: An information-processing approach. *American Anthropologist,* 1968, **70**, 508–523.

Sastri, M. I. Prepositions in *Chemical Abstracts:* A semantic study. *Linguistics,* 1968, No. 38, 42–51.

Schlosberg, H. A scale for the judgment of facial expressions. *Journal of Experimental Psychology,* 1941, **29**, 497–510.

Schlosberg, H. The description of facial expressions in terms of two dimensions. *Journal of Experimental Psychology,* 1952, **44**, 229–237.

Schlosberg H. Three dimensions of emotion. *Psychological Review,* 1954, **61**, 81–88.

Shepard R. N. The analysis of proximities: Multidimensional scaling with an unknown distance function. I. *Psychometrika,* 1962a, **27**, 125–140.

Shepard, R. N. The analysis of proximities: Multidimensional scaling with an unknown distance function. II. *Psychometrika,* 1962b, **27**, 219–246.

Shepard, R. N. Attention and the metric structure of the stimulus space. *Journal of Mathematical Psychology,* 1964, **1**, 54–87.

Shepard, R. N. Metric structures in ordinal data. *Journal of Mathematical Psychology,* 1966, **3**, 287–315.

Shepard, R. N. Some principles and prospects for the spatial representation of behavioral science data. Paper presented at MSSB Advanced Research Seminar on Measurement and Scaling, June 1969.

Shepard, R. N., and Chipman, S. Second-order isomorphism of internal representations: Shapes of states. *Cognitive Psychology,* 1970, **1**, 1–17.

Sherman, C. R. Nonmetric multidimensional scaling: The role of the Minkowski metric. Chapel Hill, N.C.: Psychometric Laboratory Report No. 82, April 1970.

Slobin, D. I. Soviet methods of investigating child language. In F. Smith, and G. A. Miller (Eds.), *The genesis of language.* Cambridge, Mass.: M.I.T. Press, 1966.

Sokal, R. R., and Sneath, P. H. A. *Principles of numerical taxonomy*. San Francisco: Freeman, 1963.

Steinberg, D. D. Analyticity, amphigory, and the semantic interpretation of sentences. *Journal of Verbal Learning and Verbal Behavior*, 1970, 9, 37–51.

Stenson, H. H., and Knoll, R. L. Goodness of fit for random rankings of Kruskal's nonmetric scaling procedure. *Psychological Bulletin*, 1969, 71, 122–126.

Strawson, P. F. *Introduction to logical theory*. New York: Wiley, 1952.

Stringer, P. Cluster analysis of non-verbal judgments of facial expressions. *British Journal of Mathematical and Statistical Psychology*, 1967, 20, 71–79.

Sturtevant, W. C. Studies in ethnoscience. In A. K. Romney, and R. G. D'Andrade (Eds.), *Transcultural studies in cognition. American Anthropologist*, 1964, 66, No. 3, Part 2 (Special Publication).

Tomkins, S. S., and McCarter, R. What and where are the primary affects? Some evidence for a theory. *Perceptual and Motor Skills*, 1964, 18, 119–158.

Torgerson, W. S. *Theory and methods of scaling*. New York: Wiley, 1958.

Torgerson, W. S. Multidimensional scaling of similarity. *Psychometrika*, 1965, 30, 379–393.

Torgerson, W. S. Multidimensional representation of similarity structures. In M. M. Katz, J. O. Cole, and W. E. Barton (Eds.), *The role and methodology of classification in psychiatry and psychopathology*. U.S. Department of Health, Education, and Welfare, 1968.

Tucker, L. R., and Messick, S. J. An individual difference model for multidimensional scaling. *Psychometrika*, 1963, 28, 333–367.

Ullman, S. *Semantics: An introduction to the science of meaning*. New York: Barnes and Noble, 1962.

Wallace, A. F. C. The problem of the psychological validity of componential analysis. In E. A. Hammel (Ed.), *Formal semantic analyses. American Anthropologist* 1965, 67, No. 5, Part 2 (Special Publication).

Wallace, A. F. C., and Atkins, J. The meaning of kinship terms. *American Anthropologist*, 1960, 62, 58–79.

Ward, J. H., Jr. Hierarchical grouping to optimize an objective function. *Journal of the American Statistical Association*, 1963, 58, 236–244.

Ward, J. H., Jr., and Hook, M. E. Application of a hierarchical grouping procedure to a problem of grouping profiles. *Educational and Psychological Measurement*, 1963, 23, 69–81.

Weinreich, U. On the semantic structure of language. In J. H. Greenberg (Ed.), *Universals of language*. Cambridge, Mass.: M.I.T. Press, 1963.

Weinreich, U. Explorations in semantic theory. In T. A. Sebeok (Ed.), *Current trends in linguistics*, Vol. III. The Hague: Mouton, 1966.

West, M. (Ed.), *A general service list of English words*. London: Longmans, 1953.

Wexler, K. N. Semantic structure: Psychological evidence for hierarchical features. Paper read at Research Workshop on Cognitive Organization and Psychological Processes, Huntington Beach, California, August 1970a.

Wexler, K. N. Embedding structures for semantics. Paper read at meetings of Mathematical Psychology Group, Miami Beach, Florida, September 1970b.

Wexler, K. N., and Romney, A. K. Some cognitive implications derived from multidimensional scaling. Paper presented at MSSB Advanced Research Seminar on Measurement and Scaling. June 1969.

Young, F. W. A model for polynomial conjoint analysis algorithms. Paper presented at MSSB Advanced Research Seminar on Measurement and Scaling. June 1969.

Young, F. W. Nonmetric multidimensional scaling: Recovery of metric information. *Psychometrika,* 1970, **35,** 455–473.

Young, F. W., and Torgerson, W. S. TORSCA, a FORTRAN IV program for Shepard-Kruskal multidimensional scaling analysis. *Behavioral Science,* 1967, **12,** 498.

Author Index

A

Abelson, R. P., 6, 103, 208, *252*
Allport, F. H., 100, *252*
Anisfeld, M., 87, 99, *252*
Arm, D. L., *255*
Atkins, J., 2, 5, 58-59, 61, 81, 243, *257*
Attneave, F., 12, 20, 24, *252*
Ayer, J. G., 190, 192, 193, *255*

B

Baltes, P. B. *256*
Barton, W. E. *257*
Beals, R., 28, *252*
Bendix, E. H., 7, 149, 167, 169-172, 184-185, 187, 238, *252*
Bennett, D. C., 125, *252*
Bennett, J., 148, *252*
Block, J., 6, 102, 105, 108-110, 123, *252*
Bolinger, D., 244, *252*
Boucher, J., 211, 231, *252*
Boyd, J., 3, 10, 14, 18-19, *256*
Brown, R., 85, 149, *252*
Busacker, R. G., 14, *252*

C

Carroll, J. D., 26-28, 35, 249, *252*
Chang, J. J., 26-28, 35, 249, *252*
Chapanis, A., 5, 42, 56, *252*
Chipman, S., 4, 106, 107, 226-227, 232, 244, *256*
Clark, H. H., viii, 2, 6, 11, 126-129, 133, 141-144, 211, 242, *252*
Cliff, N., 4, 26, 103, 226, 232, *252, 253*

C

Clifton, C. E., viii
Cole, J. O., *257*
Collins, A. M., 249, *253*
Constantinescu, P. A., 29, 37, 103, *253*
Coombs, C. H., 20, 23, *253*
Cooper, G. S., 6, 125-127, 145, *253*

D

D'Andrade, R. G., 2, 5, 58-61, 80-81, 105-106, 243, *253, 256, 257*
Deese, J., viii, 2, 6, 86, 99, 145, 239, 241, 250, *253, 254*
Degerman, R., 35, 37-38, 122, 239, *253*
de Saussure, F., 3
Descartes, 100
Dietze, A. G., 107-108, 123, *253*
Dixon, T. R., *255*

E

Ekman, G., 6, 56, 107-108, 110, 123, *253*
Engen, T., 102-103, *253*
Erdös, P., 17-18, *253*

F

Feldman, S., *252*
Feovanov, M. P., 125
Fillenbaum, S., 6, 86-87, 99, 145, 246, *253, 254*
Fillmore, C. J., 7, 125, 170, 191-194, 204, 206-207, 245, *253, 254*
Fodor, J. A., 1, 59, 244, *254*
Funk, S. G., viii

259

G

Gerbner, G., *253*
Gleitman, L. R., 161, *254*
Goulet, L. R., *256*
Green, P. E., 26, *254*
'Greenberg, J. H., 211, *254, 257*
Guttman, L. A., 20, *254*

H

Hammel, E. A., 2, *253, 254, 257*
Heider, F., 190, 206, *254*
Helm, C. E., 5, 25, *254*
Henley, N. M., 2, 99, *254*
Hobbes, 100
Hook, M. E., 29, *257*
Horan, C. B., 25, 27-28, 35, *254*
Horton, D. L., *255*
Hyman, R., 24, 248, *254*

I

Isaac, P. D., 20, 25, *254*

J

Jakobovits, L. A., *255*
Johnson, S. C., 11-12, 29-30, 32-34, 36, *254*
Johnson-Laird, P. N., 148, *254*
Jones, L. V., viii, 6, 86, 145, *253, 254*

K

Kanouse, D. E., 208, *252*
Kao, R. C., 23, *253*
Katz, J. J., 1, 59, 168, 171-172, 232, 244, *254*
Katz, M. M., *257*
Kintsch, W., 40, *254*
Klahr, D. A., 21-22, *254*
Knapp, M., 87, 99, *252*
Knoll, R. L., 21-22, *257*
Koch, S., *252*
Krantz, D. H., 28, *252*
Kruskal, J. B., 12, 20-21, 26-27, 35, *254*
Kuusinen, J., 210, *255*

L

Lehiste, I., *253*
Levy, N., 102-103, *253*
Lingoes, J. C., 20-21, *255*
Livant, W. P., 3, 10, 14, 18-19, *256*
Lyons, J., 1, 11, 41-42, 58, 86, 97, 243, 251, *255*

M

McCarter, R., 100-101, *257*
McDougall, W., 100
McGee, V. E., 20, 26-27, 35, *255*
McNeill, D., 249, *255*
McQuitty, L. L., 29, 107, *255*
Messick, S. J., 25, 35, 138, *257*
Miller, G. A., 2, 9, 11-12, 29-30, 49, 142-143, 187, 193, 204, 206, 209, 230, 237, 245, 247-248, *255, 256*
Minsky, M., 249, *255, 256*
Morris, T. W., 26, *254*

N

Norman, D. A., *254*
Norman, W. T., 105, *255*
Noyes, H. L., 2, 99, *254*
Nummenmaa, T. 110, *255*

O

Ornan, A., viii
Osgood, C. E., 2-3, 7, 101-102, 105, 110, 122, 190, 192-194, 203-204, 207, 209, 211, 230-231, 239-240, 247-248, *252, 255*

P

Peay, E. R., Jr., 35-36, 104, *256*
Plutchik, R., 110, *256*
Postal, P. M., 1, *254*

Q

Quillian, M. R., 249, *253, 256*

R

Rapoport, Amnon, 3, 10, 14, 18-19, *256*
Rapoport, Anatol, 3, 10, 14, 18-19, *256*
Reibel, D. A., *254*
Reichenbach, H., 148-150, *256*
Rényi, A., 17-18, 19, *253, 256*
Riegel, K. F., 125, *256*
Romney, A. K., 2, 5, 58-61, 80-81, 243, *256, 257*
Roskam, E. E., 20, *256*
Ross, J., 26, *256*

S

Saaty, T. L., 14, *252*
Sanday, P. R. 81, *256*
Sastri, M. I., 125, 127, *256*
Schane, S. A. *254*
Schlosberg, H., 6, 100-103, *253, 256*
Schopler, E., viii
Sebeok, T. A., *254, 257*
Seifer, S., viii
Sermat, V., 6, 103, *252*
Shepard, R. N., 4-5, 8-12, 20, 22-25, 39, 51, 56-57, 81, 103, 106-107, 226-227, 232, 240, 244, *256*
Sherman, C. R., 24, *256*
Slobin, D. I., 125, *256*
Smith, F., *256*
Sokal, R. R., 9, 29, *257*
Sokhin, F. A., 125
Sneath, P. H., 9, 29, *257*
Snell, P., viii
Steinberg, D. D., 247, *255, 257*
Stenson, H. H., 21-22, *257*
Strawson, P. F., 6, 148-149, *257*
Stringer, P., 103-104, *257*
Sturtevant, W. C., 85, *257*
Suci, G. J., 3, 209, 230, *255*

T

Tagart, J., 148, *254*
Tannenbaum, P. H., 3, 209, 230, *255*
Tomkins, S. S., 100-101, *257*
Torgerson, W. S., 9, 11, 12, 20-21, 24, 28, 57, 182, *257, 258*
Tucker, L. R., 5, 25, 35, 138, *254, 257*
Tversky, A., 28, *252*

U

Ullman, S., 168, 250, *257*

V

Vlek, C. A. J., *255*

W

Wallace, A. F. C., 2, 5, 58-59, 61, 79, 81, 84, 243, *257*
Ward, J. H., Jr., 29, *257*
Wason, P. C., 148
Weinreich, U., 2, 6, 125, 149, 188, *257*
Well, A., 24, 248, *254*
West, M., 125, *257*
Wexler, K. N., 5, 7, 59-60, 80-81, 171, 185-187, *257*
Wundt, W., 100
Woodworth, R., 103

Y

Young, F. W., viii, 4, 11, 12, 20-21, 23, 26, 28, 103, *253, 257, 258*

Subject Index

C

City Block model, 24
Class quantitative procedure, 35, 37–38
Cluster analysis, 12, 28–35
  cliques and, 35–37
  of color names, 48–51
  of conjunctions, 159–161
  Connectedness method of, 30–31
  Diameter method of, 30–31
  Direct Grouping method and, 31
  of emotion terms, 115–118
  of Good–Bad terms, 217–222
  of HAVE verbs, 177–181
  of kinship terms, 68–73, 78
  labeled trees and, 29, 34–35
  MDS and, 37, 39, 73–74, 78–79
  of prepositions, 135–139
  of pronouns, 91–93, 96–97
  statistical properties of, 33–35
  techniques of, 2, 29, 37–38
  of verbs of judging, 196–199, 201–202
Clusters, *see also* MAXC clusterings
  diameter of, 32
  distance between, 34, 72, 138
  significance of, 33, 35, 49, 72, 177
  strong, 29
  value of, 29
  weak, 29
Color names, 41–57
  cluster analysis of, 48–51
  completely connected undirected graphs, 46–47
  cycles of order k, 47–48
  domain of, 5, 11, 24
  employed in present study, 43
  Euclidean representations of, 52–55, 57
  graph analysis of, 44–48

Color names—*cont.*
  MAXC clusterings of, 49–50
  MDS analysis of, 51–55
  node degree in trees, 44, 50, 55
    in undirected graphs, 47
  pairs of adjacent nodes in trees, 44–45, 55
  popularity bias of, 44
  space of (CNS), 41–42, 56–57
  stress values of, 52, 55
Completely connected undirected graphs
  of color names, 46–47
  definition of, 17
  of emotion terms, 113
  of kinship terms, 66–67
Componential analysis
  of kinship terms, 58–61, 79–80, 84
  methods of, 2
  of pronouns, 85–87
Conjunctions, 148–167
  cluster analysis of, 159–161
  combinatorial, 6, 149–151, 162–164, 166–167
  contrastive, 6, 149–151, 162–164, 166–167
  domain of, 6
  employed in present study, 151
  Euclidean representations of, 161–162, 164
  graph analysis of, 157–159
  in logic and in vernacular, 148–150
  MAXC clusterings of, 159
  MDS analysis of, 161–162
  node degree in trees, 158, 163
  pairs of adjacent nodes in trees, 158–159, 163
  sentence completion task, 150, 152–157, 165–166, 246

Conjunctions—*cont.*
  stress values of, 162, 164
  subordinating, 161–162
  syntactic conditions of use, 166–167

D

Data
  dominance, 8
  profile, 8
  proximity, 8, 9
Direct Grouping method, 10, 11, 32
  cluster analysis and, 31
  with Good–Bad terms, 215–217,
    221–222, 227–230
  with HAVE verbs, 175–177, 181–183
  with prepositions, 133–134, 138–142

E

Emotion names, 100–124
  analysis of Block's data, 109–110, 123
    of Ekman's data, 107–108
  cluster analysis of, 115–118
  completely connected undirected graphs,
    113
  cycles of order k, 114
  domain of, 6
  employed in present study, 109–110
  Euclidean representations of, 118–119
  graph analysis of, 111–114
  MAXC clusterings of, 115
  MDS analysis of, 118–124
  node degree in trees, 111–112
    in undirected graphs, 113–114
  pairs of adjacent nodes in trees, 112
  popularity bias of, 112
  previous studies of, 107–110
  as referring to internal experiential
    states, 105–107, 124
  stress values of, 118–119
  studies of facial expressions and, 6, 102
  trait names and, 105–106
Emotions
  analysis of Stringer's data, 104
  data collection and analysis methods,
    102
  dimensional approaches to, 100–101,
    103
  studies of facial expressions, 101–105
  typological approaches to, 100–101,
    103–104

Euclidean representations
  of color names, 52–55, 57
  of conjunctions, 161–162, 164
  of emotion terms, 118–119
  of Good–Bad terms, 223–230
  of HAVE verbs, 181–183
  of kinship terms, 73–77, 81–82
  of prepositions, 139, 141
  of pronouns, 93–94
  of verbs of judging, 199–201

G

Good–Bad terms, 209–234
  antonymous, 210–211, 225–226
  cluster analysis of, 217–222
  Direct Grouping data, 215–217,
    221–222, 227–230
  domain of, 7, 170, 209–210
  employed in present study, 212
  Euclidean representations of, 223–230
  Evaluation factor, 8, 209–210
  graph analysis of, 213–217
  grouped together in pairs, 216–217
  item selection, 210–211, 233
  marked and unmarked, 211, 231
  matching analysis of, 7, 210, 225–231
  MAXC clusterings of, 218–222
  MDS analysis of, 222–230
  node degree in trees, 213–214
  pairs of adjacent nodes in trees, 214–215
  popularity bias of, 215
  stress values of, 222–223
  as syncategorematic, 232–233
Graph analysis
  of color names, 44–48
  of conjunctions, 157–159
  of emotion terms, 111–114
  of Good–Bad terms, 213–217
  of HAVE verbs, 172–175
  of kinship terms, 62–68, 79, 83
  of prepositions, 131–134
  of pronouns, 88–91, 97
  of verbs of judging, 194–196

H

HAVE verbs, 168–189
  Bendix's analysis of, 7, 170–171,
    184–185
  cluster analysis of, 177–181

HAVE verbs—*cont.*
  Direct Grouping data, 175–177, 181–183
  domain of, 7, 170–171, 236
  "embedding structures" model of, 171, 185–187
  employed in present study, 173
  Euclidean representations of, 181–183
  graph analysis of, 172–175
  grouped together in pairs, 175–176
  Katz's analysis of, 171–172
  MAXC clusterings of, 177, 180–181
  MDS analysis of, 181–183
  node degree in trees, 173
  pairs of adjacent nodes in trees, 173–174
  popularity bias of, 174–175
  stress values of, 181
  weighting of features, 188
  Wexler's analysis of, 7, 171, 185–187
Hierarchical clustering, *see* Cluster analysis

I

Item selection, 233, 236, 247

J

Judgment criterion, similarity vs. relatedness in meaning, 242–243

K

Kinship terms, 58–84
  cluster analysis of, 68–73, 78
  completely connected undirected graphs, 66–67
  domain of, 5, 11, 24
  employed in present study, 59
  Euclidean representations of, 73–77, 81–82
  family relation criterion, 61, 69, 82, 241
  graph analysis of, 62–68, 78, 83
  MDS analysis of, 73–79
  mutual affection criterion, 61, 69, 82, 241
  node degree in trees, 62–65
    in undirected graphs, 67
  pairs of adjacent nodes in trees, 63, 65–66
  popularity bias of, 63

Kinship terms—*cont.*
  RD model, 59–61, 69, 72–74, 77–78, 80–81, 84, 243
  stress values of, 73–74
  WA model, 59–61, 69, 71, 74, 80–81, 84, 243
  weighting of features, 82

L

Linear graphs, 14–20
  complete, 14, 16–17
  connected, 15
  cycles in, 15, 18
  definition of, 14
  directed, 15
  "evolution" of, 11, 19–20
  labeled, 15
  random, 17
  simple, 14
  statistical properties of, 17–20
  undirected, 10, 15

M

MAXC clusterings
  of color names, 49–50
  of conjunctions, 159
  definition of, 34
  of emotion terms, 115
  of Good–Bad terms, 218–222
  of HAVE verbs, 177, 180–181
  of prepositions, 135–138
  of pronouns, 91
  of verbs of judging, 196, 198–199, 201–202
MDS analysis, 20–28
  cluster analysis and, 37, 39, 73–74, 78–79
  of color names, 51–55
  of conjunctions, 161–163
  of emotion terms, 118–124
  of Good–Bad terms, 222–230
  goodness of fit measures, 20–22, 39
  of HAVE verbs, 181–183
  individual differences in, 25–28, 248–249
  of kinship terms, 73–79
  metric determinacy, 23–24
  Minkowski exponents, 23–25
  of prepositions, 139–141

MDS analysis—*cont.*
  of pronouns, 93–94, 97
  techniques of, 11
  of verbs of judging, 199–203

N

Node degree in trees
  of color names, 44, 50, 55
  of conjunctions, 158, 163
    definition of, 18
  of emotion terms, 111–112
  of Good–Bad terms, 213–214
  of HAVE verbs, 173
  of kinship terms, 62–65
  of prepositions, 131
  of pronouns, 89
  of verbs of judging, 194–195
Node degree in undirected graphs
  of color names, 47
  definition of, 18
  of emotion terms, 113–114
  of kinship terms, 67
Nonmetric multidimensional scaling, *see*
  MDS analysis

P

Pairs of adjacent nodes in trees
  of color names, 44–45, 55
  of conjunctions, 158–159, 163
  definition of, 19
  of emotion terms, 112
  of Good–Bad terms, 214–215
  of HAVE verbs, 173–174
  of kinship terms, 63, 65–66
  of prepositions, 131–132
  of pronouns, 89–90
  of verbs of judging, 195
Pairs of terms grouped together
  of Good–Bad terms, 216–217
  of HAVE verbs, 175–176
  of prepositions, 134
Perceptual separability hypothesis, 24
"Point of view" analysis, 25–26, 248
Popularity bias, 19, 43–45, 63, 90, 112,
  132, 174–175, 196, 215
Prepositions, 125–147
  Clark's analysis of, 128–129, 143–144
  cluster analysis of, 135–139

Prepositions—*cont.*
  Cooper's analysis of, 126–127, 145
  Deese's analysis of, 6, 145
  Direct   Grouping   data,   133–134,
    138–142
  directional, 137, 145
  domain of, 6
  employed in present study, 130
  Euclidean representations of, 139, 141
  graph analysis of, 131–134
  grouped together in pairs, 134
  locative, 6, 125, 126, 137, 144
  MAXC clusterings of, 135–138
  MDS analysis of, 139–141
  node degree in trees, 131
  pairs of adjacent nodes in trees, 131–132
  polysemous, 125, 127
  popularity bias of, 132
  stress values of, 139
  weighting of features, 145–146
Pronouns, 85–99
  cluster analysis of, 91–93, 96–97
  componential analysis of, 85–87
  confusion in learning, 6, 87, 95–96,
    98–99
  Deese's analysis of, 86
  domain of, 5–6
  employed in present study, 88
  Euclidean representations of, 93–94
  graph analysis of, 88–91, 97
  MAXC clusterings of, 91
  MDS analysis of, 93–94, 97
  node degree in trees, 89
  paired-associate   data,   87–88,   94–96,
    98–99
  pairs of adjacent nodes in trees, 89–90
  popularity bias of, 90
  stress values of, 93, 96
  weighting of features, 85–87, 92, 94, 97
Proximities
  conditional matrix of, 10, 20
  derived measures of, 9–10
  direct measures of, 9–10
  rectangular matrix of, 10, 20
  symmetric matrix of, 10, 20

S

"Second   order"   isomorphism,   106–107,
  227, 244

Semantic domains, 2–5, 8, 11, 168–172, 235
  data analysis, 238–240
  discovery procedures, 237
  hypothesis testing, 237
  ill defined, 7–8, 169–170, 209–210, 236
  item selection, 236
  relations among, 249–250
  well defined, 5–6, 8, 168–169, 236
Semantic field, *see* Semantic domain
Semantic interaction analysis, 2, 248
Semantic markers, 58–59, 125, 172
Semantic space, 3–4
Semantic structure, 1–5, 13
  choice among competing models, 59–61, 80–82, 243
  contingent upon task set, 241–242
  "conventionalist" position, 241
  individual differences in, 248–249
  interpretability as selection criterion, 240
  memorial techniques in study of, 87, 99, 246–247
  present work compared with other approaches to, 247–248
  psychological validity of, 59, 241
  "realist" position, 241
Stress
  of color names, 52, 55
  computation of, 21
  of conjunction, 162, 164
  cut-off points, 22, 52, 119
  determinants of, 21
  of emotion terms, 118–119
  of Good–Bad terms, 222–223
  of HAVE verbs, 181
  of kinship terms, 73
  Monte Carlo study of, 21–22
  of prepositions, 139
  of pronouns, 93, 96
  of verbs of judging, 199–200
Syncategorematic terms, 232–233

T

Trees
  cluster analysis and, 29, 34–35
  definition of, 15
  distance in, 16
  endpoints of, 18
  labeled, 16, 64
  method of construction, 10, 15–16, 55–56, 238–239
  random, 18
  statistical properties of, 18–20
  unlabeled, 64

U

Ultrametric inequality, 49

V

Verbs of judging, 190–208
  cluster analysis of, 196–199, 201–202
  domain of, 7, 170, 190
  employed in present study, 194
  Euclidean representations of, 199–201
  Fillmore's analysis of, 7, 191–192, 204–207
  graph analysis of, 194–196
  illocutionary force of, 191, 193, 207
  MAXC clusterings of, 196, 198–199, 201–202
  MDS analysis of, 199–203
  node degree in trees, 194–195
  Osgood's analysis of, 7, 190–191, 203–204, 207, 248
  pairs of adjacent nodes in trees, 195
  popularity bias of, 196
  presuppositions of, 191, 193, 206–208
  role structure of, 191–192, 207
  semantic interaction analysis of, 191, 248
  stress values of, 199–200